THE DIFFERENCE BETWEEN A MAN AND A WOMAN

Theo Lang

THEO LANG was born in Bradford, Yorkshire. He left school at the age of fifteen to earn his living and from being a farmer's boy he became a journalist and eventually a Fleet Street executive. He has had homes in London, Paris, Rome, Glasgow and Tangier and at one time maintained a castle in Scotland, a penthouse in Mayfair and a villa in the south of Italy. Now he has only one home, a villa overlooking the Mediterranean on the Sorrento peninsula, but, a compulsive nomad, he is travelling through Europe, North Africa and the Middle East looking for a new place to live.

Theo Lang wrote his first novel on a guard-room table when in the Army, and has since published thirteen more books. He has recently been working on another novel and a play.

The Difference Between a Man and a Woman
THEO LANG

SPHERE BOOKS LIMITED
30/32 Gray's Inn Road, London WC1X 8JL

First published in Great Britain in 1971
by Michael Joseph Ltd
© 1971 by Theo Lang
First Sphere Books edition 1973

TRADE
MARK

This book is sold subject to the condition that
it shall not, by way of trade or otherwise, be lent,
re-sold, hired out or otherwise circulated without
the publisher's prior consent in any form of
binding or cover other than that in which it is
published and without a similar condition
including this condition being imposed on the
subsequent purchaser.

Set in Intertype Lectura

Printed in Great Britain by
Hazell Watson & Viney Ltd.
Aylesbury, Bucks

ISBN 0 7221 54127

Contents

ACKNOWLEDGEMENTS . . . 9

INTRODUCTION . . . 13

PART ONE: THE DIFFERENCE IN BODY

1 HOW THE DIFFERENCE BEGINS . . . 17
  1. Our First Lesson in Sex
  2. Nature is a Woman
  3. Female Egg but Mixed-up Sperm
  4. Parents Who Prefer Boys

2 WHY ONLY TWO SEXES? . . . 36
  1. Penis or Clitoris
  2. Testicles or Ovaries
  3. The Sex Messengers
  4. Boy or Girl? Or . . .?

3 MALE AND FEMALE SHAPES . . . 56
  1. Which is More Beautiful?
  2. Woman's Difference is Fat
  3. Breasts and Hips; Voice, Skin and Hair

4 'THE WEAKER SEX' . . . 75
  1. Women Live Longer
  2. Boys are Born Weaker
  3. A Matter of Strength
  4. 'Stronger Heads' Too
  5. The Mystery of Menstruation

PART TWO: THE DIFFERENCE IN DESIRE

5 SEXUALITY TAKES SHAPE . . . 103
  1. The Birth Trauma
  2. The First Denial
  3. The First 'Love Affair'
  4. Penis-Envy
  5. Handsome Boy! Pretty Girl!
  6. Youth or Maiden

6 THE ACT OF SEX   150

   1 Learning How to Make Love
   2 Hymen and Virginity
   3 The Different Orgasm
   4 Change of Life: Woman's and Man's
   5 Man's Biggest Fear

PART THREE: THE DIFFERENCE IN MIND

7 NO WOMAN BEETHOVEN   195

   1 Woman's Higher I.Q.
   2 Women Writers, and Others
   3 'She Has Never Had The Chance'

8 WOMAN'S SMALLER BRAIN   223

   1 The Subtle Knot
   2 A Ten-per-cent Difference
   3 The Descent from the Trees
   4 Again, the Mystery of Menstruation

9 WOMAN'S INTUITION   263

   1 Sense of Humour
   2 'Woman's Intuition'

PART FOUR: THE DIFFERENCE IN LIFE

10 THE LAWS OF SEX   281

   1 First Man and First Woman
   2 Sex Taboos
   3 Who Proposes?

11 WHY TROUSERS? WHY SKIRTS?   305

   1 Who Chose the Fig Leaf?
   2 Sex in Fashion
   3 When Breasts Are Masculine

12 THE EMANCIPATION MYTH   346

   1 Men Must Work, and Women Must Weep
   2 How Woman Rules

PART FIVE: THE MEANING OF LOVE

13 THE MEANING OF LOVE   367
   1 'Making Love' or Being in Love
   2 Sex in the Brain
   3 The First Lovers

SELECTED BIBLIOGRAPHY   386

INDEX   395

TO ROY

whose generosity made
it all possible

Acknowledgements

In thanking those who have helped me with this book courtesy demands that I should first thank the doctors and scientists; some of them were friends, but who readily and generously gave me advice and tolerantly allowed me to plunder their work.

In particular I must express gratitude to Dr. W. Grey Walter and Dr. Peter Nathan for warnings against error as much as guidance, and to Dr. Donald Mackay who, as Medical Superintendent of one of the greatest post-graduate teaching hospitals in the world, guided me to specialists in several fields. Special thanks are also due to Mr. R. H. Horsman, former deputy secretary of Hammersmith Hospital Board of Governors, who so readily volunteered to act as 'surveyor in chief' of the operation of checking and cross-checking corrections and suggestions made by distinguished specialists at each stage of this book.

I must also thank members of the staff of the Reading Room of the British Museum who led me to little-known sources reporting some scientific findings which, as they had not been widely published, I should otherwise have missed. For more specialised library research my thanks are due to Jon North, librarian, who kept me informed of the latest authoritative reports and opinions in current medical and biological inquiry, as well as to his biologist wife, Jane North, whose pointed questions led me to frame my opinions in a more comprehensively informed manner.

Thanks are also due to Dr. E. M. Horowitz, who was among the first to hear of my ambition to write this book, for his encouragement and comments; to other doctors whose valuable comments and advice are mentioned in the text; to Mr. Robert Cook for his literary and typing assistance; and to Mrs. Jean Langton, whose secretarial assistance initially involved the typing and cataloguing of some 150,000 words of research notes and subsequently the continual retyping and checking of innumerable first drafts of the book. As for my many publishing and newspaper friends and associates whose comments and advice stimulated me in my work, they know, without published mention, how grateful I am for their interest and encouragement, though I feel in duty bound to single out for special thanks Mr. Michael Christiansen editor of the *Sunday Mirror* for the stimulus of his enthusiasm when I first outlined my project, and to Mr. Charles Roger, now of the *Daily Mirror*, for his generous advice and encouragement as the work progressed.

As this book is intended for the general reader and has no pretence of being a book of reference, I originally decided not to include a bibliography, feeling that by doing so I should be making pretentious claims to scholarship. However, I am now acutely conscious of my great debt to many authors and scientists whose books and papers have helped me; sometimes directly with facts and findings, but more often indirectly by suggesting new ideas or indicating fresh fields for inquiry and comment. My acknowledgement of this assistance is implicit in my listing the books which have most helped me. I realise also that I owe to my readers some indication of sources where they can find more detailed and more authoritative information on any subjects in this book that arouse their especial interest.

Among the authors Margaret Mead is one to whom I must express particular gratitude. I first read her *Male and Female* in a frenzy of underlining disagreement, yet this was the book which eventually fired me with an ambition to write for the general reader an account of masculine and feminine differences in our own society; an ambition which eventually was transformed into the decision to write a popular sexual-anthropological survey of ourselves that would be at once more intimate and personal than any of the sociological studies now being published and more biologically and psychologically comprehensive than, for instance, a Kinsey Report. In the course of this work I became aware inevitably that many of my hasty underlined objections to *Male and Female* were mistakes in my comprehension, but also I became deeply envious of the graceful literary style in which Margaret Mead can convey scientific observations and wise opinion. Another author to whom I owe a special debt is Loren Eiseley. This writer, who presents the richest and wildest fancies and the most imaginative and sometimes untenable theories in the cadence of poetic truth dazzles one with his magnificent impudence. I came upon his *The Immense Journey* at the very moment I was beginning my first draft of this book. In my attempt, admitted, to manhandle science to serve my arguments, I could have found no better morale booster.

As I collected an ever increasing number of books and papers my research led me into some of the remoter byways of scientific inquiry. I found myself tempted into entranced study of papers bearing such alluring titles as *On the Absence of any Relation between Coffee Consumption of Parents and the Sex Ratio of Their Children*, and *Sex Attractant of the Black Carpet Beetle*, as well as one title where I thought it necessary to warn my typist to be particularly careful about the spelling, *The Sex Odour Problem of Boars*. Although every one of these inquiries was of absorbing interest, such papers proved to have no direct application to my book. Therefore, to avoid presenting a bibliography of inordinate length I include only titles of books and papers which come under four headings: (a) those from which I have made direct quotation in my text; (b) those which, though not directly quoted, have provided background information, including those which were always beside my desk for reference and inspiration during my work; (c) those which are not scientific works but were no less valuable for the arguments they made and the points of view they presented; and (d) those which will be helpful to any readers who might wish to study any particular aspect of the male-female difference in greater detail.

To avoid giving footnotes, which I considered a too scholarly device for this book, I have specifically acknowledged my sources in the text, but I must here express particular thanks to authors (and/or their publishers) who have given me permission to quote extracts from their works: To Simone de Beauvoir, *The Second Sex* (and her publishers Alfred A. Knopf Inc., New York); J. A. C. Brown, *Freud and the Post Freudians* (Penguin Books Ltd., London); C. O. Carter, *Human Heredity* (Penguin Books Ltd., London; Ernest Crawley, *The Mystic Rose* (Methuen & Co., Ltd., London); Michael H. Day, *Fossil Man* (Paul Hamlyn Group, London); Helene Deutsch, *The Psychology of Women* (Grune & Stratton, New York Research Books, London); Christine Doyle, from a report of an interview, 10th August 1969 (*The Observer*, London); H. J. Eysenck, *Uses and Abuses of Psychology* (Penguin Books Ltd., London); J. C. Fluegel, *The Psychology of Clothes* (The Hogarth Press Ltd., London); Sigmund Freud, *Complete Psychological Works* (The Hogarth Press Ltd., London); Betty Friedan, *The Feminine Mystique* (Penguin Books Ltd., London); Arnold Gessel, *The First Five Years of Life* (Harper & Bros., New York); Brian Glanville, from an article on women in sport, 31st August 1969 (*The Sunday Times*, London); Norman Haire, *Hymen, or the Future of Marriage* (Routledge & Kegan Paul Ltd., London); W. Hamilton, from his introduction to *The Symposium of Plato* (Penguin Books Ltd., London); D. O. Hebb, *Textbook of Psychology* (W. B. Saunders Company, Philadelphia); George William Henry, *All the Sexes* (Holt, Rinehard & Winston Inc., New York); Ruth Martin from an article on the female orgasm (*Woman's Own*, London); Margaret Mead, *Male and Female*, (Victor Gollancz Ltd., London); A. S. Romer, *Men and the Vertebrates* (University of Chicago Press, Chicago); Bertrand Russell, *A History of Western Philosophy* (George Allen and Unwin, Ltd., London); and Kenneth Walker, *Human Physiology*, and *The Physiology of Sex and Its Social Implications* (Penguin Books Ltd., London).

Introduction

It is my ambition in this book to bring together for the first time in one volume and under one title multifarious aspects of the difference between men and women. To say that no scientist could write such a book might sound presumptuous. Though it could be true to say that few scientists would attempt to write it. For a scientist must confine himself, at least in his published writings, to the discipline or disciplines in which he has specialised and in which he is a qualified and accepted authority. So if a biologist were writing under this title he would restrict his personal observations and arguments to the biological difference between man and woman. Similarly a sociologist would restrict himself to the sociological differences; and so on.

It is different for a writer. The writer is free to roam. Like a pirate he raids the treasures of learning amassed by others, chooses the richest nuggets and sells the loot to his readers. That is what I am doing in this book. The loot will be raided from many sciences, particularly the sciences of biology, anatomy, physiology, cytology, embryology, foetology, endocrinology, anthropology and sociology. Also it will be necessary to seek out opinion, arguments, legend and romance in the realism of art, literature, history and politics, and even in linguistics and law. Such an exploration might seem daunting, might seem to threaten a ponderously scholastic result, but we shall make our journey together as laymen, a bit wide-eyed and innocent and wondering, trying to translate everything that we discover into layman's language. By doing so we shall, I hope, invest this report with interest and excitement and, more important, some measure of the beauty its subject deserves.

I think that a word about the structure of this book will be helpful to my readers. After first conceiving the idea of the book I made many experiments to design a structure which would present a vast and complex subject in a readable way. Each experiment brought me back to what I call a 'chronological plan'. By that I mean a plan which tells the story of the difference between man and woman in chronological sequence. We begin with the fertilisation of the egg, and from the conception of male or female embryo in the womb we continue through pre-natal life, babyhood, infancy and puberty to the sexual maturity of adult man and adult woman. This, I have decided, is the only logical plan. But I do see in it one possible disadvantage. It means that the opening chapters might be concerned more with the intricacies of science than with flesh and blood; more with such things as sperm and ovaries, chromosomes and hormones, than with those things which promise to be more interesting: the bodies, minds, habits and sexual attitudes of the men and women we know. Yet I am encouraged by the fact that for my own part I found the biological forming of our sex differences as exciting to study and as exciting to write about as are men and women themselves. I hope my readers might share that interest.

The impatient reader however, the reader who wants to get down immediately to learning how different he or she is from her or him, can use the table of contents as a guide to chapters of particular interest, for all the chapters are so designed that each one can be read independently of the others, though as author I naturally hope that any chapter read in that way will tempt the reader to go back or forward and read all the others. My attempt to make each chapter 'self-contained' inevitably results in occasional repetition when, by way of explanation, facts essential to other chapters have to be referred to again. But I decided occasional repetition was preferable to cumbersome cross-reference. Similarly, because this book is not a technical scientific book, I have avoided the use of footnotes. Authorities quoted are acknowledged in the text. My immense debt to those authorities and to the scientists and doctors who have helped me with personal comment and advice is acknowledged in the biblography at the end of the book.

PART ONE

The Difference in Body

. . . male and female created He them

GENESIS

1 How the Difference Begins

The boy has a penis; the girl has not.

Each of us discovered that anatomical fact in our different ways. If we were lucky enough to have baby brothers and sisters, we made the discovery gradually and cumulatively, noticing penis or no-penis while baby was being dressed or bathed or having its nappy changed. If we had no brothers and sisters, we satisfied our curiosity more furtively and deliberately, and perhaps a little later in life, under bushes in a garden, behind a wall at infant school, or in some other private retreat.

My own childhood memories are woefully fragmentary, almost pathologically so, but my memory of the moment when I discovered that the body of my favourite playmate lacked such a tassel as my body possessed is vivid enough to have survived to this day with all its attendant details of scene and scent and sound; and I hold firmly to the opinion that she and I can be numbered among the lucky ones in that this sexual revelation burst upon us amid the clean sane beauty of a sunlit Yorkshire meadow during an interval between picking flowers. The girl found the difference so diverting that she curled up in giggles, but then, to mollify any affront to my pride such derision might have caused, she honoured my masculinity with a decoration of cowslips. All that years before Lady Chatterley.

A colleague interrupts me here to say that he has no recollection at all of the occasion when he first made the penis-no-penis discovery. He is not unusual in that. The majority of the memories a child retains are pleasant memories. Unpleasant memories are always more likely to be repressed than are pleasant ones. 'We all block the recalling of some unpleasant past experience,' says Professor Ian Hunter, 'and our lives are the happier and better for it.' Many people therefore do not remember the penis-no-penis discovery because it was probably made in circumstances which seemed in some way disagreeable to the child, in circumstances tinged with disquiet or feelings of guilt, or in circumstances accompanied by parental anger or warning or censure. If that happens, the memory is suppressed, is buried in the subconscious beyond conscious recall.

However, before a child becomes conscious of having a penis or lacking one it has become aware of innumerable other social sex differences. Little boys wear trousers, but little girls wear skirts. Little boys have their hair cropped, but little girls keep it long and tied with ribbons. Little boys play rough games, scuffle in the mud and flourish toy pistols, but little girls are prissy, careful of their frills, and pretend to be mummies at mincingly polite dollies' tea-parties. Undoubtedly these differences in dress and conduct awaken our sexual curiosity. The sex difference becomes the big 'Why?' of our infancy. Eventually, if the 'Why?' is not answered by accident, some of us are bold enough to answer it deliberately, to uncover that unspeakably mysterious difference which, hidden under trousers or skirts, is so fascinating to unveil and peep at and so agreeable to fondle with innocent but vibrantly exploratory fingers. Indeed we find the examinations we make of this particular difference between boy and girl so disturbingly exciting that we know by instinct that it is better to keep any news of our intimate explorations from the ears of adults who, we guess, would be censorious and restrictive.

A child is, of course, impressed by the penis-no-penis difference in male and female bodies. In a child's eyes it naturally looks a quite staggering difference, far more important than it actually is.

Some people never grow out of the childish belief that possessing penis or vagina is the only important distinction between man and woman. When discussing the title of this book an American publisher said that there was hardly need to write anything; the whole story could be told by two photographs of frontal nudes. The publisher said that as a joke, but there really are people who think that the entire difference between man and woman could be demonstrated as easily as that. Those are adults whose sexual ideas and sexual imagination are retarded. Their concept of sexuality is forever arrested at the primitive level of childhood's furtive peeping and fingering. All their sexual desires and all their sexual activity, in short all those things which they mistakenly dignify with the word 'love', never rise higher than the groin. It can be taken as a rule that the less mentally mature an adult is the more importance he or she will attach to penis or vagina. The more incapable an adult is of performing the higher human processes of thinking and reasoning and imagining in the proper location for such processes, above the neck, the more he or she will be governed by what goes on below the waist. Incidentally, this childish fixation on penis or vagina is as common in retarded homosexuals as it is in retarded heterosexuals: such people, homosexual or heterosexual, are ready-made customers for the quick crude genital commerce of male or female prostitute.

Those frontal nudes, interesting and attractive though they are, tell us only a fraction of the story of sex differences. Penis or vagina, which seem so important to us when we are children and such sources of pride and joy when we are adult, are not actually distinctions between man and woman; not even, in the strictly biological sense, necessary for reproduction. In fact they are defined, along with such things as the hairs on a man's chest and a woman's breast and fatty hips, as nothing more than *secondary* sexual characteristics. The *primary* characteristics of sex, those decisive differences which do not show up on any studio photograph and are difficult enough to find even with X-ray or microscope, are biological and biochemical; differences of glands and hormones and chromosomes.

However much or little we know about those inner biological differences most of us, when we assess masculinity or femininity, appreciate sex differences that seem more important than differences in physical shape. Men and women move differently and talk differently; they conduct their lives and their vocations differently; they have different attitudes of thought; they have different emotions. Are these differences determined by our sexual shape? Or are they forced on us by social conditioning, by society teaching us how to be male or how to be female? What about sex differences in aptitudes and skills and intelligence? Why has woman's record in intellectual achievement been so much less than man's? And how do we account for certain attributes being considered masculine and others being considered feminine? What, for instance, about 'woman's intuition'?

Finally, what about that fundamental difference between the sexes, the difference between male and female love? Man is the lover: woman is the loved. This, I believe, is the most important difference of all; a difference that has determined the whole pattern of human evolution and the whole shape of human civilisation. But before that can be explained we have to know something about the physical and psychological construction of male and female humans.

1 OUR FIRST LESSON IN SEX

'Da ... da ... da. Ma ... ma ... ma.' The smacking of tongue against palate and the pressing and parting of lips are more like movements of eating and sucking than of speech. Yet these burblings are the forerunners of words, and eventually the words take shape.

'Dadda! Mamma!' Those are among our first words, sometimes the very first, and they are the most significant in our vocabulary. Significant because by uttering them we are doing more than announcing the dawn of our intelligence as humans and making our first tentative exercises in the greatest of human talents, the talent of speech. We are also showing that we have reached the stage when we can see other humans as separate individuals, can distinguish one face from another. What is more, we can already see the difference between man and woman. Man is father. Woman is mother. Our sexual education has begun.

Just as a child who is learning to read must first learn to recognise the differences in the shapes of printed letters long before it can be expected to appreciate the complexities of thought which those shapes are capable of conveying, so does the baby recognise father and mother as man and woman long before it can appreciate the infinite complexities of behaviour and, sexual destiny written into the difference between male and female.

Our simple dadda-mamma concept of masculinity and femininity cannot survive beyond babyhood. It is soon overlaid by other sexual knowledge. We collect more data. By using father and mother as archetypes we learn to distinguish other men from other women. By measuring our playmates against ourselves we know which is a boy and which is a girl, learning to approach each in a different way and to expect from each a different response.

How do we learn all this? Not because the little boy has a penis and the little girl has not, for we distinguish differences between male and female long before we notice that novelty. Then how? No one deliberately and studiously teaches us.

There is never need for anyone to tell us. 'This is a man' or 'This is a woman'. We acquire the knowledge for ourselves. We learn in the way in which the human learns all the habits of life: from things seen and heard and felt. Information flows into us through our eyes and ears, and nose and mouth, and through every nerve ending of the sensitive human skin of our fingertips and lips and belly and genitals. Each intimate attention by our mother, each laughing encounter with our father, each meeting with uncles and aunts, brothers and sisters, boys and girls adds to our store of knowledge. From faces that look down on us, from hands that caress us, from arms that lift us, we learn that male and female differ in shape and size and hairiness.

By the time we begin noticing the exaggerated difference between masculine and feminine clothes we are also becoming aware of differences far more subtle. Different tones of voice; different ways of moving and walking and running; different emotional responses that are accompanied by different laughter; different tears and different angers. As well as also becoming aware of one markedly sexual difference, one which we accept for the time being without any sense of mystery or prurient curiosity, the different male and female postures for urinating.

Equally without questioning it we accept our society's pattern of masculine and feminine behaviour, taking it for granted that man and woman assume differing duties and perform differing chores in the home and around it. With the result that when the time comes when we can move around and exercise freedom of choice we fashion our conduct on the examples set by father and mother, adopting our individual pattern of masculinity or femininity and showing preference for the toys and play that are suitable to our sex.

We would have done the same wherever we had been born. In other parts of the world many of the sexual symbols which distinguish male from female would have been completely reversed from the ones we know in our society, or might not have existed at all. The women around us might have worn trousers or pantaloons and the men have worn kilts or skirts of grass. Or both might have been robed alike in sarong or skins or beads. We might have been born into a society in which women were the labourers, the tillers of soil and makers of pots, carrying all burdens 'because their heads are stronger', and where the men were painted dandies leaning over the garden fence giggling and gossiping. Even the postures adopted by male and female in urinating could be the reverse to what we know in our society, for in some primitive societies men squat and women stand during the process; as, according to Herodotus, was the custom in ancient Egypt. Nevertheless in any society we would grow up knowing without doubt which was man and which was woman, and the first words any baby would lisp would be the racial equivalent of Dadda and Mamma.

The baby is right. Not knowledge, which comes later, but instinct, with which all of us are born, has led the baby unerringly to the fundamental difference between man and woman. Man is father: woman is mother. That is the difference more profound than any difference of dress and custom which we later notice, more decisive than the outspoken differences of male and female genitals. All man's flamboyant regalia of penis and testicles and all woman's rounded hips and burgeoning breasts are secondary to the primary sexual difference between man as sperm-carrier and father and woman as egg-breeder and mother.

The time will come, of course, when our masculinity or femininity matures and our bodies stir to the teasing and demands of awakening sexuality. Then those secondary characteristics, the difference in genitals and breasts, the difference in shape and odour of man and woman, will seem to us to be emphatic and desirable differences between male and female. When that time comes our innocent conception of man as father and woman as mother, though still persisting on the threshold of consciousness, will be engulfed in the clamant desire of male for female and female for male. Then the same senses with which as children we learned to see and to know the differences between man and woman, the senses of sight and sound and smell and touch, will come into sexual use. We shall employ them first to observe, then to explore, and finally to enjoy the sexual difference in ecstasies of pleasure and pain. Though, by now intelligently adult, we shall transmute the messages transmitted from our sensory organs, shall have the capacity to enrich sensual sensations with intellectual sensations; with passion, with imagery, and, on occasion, with love.

By that time we shall have come full circle. We in our turn shall have become wholly male or wholly female, father or mother. By that time too we might realise that the physical differences which we find so entrancing and stimulating are a lure, the baited trap, the beautiful and complex duality Nature has designed to seduce us into the performance of our human duty.

As it is in this book our ambition to make the complexity and also the natural and entrancing beauty of that sexual duality explicit there is only one way to begin our story. We must begin it by describing the way Nature decided what sex, male or female, we should be and how, in making that decision, she designed the symbols, masculine or feminine, that our bodies would wear.

The decision was made before we were born: some nine months before, at the beginning of our pre-natal existence. It was made at that moment when one spermatozoon, a single microscopically-minute tadpole, only 1/50,000th to 1/60,000th of a millimetre from head to tail and only one of a wave of about 260 million of other tadpoles which had been bred in our father's testes and ejaculated through his penis into our mother's vagina, wriggled with flaying tail into her uterine tube and there, beating odds of 260-million-to-one against him, found and won the prize of the awaiting egg, 85,000 times bigger than himself, pierced the membrane of the egg, entered it, was swallowed up by it, and fertilised it. The other spermatozoa, the 259,999,999 losers, died. To the winner went the reward of having created a human life. We were on our way. We were already irrevocably destined to become man or woman.

2 NATURE IS A WOMAN

Woman is the balanced one; man is a bit odd. At least that seems to be the opinion Nature expresses in the biochemical processes which she has designed for the creating and perpetuating of life.

Incidentally, notice how in that last sentence we have revealed our instinctive recognition of Nature's sex. Without thought of questioning the word, we automatically refer to Nature as 'she'. It is true that when we are speaking rhetorically of humanity we use grandly masculine terms: when we refer to human beings in the mass, whether they are men or women, we use the word 'mankind' or '*man*'. But when we try to give a name and the semblance of personality to the generative force which gives life to our earth and everything upon it we resort to the feminine pronoun, demonstrating in our vocabulary the primeval concept of Mother Earth, the maternal source of existence. Indeed when we are speaking of Nature in her benign and reproductive moods we honour her with the title 'Mother Nature', saluting her as the universal mother and housewife compared with whom any male God we might dream up and invest with awful power seems only the rather fussy and constantly overworked business manager to a matriarchal producer and dispenser of wealth. Biology beautifully demonstrates this aspect of Nature as mother and housewife. Despite her sometimes awful anger when she ravages our homes with earthquakes and dusts the oceans with hurricanes she can in matters of detail be exquisitely precise and rigorously systematic.

Above all she likes symmetry. She likes things to be spherical, or at least rounded in their overall contours: plants, eggs, seeds, cells. And she likes to arrange these creations symmetrically, most often preferring them, like vases on a mantelpiece, in pairs: twin leaves on the stem of a flower; two arms and legs, two lungs and kidneys, two breasts and two testicles on bodies; two eyes and nostrils on faces; two frontal lobes to a centrally balanced brain.

This pattern of evenly balanced pairs is obligatory by physical law. The force of gravity which holds everything close to the breast of Mother Earth, the dominant force which keeps us all securely on our home ground instead of being whirled into space and which controls every instant of our life and determines the structure of every millimetre of our being, does more than make apples fall from trees. It plays its part even in our sex life, including such refined mechanics as drawing testicles down from the warmth of summer-heated bodies so that the spermatozoa will enjoy the cooler temperature they need to retain active life, and lowering the weight of milk-filled breasts to the upturned suckling. Because of the force of gravity living mobile creatures must have their organs and their weight evenly disposed on a central axis.

Vertebrates, humans and all back-boned animals, are bilaterally symmetrical, one side of the body being in general a mirror-image of the other. Except, you remark, for the heart. Why that organ, that single governor of the vital circulation of the blood, should be on one side is, as Chesterton remarked, indeed 'uncanny'. He poetically described the phenomenon as 'a silent swerving from accuracy . . . a sort of secret treason' against Nature's law of symmetry, and added, 'No one has any idea why'.

Nature's theme of pairs is seen in its most fascinating and exquisite form in the innermost recesses of life, in the paired arrangement of the chromosomes in the nucleus of the organic cell. It is in that minute chamber, the cell where we can see the beginning of the difference between man and woman, peering through our microscopes into that laboratory where our sexual differences are chemically manufactured.

Cells are often described as 'the building blocks' of life, the bricks used for the building of everything that lives, of every plant and insect and fish and bird and beast. If we describe cells as bricks, then we might describe the chromosomes within the nucleus of the cell as the templates which decide the shape into which the cell must grow and the architectural position it must occupy in the final structure.

The chromosomes are infinitely minute rods clustered in the heart of the animal cell. Individually they look something like a child's drawing of matchstick-men or letters from the alphabet of some early script. A script they certainly are, for precise instructions of what we shall become are meticulously sketched on the chromosomes. Each chromosome consists of hundreds or thousands of genes strung along, like information in a vast encyclopedia, in coded clumps of acids which dictate to the cell what its function in life must be; whether it must become skin or flesh, muscle or bone, as well as the size and shape of the organ of which it will form a part.

In order that life can continue, that organs can take shape and grow, cells must multiply. They do so by splitting into pairs. When the cells split, the chromosome instructions are not lost, for when a cell is dividing to become two cells the chromosomes also split along their length. One half of each chromosome goes to one cell and one half to the other, with the result that both cells now have an identical complement of genes. So the genetic instructions have been duplicated, like a letter in a typewriter. Now two cells instead of one know precisely what is expected of them.

In the body cells of most animals, including the human animal, the chromosomes are arranged in pairs, in two sets identical or nearly identical in size and shape. One set has come from the egg, the other set has come from the sperm.

Different species of animals have different numbers of pairs of chromosomes. A mouse, for instance, has twenty pairs; a horse has thirty; your cat has nineteen. The human being has twenty-three pairs.

Upon these little rods our future depends. They decide most of our physical and quite a lot of our mental development. The genetical instructions printed in the acid code dictate whether our skin will be black or brown or yellow, or what we call white; whether our hair will be blonde or brunette, curly or straight; whether our bodies will be tall or short; and even such details as whether our brows will be high or low, or whether our buttocks will stick out or not. These genes can doom us to deformed legs and a limp, or help us to win Olympic races.

If they are not doing their job healthily and properly genes can endow us with such oddities as deformed fingernails and kneecaps, can weaken our ability to taste food, or can overdevelop our muscles in uncomfortable places. Some defects inherited in our genes we shall transmit to our children and our grandchildren and their grandchildren. In 1969 medical researchers in America investigating one of the rarest forms of diabetes traced it back to Scotland and came to the conclusion that it had been brought across the Atlantic in the genes of a particular party of Scottish colonists who had arrived at Halifax in Nova Scotia in 1761. The genes we inherit can determine even our mental ability, might even dictate whether we shall be a genius or a moron, an Einstein or a politician. The fateful importance of chromosomes was discovered in 1902 when a Dane, W. L. Johannsen, recognised their importance in heredity. In the same year C. E. McLung discovered their sexual power. Of the twenty-three pairs of chromosomes in the human cell there is one pair whose function is to decide the sex, the sexual shape and sexual purpose, of the human egg. Scientists have conveniently labelled these sex-chromosomes as 'X' and 'Y'. The X-chromosome is the female one; the Y-chromosome is male.

They are fairly easily recognised from the other pairs because they are so odd. Here Nature has had to depart from her theme of balanced pairs, and in doing so she seems to express in biochemical language her feminine prejudice. For the female chromosome, the X, is large, equal in size to the majority of chromosomes in the cell, and compared with her the male chromosome, the Y, is tiny, a mere mite. Incidentally he has fewer genes.

At this stage, just in case some scientist interrupts (as scientists are inclined to do and have the right to do when laymen are dangerously simplifying and translating their findings), with a grumbling observation that we have oversimplified the story, we must admit that it is risky to talk loosely of *male* and *female* chromosomes. Actually it is the complex of genes in the chromosome which governs the extent of masculinity and femininity, and in that respect chromosomes can be as mixed-up as some of we humans sometimes are. So the sexual characterisation of the chromosomes is not always in accordance with the sex it might appear to be. However it will be simpler and more understandable here to refer to *male* chromosomes and *female* chromosomes as boldly as we refer in real life, in drawing room or in bed, to men and women.

3 FEMALE EGG, BUT MIXED-UP SPERM

If Nature had been adamant, if she had insisted in adhering, even at the basic cellular level of life, to her obsession with balanced pairs, those sex-chromosomes would have had to be of equal size and equal weight. However, as life has to go on and the species must be perpetuated, Nature had to make a concession. She had to forgo her preference for symmetry and introduce that odd little chromosome, that undersized by-product the male.

Confronted with such positive evidence of Nature's biochemical prejudice, the male will probably look around for something to support his pride in his masculinity. He will almost certainly claim that although he is cast in a smaller and inferior role biochemically, it is nevertheless the male who is the active and dominant performer in the creating of life, whereas the female is merely the passive and receptive vessel for his seed. After all, he will say, the female has to wait with her unfertilised egg until he has manufactured and ejaculated that precious sperm, the vital product of manhood. It is significant that the vulgar word for sperm, 'spunk', is often also used to indicate those masculine qualities which any man, or for that matter any boy, ought to have 'in him'.

It is indeed natural to imagine that the virile spermatozoon is a muscular masculine invader and the egg is a quiescent virginal victim of his forceful entry. Nature must smile at such conceit.

Yes, the egg is feminine, wholly and undeniably so. When it has reached maturity and, lodged in the uterine tube, awaits fertilisation, it contains one feminine X-chromosome. But, alas for masculine pride, no comparable status of irrefutable sex can be claimed by spermatozoa *en masse*.

It is true that spermatozoa do behave like soldiers. In what we could describe as a typically masculine attitude of attack and conquest the millions-strong army of tadpoles surges forward and upward with a vigorous wave-like motion; as relentlessly as a swarm of salmon on their way to the spawning ground, and for the same purpose. Indeed they can, like salmon, go against the current of any descending fluid, either that of the female secretions or even the seminal fluid in which they are suspended, and by the forcefulness of their own vigorous tail-flaying activity reach the womb and the ovaries.

Even in their determination to survive against all odds until they have done their job spermatozoa seem courageously masculine. The wave of sperm will survive through some thirty-six hours needed for the journey from the mouth of the womb to the egg. There the successful one makes his conquest. His millions of brave comrades carry on, missing and presumed dead, into the abdomen: a man's picture of a gallant army lost but one hero conquering.

Yet the truth is that only fifty per cent, about 130 million, of those creatures who appear so energetically and essentially masculine in behaviour are male: the other 130 million are female.

Because of this biochemical male-female mixture in the spermatozoa the sex of the resulting baby is a matter of fifty-fifty chance. The sex of the baby depends entirely on which kind of spermatozoon wins the egg. It might be a female spermatozoon: in which case its X-chromosome will mate with the egg's X-chromosome to form the symmetrical X-X pattern characteristic of the female cell. Or it might be a male spermatozoon who gets there first with his Y-chromosome: in that case we shall have that odd unbalanced X-Y pair of one big and one little chromosome which designs a man.

Many ideas have been advanced to suggest ways in which the gamble can be influenced to favour the X or Y spermatozoon. Some of the ideas are divertingly bizarre. One, for instance, suggests that alcohol imbibed too freely at the wedding breakfast is the cause of more first-born children being male than female. It is argued that an intoxicated man is more likely to beget a boy than a girl. This, by the way, is not the freakish belief of some superstitious peasants: it is an opinion expressed in all scientific seriousness, founded on the theory that male spermatozoa are slightly more vigorous than female spermatozoa. Therefore, the argument continues, if the father is guilty of any habits that can have an adverse effect on his sperm production, if for instance he drinks too much before the wedding night, the male spermatozoa, being stronger and more resistant, 'able to hold their drink better', have more chance of winning that race to the egg than have the weaker intoxicated females.

Well, one German geneticist actually put the theory to the test: though he did it in his laboratory, not at a wedding breakfast. He intoxicated a flock of male mice and then let the drunken creatures roister among their wives. The result was 120 baby males and 100 females, as against the 80 males and 100 females previously recorded when the fathers had been stone cold sober. Apart from any significance there might be in the male-female proportion in those figures, it is surely interesting to note that mice when drunk have 40 more children than when they are sober.

Not only drinks at the weddings but now the smoking habits of fathers and mothers are being investigated as a possible influence on the sex of their children. This inquiry was sparked off by investigations in Japan among people who had been exposed to atomic-radiation. Scientists there claimed that a most sensitive indicator of damage to the genes was the sex ratio of male and female births from exposed parents.

A father transmits his X-chromosomes to his daughters, and his Y-chromosome to his sons. But the Y-chromosome, as we have mentioned, has far fewer genes than the X-chromosome. Therefore the damage it might suffer from radiation is relatively much less. The X-chromosome, having many more genes, is more liable to be damaged. If a human egg is to be fertilised to produce a female, it must receive an X-chromosome from the father's sperm. But if the father's X-chromosomes have been decisively damaged by radiation then his Y-chromosomes will have the best of the odds in the race. That father is therefore likely to have more sons than daughters. On the other hand if the mother has been exposed and the father not, the damage to her X-chromosome, if the damage is not excessive, will be counterbalanced by the father's healthy X-chromosome. If the damage to her X-chromosome is dominantly excessive, then she too has less chance of having daughters. If her damaged X-chromosome meets up with a Y-chromosome, there will be no counter-balance from the father and the net result will be a lower proportion of sons. We can sum up all these possibilities in a kind of mathematical genetic equation: exposed fathers can be expected to produce more sons than non-exposed fathers, but exposed mothers can be expected to produce fewer sons than non-exposed mothers.

From these findings comes the smoking theory. It is suggested that tobacco smoking might cause genetic mutation in the same way that radiation can. Some geneticists now believe that smoking exposes human beings to the most significant genetic mutagen known, ionizing radiation. Surveys of the sex-ratio of children born to smoking and non-smoking fathers and mothers have already been made. The statistics collected have not confirmed the geneticists' theory as strongly as in the radiation investigation, but the inquiry is continuing.

In less sophisticated circles, in villages of France and Italy where people know nothing about genetics, wise folk say there is an infallible way of ensuring the birth of a boy: the father must wear his hat when he performs the necessary act. So far as I can ascertain no scientist, German or otherwise, has yet put that uncomfortable and rather ill-mannered operation to the test with men; and it would be difficult to get a mouse, even if it were drunk, to wear its hat. When I discussed the legend with an English psychologist, however, he pointed out the possible traumatic effect on the baby's mother if she did not know the colour of its father's hair.

Champagne at weddings, drunken mice, cigarettes and hats apart, so far as we can see the ultimate sex of the baby is still a gamble. Up to now neither science nor superstition has found a way of controlling the throw of the dice, although Kenneth Walker in *The Physiology of Sex* says that if 'male-determining and female-determining sperms differ in size, some method of separation, for example by careful centrifugalisation, may eventually be found. This will allow of the artificial insemination of the female with the required type of spermatozoa, so that the birth of a male or a female may be obtained, according to desire.'

Sometimes the neat X-Y or X-X pattern is upset by an extra chromosome pushing itself into the grouping. Babies with such chromosomal abnormality are found to be smaller at birth than babies with the normal 46 chromosomes. But when, as happens in about one male in 500, the intruding extra chromosome is a Y, this makes an X-Y-Y grouping. For some time this grouping has been associated with extra tall men, but recently a more unwelcome possibility than tallness has emerged. That extra Y, it is believed, might cause its possessor to have criminal tendencies and lower intelligence.

In a Brooklyn laboratory a physiologist has managed to produce 'super-male' fish with an abnormal pattern of only Y-Y chromosomes and he finds that they behave in a manner somewhat analogous to the behaviour of some X-Y-Y human males. Like those 'tall men' the Y-Y fish are more competitive in sexual pursuit of females and more inclined than are their normal X-Y fellows to threaten and chase off rivals. The physiologist is also waiting to see if his 'super-males' have shorter lives than other males, in which case the extra Y-chromosome might be the cause, and this could possibly be one more clue towards discovering why men have shorter lives than women.

Some doubts are now being expressed whether that male Y-chromosome is as important as was thought. Even the male himself might not be necessary for the procreation of life. Simone de Beauvoir seizes upon this idea with characteristic enthusiasm, welcoming the possibility that 'in time the co-operation of the male will become unnecessary in procreation —the answer, it would seem, to many a woman's prayer'.

We hasten to point out that this feminist hope is not founded on anything so crude as the prospect of universal artificial insemination, but arises from the bold suggestion now being made that perhaps male sperm is not always necessary for reproduction. It is now generally accepted that all the things really needed for the building of a living creature are stored within the egg. The German-born biologist Jacques Loeb, working on this theory in America, found that merely by altering the interacting pressure in the unfertilised eggs of such lower forms of life as sea-urchins and frogs' eggs which had never received sperm from the male became fertile and produced larvae.

We know that virgins can give birth to children. The phenomenon known as parthenogenesis, colloquially called 'virgin birth', when a female egg develops and reproduces life without being fertilised by a male spermatozoon, does actually occur in lower animals. Sperm need not of itself contain any 'seed of life' at all. It need be no more than a ferment. Its sole function can be to act as a simple chemical stimulant that stings the self-sufficient egg to the creation of life. Simone de Beauvoir reports scientific findings that in certain species the egg can thus be stimulated to cleave into two and develop an embryo without any sperm at all. All the egg needs is nothing more than a drop of acid or even the prick of a needle. This, however, is yet another experiment that no one as yet has put to the test with humans.

At present the emphasis in conditioning fertilisation is mostly on techniques of artificial insemination, a process which seems to many to be one of the scientific discoveries of our day. Actually it was performed some 600 years ago. The first known product of artificial insemination was a foal born after an Arab horse-breeder had stolen semen from a famous stallion and carried it on a cloth to a mare in his stables.

4 PARENTS WHO PREFER BOYS

If ever we do reach the stage of sophisticated tampering with human spermatozoa or with the human egg, and if at the same time we can learn how to control the ultimate sex of the progeny, the result would almost certainly be the birth of more boys than girls. For despite Nature's prejudice in favour of the female, human beings show a contrasting prejudice in favour of the male. More parents want to have a male child, at least as the first-born, than a female child.

A survey made in the U.S.A. showed that if parents could have freedom to choose the sex of their child there would be a surplus of more than 300,000 boys a year. Psychologists studying the reasons given by the parents came to the conclusion that most mothers want a boy because the male child will be a substitute for the father, and most fathers want a boy because they believe that boys are more certain than girls to achieve success in competitive masculine-orientated society.

In other societies and in other times this preference for male children is seen in more exaggerated forms, even to the extent of letting female children die. In some communities the preference is dictated by the dominant belief that man is more important than woman. The Korava people of southern India, for instance, believe so much that the life of the man is more valuable than that of a woman, that during a wife's pregnancy it is the husband who is carefully tended and nursed. The male-preference is expressed, poetically, but brutally, in a Turkish proverb. 'If a daughter is born to thee, better she should not live. Better she should not be born, or, if born, better the funeral feast be with the birth.' And a Kirghiz proverb says, 'Keep not thy salt too long or it melts away to water. Keep not thy daughter, or she becomes a slave.'

Yet modern science now comes up with suggestions that much as parents might prefer boys Nature, characteristically, makes it easier for the girl to be born; makes it easier not during birth but biochemically before birth. Ever since Freud declared that sexuality was not an adult monopoly but existed in the body and mind of the baby at the breast, psycho-analysts could not be content to restrict their inquiries to the psychological upsets of the patient on the couch. To find the roots of these upsets they had to go back further and further, to childhood, to infancy, to babyhood. Recently they have begun to ask if they might go even further back? Is it possible that the roots of adult preoccupations and fears and disturbed sexuality are implanted *before* birth? This question brings psychiatrists and physiologists together to study what happens to us during our nine months of pre-natal life. Together they are finding clues leading to the belief that at least some of our mental future is designed, just as much of our physical future and our sex is designed, in the womb.

Experiments at Rochester University in New York have shown that shocks suffered by a mother can affect the mentality of her offspring. Pregnant rats have been put into a state of anxiety by a series of electric shocks. Young rats from mothers who had not suffered these anxieties proved to be normally bold and exploratory in any fresh environment. But rats that had been in the womb when their mothers had suffered anxiety shocks were utterly different creatures; so frightened that they could not move. They also showed greater susceptibility to disease.

At Yale New Haven Hospital in Connecticut experiments with sheep have shown that eye movements made by unborn lambs are remarkably similar to eye movements made by humans when dreaming. Then do we human beings dream before we are born? Dr. Edward Quilligan thinks that 'there is a possibility that the foetus dreams while in its intra-uterine environment. If this indeed is true, the foetus must receive some stimuli which would constitute the matrix for its dreams. And if it is receiving stimuli, then indeed it would be possible to condition the foetus in the womb by providing proper stimulus.'

If unborn babies do dream, are the dreams of unborn boys different from those of unborn girls? Even that is possible. Current research is exploiting the possibility that we might experience some kind of sexual stress even when we are in the womb. Although the pregnant mother might be no more than curious as to whether her baby will be boy or girl, might have no conscious preference for one or the other, unknown to her her body might be expressing a sexual preference, might be reacting differently to a male foetus than it would to a female foetus. This theory arises from the suggestion that the biochemical reaction in a pregnant woman's body differs according to the sex of the foetus. After all, the argument goes, the mother is female, so it does seem possible that her biochemistry will have an *affinity* with the female, but should the baby be male her biochemistry will be in *contrast* to the male.

Such biochemical possibilities seem so mystical that we can get the impression that science is coming almost full circle, is approaching a point at which it will confront ancient superstitions once accepted as truth. To our knowledgeable and speculative twentieth-century minds the beliefs of ancient man and of modern primitive peoples seem bizarre and irrational. Well, to their minds many of our latest discoveries and daunting theories would seem equally bizarre and irrational. We can almost imagine that in the science-fiction future of tomorrow scientists might find reasons for some of the extraordinary and colourful superstitions which primitive people attached to pregnancy and birth. Although it can hardly be expected that any scientist will ever prove the warning given to a pregnant woman by the Galelareese Indians of Halmahera that if she eats two bananas that have grown on the same stalk she will give birth to twins, perhaps it might be discovered that a mother's pregnancy can be biochemically determined by influences considered equally superstitious.

However we have not reached that stage yet. So far as we can at present ascertain, parental preferences for boy or girl have no influence at all on the end result. Although the physiologists are juggling with spermatozoa and testing mechanical means of separating Y's from X's, so far as normal copulation is concerned we still find it difficult, to say the least, to pick the winner in a race in which there are 260 million runners. The common method of fertilisation is still that of shooting a flood of mixed male and female tadpoles more or less in the direction of the womb. It does seem a haphazard process, yet by the law of averages the fifty-fifty sex balance of the spermatozoa results in an almost equal number of male and female births.

Almost equal. There is a slight excess of males. Statistics from most countries (and, where available, from most racial groups) show more boys born than girls. The number of male conceptions, when one takes into account the higher number of miscarriages and stillbirths with male children, might even be as many as 120 to every 100 female conceptions. British statistics show some 105 to 108 boys born for every 100 girls; so each impregnation in Britain has about a 52 per cent chance of resulting in the birth of a male.

One explanation for the excess of male births suggests it is because although *all* men are masculine some are *more* masculine than others, and that the more masculine fathers probably have a tendency to produce more males than females. As in most societies it is the man who initiates or forces copulation it is likely that the more masculine types exercise their male prerogative more forcibly and constantly than the others; thus more males than females are fathered.

Yet, and here again we can suspect Nature of continuing her sex prejudice, boys are more likely to be still-born than girls. This is true of every country where birth-statistics are compiled. Also the mortality of male children in the first year is much greater than that of female children. In fact infant boys are notably more delicate and more difficult to rear than infant girls, with the result that, particularly and noticeably in Europe, the surplus of males at birth changes to a surplus of females among adults. We shall deal with this in greater detail when we discuss the 'weaker sex' in Chapter 4.

So, by and large, the human race is kept to a fairly even balance of the sexes, and even if doctors do become more successful in saving the lives of more boys with more effective gynaecological and post-natal care, perhaps any resulting excess of males over females will still be corrected by the increasing hazards of human life; the excess males being eliminated, in large numbers by warfare and in small numbers by motor-cycles or other lethal masculine toys.

2 Why Only Two Sexes?

It is surprising that there are only *two* sexes.

Nature's mechanism for manufacturing male or female is delicately and superbly designed, and it works, on the whole, efficiently. Only on very few occasions does it misfire, and then the result is not so decidedly male or female as might be desired. But if we remind ourselves of the infinite number and complexity of parts needed in sex engineering we find ourselves surprised that the sexes are not more varied and mixed-up than they are.

Indeed we ought to marvel how humans even come out in any consistent shape at all. Think of the biological processes involved, not only in the details of moulding membrane and genital tissues into masculine and feminine sexual organs, but in the overall construction of a human anatomy; the building of a torso with four limbs, the fashioning of entrails, bone, skin and muscle, the weaving of the nerves, the construction of the electrical complex of the brain, as well as the chemical composition of the hormones, those secretions confected by our endocrine glands.

When we study all these intricate processes we are dully unimaginative indeed if we do not catch our breath in wonder that human beings turn out so much like each other and have so many physical characteristics in common, and that the only notable difference between them is represented by two recognisably differentiated types, man and woman. There are, of course, racial differences of colour and shape and size. But we must not attach too much importance to those: they are merely superficial colorations of the universal beautifully constructed uniform two-legged prehensile vertebrate that is a human being.

Within each sex there are, as we know, subtle differences in the intensity of masculinity and femininity even where there is no uncertainty in sexual tendencies. But fortunately for our sanity and certainly fortunately for our pleasure we are by and large distinguishably male or female, each equipped with a recognisable reproductive sexual appliance appropriate to our sex, which, though it might differ in size or colour from man to man and from woman to woman nevertheless comes in familiar and understandable pattern: a penis for the man, and a vertically cleft (legends to the contrary about oriental women can be discounted) *mons veneris* for the woman.

The different shapes of male and female sexual instruments seem to express in a bold physical manner the significant differences between masculinity and femininity. Because we humans are thinking beings, beings who can not only see the shape of things but can also think about them, reflect on them and speculate about them, it is understandable that we accept almost subconsciously that the protruding penis of the man and the infolded vagina of the woman illustrate the psychological differences between man and woman. Thus we think it natural that man should be, like his penis, an outward, thrusting, and boldly obvious character, and woman, like her concealed vagina, should be an inward, receptive, secret and mysterious character.

That assumption is a little too facile. There are, as we shall discover later when we investigate the differing sexuality of man and woman, hazards in all sexual generalities, and now we must study closely something which will warn us against making glib judgments not only about psychological differences between the sexes but also about physical differences. We are going to see the way in which our apparently so different sexual organs arrive at the shapes we know so well.

1 PENIS OR CLITORIS

During the fourth week of pre-natal life, from twenty-one to twenty-eight days after the spermatozoon has fertilised the egg, the human embryo, only seven millimetres long, is just recognisable as a human 'seedling'. Already fairly easy to see is the curve of the spine, at one end a tail and at the other the bulb which will develop into a head. In the head a perceptive layman can see two blister-like sacs; these are the optic vesicles which will become eyes. A more trained observer can detect other signs of human formation. A bulge shows the location of the heart which begins beating during this stage of embryonic development. Also detectable are rudimentary beginnings of a brain and a nervous system.

Sexual development comes a few days later. The initial indication of genital formation is at this stage nothing more than the thickening of the covering of the genital area, but during the next week the sexual organs begin taking shape. But there is as yet no clue whether they will be masculine or feminine.

It is salutary for each of us, man or woman, to be reminded that at this stage of our pre-natal life we are genitally neither male or female. Although the X-Y or X-X pattern of chromosomes has dictated our eventual destiny we are beginning life, as do all other vertebrate, as hermaphrodites. We possess the rudimentary organs of man and woman, but, in the words of Kenneth Walker we are 'sitting on a hermaphrodite fence', prepared to move in either direction.

All there is in the genital area is what is known as the genital tubercle, a kind of bulb which must grow and blossom before the genitals can be recognised as male or female. This domed eminence grows and lengthens, and becomes, in both male and female, a phallus. This phallus will grow into either male penis or female clitoris. It is surrounded by, or for the sake of illustration we might say it is rooted into, four genital folds. These folds are not as yet sexually differentiated. Later they will develop either into labia, the characteristic outer and inner lips of the woman's vaginal entrance, or into a scrotum, man's characteristic pouch which is designed to receive and protectively hold the testes. In their early primitive form, however, male and female genital folds look alike. Both have a noticeable cleft dividing them left and right. If the foetus is to become a female baby, this cleft will remain a cleft and become the pudendal cleft, the entrance to the woman's vagina. If the foetus is to become a male baby, the cleft will close up, knitting into that seam which is easily visible down the centre of a man's scrotum.

More dramatic, however, is the development of the phallus into penis or clitoris. It is a vivid demonstration of the basic equality and similarity of the genital possessions of man and woman. Man has the distinction of having a larger penis in proportion to his size than any other vertebrate. Woman also has something equivalent to a penis, her clitoris. It is tiny compared with man's, though in abnormal circumstances it can be so unusually large and cylindrical as to resemble the male organ, and there is at least one recorded instance of a woman having a clitoris two inches long which, said the woman, was three inches long when fully 'erect'. The clitoris is not in fact capable of a genuine erection like that of the penis. It is, however, richer in nerve ends and consequently more excitable.

In a similar way man possesses vestigial female organs, so that he will always have in his body evidence that he began existence in the essentially female structure of an egg. As his masculinity becomes defined those feminine parts atrophy and become ineffective, but he will always have what can be described as a miniature uterus, as well as miniature nipples and other female structures.

Right into the twelfth week of its life the foetus continues to possess the rudiments of both male and female genital systems. It is hardly true to say that the sexual characteristics of one sex *assert* themselves; it is more true to say that the sexual characteristics of the other sex disappear.

It is before this, however, in the eighth week of pre-natal life, that we see clitoris and penis assuming their differing shapes and taking up different positions. In the early stages of the process the female phallus is, oddly enough, longer than the male phallus. Like a penis it will develop the sensitive head we call the glans, and will grow a prepuce in the same way that the male phallus grows a foreskin. The female phallus, however, retires behind the genital folds as they develop into female labia.

The changes in the male are more rapid and extensive than those in the female. In view of what has to happen this is understandable. The male's genital organs have a much more gymnastic exercise to perform. They have to advance out of the body; the phallus has to become a protuberant organ and must draw the genital folds behind it to form the scrotum. To protect the penis in so exposed a position and to insulate the tender and sensitive glans from the rigours it might encounter in the 'outer world' the prepuce grows forward, covering it in a sheath of skin.

That founder of classical medicine and natural science, Hippocrates, who held the belief then current that woman was an incomplete being, only 'half human' and inferior to man physiologically and otherwise, put forward the imaginative theory that the genital organs of woman were not really different from man's at all; only in man they were expanded and made visible by his natural warmth and superior vigour, and in woman they had to remain concealed in her body because she was colder and feebler in constitution.

There is one difference between penis and clitoris which is

more emphatic than difference of size or position. In the female the duct leading from the bladder, the urethra, remains distinct from the clitoris: in the male it becomes enfolded in the penis. The result is that the male organ eventually has a double job to do: it not only has to transmit urine from the bladder but also has to transmit sperm from the testicles. A woman's clitoris has no anatomical importance or function at all, except as an instrument of sexual pleasure and is thus important to a woman's sexuality.

2 TESTICLES OR OVARIES

During the period when penis and clitoris are assuming male and female shape and position, another process far more important to masculinity and femininity is taking place. Visually it is less dramatic than the formation of the sexual organs, but it is more essential to the difference of man and woman, for it is the process which really decides which one is to be father and sperm-carrier and which one is to be mother and egg-breeder.

Sperm is produced in testicles; eggs are produced in ovaries. When they first appear these sexual glands look alike, but eventually they also take up an appropriate male or female position. Here again the female's development is slower than the male's. The ovary takes longer to attain defined sex than does the male testes. Also here again we see a similar pattern of feminine retention and masculine extrusion, for just as the female retains her clitoris inside the body and man thrusts the penis out of his, so does the female retain her ovaries and the male expel his testes.

A woman's ovaries are two almond-shaped glands. So are man's testes. Though his almonds are a little plumper in shape than hers. Ovaries are about three centimetres long, one-and-a-half centimetres wide, and about one centimetre thick; they lie to the left and right of the womb and are estimated each to contain one million ova. The vital statistics of the testes are roughly twice those of the ovaries: four to five centimetres long, two-and-a-half centimetres wide and three centimetres thick, and they are on average more than three times heavier than ovaries. In the scrotum they also hang left and right. By the nature of things they have to be more prodigal in production than the ovaries. To make fertilisation certain they produce around 260 million spermatozoa for each ejaculation. Incidentally the left testis hangs a little lower than the right. One assumes that this uneven disposition is responsible for the preoccupations of the tailor and the intimate question he must ask when he measures a man for well-hung trousers.

When the female foetus takes on defined female shape the ovaries are retained near the entrance of the uterine tube by an attachment of muscular membrane. This attachment anchors them in the desired position and restricts their movement until they are brought into operation for the first time to produce eggs. After the first baby the position of the ovaries can vary considerably in different women, and they probably never return to the position they occupied during nulliparity. For some months testes are similarly anchored in an internal position, but in the seventh month, as though suddenly waking up to their destined purpose, they descend rapidly to the scrotum to take up their working position in that characteristic masculine purse, the factory in which they will eventually perform their lifelong industry of sperm production.

In that short summary of the development of testes and ovaries we have described the all important and specific sexual difference between man and woman, the creation of glands that produce either sperm or eggs. The more visually obvious differences of penis and clitoris are merely secondary anatomical differences. In determining sex the determinant organs are the sex glands, the testes and ovaries. When these glands have been transferred between male and female animals in laboratory experiments the sexual behaviour of the animals has switched. Testes transferred to female animals make the females assume the sexual desires and sexual postures of the males: ovaries transferred to males make the males act like females.

But one thing discovered during these experiments seems especially significant. It is easier to transform an animal into a male than it is to transform it into a female. This has been found to be so with fowls, guinea pigs and rats. It seems to be the same with human beings, but I shall refer to that in detail a little later when I discuss cases of sex-change operations in humans of my own acquaintance.

The fact that by experimental tampering with the sex glands we can more easily make animals male than we can make them female seems to be additional confirmation of Nature's pro-female prejudice, as though Nature is apparently prepared to agree fairly readily to the creation of males, for after all, as she has biochemically expressed, males are to her merely hybrid throwouts, but when it comes to the question of creating females Nature protects her copyright against infringement and resists experimental tampering.

Man has been tampering with sex glands for centuries. Castration was one of the first surgical operations ever performed. When man wanted more tractable animals for placid labour or wanted plumper animals for better eating he extracted the testicles of bulls and boars. To make his mount more obedient he extracted the testicles of the stallion. For heavier fowls he castrated cocks and they became capons. He went further. He castrated human beings. To retain the loveliness of treble voices in his theatres and choirs he castrated boys. To protect his women from competitive attention he created eunuchs for his courts and harems.

How primitive man discovered the effects of castration we can only imagine. Probably he made the discovery by observing the results of accidents suffered by males, human or animals, or by observing the effects caused when he punitively mutilated males captured in war. In any event, he performed it as merely rule-of-thumb surgery. Although he saw what happened to males when their testicles were removed, how and why it happened he could not know until scientists had the instruments necessary for probing the biochemical secrets of life.

3 THE SEX MESSENGERS

This brings us to the fundamental chemistry of the difference between a man and a woman. Now we must peer into the inner recesses of physiology and examine the work of those backroom boys, the endocrine glands, and the secretions which these glands produce. We call the secretions hormones. They are the chemical messengers who carry information along a chain of communication which is supplementary to that other communication system provided by our nerves.

In this exploration we must face up to the realisation that neither of us, neither man with a penis nor woman with a clitoris, is so wholly masculine or feminine as we like to believe. The hormones which determine our sex are not exclusively masculine in a man and feminine in a woman. Every person throughout all his or her life possesses both male and female hormones. Nor has it as yet been determined to what extent the relative proportion of male and female hormones in our bodies decide our masculine and feminine behaviour. At least it has not been discovered at the time of writing. But researchers have reached the stage when they can assume that both the production and the utilisation of our sex hormones is governed primarily by, (one) the complex influences our endocrine glands exert on each other, and, (two) by the demands the body makes for a supply of the hormones in particularly desires for its anatomical male or female needs.

More than two hundred years ago a physician at the court of Louis XV of France, a Monsieur Bordeu, argued the possible existence of biochemical influences in the human body. He based his assumption on observations he had made, but no laboratory techniques of his day could establish his theory that every organ in the body was a workshop which produced some particular substance which passed into the blood. If any of these substances were missing, he continued, then the harmony and anatomical integrity of the body were thrown off balance. He was right, but it was not until the beginning of this century that the first hormone was discovered by a European physiologist at University College, London, on 16th January, 1902.

This happened when the English physiologist, Ernest Starling, was investigating the origin of the pancreatic juices which are produced in our intestines so that we can digest our food and absorb its nutriment. For his investigation he had completely severed from the mucous membrane of the small intestine all the nerves which, so far as was then known, were in sole control of its absorptive processes. He then introduced into the membrane a few drops of hydrochloric acid. Pancreatic juice began coming from the small intestine. So the intestine was operating under the stimulus of the acid. But how did it receive its knowledge? It had no nerves to transmit to it the information that the acid was acting as a stimulant. Yet it was behaving just as it would have done had it been responding to messages sent by nerves. Why? How?

Starling answered the questions with words as perceptive as those uttered by Monsieur Bordeu in the eighteenth century: 'It must be a chemical reflex,' he declared, and this belief put him on the track of the body's second system of communication, the chemical one. When he had succeeded in extracting the chemical from the intestine he called it, because it was secreted in the membrane that he had examined, secretin. He was sure that physiologists would now discover what Monsieur Bordeu had already guessed: that other organs manufactured other secretions.

They did discover them, many of them, and called them 'hormones', from the Greek word 'hormnein' which means to set in motion or spur on; actions which the secretions do perform in the body. Not until twelve years after Starling's discovery was the next hormone discovered. This was thyroxin, a secretion in the thyroid gland which, another thirteen years later, was used to spectacular effect on patients suffering from thyroid deficiencies and converted pitiably retarded cretins into normally growing beings.

After physiologists had discovered the powerful influence of the hormones, the question inevitably asked was whether hormones also influenced sexual development. It was already known that when sex glands were poorly developed, or became diseased, changes in sex attitudes and in secondary sexual characteristics often occurred. Fowls born as hens had changed into cocks because their ovaries had been destroyed by tuberculosis, and miniature testes had taken their place. But was it possible that, apart from malformations caused by disease, malformations could also be caused by an imbalance of hormones? Could there be such things as *sex* hormones?

That question had already been answered in China in the twelfth century. We now know that nearly 800 years before Starling's discovery at University College, in the days when Europe was still an uneasy conglomeration of feudal states and west was divided from east by a vast and rarely explored barbaric no-man's-land, Chinese scientists were using crystalline steroid hormones for the medical treatment of imbalances for which our twentieth-century doctors prescribe sex hormones today.

The sex hormones are found in the obvious places: the male hormones in the testes and the female hormones in the ovaries. In naming them European scientists went to classical languages. They christened the male hormone testosterone. The obviously masculine prefix comes from the Greek *testo*, meaning solid; the added *sterone* indicates something belonging to this hormone. The name given to the female hormone, oestrin, is even more illustrative, even more mischievously well-chosen, for the Latin *oestrus* and the Greek *oistrus* can mean a gadfly or a sting of some vehement desire. It can even be used as an epithet for anything that drives one mad. How apt! For the messages transmitted through a female's body by these chemical couriers which carry oestrogen compounds are the messages that arouse her to her intense and periodic sexual urges. Deprive a female cat, for instance, of these chemicals and she will no longer assume her periodic attitudes of sexual invitation and receptivity to the tom. So emphatic is the sexual provocation of this hormone that if the back of a male mouse is touched only lightly every day with a tiny brush dipped in the secretion, the animal evinces profound changes towards femininity.

The tissues of both internal and external reproductive organs which the embryo develops while in the womb can be described as hermaphrodite, for it can develop either male or female organs, and the development of one set of tissues and the suppression of the other is partly dependent on whether the prevailing hormonal chemical influence to which the embryo is subjected by its developing gonads is androgenic or oestrogenic. Whatever the genetic constitution of the embryo it is possible to cause either set of tissues to develop by administering androgenic or oestrogenic hormone.

We have mentioned that all of us, men and women, have both male and female hormones in our body. It would seem obvious that if the male could get rid of his female hormones and the female get rid of her male ones, we should have immaculately undeniable masculine and feminine beings. Possibly, if they lived at all, yes. But almost certainly they would be sexually sterile or frigid. For it does seem that without that modicum of 'other sex' in our hormones we would be sexually inert. Experiments currently being made at Birmingham University, England, indicate this. The experiments are being performed on Rhesus monkeys by Dr. B. J. Everitt and Dr. J. Herbert of the anatomy department there. They are reaching the conclusion that females need male hormones to stimulate their sex life.

Every female has small amounts of the male androgens, secreted principally in the cells of the outer layer of the adrenal gland. It is now also established that doses of the male testosterone do enhance the libido of women and the sexual receptivity of female monkeys. But, apart from administered doses of testosterone, what would happen to a woman if she herself was not secreting her normally produced male hormone? Would her libido be reduced? These are the questions the two doctors are trying to answer. The results they report on the monkeys seem to our layman's eyes most dramatic.

The doctors have found that if the cells of the adrenal glands in the female monkey are prevented from producing *male* hormone the female monkeys lose some of their sexual urge. They become less receptive, they present themselves to the male less often, and they may even refuse to allow the males to mount. Males that do mount take longer to ejaculate, presumably because they are less stimulated by the female. Experiments of this kind can hardly be performed on humans for merely experimental purposes, but in the course of necessary operations on women it has been found that the removal of both ovaries and adrenal glands tends to decrease sexuality more than does the removal of the ovaries alone. The suggestion therefore can be made that the male androgens in the adrenal gland are as necessary to a woman as they have proved to be in female monkeys.

Hormone problems have already reached the dining table. A Scottish cheese has been banned from Italy because, an Italian Government Official said, 'we are already among the most emotional people in the world with a very high birthrate, and my Government feel it would be wrong to import anything that would make things worse'. But how could Scottish cheese affect Italian emotions and the birthrate? Because the milk from which it is made on the island of Islay could not be guaranteed to be free of oestrogen. No Italian cheese can be sold in Italy unless it can be certified as free from oestrogen, and as the Scottish cows were probably absorbing oestrogen on their different grazing grounds it was impossible for the Scottish cheese makers to give a complete guarantee unless every single gallon of milk was tested. We can understand the Italian point of view; over the last seven years their population has increased by 2,687,000 to 52,958,000, even without Scottish cheese.

The influence of hormones has been detected in the classroom also. A woman doctor recently made the astonishing discovery that a hormone used in the birth-pill was producing what was described somewhat sensationally in newspaper reports as a 'race of super-children'. She found that the babies of women who had been given progesterone to correct certain blood deficiencies during pregnancy were able to stand unaided and walk earlier than other children; when they went to school they shot ahead of other pupils in study.

The power of hormones is perhaps best illustrated by describing the effects caused by one secretion in the pituitary gland. This chemical messenger carries the message 'Produce milk'. When a tomcat is injected with it his body obeys the command and the tom actually gives milk. Not surprisingly this hormone, prolactin, has been described as 'mother love in bottles'.

On the other hand, if a female rat is injected with male hormones, her clitoris becomes a penis. Male hormones added to water in which female tadpoles were swimming caused the females to grow into outwardly male frogs which were nevertheless genetically female.

As is plain from these experiments with mixed-up mice and frogs, hormones do not need to be injected to have an effect on the body: they can be absorbed through the skin. Consequently they have been medicinally incorporated in ointments. In fact the complex interaction of hormones can be demonstrated by one final example. When used in an ointment male hormones can remedy deficiencies of a *man*'s testicles, yet they can also alleviate symptoms of secondary carcinoma in a *woman*'s breasts.

It must be understood therefore that it is not just a simple case of a man possessing and needing male hormones and a woman possessing and needing female hormones. It is true that the secretions of the testes and ovaries are sexually specific, one designs masculinity and the other designs femininity, but both are biologically necessary to both man and woman.

In accordance again with Nature's pro-female prejudice the female is far less dependent on her sex hormones than the male is. If, for instance, the ovaries are extracted from a newly-born female rat, the deprivation does not slow down the development of the animal's female genitalia; the rat goes on growing into a recognisable female. It is different with the male. He cannot do without his supply of male hormones if he wants to become a true male. Deprived of them he can no longer grow his genitalia. It does seem that whereas the male has been left helplessly dependent upon his supplementary endocrine system, the egg and female have been designed to continue regardless.

This mere sketch of some of the fascinating intricacies of the sex hormones brings us back to our theme of Nature's prejudice in favour of the female. We have glimpsed why the prejudice has to exist and how it is biochemically expressed. The female is the basic mammal; the male a more highly differentiated one emanating from the female by the action of the male hormone. So a man should be considered not only as being 'born of woman' but being actually 'created' from woman, provided by Nature to perform his small stimulating role in procreating human children.

So much for the legend of Adam and Eve. We are indebted to Helene Deutsch for her neat summary of how, before Genesis was written, an ancient Sumerian legend told the story of the creation of man and woman in a fable closer to biological fact.

'My brother, what hurts thee?'
'My rib hurts me.'
'The Goddess Ninti I have caused to be born for thee.'

When the Hebrews translated the story they made a mistake. In Sumerian the word 'ti' meant rib; but it also meant 'to give life'. The Hebrews translated 'Ninti' as 'Lady of *the Rib*', which title suggested that man had given a rib for the creation of a sexual companion. But what the Sumerians had really meant by 'Ninti' was 'Lady Who *Gives Life*'. Biology has taught us they were on the right track. Woman is the basic creation and out of her comes man. Perhaps Genesis tells us otherwise only because it was written by a man.

4 BOY OR GIRL? OR...?

The baby is born. It is delivered, and the cord is cut. It is swung by its ankles and slapped. It breathes. It wails. The doctor smiles and says, 'It's a boy!' or 'It's a girl!' But sometimes he does not smile.

On rare occasions the doctor cannot be sure of the baby's sex. Even the genital organs, the sexual apparatus which we expect to be the recognisable insignia of the baby's sex, might not after all be distinctively masculine or feminine. If one of the delicate processes of sexual pre-natal growth has not functioned accurately, even a medical man can sometimes be in doubt as to whether the baby is a boy or a girl.

Male babies are more likely than female babies to suffer from physical defects of their genital organs. In the male baby, for instance, the urinary duct from the bladder to the penis sometimes does not run the whole length of the penis. Instead of finding its way out at the tip of the glans it forces an outlet at the base of the glans. In more severe cases of this particular malformation the urethra, ending even further away from its proper goal, emerges just in front of the scrotum at the very base of the malformed penis.

However, in such cases the baby has at least some kind of penis, even if not a properly formed one, and on this a doctor can decide the baby's sex. It is far more difficult for the doctor when he faces rarer occasions in which the genital folds have failed to fuse in proper masculine pattern. The folds, instead of developing into the familiar united and seamed sac, the scrotum, have remained divided, and, as often does happen along with this malformation, the testes have not descended. The genital folds of such a baby can bear so striking a resemblance to the feminine labia that these male children are often mistaken for girls.

Often comparatively simple surgery can correct genital malformations, but sometimes the sexual mix-up has deeper organic complications, so that later in life not only the genital organs but also the secondary sexual characteristics of hair-growth and breasts and overall bodily shape tend to assume forms completely contradictory to the sex dictated by testes or ovaries.

Persons who suffer from such mix-ups are often popularly referred to as 'hermaphrodites', but the term 'hermaphroditism' really means the presence in one body of the reproductive glands of both sexes, and humans of that mould are so rare as to be almost unknown. One of these rarities is now living in Holland; a person who is genetically female but is able to produce sperm and is actually married to a woman. Such persons of uncertain sex as we more commonly encounter have physical characteristics much less grossly contrary to their glandular sex, and the correct term to use for them is 'pseudo-hermaphrodites'.

Society has not yet reached a stage of cynical indifference to the individual human being which would permit scientists to perform experiments on humans like the sex-changing experiments they are performing on animals. At least, not merely to satisfy scientific curiosity. But on occasions it is desirable to attempt surgical or other corrective treatments to sort out human beings who are suffering from sexual ambivalences.

We all know how a sexual mix-up can cause the personal tragedy of making a person feel an outcast from society, and how, under the mental stress of this situation, that person can become psychotically disturbed. Fortunately public opinion is becoming better informed and more liberal-minded on this subject. Sexual deviation *per se* is no longer considered a crime. Later, we hope, it will no longer be considered either a social stigma or even a social oddity. When this second aim is achieved the word 'queer' will be used in its true sense and not as a derogatory name for a deviant.

The physical mix-ups suffered by pseudo-hermaphrodites would not in themselves be all that serious were they not nearly always accompanied by psychological ambivalence as well. Persons physically ambivalent are often plagued with a confusing mixture of sexual attitudes and desires; two sexes merge in the one person not only physically but also mentally. Although a surgeon or physician might be able to correct the physical defect, the mental defect remains.

For instance treatment with appropriate hormones could possibly restore the balance of a female who has ovaries which have developed imperfectly or have atrophied because of some biochemical error and consequently she has some of the desires and attitudes of masculinity. But quite often a pseudo-hermaphrodite with an organic defect of that kind is also obsessed with exaggerated emotional uncertainty about her true sex, and however successful surgical or medical remedies might be physically the psychological uncertainty cannot be entirely dispersed. For this reason medical men are nowadays becoming cautious about attempting treatments, and some psychologists are criticising doctors and surgeons for attempting treatments which, they argue, do not correct the mental and inherited sexual disharmony but actually aggravate it. Nevertheless there are cases where surgical or medical correction of sexual abnormalities does help an individual to overcome the psychological upset caused by those abnormalities.

In recent years I have met and written about individuals who have undergone so-called 'sex-change' operations. One of these was a much publicised person who had been considered masculine to the extent of having achieved military distinction in the war and married a woman. But throughout supposed 'boyhood' and early 'manhood' she had been worried by certain feminine characteristics of her body and by her abnormal genitals. Eventually doctors advised her that she was really a woman. Rather than accept the fact she attempted suicide, but finally she agreed to a series of operations. When I met her she was making a courageous and on the whole successful attempt to drill herself to femininity; trying not only to live as a woman, but also to walk and move like one, to give to her movements the subtle difference which we recognise as feminine; a feminine way of sitting, of lighting and smoking a cigarette, even of carrying a handbag and placing it on her lap. She was having to unlearn all the years of social conditioning when, as a 'boy', she had tried to conduct herself in masculine fashion.

This woman was an intersexual. Intersexuals are one of the two main groups involved in the question of 'sex change': persons whose sexual ambivalence is physical and noticeable at birth in those rare cases when it is virtually impossible to tell from the genital organs whether the baby is male or female. The other main group are trans-sexuals: individuals who appear to be physically normal men and women yet have a passionate desire to belong to the other sex. Felix Boehm reports that many male patients can describe in fantasy how pleasant it would be to be a woman and have intercourse as a woman even when feminine tendencies do not play any special part in their lives.

If there were only those two groups, intersexuals and trans-sexuals, the problem would be difficult enough, but actually there are complicated variations among even these groups. The physical differences of penis or no-penis, testicles or ovaries, uterus or no-uterus, are not always sufficient indication of sex.

A basic indicator of sex is the genetic sex which is indicated by the chromosomes. A leading article in *The Lancet* in 1959 declared 'There must be one or two genetic females in every battalion of the British Army, and a few such cases on nearly every practitioner's list'.

Other sex indicators are: gonadal sex, indicated by the growth of testes or ovaries whose development is controlled by the chromosomes; phynoptic sex, indicated by the growth of the genitals which are the visible apparatus of gender; and behavioural sex, indicated by the sex which the individuals believe or have been conditioned to believe themselves to be.

If these four sex indicators always agree, all would be well. But often they conflict, and the same body can have both male and female indicators, so that, for instance, one person might have male chromosomes and normal testes yet have female external genital organs. Another can have female chromosomes and normal ovaries, yet have male external genitals.

Because of this the most eminent doctors agree with Dr. C. J. Dewhirst, one of the world's leading authorities in the problem of sex deviation, that 'it is virtually impossible to arrive at a hard-and-fast definition of sex. There are always exceptions'.

Apart from the fact that the existence in both sexes of both male and female hormones is alone sufficient to forbid any human claiming to be completely male or female, there are in all men and women other subtle gradations of masculinity and femininity, both biological and psychological, to support the claim made by Dr. Biedl that 'the pure man and the pure woman are extreme cases which are scarcely met with'.

When the most sophisticated instruments of medical science cannot make a 'hard-and-fast definition' of sex it is not surprising that the blunter instrument of the law gets itself into a hopeless mess and emerges as more than usually an ass when it attempts to decide what is male and female. The law's dilemma was recently highlighted in the case of the former merchant seaman, George Jamieson, who after a supposed sex-change by surgery became an attractive and much sought-after model, April Ashley, and eventually married the Hon. Arthur Cameron Corbett, son and heir of Lord Rowallan, former Chief Scout of the Boy Scout Association. The husband's petition to have the marriage annulled on the grounds that his 'wife' was a man faced the High Courts for the first time with the task of giving a judicial answer to the question: 'What is a woman?'

Mr. Justice Roger Ormrod, himself a doctor, ruled that April Ashley was not a woman for the purpose of marriage, was biologically a male and had been so from birth. The medical evidence proffered suggests that April Ashley was a trans-sexual; apparently a normal physical male when born but with the desire to be a female. Mr. Justice Ormrod had to base his judgment to some extent on those four sex indicators mentioned above. Tests made by a Cambridge professor had revealed only male cells, therefore she was of male chromosomal sex. She had had testicles prior to her operation, therefore she was of male gonadal sex. She had had genitals without any evidence of internal or external female sexual organs, therefore she was of male genital sex. Even psychologically she was male: a biological male with trans-sexual tendencies. The judge agreed with medical witnesses that the biological sexual constitution of an individual is fixed, at the latest, at birth, and could not be changed by medical or surgical means. The judge referred to April Ashley's 'pastiche of femininity'. 'Her outward appearance,' he said, 'at first sight was convincingly feminine, but on closer and longer examination in the witness box it was much less so. The voice, manner, gestures and attitudes became increasingly reminiscent of the accomplished female impersonator.'

So far as legal arguments about marriage and divorce are concerned it is impossible to see how a judge could make any other judgment, though Dr. Harry Benjamin, eminent New York endocrinologist, described the judgment, as 'cruel and illogical'. 'In practical life,' he continued, 'the definition of a man is a person who has male sex organs. April Ashley has a vagina, so she is a woman.'

Society would no doubt agree more with Dr. Benjamin than it would with Mr. Justice Ormrod. If, her lawyer said later, she was sent to hospital, she would be put into a woman's ward; if she were sent to prison, it would be to Holloway, not Brixton. Bureaucracy has shown a similar attitude to her. She has a passport in the name of April Ashley and has a woman's National Health Card. She was not, however, allowed to have her birth certificate altered. That could only be done if she had been an intersexual and the original description of her sex had been proved medically incorrect.

Another fairly common sexual deviation is transvestism. This is when a person has a compelling desire to wear the dress of the other sex. It is commonly confused with homosexuality, but actually practically all male transvestites are heterosexual in their sexual desires.

Dr. Konrad Lorenz described two such masculine transvestites. 'One of them such a beautiful "girl" that you were surprised to see her. He talked of himself as a female but he was not in the least homosexual: he had a double life, as a man and as a woman. The other was a locomotive driver on the railway who did exactly the same thing. He had a wife and children in a perfectly normal way and, just as some men go boozing for some days, he changed into a woman for a few days.' At the same symposium at which Dr. Lorenz made this report Dr. Frank Fremont-Smith commented on a tribe in southern Sudan 'where transvestism is part of the social organisation and there are actual marriage ceremonies between males, one dressed as a woman and the other as a man', and Margaret Mead pointed out that such marriages occur in various parts of the world.

At a recent conference in London psychiatrists and social workers listened to a paper read by a Dr. Virginia Prince, an attractively gowned 56 years old blonde from Los Angeles. Only after the conference was 'she' revealed as Dr. Charles Prince who during the previous 15 months had been courageous enough to accept his transvetism as part of his character and had worn woman's dress. Reporting on this case Christine Doyle, medical reporter of *The Observer* said:

'Dr. Prince said the lives of many transvestites were reduced to misery sometimes resulting in suicide because they thought that their compulsion to dress as the opposite sex meant they were homosexual. "Only in recent years have psychologists come to realise that sex and gender are not the same thing, and that the sexual variant known as homosexuality is not the same things as the gender variant known as transvestism."

'Dr. Prince blamed the rigid polarisation of Western society. "Modern psychology accepts the fact that while one is born with a sex, one learns a gender." Many children whose sex was mistaken at birth grew up psychologically as the wrong sex, but might cope adequately until their identity was unmasked. Since there are many overlapping traits and characteristics in both men and women, Dr. Prince does not find it surprising that with some men the feminine traits do not get completely "turned off" during childhood and adolescence. By dressing as a woman, contact is established with the part of himself that society demands him to suppress. "But doctors, psychiatrists, police and employers have little understanding or no information about this phenomenon. The result is a lonely, guilt-ridden, fearful and ashamed person who locks all his feelings inside himself. Few are "cured". Dr. Prince is not advocating transvestism, but is pressing for more understanding by psychiatrists so that transvestites can learn to come to terms with their handicap.'

The fact that transvestism should not be confused with

homosexuality seems to be emphasised by J. Housden's report that he knew 'eleven transvestists who have never presented themselves for medical help. Although some of these were expert at mimicking women when they wore female clothes none of them appeared anything but completely masculine in their normal attire.'

One truth emerges from the most superficial study of sexual deviations. Social attitudes which we have inherited through centuries of cultural conditioning have created a climate of opinion which prefers, and on occasions stridently demands, that masculinity and femininity should be clearly distinguishable. The result is that a basic necessity for individual happiness and confidence in present-day society is for a man to feel assured beyond all doubt of his manhood and a woman of her womanhood. One fears that the time is still far distant when a sexual deviant might find equal happiness and equal confidence in the knowledge that he or she is formed of a more varied, more complicated, and, possibly, far richer sexual mixture.

However, there exists already a whole library, one that is constantly being added to and threatens to become almost boringly multitudinous, on the subject of sexual deviation. It would be easy enough to write into this book any number of morbidly interesting stories and case-histories of sexual deviants. Immediately there springs to mind the argument about the Russian 'woman athletes' and the Polish sprinter Ewa Klobukowska who was barred from racing with women because doctors said, in strangely vague terms, that she 'had one chromosome too many'. We remember also reports of bizarre changes of sex such as those I have mentioned. Sailors, a fighter-pilot, even a champion boxer have become women, model-girls and wives. But the subject implicit in the title of this book is vast enough on its own and we must confine ourselves to that title and study only the difference between normal men and normal women. Though never for a moment must we forget that 'normal' is a word capable of wide variations of interpretation along that broad spectrum which stretches between the man whom we consider ideally masculine and the woman whom we consider ideally feminine.

3 Male and Female Shapes

'You can tell a woman by her throwing ever so far off.' A Greek contemporary of Aristotle said that more than 2,300 years ago, and we know just what he meant. Imagine a human figure 'ever so off', motionless and too far away for us to see its sexual shape sufficiently to distinguish with certainty whether it is male or female. Then it throws a stone, and from the way it moves we know at once whether it is man or woman. If it walks, we also know. Even more so if it runs; for then, if it is a woman, its feet will make little semi-circular movements and its hips and buttocks will sway in unison. We can be equally sure of its sex if it calls out to us.

Those visual and aural observations from a distance are in a way similar to a baby's dawning appreciation of the sex difference in the movements and sounds made by men and women hovering around the horizon of the cradle, but when the human figure moves closer to us and we can see its shape more clearly we can tell from shape alone whether it is masculine or feminine, quite apart from the clothes with which it might emphasise or attempt to conceal its sex.

The difference in male and female shape was described in a beautifully illustrative way by the ancients of Aristotle's day. They said that the trunk of either a man or woman could be likened to an ovoid figure. Like an egg, the human shape had a large end and a small end. But in a man the large end is at the top; in a woman the large end is at the bottom. The shoulders of a normally developed man have a greater diameter than his hips; a woman's hips have a greater diameter than her shoulders. In a man, however, the difference in the size of shoulders and hips is considerable; in a woman it is only slight.

Personal observation will show us that in many men and women the egg shape is not very emphatically masculine or feminine. In some the egg even seems the wrong way up for their sex. An inappropriate balance of hormones can cause this. For instance, if a man suffers from a deficiency in his testicular secretions, he will grow fatter and more rounded in the wrong places, and his figure will assume an overall shape more like that of a woman, the more so according to the seriousness of his defect. On the other hand an ovarian deficiency in a woman will make her thin.

1 WHICH IS MORE BEAUTIFUL?

However, as we are now going to compare man and woman in physical detail let us assume that our two specimens are strongly defined masculine and feminine humans; such a man and a woman as we can call, with the necessary reservations, normal. In fact, let us imagine they are *ideal* physical examples, like a man and a woman we might see in certain painting and sculpture; the male body powerful and muscular, the female body voluptuously soft and curvaceous.

We do see male and female bodies even more emphatically different and presented less artistically and more stridently in pin-up pictures of full-breasted wide-hipped girls and in photographs of muscle-men in male-beauty magazines. We see them represented even more crudely in the graffiti of public lavatories. In those malodorous studios lonely amateurs who attempt to portray the sexual difference use curving outlines for women and angular lines and straight protuberances for men.

The men and women we meet in daily life are not so exaggeratedly different in overall shape as all that. But we do take it for granted that there should be distinctive differences.

Man is the larger. He nearly always has bigger bones, and his body weight is on average some ten per cent more than that of a woman. At maturity he is, according to Morris's *Human Anatomy*, 19.3 times heavier than his 3.4 kilograms at birth, whereas the woman is only 17.3 times heavier than her 3.2 kilograms at birth.

Man's figure is more strikingly erect and closely knit; his bone structure is so visible that we can locate the prominent points of his skeleton; and his muscles are conspicuously defined. Man's rugged outline suggests physical energy. Man looks to be built for action.

The woman is altogether smaller and rounder. Even if she has trained and strengthened her muscles they are hidden by the fleshy curves of large hips, breasts, abdomen and flanks. As a result her figure, in contrast to man's appearance of activity, suggests an attitude of repose.

The woman's abdomen is much more rounded in its lower part than a man's; this effect is heightened by the much deeper depression of her navel. Her abdomen is also longer, proportionately, than a man's, with a greater distance between her navel and her genitals. This longer and rounder abdomen is fashioned to suit her reproductive needs, but those artists who dotingly emphasise it in portraits of nudes do not do so in appreciation of that biological necessity but because they consider a full and rounded abdomen as one of woman's particular charms. This opinion is shared by the average man, whose own abdomen, at least until age or indulgence alters its outline, is comparatively flat and inconspicuous.

The woman is more slender at the waist, just above the loins. Whereas the man's chest narrows abruptly into hips and loins, the woman's chest, after narrowing considerably below her bosom, swells out into the hips, suggesting that hour-glass outline which ardent Latins sketch extravagantly in the air when describing the ideal shape of a girl friend.

Apart from the difference in overall shape there are structural differences. Most obvious are the contrasting proportions in limbs and bodies. The woman's head, *in relation to her total weight*, is longer than the man's, and her neck is shorter. Her legs are noticeably shorter in proportion to her trunk than are a man's to his.

Which design, male or female, is more beautiful?

The question is often asked. Only a moment's thought reveals it as futile. The male is neither more nor less beautiful than the female: if both are perfectly constructed humans they are equally beautiful. A claim that one is more beautiful than the other is usually a measure not of the speaker's aesthetic judgment but of the speaker's sexual preferences and desires. But when faced with the beauty of the human body even scientists are sometimes tempted to depart from objectivity and step beyond anatomical measurements to venture opinions on relative beauty. For instance, Wilhelm Heinrich Busch, a German doctor: 'The external appearance of woman is more comfortable to harmony and beauty than that of a man. Her proportions are at once rounder and more delicate; whereas the man's are angular and rough hewn.' The slighted male might find comfort in the opinion of another German, H. T. Finck, who described the Englishman as 'far and away the most beautiful animal in the world' by virtue of his regular features, his beautiful eyes, his fresh complexion, and 'the slender disciplined build of his body.' Or what about Schopenhauer? He declared that for a man to see any beauty in woman, 'that squat, narrow-shouldered wide-hipped and short-legged sex', was nothing but a delusion of the 'masculine brain clouded with the fumes of instinct'.

Darwin, on the other hand, took the usual masculine view that women are far more beautiful than men. He claimed that their superior beauty was one extra piece of evidence in the vast structure of his theory of natural selection. It would be inevitable that the most attractively shaped and desirable woman would be the ones most in demand by the men of their day. The children of such unions would inevitably inherit some of, if not all, that beauty. Therefore each succeeding generation would enhance the general beauty of the womenfolk.

Perhaps Darwin's theory could explain why the majority of women in our civilised society are sadly not all that beautiful. Whereas among primitive peoples nearly all the girls and women are physically perfect according to the standards desired in such societies, in our civilised societies women who reach our ideal of physical perfection are in a minority. The way in which civilised man chooses his female mate could be responsible for that. A man of a primitive tribe will almost certainly choose his woman for her looks, and the most stalwart man will be the one powerful enough to get the pick of the bunch or the one most sought after by the girls, and the resultant daughters will, as Darwin would expect, be beauties. Western men, on the other hand, most often chooses his wife not because she is beautiful, though it is nice if she happens to be so, but for social and family reasons, for her amiability or her cooking, sometimes for her bank-balance and sometimes even for her brains. None of these desirable attributes, not even cash or brains, can be expected to play much part in fashioning beautiful children.

However, beauty is in the eye of the beholder, and particularly if the beholder is a lover. To the question so often whispered in the drawing-room or cocktail bar 'What on earth can he see in her?' the answer is that the man sees far more in her, finds far more attraction in her, than can ever be seen by the casual observer. Against all the physical evidence by which another might judge a woman as lacking grace or beauty, the man sees the woman he loves as physically desirable. He has to do so. Except in the rare circumstances of blind and unselective rape a woman must be in some measure physically attractive to a man before he can be roused to fulfil his sexual role.

The woman has a different approach. She can appreciate male beauty, though very often is chillingly objective about it, but she does not demand beauty in her love object nor need to imagine her love object is beautiful. She can be roused to perform her sexual role without demanding that her mate should be at all beautiful physically.

Asked to imagine an ideal woman any normal man will first almost invariably picture her as physically beautiful. Talking about her he might in fact not go further than describing her body and the colour of her hair and her other physical attributes. A woman on the other hand might be completely unable to picture her ideal man physically; and is much more likely to enlarge on his character, his ability, his mentality and his kindness. Nietzsche's glib allegation that all that was needed to please any pious woman was 'a saint with beautiful legs, still young, still innocent' shows remarkable ignorance of female taste and desire. Of the qualities Nietzsche lists innocence is the only one that could strongly appeal to the normal woman. The other attributes would be important, only to women of more than normal sensuality. With such women youth would be an attractive attribute in the love-object, but even so only the most licentious of women would pay special attention to 'beautiful legs'.

Standards of beauty change from era to era and from race to race, but it is remarkable that the change in beauty is almost entirely among the women. It can be argued that by and large the ideal male has stayed the same for centuries and is more or less the same from race to race. But women come in all shapes and sizes; fat for some races, slim for others; sometimes with enormous buttocks, at other times with thighs like boys'. The more primitive races maintain a regular standard of feminine beauty; sophisticated societies such as ours change the standard according to fashion from era to era. In all societies however the general tendency is for men to prefer women shorter than themselves and for women to prefer men taller than themselves. Beigel suggests that women who want men nearer to their own height are expressing a need for ascendancy, and men who desire taller women are actually satisfying repressed infant sexual desire to possess the forbidden parent figure.

2 WOMAN'S DIFFERENCE IS FAT

One factor responsible for woman's overall shape being so different from man's is, to put it brutally, fat.

Nearly 2,000 years ago Plutarch put on record a grisly observation. 'Experience at funerals,' he said, 'shows that the bodies of women are hotter than those of men. Those whose business it is to burn bodies always add one woman to every ten men. This helps the burning of bodies because the flesh of women is so fat that it burns like a torch.'

The anatomist has to have an equally matter-of-fact approach, and he describes all those alluring curves and roundnesses and declivities which man finds so lovely and so sexually exciting as 'deposits of fatty tissue'. In fact the accumulation of fat on a woman's thighs and buttocks is so pronounced that it can be considered as one of the female's secondary sexual characteristics. By a strong effort of will some women can slim away their fatty deposits, but if they do it to excess the result can often be sagging or wrinkled skin where once were full-fleshed feminine curves.

In contrast to woman's fatty deposits man's sexual characteristic is his muscle. This sexual allocation of muscle and fat suits male and female psychological attitudes: man's muscles accord with his tendency for strenuous exercise, woman's fat accords with her tendency to adopt more placid postures to conserve her energies. Likewise muscles and fat are suited to male and female sexual and parental duties. For copulating mates it is suitable to have a muscular man and a plump receptive woman; as parents it is desirable to have a muscular hunting or fighting father and a comfortable and warm nursing mother. Corpses found at Pompeii and Herculaneum are said to show that the men had made forceful muscular resistance to the catastrophe whereas the women had clasped their children in attitudes of unresisting acceptance.

Man's bigger bones and muscles and woman's smaller bones and fatty deposits are forecast in the bodies of children by physical tendencies which have little if anything to do with post-puberty maleness or femaleness. Dr. Tanner points out that in little boys there is more mesomorphy and in little girls more endomorphy.

Mesomorphy is the type of body build in which the predominating tissues are derived from the mesoderm, the middle layer of the three primary germ layers of the embryo. Among these tissues are connective tissues, bone and cartilage and muscles, and therefore mesomorphy results in a type of body in which there is a relative preponderance of connective tissue and bone and muscle, usually with heavy hard physique of rectangular outline. In endomorphy the predominating tissues are derived from the entoderm, the innermost of the three primary germ layers of the embryo. This provides the covering and linings of the pharynx, respiratory tract, digestive tract, bladder and urethra. Therefore the endomorphy in little girls results in a relative preponderance of soft roundness throughout the body, with large digestive viscera and accumulations of fat, the body usually presenting large trunk and thighs and tapering extremities.

Police reports and detective fiction have taught us that even the smallest part of a body, even one bone from a skeleton can be identified as male or female. Some clues are so pronounced as to be detected at a glance. A woman's skull, for instance, is just that bit nearer than a man's to spherical shape, and its ridges and protuberances are fewer and slighter. In a woman the length of the skull from brow to chin is less, not only relatively less in proportion to her own size, but also absolutely less than in a man.

The skull difference is a profoundly significant difference. Because the skull of a woman is more like an infant's in its lack of overhanging brows and less corrugated, bearing, one might say, fewer of the wrinkles of human time, the implication is that woman is behind man in evolutionary development. As her skull is smaller than man's the brain within that bony casing is also smaller. This difference has implications which deserve fuller investigation and discussion, and we shall devote a separate chapter (8: *Woman's Smaller Brain*) to it. Here we restrict our observations to noting how woman's smaller and differently proportioned skull affects her outward appearance generally. The lower forehead combines with smaller nose and mouth and smoother and less pointed chin to make woman's face smaller and rounder than a man's. Embellished with soft and fleshy curves it becomes characteristically feminine.

All those differences in outward appearance are distinctive enough to be easily observed. Hidden within the human body, however, are anatomical differences less easily observed. Two bony differences, for instance. A simple one is that a woman's collar bone is shorter than a man's. A more complicated one is a difference of her coccyx. The tail end of the spine is usually composed of four spinal vertebrae; but sometimes it has five, and that extra vertebra is found far more often in woman than in man. Some physiologists have suggested that this supports the suggestion that woman is an evolutionary step nearer to our primeval tailed ancestors. Late in life the coccyx often fuses into the vertebrae above it, the vertebrae which form that portion of the spine known as the sacrum. This fusion is likewise found more frequently in women than in men.

Other anatomical differences that have been considered as indications of woman's retarded evolution are her shorter stature; the higher index of delichocephaly (longheadedness in which the breadth of the skull is less than four-fifths of its length) and more pronounced prognathism (protruding jaws and low facial angle) which are both more frequent among women than among men; and the greater frequency in women of hypertrichosis (excessive growth of hair) with a corresponding infrequency of baldness among women.

Of the many structural differences between the sexes, some minute and complex, let us choose some more easily accessible for comparison: some which any reader with a co-operative spouse or an amenable girl-friend or boy-friend can personally examine with less embarrassment than might be caused by comparing the coccyx.

Legs and arms for instance. Man's legs, as we noticed when we compared the proportions of the male and female shapes, are longer than a woman's in proportion to his whole weight and to his trunk. Artists very often tell lies about woman's legs. In a desire to idealise the female form they often portray women with legs relatively longer in proportion to the trunk. Such legs are rarely seen in women, and certainly never in a woman whom we would describe as typically feminine in shape.

Arms show marked male and female differences. Man's forearm is relatively longer than his upper arm whereas woman's is relatively shorter. Measurements made of children in American schools showed girls' arms as consistently shorter in their entire length than boys' arms, and their forearms are even more markedly shorter. This difference in the proportion of forearm to upper-arm is considered as responsible for girls and women throwing with a different action and in less forceful style than boys and men: as noticed by that Greek 2,300 years ago.

Not only in length but also in shape the male arm differs from the female. This difference can be seen in childhood: a boy's arm is flatter than a girl's, and in later life becomes a much more muscularly defined limb and far less rounded than woman's. Artists show preferences for male or female arms. When painting angels for the churches and altar pieces of Renaissance Italy many painters gave their cherubs girls' arms. Others, including Andrea del Sarto, gave them boys' arms; either because they thought that angels should be boys or because they thought boys more beautiful.

Investigating finer details we find that in a woman's hand the second metacarpal (that is the second of the five bones in that part of the hand between wrist and finger) is relatively longer than the other metacarpals. This difference in the female hand is seen in the earliest weeks of life, so it is obviously a primary female difference and more fundamental than those secondary sexual characteristics that appear later. A woman's fingers are narrower than a man's and more pointed. As Havelock Ellis observed, 'A man is a man even to his thumbs . . .' True enough. A man's thumb is relatively longer than a woman's; so is the big toe. It is only in recent evolution (let us say in the last million or fewer years) that our ancestors found a long thumb and a long big toe useful. When we began walking on our feet we used our hands to grasp weapons and utensils, and possibly used them also to grasp any female who might be around. Woman's thumbs and big toes have not developed as quickly as man's. She probably needed them less; her domestic chores as mother and housewife demanded less grasping. Havelock Ellis continued: '. . . and a woman is a woman down to her little toes.' True again. But here woman seems to reverse the trend seen in her thumbs and big toes: in her little toes woman is paradoxically ahead of man in evolutionary change. When our arboreal ancestors came down from the trees and stopped chasing along branches after their food a full complement of grasping toes became less necessary, and by now the third joint on our little toe is being phased out as redundant. Statistics suggest that women are getting rid of that third joint much more quickly than men are. In a recent examination of 111 human feet the middle and end phalanges of the little toes were found to be in a state of fusion in 41.5 per cent of the women, but in only 31 per cent of the men.

3 BREASTS AND HIPS; VOICE, SKIN AND HAIR

A smaller and rounder figure, shorter arms and legs, fatty deposits instead of muscles, a trunk with the broad end of the egg at the bottom. These, then, are some of the characteristics of the pattern imposed on the human being chosen to be a mother. As Nature's primary concern is the preservation of a species, a woman's body had to assume the shape best suited for conceiving and bearing children. How the woman would get along with such a body was up to her. We see for ourselves how she does get along with it.

Look how she moves. How differently from a man! We have seen how feminine proportions of her arms and feebler feminine muscles make her throw in feminine style, but now let us watch her walk. See how that broad end of the egg makes her gait so unmistakably feminine. There is a structural reason for that.

Of all parts of the body the leg is the one that grows most rapidly; and in maturity its sexual differences are impressive. Because of fatty deposits a woman's thigh has a circumference measurement greater than that of a man's: not *relatively* greater but *absolutely* greater. It is the only part of a woman's body of which that can be said. The average difference in girth is $1\frac{1}{4}$ inches. The woman's thigh, however, tapers so rapidly that its lower part just above the knee is scarcely, and sometimes not at all, larger than a man's, and as the whole thigh is naturally shorter than a man's a woman's thigh has a distinctly recognisable female contour. Furthermore it is set at a different angle to the body, and this makes a strong effect on the way she walks.

That different angle is caused by her wider pelvis. The broad end of the egg is broader not only because of its fatty deposits but also because underneath that flesh is a wider pelvis, fashioned on the ample lines necessary to motherhood. That wider pelvic structure results in woman's thighs being set wider apart at her hips. From there they slope inward to the knees: in fact sometimes they slope inward so much that they give many women the appearance of being knock-kneed.

Look again at a woman trying to run. Watch her hurrying to a bus-stop. It is not her high-heeled shoes that give her that appearance of instability: it is her inward-sloping thighs which force her into making alternative semi-circular rotations of her legs to propel herself along. There are, of course, sportswomen who do not run in so feminine a style. These women, we notice, have less fatty deposits on their thighs and have longer slimmer legs. It can hardly be believed that the physical training performed by these women has altered the shape of their anatomy so radically. It is more likely that the legs they have grown were always less emphatically feminine and that this factor is what helped them to excel at sports and encouraged them to competitive efforts. Yet even in the sport of running the leg movement of the fastest women runners, apart from those recent champions of doubtful sex, is different from that of the long straight piston thrust made by the legs of men runners.

When we watch the non-athletic women running for the bus we notice that those semi-circular rotations of her legs cause a pronounced sway of her buttocks. This undulation of the *derrière* is an especially feminine trait. Indeed in sexual imagery this bottom-swaying is so suggestive of femininity that a woman who wants to arouse sexual interest in the male and to excite him into appreciation of her alluring difference will exaggerate her side-to-side sway. German scientists recently made a film from which they could study woman's walking movements analytically. The film showed that a woman moves her hips and legs together when walking, and that 'as the thigh and leg swing forward for each step, the lateral flexion of the whole trunk causes a slight rise of the hip line and dip of the shoulder'. And so on. In short, the conscientious scientific analysis merely confirmed what any man sees on any pavement where provocative ladies parade and attract their clients' attention by emphasising their femininity.

But many other movements a woman makes, much slighter movements than those involved in walking or running, are performed in a peculiarly feminine manner. For example, when some women talk animatedly and gesture with their hands they do so with a flapping from the wrists which is so typically feminine that effeminate men or female impersonators use it as a feminine 'signature'. The same can be said of woman's special manner of moving her hands and arms when she pulls a coat or wrap close under her chin. A man need reproduce only this one gesture to raise suspicion of effeminacy or a laugh, depending on circumstances.

Another secondary sexual characteristic which a woman can use as a sexual attractant is her bosom. Breasts differ in shape from woman to woman. One attempted classification grouped them into four types: 1. bowl-shaped, like a half tangerine; 2. hemispherical, like a half or three-quarters of a round apple; 3. conical; 4. goat's udder. Such adult males as find the breasts irresistibly attractive parts of a woman's body show particular preference for one type more than the other. Personal discussions have led me to the belief, however, that the younger the male or the less mature in intellect, the more he craves a bigger helping. It is of course natural for the young to be sensually greedy, to demand quantity rather than quality. Older males whose sexuality has remained at a merely physical and conceptually immature level have also an erotic preference for big breasts. More sophisticated males prefer breasts to be small and firm, perhaps because such breasts suggest, nostalgically, such things as youth and innocence and virginity.

Incidentally woman's two breasts are not as symmetrical as mass-produced brassières would suggest. The left breast tends to be slightly more developed than the right because it has more galactophore canals, the milk ducts.

One man-woman difference in this part of the body is that the distance between the nipples is often relatively greater in a man than a woman. One theory is that this is because woman has to employ a large area of skin to provide for the convex growth of her breasts, and as the skin at the side of her body yields more easily to the pull of that development her nipples consequently move nearer together.

Research is currently being conducted into probable differences in skin sensitivity between man and woman. We do know that a woman's skin appears generally softer and more delicate in texture and a shade lighter in colour than the skin of a man. In fact those rosy cheeks which poets praise in a woman are actually the result of blood shining through her more delicate skin. Unusually delicate skin in a man is looked upon as rather a feminine trait; whereas a woman whose skin has not the expected feminine delicacy is considered a bit masculine and could be called, with appropriate choice of the word, 'a tough woman'. But is woman's skin not only more delicate but also more sensitive? Accepting that it is, psychologists have suggested that the feminine sensitivity has primeval sexual origins. Early woman, they argue, suffered rape by man. Certainly the mind of earliest man was not filled with thoughts of romance and love and marriage when he seized the most attractive or probably merely the most available female and copulated. Helene Deutsch suggests that woman learned from this violent embrace of primeval rape to enjoy being, as we still say, 'covered'. Early woman learned to welcome man's whole male body pressing on all parts of her and the man's hands gripping and stroking every area of her skin. Also, not having a penis, a prominent external sexual apparatus where tactile sexual sensations could be enjoyed, she compensated for the lack by transferring sexual sensations over the whole surface of her body.

This overall sexual sensuality can be associated with woman's apparently greater susceptibility to blushing. Havelock Ellis described the male erection as 'a blushing of the penis', and there are sound physiological reasons for the phrase: both phenomena are caused by the rush of blood to a certain area.

The immense network of sensory nerves on the skin spreads the sense of touch over our whole body, makes every part of us responsive to tactile sensations caused by pressures, tickling, caressing or pain. The more 'sensitive' the skin is, the more intense are those sensations. Close similarities in structure have been found in the terminals of the sensory nerves of the skin and the corpuscles found on the glans penis, the clitoris, the prepuce of the clitoris and the larger labia. This similarity evoked from Iwan Bloch the comment that consequently 'the entire skin may be regarded as a huge organ of voluptuous sensation'. It can well be that woman's sensitivity of skin is responsible for her being usually more abundantly equipped than man with those areas of the body called erotogenic zones, parts of the body which, when caressed or assaulted, inflame erotic desire. Skin eroticism can likewise account for the particular pleasure woman finds in contact with materials such as silk and velvet and fur. The subconscious sexual delight a woman experiences when these materials wrap her body, a delight which is cultivated by any man who dresses a wife or mistress, has possibly had tremendous economic and commercial results in raising the market value of certain fabrics.

Closely allied to the difference in skin is the difference of hair growth. The human body wears two kinds of hair; hairs that are strong and visible, and hairs that are softer and finer and on occasions hardly visible at all. Roughly speaking *hair* is a male symbol and *down* a female symbol; this apart, of course, from the long tresses of a woman's head-hair.

All of us, both men and women, are covered with down before we are born. In about the fifth pre-natal month the foetus sprouts fine down, not only as eye-lashes, eyebrows and head-hair, but over the face, breast, belly, back and limbs. It grows particularly luxuriantly over the sacrum where a regular hairy tail appears. Except in abnormal cases this down reaches its peak of growth during the seventh month and then declines.

A man does have down, but whereas it is hardly noticeable on his body, on a woman's body it is very much in evidence; on her cheeks, her back, the outer surfaces of her arms and her shins. Blondes usually have denser down than brunettes, though being naturally so much paler on blondes it is not so apparent. A woman retains this infantile characteristic more than a man does, and it possibly plays its part making her skin more sensitive to touch than a man's.

The fact that it is during puberty when hair sprouts under the armpits and over the genitals of both boys and girls has led to sexual significance being attached to hair. The males of some eastern races have very little body hair, but western man has more or less thick hair on many parts of his body, and a hairy chest is looked upon, erroneously, as a confirmation of masculine strength and sexual virility.

I have seen it argued, however, that aesthetically hairiness mitigates against physical beauty. Sculptors and painters, it is pointed out, prefer female figures, or androgynous ones, or boys, because with them the lines of body and limbs are clearly seen, not 'lost' in hair covering, and some sculptors and artists actually reject otherwise perfect physical male models because they are too hairy. Women, because they are not so much concerned with outward physical appearance of their love-objects do not express strong preferences for or against hairiness, though we remember that Rebekah loved 'smooth' Jacob more than 'hairy' Esau.

Much physiological attention has always been paid to a marked sex difference in the growth of hair above the genitals. It is always noticeable that a woman's hair at that point ends in an abrupt horizontal line, whereas a man's extends in triangular disposition towards his navel. Psychologists examining the bodies of sexual deviants remarked that the pubic hairs of some males with feminine tendencies show the feminine pattern of abrupt horizontal termination above the genitals. But this observation should not lead us into the mistake of thinking that the actual pubic hair of male and female spreads over a different area. The upward continuation of hair above a man's pubic area is not a continuation of his pubic hair; it is part of the general extra hairiness of his body.

Although most western men are likely to have thin head hair or be bald by middle-age, man remains much the hairier of the two sexes, for in addition to his masculine moustache and beard, his eyebrows become longer and stiffer, and he also sprouts strong hair in his ears and nose and anus, as well as on his back and the outer surfaces of his limbs.

Woman's hair growth is almost exactly contrary. The hair on her head grows thickly and to varying but always considerable length. Her pubic hair is normally bushier than a man's, and the individual hairs are also bigger. One portion of the human body which is sometimes strongly hairy in a man is never so in a woman: that is the outer lateral surface of the upper arm in the region of the shoulders.

Earlier we imagined a human figure too far away for us to see if it were male or female, and we said that if it called out to us we should know by difference in voice whether it was a man or woman. This difference in tone of male and female voice is by no means peculiar to humans. Even if the figure had not been human but had been animal we should (with certain animals, and if our ears were trained to distinguish animal calls) know whether it was the male or female of the species. In many animals (the bitch, the mare and the hen, for example) the female has the weaker and more high-pitched voice.

The difference in voice is caused by a sexual difference in anatomical detail: the size and construction of the larynx. The larynx, the upper part of the windpipe, is a sphincter whose actual primary necessity is to enable us to breathe and live at all; only secondarily is it used as an organ of voice. The pitch and note of the voice are governed partly by the size of the resonance chambers and particularly by the length and tension of the vocal cords. The number of vibrations made by the vocal cords per second determine the nature of the sound, just as they do on a stringed musical instrument. The shorter the vocal cords, the higher will be the pitch. The average length of a man's vocal cords is 18 millimetres; woman's are much shorter, 13 millimetres. The entire male larynx is about one third larger than a female's.

The average man's voice is between 130 and 145 cycles a second, the average woman's between 230 and 255. The voice of a woman is therefore around middle C, an octave higher in pitch than a man's. Men with female characteristics notoriously speak and, especially, laugh on a higher note than the normal male. Women with male characteristics speak in lower tones.

The larynx is another part of the human body in which woman seems to be more 'infantile' in development than is a man, for even when a female becomes adult her larynx is high in her neck, its original position in infancy and higher than it is in a man's neck.

At puberty the larynx develops more strongly in a boy than in a girl. The opening between the vocal folds doubles in length in the boy; in the girl it increases by roughly only one third. Consequently the boy's voice 'breaks' and becomes markedly deeper in tone. A similar change does occur in girls, but far more slowly and with much less effect on her tone. The break of the voice is a distinctive sign of male puberty, and consequently the male voice has more acute sexual significance for a feminine hearer than the unchanged female voice has for a man.

Civilisation has affected the development of the larynx and tone of voice. In primitive peoples the larynx is, as compared to the larynx in civilised societies, comparatively undeveloped, and their voices usually tend to be high and shrill.

The effect sexual biochemistry has on the larynx and voice has been noted in our reference to the effect of castration. If castration is performed on a boy before puberty his larynx remains childish, more like that of a girl's. A fact of probably sexual significance is the observation made by some researchers that both the voice and the larynx of prostitutes tend to take a masculine direction.

Just as mere millimetres of difference in larynx can alter the tone of voice, so mere millimetres of difference in our anatomy can alter our outward appearance. For example, let us look at some dimples.

Just above the cleft of our buttocks is a lozenge-shaped space where the flesh covering our spine seems thinner and tauter than elsewhere. This lozenge is called the Michaelis Rhomboid, in honour of a German gynaecologist, Gustav

Michaelis, who spent a lot of his scientific time examining it. It marks the position in our spine of the sacrum, a triangularly shaped bone built up of five spinal vertebrae and wedged at the back of the hip bones. The limits of the lozenge are sometimes marked by four dimples, one on either side and one at top and bottom. If a man does have those dimples the ones at the sides are always several centimetres nearer to each other than they are on a woman. In a young nicely plump young woman the dimples are quite large and deep and the enclosed lozenge very well defined. Those who have access to such treasures can study this feminine characteristic for themselves: otherwise many present-day photographs, even on the sleeves of gramophone discs, can provide the opportunity of comparing masculine and feminine Michaelis Rhomboida.

We come now to a very tender subject, tender not only physically but also emotionally: the bladder. There is a vulgar phrase which, even in this candid book, one is reluctant to put into print. Anyhow all of us must know the phrase: it describes what a person, particularly a woman, might do to herself or himself with laughing too much. Considering how extremely sensitive the bladder is it is not surprising that it is highly susceptible to any kind of excitement; to sensation of heat or cold or pain, as well as emotional sensations. The bladder has been proved to be even more responsive to sensations of touch than that infinitely delicate part of our body the iris of the eye. The female bladder is apparently more sensitive than the male bladder. This, it would seem, might even apply in animals. Arabs believe that a mare is ready for service by the stallion when she reaches such a pitch of sexual excitement that she urinates at the mere sound of his neigh.

There has been a great deal of argument as to why many women seem to 'spend more pennies' than men. The arguments are not economic ones, about woman's extravagance or the unfairness of her having to pay at all, but physiological arguments about why the necessity arises, or seems to arise, more frequently with women than with men. The conclusion reached is that this is because frequency of urination is caused by nervous rather than anatomical factors. The feeling of urgent need to spend that penny is not a matter of how much urine is in the bladder but by a nervous contraction of the bladder around what urine it contains. This nervous contraction of the bladder does happen, as most of us would confirm from everyday observation, more often in women than in men.

This is why women are usually chosen as subjects for any analytic examination of bladder sensitivity. In one recent investigation researchers tested a number of young women with a plethysmograph specially adapted for the experiment. A plethysmograph is an instrument used to measure variations in the size of an organ and the amount of blood in the organ or passing through it. The experimenters found that even slight physical contact such as touching the back of one of the young ladies' hands caused the female bladder to contract. It also contracted when a young woman was spoken to or when she herself was speaking, or when she had to do anything involving any mental effort at all on her part. The experiment also confirmed that fear or anxiety or suspense likewise causes the female bladder to contract. As contractions of the bladder cause the sensation of needing to urinate, these findings suggest reasons why woman's sensitivity, both physical and mental, can cause her to spend more pennies.

There is a visual anatomical difference between the bladders of men and women. Man's bladder is somewhat ovoid; woman's is rounder and is, relatively to her body size, also larger. But it has been argued that woman's bladder is larger primarily because of 'unnatural habits of distension, the result of social causes'; which means, in less euphemistic terms, that the female bladder is distended because women don't ask to leave the room as often as they should, either through a sense of modesty or for lack of a penny or anywhere to spend it. It was the same centuries ago. The second century physician Aretaeus reported that owing to retaining their urine during banquets women suffered from bladders which, because of being overdistended, had lost their normal contractile powers.

Women are more sensitive to odours than men. Kenneth Walker refers to experiments made by Alice Thayer in the U.S.A. which suggests that girls are 'considerably more influenced by odour than are boys' and that 'smell sensibility increases in girls after puberty'. It has been found that the acuity of the sense of smell in women is regulated by their female sex hormones and varies in sensitivity with the menstrual cycle. In fact Walker argues that although woman's use of perfume has a sexual significance she uses it 'for her own pleasure as much as for that of her mate'.

The most important difference between the skeletons of man and woman is one which exquisitely demonstrates how architecturally precise Nature can be in equipping woman for her prime duty, motherhood. This difference is the difference in the shape of the pelvis. We have noted earlier that difference in the pelvis causes difference in body shape and movement, but now let us examine the pelvis itself as a magnificent piece of physiological engineering. Since the time when it was originally designed for our arboreal ancestors it has had to be modified through millenniums of back-to-the-drawing-board improvements until it became an appropriately up-to-date appliance for a creature who wanted to walk erect; a posture unnatural for an animal but preferred by humans.

Nevertheless, the instrument, however much it was adapted, had always to be manufactured in masculine and feminine ranges. The pelvis of the modern male is long, narrow and strongly built. One important masculine characteristic is that the margins of its pubic arch are turned a little more inside out than in a woman's pelvis in order to accommodate comfortably the root of that masculine appliance the penis. The female pelvis is built in more broad and shallow lines to suit her occupation of child-bearing. A human baby's head at birth is fairly large. Consequently the pelvis built for a woman has to be wider and altogether more ample than a man's, and its depth also has to be diminished so that the baby's head can get through speedily and unharmed.

An Edinburgh scientist, Professor R. W. Johnstone, once said: 'Despite any arguments to the contrary, reproduction is the greatest function of womanhood, and certainly it is the only one in which Mother Nature takes any special interest. She is almost obsessed with the one idea: reproduction of the species.' Many years have passed and many changes in woman's social state have occurred since Johnstone made that flat statement. But the words are still true, and the design of the pelvis is one of the feminine characteristics underlining them.

4 'The Weaker Sex'

There are certain hours of the day, in certain streets and tea-shops and department stores when one suddenly gets the impression that the world is populated with elderly women. The impression is intensified by experiences in famous cities and holiday resorts during the tourist season. The windows of those long buses, particularly those whose tours originate in the United States, frame row upon row of eagerly staring blue-rinsed matrons, most of them, one is certain, widows whose husbands have died of thromboses and ulcers while amassing the fortunes now being spent on gay hats, tourist souvenirs and package holidays. On the pavements of industrial cities one sees these women's less well endowed sisters. Many of them are not in very good shape. Having eaten too much or having sustained themselves on an ill-balanced diet they have grown broad in the beam, their feet are bad, and surgical bandages or elastic stockings support their varicose veins. In contrast there are others as bony as old birds, and as perky. Yet the majority, fat or lean, agile or not, bravely defy their years, spend hours at the dress-racks fingering 'young matron modes' and as much of their pensions as they can afford at the hairdresser. Rich or poor, fat or lean, nearly all these elderly women seem determinedly durable and tenacious of life.

Actually our momentary impressions are correct. We have no need to go around counting heads. Population statistics prove us right. There are more old women in the world than old men. We are right too in detecting an extra durability in women. Women *are* more durable than men: that is why they live longer than men.

That last fact should of itself be enough to restrain us from using carelessly the time-worn phrase 'the weaker sex' when we refer to women. Actually there are many other facts to show what an ill-based phrase that is. When we study those facts, we shall find emphatically confirmed the suggestion we made earlier that Nature invariably shows preference for the female of the species. Biological facts and statistics prove that man, despite stronger muscular power, is in most other respects actually the weaker sex.

Nature's feminine prejudice is understandable. To Nature

the woman is necessary and precious: she is the mother. The man is dispensable. His work for Nature is over in a couple of minutes or even less: the woman has a job for life. Because whereas the man makes his one necessary contribution to the perpetuation of the species with the speedy ejaculation of sperm, the woman's job has at that moment only just begun. She must gestate the fertilised egg for nine months and then give birth to the child. She must suckle and nurse and rear it through babyhood and infancy. The sperm-carrier may stay around out of a sense of duty or love; he may even be compelled to stay around by the conventions and laws of society; but his presence is not physically necessary.

So the woman has to be built in more durable fashion. Being fashioned so she has a better chance of living longer.

1 WOMEN LIVE LONGER

Most husbands reading these words will die before their wives do. Out of every three men in the United States and Britain who have managed to live into their mid-thirties one will die before he is 65. Only one woman in five will do that.

All of us, men and women, have nowadays a chance of living longer than our parents did. The discovery of antibiotics, the development of new techniques in surgery, the improvements in hygiene and social conditions help to protect us against dying before our time. But even so man's time comes earlier than woman's.

In just under 40 years medical science has made such advances in its battle against one-time killer diseases that each of us has been given a bonus of a possible eleven or twelve years more on this earth. The important point to notice is this: the *eleven* possible extra years apply to my male readers; the *twelve* apply to my female readers. For although statistics prove that both men and women are living longer, the fact emerges that women are doing better out of the bargain than men. The expectancy of life for a woman always was more than that of a man, but the gap of years between the sexes is actually widening. In 1930 a man could be expected to live to be 56 and a woman to 60. The latest statistics show man's life expectancy is now 67; woman's has leaped to 72. So in only 40 years woman has gained an extra year's lead over man.

Even when approaching their century women have a better chance of lasting than men. According to the life expectancy figures published by the Institute of Actuaries a woman of 93 can expect to live 3.13 years more, but a man of 93 can expect to live for only 2.48 years. The last expectation of life the tables quote is at the age 99, when a woman can expect to live to be 101.09 and a man to be 100.73.

Every country where reliable expectancy-of-life figures are available shows the same trend.

Longer life is not an unmixed blessing for the woman. Nowadays two out of every three of the over-65's in the population are women. This means that old-age becomes increasingly woman's problem; a problem not only of becoming old herself but also of having to look after the aged, because that has always been considered traditionally woman's work.

Most of the aged women are widows. Indeed widowhood has become for woman the inescapable and often sad version of man's retirement. A man's retirement marks the end of his working life, and any shock or chagrin experienced is softened by the gold watch and good wishes of his colleagues, the sensation of being relieved of the necessity of daily wage-earning, and the prospect of pottering around his garden. Compared with this woman's 'retirement' is a sad fading out, signalled by the sometimes sudden loss of her husband and leaving her with little to do and the threat of loneliness.

Why is it that men die so much sooner than women? The conditions of modern civilization, the pace of life and work, are sometimes blamed. It is undeniable that in our fast-moving competitive society the average man lives at a constantly higher pressure than does the average woman, and because of this he generates and uses up nervous force more rapidly. Consequently a man is more likely to suffer premature death than a woman; more likely to die at a comparatively young age from such things as ulcers and heart diseases and other illnesses caused by the stress and abuses of modern life.

It is also a fact that however much civilised society attempts to protect life and to guard men and women not only against premature death from disease but also from accident, the average man inevitably faces more dangers of early death in spheres of work and sport and adventure than the average woman does. More males than females suffer accidental death. This trend begins at the early age of three. In England and

Wales, for example, 387 boys but only 57 girls were drowned in one year.

The fact that we take it for granted that boys rather than girls are likely victims of accidents at play is surely indicated by the wording of a sentence in an article about the dangers of the pike that came to my notice a day or two ago. 'Ducks, swans, other pike and even small boys have been attacked by this killer.' No mention, one notices, of attacks on small girls.

The sex disparity in the rate of accidental death increases up to the age of thirty. By that age in some countries fifteen times more men that women suffer death by accident.

Nor is it always disease or accident that carries men off prematurely in our modern society. More ageing men than ageing women commit suicide. Here again the stresses of modern life might be the cause. Most men do face more worries and responsibilities than women, particularly financial and status worries, and might therefore be more prone than women to decide they have had enough of it and make their own quietus. Though it might be argued that this proves that men are the weaker vessels and succumb more easily to despairs, whereas women take the rebuffs and disappointments and tragedies of life with more resilience. It certainly can be established, by statistical evidence as distinct from theoretical argument, that severe illnesses arising in old age as the result of psychiatric disorders are more common in men than in women.

But more significant than social statistics is the fact that also among primitive peoples who suffer none of the stresses and hazards of civilisation women still live longer than men. In fact most primitives, knowing nothing about statistics, accept it as a commonplace of life that the female is stronger and more likely to survive than the male. It was always the custom of the Indians of North America, for example, to nurse a boy child with more care and indulgence than a girl child, because they believed that a baby boy was weaker and, unless he received more attention, was more likely to die.

Illnesses to which women are more prone than men are generally linked in some way with woman's feminine destiny. For instance it is claimed that nearly all diseases of the thyroid gland are more frequent in women than in men, and certainly this is so with goitre. The significance here is that the thyroid is directly linked with woman's sexual metabolism, particularly with pregnancy.

The ancients believed that the slenderness of a woman's neck could indicate she was a virgin and said that by measuring the necks of brides they could establish whether they were virgins or not. The belief was no doubt based on such discoveries as the one made by Democritus, contemporary of Socrates. This remarkably observant anatomist remarked that women's necks swelled during pregnancy. Now, 2,000 years later, doctors agree that all sexual activity in women is accompanied or preceded by hyperactivity of the thyroid. It swells at the very first menstruation and it is not uncommon for it to increase at every subsequent menstruation. In fact it has been claimed that the thyroid plays a leading part in dictating the metabolism of the whole body, the male body as well as the female, to make it perform its generative functions. Certainly any thyroid deficiency can cause a breakdown of these functions; the development of the genitals may be retarded, menstruation may be irregular, puberty upset or delayed, or the uterus may atrophy. Indeed in some cases of thyroid deficiency in a woman her whole libido may be destroyed and her mentality become apathetic.

The fact that more women than men become grossly fat is considered due to upsets in the metabolism. Morbid obesity, about twice more frequent in women than in men, may be due to the thyroid or pituitary deficiency which is associated with that failing energy of the body's sexual system so often occurring after the menopause.

2 BOYS ARE BORN WEAKER

The 'bouncing baby boy' is not merely imagined. He is true. Baby boys *are* bigger than baby girls. At birth the male baby is already rather heavier than the female, is about one-fifth of an inch taller and has a greater chest girth.

But far from being an advantage the boy's superior size is actually a hazard. It increases the dangers a baby faces at birth. The boy is just that bit more likely to find difficulty in passing safely through the mother's pelvic outlet. This is one factor responsible for still-born children being more frequently male than female; the proportion reaching as many as 140 stillborn males to 100 stillborn females.

More male than female babies suffer some malformation of

the genitals at birth. More baby boys than baby girls suffer from physical abnormalities caused by an arrest in the developments of the embryo or by some unknown cause early in prenatal growth. Deaths per million from congenital defects average decidedly higher for males.

Even before birth the male has less resistance to disease or accident and is in greater danger of death than the female. At the time of writing research is being conducted in New York which suggests that some connection between mental disorder and the biochemistry of pregnant mothers can spell death to the male foetus. There is even a suggestion that a mother might herself suffer some toxic effects from bearing a male rather than a female baby.

At a New York hospital Dr. M. A. Taylor, a psychiatrist at New York Medical College, studied 54 pregnancies in all of which the mother had suffered an attack of schizophrenia before or after conception. To 13 women whose attack had occurred within one month of conception only girls were born. Dr. Taylor's study confirmed a theory suggested earlier by New York researchers. A survey they had made indicated that during an attack of schizophrenia there is released into the mother's blood some factor that is toxic to the male chromosome carried in the sperm or in the fertilised egg. Whenever the attack occurred in the second or third month of pregnancy male babies tended to be stillborn or abnormal.

Dr. Taylor went on to study cases where mothers had become schizophrenic within a month after giving birth. There were 29 of them; 22 of them had given birth to boys. The figures suggest that there may be some causal relation between a male birth and a later attack of schizophrenia. Dr. Taylor says this suggests that if the mother becomes acutely schizophrenic during the first month or so of pregnancy, the foetus, if a male, is destroyed, presumably by some chemical released into the blood as a result of schizophrenia. When it occurs later in pregnancy the male foetus somehow defends itself, possibly by producing large quantities of the sex hormones progesterone and testosterone. The hormones would suppress the disease in the mother, perhaps by preventing the formation of the toxic blood factor. When the child is born the mother is no longer protected by the male sex hormones of the foetus and the schizophrenia is unmasked. In support of the theory Dr. Taylor quotes clinical cases in which changes in certain sex hormone levels have been associated with schizophrenia.

An investigation into congenital deformities among school children in Glasgow revealed that among many malformations caused before birth the peculiar deformity of a third nipple was found on nearly twice as many boys as girls. The total figures collected in the Glasgow survey also showed that *twice* as many boys as girls suffered from some congenital deformity.

Hare-lip is statistically recorded as generally occurring in nearly twice as many boys as girls. One survey at St. Thomas's Hospital, London actually found *more* than twice as many males as females with hare-lip.

Dr. Carter in *Human Heredity* reports that a condition known as pyloric stenosis, a stricture of the opening from the stomach into the duodenum, is found in one of 200 boys but only in one of 1,000 girls, and says that a survey made by British doctors at Birmingham to investigate the family incidence of this condition found one brother in 16 affected as against one sister in 64.

The male baby's greater susceptibility to congenital weaknesses is similarly revealed in the statistics of much rarer deformities. One of these is known as *talipes equine-varus*. It is a type of club-foot, and it is particularly interesting to physiologists because it represents the position of the foot which is normal in adult apes but is normal in men only *before* birth. If it exists after birth, it shows there has been pre-natal arrest of development. This malformation is far more prevalent in males than in females.

Equally significant is the fact that throughout the whole world males are more liable to colour-blindness than are females. Colour-blindness is a defect common to albinism, the absence of pigment in the skin and eyes and hair, and is yet another of the congenital abnormalities found more often in male children than in female.

The fundamental extra weakness in the male is summed up in Kenneth Walker's *The Physiology of Sex*.

'Statistics show that in a country like Great Britain women preponderate over males, the preponderance increasing steadily with every decade of life. This is due to the fact that, constitutionally, males are less resistant than females. Not only is this susceptibility of the male to accident shown by the greater number of male intra-uterine deaths, but also by the higher mortality rates of males throughout the whole of life. The slightly greater vigour of the Y-bearing spermatozoa and the higher ratio of male conceptions and births are therefore more than offset by the higher mortality of the male.

'Contrary to the accepted opinion, the female is the stronger sex.'

3 A MATTER OF STRENGTH

If he overcomes the dangers of being born male, if he is free of deformities, and if he avoids the hazards of boyhood, escaping such mishaps as being drowned or being gobbled by pike, the male, despite his inherent fundamental weaknesses, will grow into a taller and heavier adult than the female. It is interesting to note here that the same applies to all mammals. In all species of mammals, with the as yet unexplained exception of the rabbit, females are smaller than males.

Another emphatic difference is one we remarked on when we discussed the different shapes of man and woman: this is the marked different in muscles. When we come to muscles we really can describe women as 'the weaker sex'.

In all human races women are muscularly weaker than men. The difference in muscular strength is, however, less apparent among primitive peoples; so much so that Sir Harry Johnston claimed that the women of one West African tribe were 'in many cases stronger and finer than the men' because their energetic life as the carriers and labourers of the community had strengthened their muscular system. But we must not be tricked by appearances into believing that even such women are muscularly stronger than their menfolk. In communities where women are usually the bearers of burdens, the men do appear to tire more easily if in some emergency they have to perform chores usually done by women. But that is not because the men are weaker. Those men would show just as much weariness if they were doing nothing more strenuous than nursing a baby for too long. This is characteristic of the male. A man usually prefers to intersperse bursts of energy between long periods of inactivity: a woman will labour on and on continuously.

The average man of any race can carry almost double his own weight, the average woman only about half her weight. A boy can carry one third more weight than a girl. The force exerted by a woman's hand is on average about one third less than that exerted by a man's hand.

Sex disparity in strengths is understandable when we compare the sum total of muscles in men and women. An average woman's muscles weigh 15 kilograms, less than one third of her total 55.3 kilogram weight; a man's are 26.1 kilograms considerably more than a third of his 65.7 kilogram weight.

Attempts have been made to calculate how many 'strong women' and how many 'weak men' there are in a given population: that is, how many women are stronger than average and how many men weaker than average. In the course of this research a series of ingenious laboratory experiments conducted in England found that on average seven out of every hundred men are weaker than the norm and seven out of every hundred women are stronger. The researchers were thus able to prescribe an easy rule-of-thumb method for anyone who might want to recruit the hundred strongest individuals from a group of one hundred men and one hundred women. All one would need to do was to select all the hundred men, then eliminate the seven weakest of them and replace them with the seven strongest women.

A woman is particularly weaker than a man in her chest muscles. Her back muscles are also very weak: this has been suggested as a possible reason for her greater tendency to backache. Out of 2,300 cases of lateral curvature of the spine recorded at one London hospital 84.5 per cent were women and only 15.5 per cent were men.

Weakest of all are the muscles of her arms, but one muscle she develops well is the latissimus dorsi. Naturally, for it is that muscle in her back which comes into play when she has to button or zip a dress at the back. Similarly the stronger development of the feminine deltoid muscle of woman's upper arm has been ascribed to the exercise this muscle gets when a woman dresses her hair.

Strongest of a woman's muscles are her thigh muscles, a strength she has exploited in dancing and ballet. Indeed it has been stated that of all aptitudes requiring energetic use of the muscles dancing is the only one in which women can physically excel men. Women do equal or even excel men in other feats of muscular dexterity, but only in circumstances where the main force is provided by some other agent, like the horse in riding or the trapeze in the circus. But in cases where all the muscular strength has to be provided by the individual performer a woman can never compete with man however much she trains to do so.

Physiologists declare flatly that whatever improved facilities modern society provides women for physical training and exercise, the basic difference of muscular strength between the sexes can never be altered: man will always, because of his anatomical build, have stronger muscular power. In golf, for instance, the woman can lift a ball only 70 to 100 yards against a man's 120 to 140 yards, and W. T. Tilden, while admitting that women were just as great *artists* on the tennis courts, said, 'Their physical limitations of height, weight, speed of foot, and bodily structure, prohibit women ever attaining a skill equal to men's.'

On the other hand Brian Glanville recently remarked that although the performances of some girl athletes, he particularised girl runners, might be equalled by a fifteen-year-old schoolboy, girls of 15 and 16 had trained to become superb swimmers and while a Johnny Weismuller would thresh helplessly in their wake, were besting records set up in the 1960's by such as Murray Rose. In a most thought-provoking answer to the question 'What is happening to girls in sport?' Glanville argued that attempts to defy the biological and psychological difference between the sexes for the sake of athletic success were undesirable. He argued that a 'girl who goes out to run, swim or play tennis for the joy of it is still being a girl. But a girl who slogs away all winter in a gymnasium lifting weights so she can beat other girls in the summer is behaving like an imitation man.'

That psychological factors do play a considerable part in turning girls to muscular sporting activity is suggested by his recollection of a girl sprinter telling him that every member of the outstanding team to which she belonged 'came from a broken home'.

The physiological effect of muscular development by women also indicates that it is contrary to essential femininity. Nature does not like it at all. Doctors have noticed that muscularly well-developed or athletic women show noticeable uterine as well as vesical inertia in childbirth. In contrast apparently weak and fragile women often carry out the processes of parturition efficiently.

In any case, neither the possessing of muscles nor the ability to develop and exploit them necessarily indicates powers of endurance and fortitude. It is well known that although so-called 'muscle-men' are capable of characteristically masculine bursts of energy in feats of physical strength such as weight-lifting and wrestling and the like they are almost invariably hypochondriacally worried and babyishly sensitive when facing physical discomforts or the slightest pains of quite minor ailments.

There is probably some significance in the fact that by all accounts most of these 'he-men' also make poor lovers. Despite an appearance of bulging masculinity they lack the sexual virility possessed by their less muscled fellows. In many instances, of course, their devotion to the development of their biceps is the outcome of their narcissism, an attribute which does not make a man a good lover. Indeed it is found that sexual vigour is stronger and is longer-lived in men who have exercised and developed their brains rather than their muscles, in painters and writers and other men of intellectual power: certainly woman's lack of muscle never detracts from her sexual urge.

Only in one part of her body has a woman stronger muscles than a man. Or so we are informed on the serious authority of a German physiologist, Dr. Thiele. He claims that the muscles in a woman's tongue are stronger than in a man's tongue. Further comment can be left to the reader.

4 'STRONGER HEADS' TOO

The anthropologist Margaret Mead tells of a South Seas people who 'regard women as the appropriate bearers of heavy burdens "because their heads are stronger than men's" '. Whether they are right in their belief that the heads of their womenfolk are *muscularly* stronger than men's is debatable, but we in the western world might confidently use the words 'stronger heads' in another sense. Our womenfolk, we could say, are better fitted to carry the heavy burdens of family problems and to endure the stresses and strains of life because they are 'stronger in the head' than man. And we should be right.

There is no need to resort to health statistics to demonstrate this. Daily observation is sufficient to show that the popular concept of woman as a swooning timorous female is a product of romantic sentimental fiction, one perhaps dreamed up by the male himself to inflate the male ego. Any man would agree that the woman he knows best, his wife or his mother, can conjure up reserves of strength and resilience that often surprise him, so much do they seem to contradict the universal concept of the weaker sex. Many a man probably believes that in this way the woman in his life must be an exception. He is wrong. His woman is not an exception.

Perhaps man has encouraged the concept of woman being 'the weaker sex' for his own personal and selfish reasons. Man always needs a woman. He needs her first as his own mother and then as mother of his children, as provider of domestic convenience and sexual pleasure. Therefore man wants a woman at hand whom he can call his own. To win such a treasure he may have to beat off competing males, and then, having secured her, he must protect her. It was comparatively simple to do this in the days when he kept her in a cave, but when cities and civilisation broke down the cave walls and substituted communities of freely mixing men and women, the man had to choose his woman by more sophisticated means than dragging her through the trees by her hair. Instead he had to serenade her with offers of comfort or wealth or power or by convincing her of his superiority, in ardour or beauty or sheer size, over other men. When he had made the capture he cemented it by draping her with the mantle of marriage; housing and clothing her in a manner suitable to his wealth or status; thus sending the signal 'Keep Off!' to other men not with a club or spear but by investing her with the accoutrements and dignity of a wife. In that way a woman became the precious and protected companion of the desirous male. Perhaps only in that way did the phrase 'the weaker sex' ever have any validity.

The status of women in our masculine-dominated society and the conventions which dictate our social sexual conduct condition her to assume an attitude of not being able to cope, of not being able to face up to the stress of life. Convention insists that she must leave it to the man, normally her husband, to protect and sustain her, or pretend to do so. But again and again we see that this attitude of dependence is merely a pose dictated by the conventions of a masculine-dominated society. We see it, for example, when a woman who throughout all her married life has appeared to need the protective guiding presence of a husband suddenly finds herself a widow on her own. If she does not find a substitute conventional prop with another man or in another family she copes with the worries of life alone and magnificently. On the other hand the man, the male who throughout his married life has appeared to be the mainstay of the marriage, crumbles. The widower is nearly always a rather helpless and pathetic creature. Remembering those matrons in the tourist buses, we might ask ourselves what comparative results we would turn up if we made a census to discover how many ageing widowers ever have the nerve to set off on adventurous jaunts across the continents.

An extract from a letter received at the time of writing this chapter pungently illustrates my point. The writer, a divorced woman, tells me that her young married daughter 'was at work on Friday, did all the household chores on Saturday, cooked a vast meal and entertained friends on Sunday, ignored the early pangs because she was winning at cards and gave birth to a son in the early hours of Monday. She is not by far the only young woman I know who has more staying power and guts than her mate . . . Men are splendid to look after and love, but they do seem to fall apart at the seams in times of crisis. I think the reason I won't marry again is because I'm prepared to cope with crises for one, but to Hell with crises for two.'

The truth is, as doctors and psychologists confirm, that the average woman can endure more mental and emotional stress than a man can endure without mental or physical breakdown. Consider for instance two of the scourges of present day society, both causally related to the stresses of modern life: alcoholism and drug-addiction, both of them afflictions arising from some emotional or mental weakness in the victims. Precise statistics are naturally difficult to obtain, but it is estimated that the sexual disparity is immense: as many as seven men to one woman. As for the advanced manifestation of alcoholism, delirium tremens, in which damage to the brain occurs, that is found almost exclusively in man.

The same disparity is seen throughout the whole range of disorders of psychological origin. The male is always more prone than the female to such upsets. One example will suffice. Men are three times more liable than women to be afflicted with stammering. In Boston, U.S.A., the exact proportion of stuttering among school-children was 1.12 per cent of all the boys and only .42 per cent of all the girls. What is more, it was found that whereas girls seemed more capable of overcoming the impediment in later life boys were more likely to contract it; with the result that the statistics of higher age groups showed even greater disparity in the percentages.

Before leaving the subject of psychological disorders we should also note than a woman is less likely than a man to become a 'crank', at least in the more extreme meaning of that word. It is impossible, of course, to count 'cranks', but it is accepted that an eccentric, that is to say a person whose existence takes a course divorced from or contradictory to the normal life and modes of society, is nearly always a person who is suffering from some congenital defect, and it is established that more men than women are afflicted in this way. There are milder types of 'cranks', people who indulge certain fads and fancies immoderately but in a mild way. One would say that there are as many women of that kind as there are men.

Sometimes certain anatomical details which at first seem to suggest that man is stronger in some particular prove to be misleading. For instance the fact that man's larynx, trachea and lungs are larger than woman's indicates that man's breathing power is stronger than woman's. It is. A series of tests at a British Air Force Training College proved that, and the tests also showed that a man can hold his breath longer than a woman can. Against such evidence how can we account for a phenomenon which Sidney Webb noted with astonishment? He noticed that women labourers toiling in salt works could endure the hellish heat of the stoves far better and for longer than men could. One theory suggests a surprising biological explanation for this. A woman, it is suggested, can get along with less air than a man because of her smaller lungs. Women, it has been found, have a greater chance of surviving than men have when exposed to charcoal fumes, and consequently it is now believed that women could adapt themselves to breathe at high altitudes where men would fall ill because of there not being enough oxygen for their more capacious lungs. If this is proved to be the case, then it might well be considered safer and more economical in the future to recruit women instead of men as astronauts.

Have men better eyesight than women? It is commonly argued that they have. In civilised and industrialised countries women are more prone than men to slight deficiencies of eyesight, although analysis of these deficiencies suggest that they could be caused by women neglecting to protect their eyesight, for research made among normally healthy people reveals no marked sex difference in visual acuity. Similar equality in visual acuity is found among primitive peoples who are not subjected to the eye-strains suffered in city life. However, statistics show that men are more liable than women to really serious defects of the eyes.

Nearly all authorities agree that deafness is also decidedly more common in men than in women. United States statistics confirm this, though admittedly the difference between the sexes is small. This could have some link with findings made by a researcher, W. S. Monroe, among infants in Westfield, Massachusetts. He said that the ability to learn to sing the scale was much more marked in girls than in boys, and that interest in music generally was much greater in girls and increased with age.

It seems to be generally agreed that woman has more tactile sensitivity than man. She is more sensitive to pain; meaning she can *feel* pain more acutely than man. Yet she suffers it with greater fortitude than man. Inevitably the explanation advanced for this feminine attribute is that woman has to be ready to endure pain by reason of her physical and psychological make-up and her function in life, because she is destined to suffer some degree of pain in her first sexual consummation and later she will suffer labour pains.

'Nothing has surprised me more than the extraordinary resignation, almost it would seem apathy, with which many women endure physical suffering and face impending death,' said Dr. H. Campbell, in his book, *The Nervous Organisation*. I myself have found that most medical men, hospital workers in particular, agree that by and large the average woman endures pain and post-operative distress with more fortitude than the average man. Evelyne Sullerot, brilliant international authority on woman's history and sociology, demonstrated this dramatically in her own life. In 1968, only three weeks after a cancer operation, she 'had to get out of bed and down to work' because her husband was out of a job. So it seems that the exhortation commonly addressed to an injured weeping boy 'Be a man!' might be better phrased 'Be a woman!'

One must not confuse *fear* with *pain*. The confusion is likely because the two often come together. Women are more easily frightened, or at least more easily *startled*, than men. But fear is a mental attitude, a phenomenon to do with the intellect. Some women might show more terror than men at the threat of pain or even at the imminence of a surgical operation, but will eventually bear the actuality of the pain with greater fortitude.

Of course there may be an accompaniment of feminine

groans and screams, even feminine hysterias, but exaggerated demonstrations of suffering are usually the symbolic sex signals which woman instinctually makes to man. She is calling for the compassion which she feels she deserves from the mate who, psycho-sexually, is basically the inflicter of pain. She is driven, because of the biological and sexual nature of her being, to perform her feminine masochistical act of being the raped and suffering partner. Incidentally she is at the same time flattering the man's brutal superior masculine strength. The attitude of exaggerated suffering of many women assumed during copulation is a good illustration of this.

When the need arises a woman can sustain greater fatigue with more stoicism than a man. We can all see this at the domestic level. A working mother and wife will continue her household chores long after the man, weary with his day of desk or work-bench or tea breaks, has come home to slippers and supper. Here again some women are clever enough to flatter man's masculine strength, and let him demonstrate it with the shopping basket or with his skill at washing-up.

Perhaps the last word on this subject of the relative strength of the so-called weaker sex should go to the seventeenth-century scholar, economist, mathematician, and anatomist, Sir William Petty. Sir William it was who revived the supposed corpse of a woman who had been hanged for murder. She married soon after and lived for another 15 years to support his opinion that 'women criminals have survived hanging much more frequently than men'.

5 THE MYSTERY OF MENSTRUATION

There is one period of life when the female is more at hazard than the male. That is when she is being fashioned into the ultimate pattern for which she was created, when she faces the stresses, physical and mental, of being prepared for motherhood. She begins menstruating.

Although through babyhood and through infancy she has been sturdier and heavier and stronger than the boy, at puberty the female really does become the 'weaker sex' for a time, less resistant to illness than the male and actually more liable to premature death. At the onset of puberty the difference in the mortality rate of boys and girls switches round in favour of the male.

This is not surprising. After all, the severe biological and biochemical changes that are needed to change a girl into egg-breeder and child-bearer can be expected to impose a heavy physical strain. More imaginatively we might suggest that Nature is here demonstrating her ruthlessness in her plan. She has one overwhelming obsession: the survival of a species. For the individual she has neither regard nor sentiment. In her determination that the female must perform her natural duty she tests female potentiality to the uttermost; making sure that only those who prove themselves fit and strong enough to become healthy fecund mothers should be allowed to survive. The others, those weaklings who cannot promise to serve her breeding demands adequately, are callously weeded out. This does seem to be in accord with the evolutionary law of the survival of the fittest, and even if our description of Nature is considered fanciful, the stark fact remains that between the fateful ages of 14 to 18 for every 100 boys who die some 120 or more girls die.

In the above title the word 'mystery' was chosen deliberately. For a mystery it certainly is, if on no other grounds than the fact that it is almost exclusively a human process. Only a few of the higher primates menstruate like a woman does: that is at a different time from ovulation. In all other animals two processes occur at the same time: at the same time that they ovulate, send eggs from the ovaries to await fertilisation, they also perform a kind of 'menstruation', a process which produces those sex odours of animal female 'heat'. These odours attract the male to perform coitus at the time most favourable for fertilization, when the egg has descended to await the sperm.

Humans are not controlled in their mating by periodic heats. Somehow and at some time humans and those few higher primates escaped from the sexual tyranny of periodicity. Instead of their sexual joys being confined to seasonal moments of rut they could indulge in them all the year round. It shows, if nothing more, a more sophisticated attitude to sex, and it is significant that only in the highest forms of animal life, only in a few anthropoid apes do we find females courting males at times when they are not in a condition to conceive.

The fact that we humans can copulate all the year round instead of being restricted to periods of 'heat' has had a profound influence in making not only our sexual behaviour but also our social behaviour different from the behaviour of animals. Generally speaking most animal vertebrates are highly individualistic and tend to congregate in herds and conduct themselves as members of a community only during periods of sexual urge. At other times of the year they are loners, bound neither to lovers nor families. Men and women, on the other hand, because they can feel sexually attracted to each other and enjoy sex throughout the year, tend to stay together. The year-round sexual urge can therefore be seen as the dominant factor in forming human society. Out of man and woman living together came the habit of living in families, in packs, in tribes, and, eventually, in settled communities. Year-round sexual awareness and mating resulted also in civilised adornments to community life: the ceremonies of sexual initiation and marriage, the framing of religious and legal proscriptions to protect marriage and family and inheritance, the building and furnishing and maintaining of homes, as well, of course, as all the sexual fears and neuroses we collected en route to highly civilised intellectualised sexuality. Indeed, if we care to risk audacious simplification, we could argue that all human society, everything we call civilised, was breathed into existence and nourished to growth by the fact that the human male can enjoy for 365 days a year what animals can enjoy only at periods restricted to the days when a female is on heat and prepared to accept him.

Later in this book I want to explore the sexual and intellectual significance of the great leap forward our human ancestors made when they began to rely more on their eyes than their noses, began to evaluate things by sight rather than sound. Somewhere in that leap forward is embedded the explanation of why woman abandoned the animal habit of sending out 'I am ready for coitus' signals by smell. Somewhere embedded in it also is perhaps the explanation of why, being no longer restricted by 'heat', woman developed, somewhere along the line of evolution from our arboreal ancestors, the sophisticated process of menstruation. Having made herself sexually available throughout the whole year, being now able to perform coitus and procreate any month, she therefore had to regularly get rid of any unfertilised eggs. Which is all she is doing with menstruation. Considered in that way the process loses a lot of the frightening importance superstitiously attached to it in the past. In fact biologists no longer consider menstruation as an essential process in woman's monthly cycle. They class it as merely an incident degenerative process of desquamation which cleans away material prepared for pregnancy.

In that way, it can be said, woman has adapted to her own purposes the animal's process of exuding sex-attractant odours. She still 'exudes', but she does it monthly; no longer to send out odours but to perform a regular 'cleaning-up' process. She times her menstruation for a fortnight after ovulation. But only when the egg has *not* been fertilised. Everything in her generative factory had been prepared for the fertilisation of the egg and the gestation of a child, but as the egg has not been fertilised it has to be got rid of to leave room for the next fresh egg which will descend from the ovaries and hopefully await the attack of a spermatozoon in the next flood of ejaculated sperm.

It was inevitable that menstruation, so unaccountable and so unique, would seem mysterious to primitive humans. Regulated, so it seemed to them, by the phases of the moon it was natural to associate it with the forces that controlled man's life, the movement of sun and stars, the decisions of gods and goddesses, spirits and demons. Speculations and fears about menstruation led to taboos that have persisted for thousands of years, not only among primitive people but also in civilised societies and even, at times, in medically informed circles.

Even so informed a man of the world as Pliny wrote, 'If a woman strips herself naked while she is menstruating, and walks round a field of wheat, the caterpillars, worms, beetles and other vermin will fall from off the ears.' Such a statement seems a typical product of antique superstition, but 1,850 years later, in 1878, the *British Medical Journal* could print the solemn medical opinion that 'it is an undoubted fact that meat spoils when touched by menstruating women', and even in this informed twentieth century menstruating women were forbidden to enter sugar refineries in northern France because 'their presence would turn sugar black'. They could even, it appears, make flowers die. In 1920 a Professor B. Schick of Vienna reported that when he mentioned a bouquet he had handed to a servant girl the night before was withered by next morning she said she should have foreseen it because she was 'having her periods'. He tried to put her statement to the test. He had two girls each hold bouquets for 16 minutes. He reported that the flowers held by the non-menstruating girl remained fresh; the others held by the menstruating girl drooped and showed decaying streaks within 16 hours, and withered in 24.

But there was a moment in medical history when one of the mysteries of menstruation seemed clear, when it appeared that a problem that had teased scientists for centuries was solved at last by an eminent gynaecologist discovering why women were smaller than men. The gynaecologist was Dr. W. Blaire Bell, author of the book *The Sex Complex*, who had reported in two medical papers, one published in 1911 in the *Proceedings of the Royal Society of Medicine* and the other in 1914 in the *Journal of Pathology and Bacteriology*, that menstruation caused women to lose abnormal amounts of that essential bone-builder calcium.

These papers caught the eye of a gifted and prodigiously industrious author who was attempting to write a vast work of sexual facts such as no one had as yet dared to publish in popular form. The author was Henry Havelock Ellis, later to be hailed as a pioneer in popular scientific study of sex. After eight years as a medical student as St. Thomas's Hospital he had, owing to an inaptitude for examinations, to be content with becoming a doctor with the licence of the Society of Apothecaries. Anyhow he was not all that interested in practising as a doctor. He wanted to be a writer and, after amassing a mountain of research, spent some sixteen years writing a vast six-volume work under the title *Studies in the Psychology of Sex*. He was so outspoken and so beautifully frank that immediately the first volume was published a prosecution was launched against a bookseller for selling it, and Ellis, fearing that he might be prosecuted, left the country, with the result that the succeeding volumes were published in America. On completing the sixth volume he declared, 'The work that I was born to do is done', but then he went on to write a seventh.

It so happened that at the time when Blaire Bell's reports on woman's abnormal loss of calcium during menstruation were published Ellis was revising yet another book on sex. In this book he was attempting to particularise research into the psychological and physiological difference between men and women, and Blaire Bell's investigations and comments burst upon Ellis as a brilliantly convincing answer to some of the questions he was asking. Why should a man's skeleton be so markedly heavier and stronger than a woman's? What makes woman's arms and legs proportionally shorter than a man's? Why are a man's thumbs and big-toes longer?

At last, said Ellis, the answer had been provided. By Dr. W. Blaire Bell. Menstruation and its resulting loss of calcium was what made woman's bones smaller than man's. Proof was provided every 29 days.

It all seemed so clear, so scientifically logical, that Ellis expanded on Bell's theories in his lively eloquent prose. Woman, he said, had a high price to pay for her role as a potential mother. When she began producing eggs and menstruating her rate of growth must of necessity be halted. In order to build all the things which make a man so physically different from a woman, long bones for arms and legs, extra protuberances on the skull, bigger collar bones, one vital ingredient is necessary, calcium. And calcium was the very thing that a woman had to deny to her own body. Instead of using calcium to build her bones she had to lay in a store of it in her uterus in case the egg was fertilised and became an embryo needing a store of calcium for building its own bones. Not only that. When the woman became pregnant she would have to use more calcium to produce milk: a necessity which must almost certainly account for her breasts frequently being tender during menstruation.

It seemed a beautifully reasonable explanation, an enchantingly logical theory, for woman's smaller body. But it was all awry. The theory was a house of cards, and the one card on which it was all raised, the card supplied by Dr. Blaire Bell, hadn't any value at all. The sad extravagance of the 'calcium loss' theory is a warning against seizing too eagerly on any speculative assumption and following it into what might seem to be reasonable theory but which is really a bog of ever deeper error.

Actually Ellis made far more out of what Bell had said than ever the doctor had intended. All that Bell had reported was that the quantity of calcium found in a woman's menstrual discharge could be as much as 30 times greater than that formed in the blood of the same woman's body. As it happened the evidence he produced to support this finding was valueless. In those two crucial papers Bell had given only *one* calcium measurement, and that one measurement was made on a woman who was suffering a severe disorder of the reproductive system. The blood Bell had examined was not even the blood of a normal menstrual flow: it had been trapped inside the woman for an abnormal length of time. To round off this story of Bell's investigation, it must also be said that even the assay method which Bell had used to determine the amount of calcium in the blood was unreliable; in his day there did not exist any assay method capable of chemically measuring particular constituents with biochemical exactitude.

Nevertheless Bell's reports were enough to spark off the enthusiastic and adventurously imaginative Ellis. Although Bell, to give him his due, had never intended to imply that calcium loss made females smaller than men, Ellis presented the findings as though this was what the doctor was proving. There was a grave lapse here in Ellis's logic. He ignored (or did he overlook?) the fact that all female mammals are smaller than their males even though female mammals do not menstruate.

Bell's papers are suspect, and the theory Ellis built upon them is not valid. Nevertheless we must not expel Ellis too brusquely. All the phenomena which he observed and conscientiously noted do seem to add up to the suggestion that in some way menstruation does have a retarding effect on woman's growth. We notice, for instance, that a girl's growth slows down as soon as she reaches puberty. Why?

In infancy and childhood a girl grows more quickly than a boy. In fact at any age a girl tends to be more advanced in the sequence of body development than a boy. Indeed from 10 to 15 the girl puts on weight and inches so much more quickly than the boy that one could imagine she could finish up as the bigger adult of the two. Between the ages of twelve-and-a-half and fifteen-and-a-half she is actually heavier than the boy. She shows her greatest gain in physical strength when she is twelve-and-a-half, two years before a boy's greatest gain. Before she begins sending eggs down to her uterus and getting rid of them by menstruation she seems to be winning the race to adult height and development.

Then, when she is around 13, she begins to show signs that she cannot stand the pace. At that age she has achieved 95 per cent of her mature height and her rate of growth slows down. At 15 the boy takes the lead, becoming rapidly taller than the girl, and then growing more slowly. At 16 the girl has reached almost her full height; she grows a little after that. Around her 20th year a girl is as tall as she will ever be, but at that age the boy is still growing and he does not reach his full stature until he is 23.

Anyone might be forgiven for finding these figures significant and asking whether slowing down of growth, coinciding as it does with the beginning of menstruation, is therefore the result of menstruation? In reply to that question biologists could retort that one could also argue, it would be no more scientifically illogical, that what causes a girl to menstruate is that she has stopped growing. The phenomena are related in so far as the female is the one who menstruates and also is the one who must grow and sexually develop in a different way from that in which a male grows and sexually develops.

For it is not because of something he has but of something he lacks which makes the male grow bigger. These are hormones known as gonadotropins. In the female their purpose is to stimulate the onset of sexual maturation and the secretion of sex hormones. It is because he does not have these hormones that the male continues his body growth.

Man's greater size is the result of the growth spurt occurring earlier in girls and being of lesser magnitude than in boys. There is considerable variation in the ages at which the growth spurt occurs. Girls can reach the maximum spurt as early as 10 or not until 14, though the average is at 12. Boys are consistently two years later in all those figures: the earliest growth spurt in a boy being around the age of 12, the latest at 16, but the average being at 14.

A deciding factor in eventual adult height is when puberty occurs. The boys or girls in whom puberty is delayed will become bigger adults than those boys or girls who began puberty earlier because they had longer to grow at pre-pubertal rate.

However, the complexity of this subject of body-growth is indicated by the fact that research is now being made into the possibility that the different growth rate of male and female might be in some measure caused by those billions of extra-large and therefore extra-heavy female chromosomes. Perhaps it is only now, when biologists can include computers among their tools of research, that such theories can be investigated.

Most girls have menstruated before their 14th birthday; in abnormal cases menstruation can begin as early as 10 or as late as 20. The healthier a girl is the sooner she will menstruate. Nature is obviously at work here: choosing the best females and pushing them into motherhood as soon as they are strong enough to face that duty, and, as we have mentioned, tending to kill off any weaklings at the same time.

In America it was found that girls of good homes and good education menstruated as much as one year earlier than daughters of labouring Irish and German immigrants. Varying averages of the age of menstruation in different parts of the world seem to confirm that if girls are better fed, better housed and better educated, they will menstruate sooner. A striking example was provided in an inquiry in Japan. It was found that menstruation in Japanese girls began at the average age of 14 years ten months, but Chinese girls in Japan did not menstruate until they were 16 and the normal age for Chinese girls in China was 17.

Puberty is coming earlier nowadays. According to information from all parts of the world where reliable statistics are available puberty appears to be becoming earlier at an average rate of about four months every ten years. This means that a girl of an average family can expect to menstruate a year younger than her mother did. It is now suggested this might be caused by artificial light, for the increase is most noticeable in cities. It is known that longer daylight in Spring stimulates the sex of seasonal creatures, and zoologists in Texas have found that the sexual activity of sparrows can be stimulated by beaming light on their brains.

There are some grounds for an optimistic view of that future, however, in the way in which menstruation, which used to be so commonly referred to as 'the curse' and had an almost traumatic effect on some girls, has been put in its place as a normal process of growing-up. So much so that even Helene Deutsch seems nowadays too dramatic when she comments that 'In the anxieties provoked by the sight or imagined presence of blood, the idea of being torn and dismembered internally plays an extremely important part'. But how intense woman's superstitious fears about menstruation once were is revealed by that same writer's comment, 'It has been observed during criminal trials that a woman will more easily acknowledge that she has committed an aggressive crime involving bloodshed than that the stain is from her own menstruation.'

In the more rational climate of today it is accepted that the healthier a woman is the less she will be affected, physically or mentally, by menstruation. An inquiry conducted under the auspices of the Industrial Fatigue Research Board resulted in the conclusion that 'the strictly physiological phenomenon' of menstruation 'has, as a rule, no noticeable effect on working capacity amongst normal healthy women ... Our own investigations lead us to believe that it has an unfavourable effect in certain subjects and in the case of certain tests; whereas for other subjects and in the case of other tests the effect may be a favourable one or there may be no effect at all. We have therefore to be on the look-out, not only for the effects on efficiency exerted by the menstrual period, but also for those conceivably exerted by other processes (especially by those of internal secretions) occurring within other phases of the monthly cycle, notably those of the pre-menstrual and post-menstrual periods and those occurring at the mid-period of the cycle at or about the time of escape of the ovum from its follicle.'

The belief that the moon has a direct effect on a woman and her regular menstruation has been dismissed as superstition. Even so some scientists speculate on the possibility that the moon and its phases can have some influence on human life. It certainly does on some animal life.

One little creature actually regulates its sex life by the moon. This is the palolo worm which lives in the fissures of the coral reefs of Samos, Fiji and Tonga islands and has engaged the attention of naturalists and zoologists for more than 100 years. The palolo worm breeds by breaking into two portions. The larger portion, three-quarters of it, fills with sperm and eggs and then swarms in enormous numbers to the surface of the water, performs its procreative functions, and then dies. The swarms always appear at dawn on the day preceding and on the actual day of the moon's third quarter in October/November. The palolo has a cousin, 'Atlantic palolo', which performs the same swarming operation in the West Indies. But this one does it at the first and third quarters of the June/July moon.

Then there is the convolute roscoffinis, a marine flat worm, who comes to the surface of the sand only at a certain phase of the moon. Even scientists, accustomed as they are to uncovering marvels, could hardly believe that so primitive a creature could be affected by the waxing and waning of the moon, let alone recognise a new or old moon. The logical solution, they argued, must be that the worms were affected not by the moon but by the rise and fall of tides over the sand. To prove this a family of convolute roscoffine and their sand was transferred to a dish in a laboratory where no tide would rise or fall. Yet, sure enough, dead on time at the proper phase of the moon, up they came to the surface of the sand.

It is a very long way from palolo and convolute roscoffinis to our modern woman slipping into the chemist for her lunar-cycle sanitary necessities. Yet that there is a link between them is argued in a speculation which takes our breath away with its imaginative implications. This link of speculation is forged in the following way. The moon affects tides: all the living land creatures we know today are the descendants of creatures which originally emerged from the sea: those primeval creatures crawled on to shores of tide-lapped rock or sand or were stranded there by rising and falling tides. Therefore, is it not probable that inherited tidal memories, immensely ancient genetically, still persist in today's living creatures, and we humans, despite all our supposed triumph over natural forces, must still respond to the waxing and waning of the same moon which pushed and pulled the seas from which our remotest of ancestors arose?

PART TWO

The Difference in Desire

The pleasure is momentary, the position ridiculous, and the expense damnable
LORD CHESTERFIELD

5 Sexuality Takes Shape

Humans have to be taught how to be male or female.

No other creatures need this education. A lion cub needs no lessons on how to grow up to be a lion or a lioness: a queer lion and a butch lioness are too bizarre to imagine. Although I am told on the authority of a circus proprietor that 'most female elephants are lesbians', an observation which he supports by what he claims is a representative case. An elderly lady elephant in his circus lavished doting protection on a younger one. When the older one died the younger was broken-hearted, refused to appear in the ring with any other companion, showed no desire to eat, and was pining away until another older lady also of lesbian inclinations joined the circus, took the girl under her protection and restored her love of life and the ring. However, the circus proprietor had to admit that most elephant troupes are composed entirely of females because male elephants, unlike male humans, are averse to being trained as entertainers. So I suspect what he thought was a proclivity to lesbianism in elephants was the result of circumstances. The poor ladies, having only members of their own sex available as objects for their emotional and sexual urges, were merely evincing the homosexual tendencies which erupt in similar one-sex communities; prisons or warships or barracks or boarding schools, and the fact that the human entertainment world is notable for a high proportion of sexual deviants has no relevance to the elephant entertainment world.

Animals in their natural state are unlikely to become deviants. Occasional outbursts of homosexual activity seen among animals are nearly always the outcome of sexual excitement during periods of heat.

With humans it is altogether different. Human attitudes of thought and human social habits have created all manner of sexual confusion. We have intellectualised sex and embroidered it with mental joys and moral terrors. Consequently our sexual desires and ambitions can be inflamed to an extent which the unimaginative animal can never know. Even the custom of dressing ourselves up in distinctive male and female livery, elaborating the coverings which were primarily designed only to conceal our genitals into clothes which emphasise our male and female differences, has intensified the visual importance of the differences in those merely secondary sexual characteristics, male genitals and female breasts, male muscles and female curves. No lion can ever be erotically excited by a lioness's strip-tease. Neither does any lion cub, nor any other young animal, ever suffer the trauma a human child can suffer when it makes the discovery that it does or does not possess a penis.

The penis-no-penis discovery is only one of many childhood experiences which can have more or less intensive influences on our development; lasting effect on our sexuality in particular and on all our mental attitudes in general. Not one of us can evaluate our individual concepts of what is male and what is female without taking those psychological shocks into account and measuring the influence they have had on us. To do this we must trace our concept of sexual differences to its source. Which means we must plod back to our sexual beginnings, to our babyhood.

Babies, let us be honest enough to admit it without sentimentality, are bores. At least other people's babies are, sharing with other people's television the tendency of being too often switched on, and usually tuned in to the same programme.

Anyhow, most of us, whether we admit it or not, are interested in ourselves. So we can enliven our interest in our investigation if we imagine that we are not studying merely any other baby but are studying ourselves. After all Sigmund Freud did that very thing in one of his earliest and most engrossing explorations into human psychology.

So let us begin by exploring the very first trauma that we experienced, the trauma of being born.

1 THE BIRTH TRAUMA

What does it feel like to be born? And does being born male feel different from being born female?

We can hope for no first-person replies to these questions. I have actually heard claims that certain persons can remember their births, but I am sure those supposed memories have been imagined or have been built-up from recitals of the event told or overheard in later years. Not even a Compton Mackenzie can remember the moments when he pushed his memory-collecting head into the world. No one can be expected to remember his or her emergence from the womb, the severing of the cord, the first slap, the first gasp for air, the first howl. No one, that is, can *consciously* remember those events. But subconsciously, yes. That's a different matter. Subconsciously birth is registered as a big moment in our lives, which indeed it is.

Throughout our formative years we experience a number of sudden changes in our sexual, physical and emotional circumstances. Each of these changes, each one necessary to our development as individual human beings, comes to us as a shock, a trauma. The first trauma of all is the trauma of birth.

Among all our experiences of life the greatest must be that of being pushed out of the enfolding security of the womb and suffering our first sensation, as it were, of space. It is a pity that at the moment of that event our mental capacities are too limited for us to appreciate what is happening and that we have not the power of speech capable of describing it. A first-person commentary on being born would be more exciting and certainly more usefully informative than any astronaut's commentary on his somewhat analogous adventure in space.

However, we can go some way towards calculating some of the excitements and fears we experience when being born. To begin with the fact that the traumatic effect is considerable can be accepted as confidently as the existence of certain chemicals was established mathematically before they were discovered. We can be sure that we could not experience being born without physical sensations, and we know that all sensations were transmitted by our nervous system from our sensory organs to our brain and imprinted there. Though at that moment in our life our brain was too primitive to evaluate the sensations and their imprints would be stored only at subconscious level.

Doctors and psychologists have nevertheless a lot of data to go on in building up a picture of the birth trauma. Doctors can assess the physical effects birth has on our bodies. They can, for intance, measure the effects of premature or delayed birth, or the effects of an easy or difficult delivery. Embryologists and physiologists can report on the baby's physical state and reactions before birth, during birth and immediately after birth. Psychologists, by combining this physical data with what is known of the social and family circumstances into which babies are born and by studying their varying psychological development, can assess the psychological effects of birth and find clues which give some idea of the emotions and sensations a particular baby might have felt at the moment of birth and the effects which these emotions and sensations can have had on its sexual, emotional and intellectual attitudes in later life.

For instance, a generally accepted theory is that one sensation a baby suffers at birth is that of being frightened of choking. In view of the physical processes involved in pushing one's head out of the womb such a fear is understandable. It is believed that the choking fear is one of the original determinants of fear in later life.

In her elegantly argued book, *Psychology of Women*, Helene Deutsch claims that the unaccountable anxieties which sometimes plague us, our craving for perfection and eternity, our mingled fears of and yet wish for death, our tormenting desires for solitude, all spring from our subconscious memories of our unity with our mother in her womb and a natural craving to return to that protective comfort. 'Man's most primitive needs and highest aspirations,' she says, 'contain energies striving for the restoration of the original union with the mother.'

This brings us to the question which we ask above, a question which at first might appear far-fetched but which, if it could be answered, might put us on the track of most profound differences between masculinity and femininity. The question is whether a boy does experience a different birth-trauma from that experienced by a girl.

There are already some faint leads to a possible answer. In Chapter I we referred to a theory currently being put forward which suggests that the biochemistry of a pregnant woman probably reacts in *contrast to* an embryo if the embryo is male or in *affinity with* an embryo if the embryo is female. We also reported on the strangely sinister findings in a New York survey which support the suggestion that there is a toxic counter-action between male baby and mother. If such theories of biochemical contrasts and affinities are substantiated we can speculate that in at least some understandable ways the sensations and emotions of birth might be different for boys and girls. To a boy birth might seem like a great relief, an escape: to a girl it might seem like a loss, an expulsion. If so, a boy's sense of fear on being expelled from the security of the womb might be to some extent relieved by the fact that he was escaping from a contrasting biochemical environment;

whereas the girl's sense of fear would be intensified because she was being expelled from an environment in which she had enjoyed biochemical affinity.

Having adventured so far into speculation, we might as well go a bit further and speculate whether such a difference in male and female birth traumas could cause some of the contrasting masculine and feminine attitudes with which we are familiar. Could that different birth trauma be one of the reasons why a boy is eager for adventure beyond the home, ready to run away to sea while his sister prefers to stay at home knitting? It certainly cannot be argued that this notable difference between masculine and feminine attitudes is entirely caused by social conditioning, by the general acceptance of a social code in which the woman is expected to stay at home and the man go off adventuring, for the different tendencies in the sexes are shown by even the youngest children as soon as they are independently mobile. Given the freedom of out of doors boys will usually troop off adventurously; girls usually prefer to play within the shadow of home.

We can imagine it was very much the same among early humans. Among our prehistoric ancestors a woman would have to stay at home in cave or lair during pregnancy or nursing. But what about the younger females? If these stayed at home while the boys roamed abroad this could be the result of a social habit, of young females copying the manners and customs of the older members of their own sex. But we can imagine even earlier tribes of humans too brutish and too intellectually infantile to be receptive of social or family customs. In such packs there would seem to be no reason why the females should not go hunting for food along with brothers, in the same way that tigresses and lionesses go hunting and killing with their males. But what if we discovered that the females of those early humans stayed at home? Then we might ask if something more compelling than custom made them do so. Was the compulsion biological? Could it spring from that biochemical *affinity* between mother and female baby?

I recall from my childhood an often quoted proverb that 'A boy is a son till he gets a wife, but a girl is a daughter for all her life'. Can we ever hope to explain this common truth of family life in biochemical birth-trauma terms? The question, like my cave-girl supposition, lies beyond scientific proof, but one is constantly tempted to spin such wild fancies. As we have already seen, and as we shall see in even more outrageous examples later in this chapter, the most learned and judicious psychologists can sometimes be lured on to pursue prejudices and fire-drakes of theory so far beyond the horizon of scientifically observable phenomena that they might be in danger of finishing up with attempts to put hats on copulating mice or advising pregnant women desirous of twins to eat two bananas that have grown on the same stalk.

2 THE FIRST DENIAL

The second emotional shock in our lives is the weaning trauma. The nipple is withdrawn. The metal spoon, silver or not, which replaces it seems an outrageously unsympathetic substitute for the alluring nipple and although we shall progress in easy stages to bowl and knife and fork and then, before we know where we are, we shall be at the cocktails and *cordon bleu* stage, we nevertheless shall always retain within our subconscious an imprint of our resentment at the refusal of the breast.

Up to the time of weaning we have had things very much as we wanted them. We have not only enjoyed generous food and warmth but our infant sexuality has been gratified without hindrance. Some of that sexual fun is now denied us.

First of all it is necessary to stress that the word 'sexuality' when used in relation to a baby's sexual excitements and responses refers only to physical sexuality, to physical excitements and responses. Admittedly some of the sexual impressions collected during this phase have lasting effects on the psychological development of male and female, effects which can be detected in the sexual attitudes of mature man and woman, but we must not fall into the trap of imagining that the sexuality of a baby is tinctured in the slightest degree with any of those mental processes of affection and imagery with which the adult embellishes physical sexual desire and with which he elevates that desire to emotional sexual love.

'Whoever has seen the sated infant sink back upon the breast to fall asleep with flushed cheeks and happy smile must say that the picture is adequate to the expression of sexual satisfaction in later life.' The writer is Sigmund Freud, caught in one of his unguarded moments. No one will deny that at moments of sexual satisfaction we do see flushed cheeks and a happy smile on the face of a gratified lover. But one can see cheeks equally flushed and smiles equally happy in any restaurant; flushings and smiles which do not indicate that their wearers have just enjoyed the felicities of successful copulation but merely register the satisfaction engendered by good food and good wine. It is very often the same with the baby. His flushed cheeks and happy smile on most occasions register nothing more than satisfaction with a generous intake of its favourite diet of milk from its favourite source; far less often do they register pleasant sensations emanating from the region of its genitals.

The baby, that 'innocent at the breast', is little more than a self-centred ravenously hungry creature possessed of only primitive lust to keep itself alive, fed, warm and comfortable. Its burbles of delight are not conscious thank-you's directed meaningfully at its doting nurse. They are merely reflex responses to the pleasant sensations that are being transmitted to its central nervous system from lips and clutching fingers and squirming legs and deliciously sensitive genitals. Screams or tears indicate no sense of sorrow or pity; they signal no more than distress and anger caused by being deprived of the sensual joys of sucking and defecating and being fondled. Were baby's mother struck dead before its eyes the baby would continue its contented gurgling for a moment or so. When later it did howl it would not be from any sense of tragedy at a mother's demise, but only because the milk was not being delivered on time.

If a baby's sexuality never developed beyond its infantile state, never collected the reason and direction and emotion that it accretes in later years, the resultant adult would be an uncomprehending sexual idiot. Even so some romantics, not lady novelists but supposedly serious psychologists, have sentimentally described the period of infant sexuality as 'the first love affair'.

The word 'affair' we might accept. After all, during the 'affair' baby's concern is to get out of it as much sensual gratification as it can, and that we must admit is as much as many adults seek when they indulge in what they call 'an affair'. But the word 'love' cannot be accepted; unless, of course, it is being used in the debased sense in which the grubbiest and hastiest copulation in a back alley is described as 'making *love*'.

Only ignorance or superstition or religiosity could make anyone believe that by some magical transfusion of 'instant' human intellect a baby is equipped with the slightest comprehension of love in the real sense of the word. Comprehension of love is something which a human acquires, in a greater or lesser degree, only after years of sexual and family conditioning and social education through infancy and childhood and puberty to maturity as man or woman.

Primitive people who have heard little or nothing about psychology and are innocent enough to care less, accept this unquestioningly. In Bali, for instance, a child less than three months old is not considered either male or female. It is not even considered to be a human, not, for instance, sufficiently part of human society to be allowed inside a temple. Consequently a Bali baby cannot be given a name: instead it is referred to as 'the caterpillar' or 'the rat'.

We do get some sexual thrills during our infant affair with our mother; or at least some infantile sexual titillation. In view of the tactile sensitivity of our genitals this is not surprising, particularly in the case of baby boys. If any observer introduced to a newly-born male is honest enough to be objective and unsentimental, he would remark not so much upon the fact that the baby has its father's eyes or its mother's nose or that its pearly fingernails are exquisite, as that it seems immoderately equipped in the genital area. First impressions of a baby boy make one think it has been designed primarily as a potentially powerful sex engine. This generous endowment might be seen as both physical confirmation of the Freudian theory of the importance of sex in infancy and a demonstration of Nature's insistence that we have a job to do.

But the sexual sensations we experience in infancy are not of our seeking. They are the enjoyable bonuses, results of caresses and strokings or accidental pressures and frictions which happen to come our way during the pursuit of what we really want from our mother's body: food and comfort and warmth, and food again. We enjoy a compost of agreeable sensations; sensations of feeding and excreting, feel of hands gliding over body and genitals, contact of lips around nipples and skin against skin, and warm and drowsy odours. Our responses are restricted, as the responses of immature adults are sometimes restricted in their so-called 'love affairs', to sucking and biting and nuzzling and occasional ecstatic squirmings. Luxuriating in a protective cocoon of female flesh and motherly attentions we turn tactile lips and greedy gums towards a woman's breast, that most entrancing object which apart from being an exciting and excitable organ or erectile tissue also provides spurts of deliciously satisfying fodder into the bargain.

We shall not remember this period of our life; not consciously remember it. Although our brain is growing at a staggering rate, it has not as yet been fed with sufficient information to be capable of evaluating the signals of sensual gratification transmitted to it by our sensory organs. Those signals are not discarded, however. As taps on the keys of a typewriter send isolated letters to the paper each sensation is imprinted on our memory bank. The first pages of elementary dictation will later be covered by more comprehensible records of conscious observation. The pleasures and pains of our first weeks of life will eventually be buried below layer upon layer of the experiences and memories than we can recall. But the early imprints on our subconscious will survive, and although we shall not be able to remember them or even recognise their effect they will colour our adult thoughts and emotions and attitudes.

Sensual desire for the mother's body will fade away as our dependence on that body fades away. Except in abnormal cases. All of us know men and women whose adoration of their mothers is passionate enough to be near-incestuous. That condition has usually been intensified by conditioning during conscious childhood, but it does have its roots in the infant subconscious. Even men completely emancipated from their mothers will nuzzle and nibble their lovers' breasts as avidly as babies seeking milk. 'A lover,' says the American psychologist Bertrand Lewin, 'loves his partner as once he loved the breast—with all the bodily pleasure and close physical comfort he enjoyed at the beginning of life.'

Doctors and psychologists say that suckling is sensually enjoyable to the baby and ideally should also be the same to the mother. It is believed to be both physically and psychologically valuable to the baby: physically because it provides the baby with the food most suitable and biochemically acceptable at that stage of its body growth, and psychologically because it provides comforting assurances of loving attention that will imprint on its subconscious a sense of security. Suckling is considered equally important to the woman and to her fulfilment as a mother.

It is true that a woman's nipples, exquisitely sensitive, are linked in physical harmony with her sexual organs. Any lover knows that the separate caressing of either nipples or genitals stimulates the uncaressed zone to sexual excitement. Through her nipples therefore a woman can give love *to* her baby and can also receive love *from* her baby. A woman might love her baby intensely but if she cannot suckle it her love falls short of the love which the baby can find only in suckling. A baby stimulated by a shower of kisses and caresses and then denied the breast can be likened to a man teased by a woman and then denied the consummation of his passion. Also the sensations of suckling can intensify a woman's love for her baby; in fact there are some women who find themselves incapable of forming intellectual or imaginative love for their children until such love is aroused by the sensations of suckling them.

Several mothers have disputed these theories with me. Some have told me that they found suckling not only unpleasant but often almost unbearably painful, and none of these would agree that their children had suffered either physically or psychologically by being denied the breast. One Boston matron pointed to her daughter and son as proof. One had been breast fed, the other had been bottle fed. Both are equally healthy physically and show every sign of being equally healthy psychologically.

However it has to be accepted that the mother's breast is inevitably the first defined object of infantile desire. To the neonate its mouth, not its genitals, is all important, and therefore the neonate's desires are first concentrated on the breast. Later the baby realises that behind the breast is a body providing other sensory satisfactions and delights, and then those desires which were formerly localised on the breast are extended to the mother in her entirety. It is for this reason that an unfortunate accident at some crucial moment in suckling or weaning, a denial of gratification or the inflicting of pain or the implanting of fear, can emboss the tapestry of pleasant subconscious memories with some unpleasant stain which, although minute in the overall psychological patterning, can be discordant enough to distort personality in later years.

The most vividly illustrative example of this which I have read is a case history reported by Otto Shaw in *Maladjusted Boys*. He tells of a boy who was sent to a special school because he showed signs of being mentally disturbed. The disturbance was mild, but the form it took was embarrassing. He had an obsessive habit of sniffing at everything, even going to the lengths of moving his nose searchingly around the bell-push at the door before ringing. It was eventually discovered that the boy was smuggling into bed with him every night a bottle fitted with a rubber teat, filled only with water but bearing a label on which the boy had written the word 'Milk'. This explained the boy's compulsive sniffing. The habit arose from the boy's constant search for his mother's breast, which, as investigation into the circumstances of his babyhood confirmed, he had been deprived of by his mother's illness.

Although the infant 'love affair' is sensual and part sexual it has, of course, no masculine or feminine bias. It is not the mother's femininity, neither her feminine shape nor her feminine character, that sensually attracts the baby. She represents only comfort and food.

Nevertheless the baby does begin its education for sexual love very early in life. It masters the primary lessons surprisingly quickly, learning basic sounds and words in the language of love. Before it has learned how to *give* love, it learns how to *get* love. It soon knows what kind of smile or what tone of gurgle beamed in what appropriate direction will win rewards of responding smiles or pleasing caresses. Having learned how to capture the love of its mother it begins flirting with any other humans around; and soon it astonishes us with its ability to express preferences, showing that it likes the presence and attentions of certain persons more than those of others. These are the first steps in forming those standards of comparison between people which in later life and in far more sophisticated form will be employed in choosing the most desired friend or sexual partner.

Correct though those Balinese are in refusing to recognise the newly-born baby as a personage, they are still this side of flattery in calling it 'caterpillar' or 'rat'. Both those creatures are at birth far more mature and developed representatives of their species than the baby is of its. Indeed it can be said that the baby is not fully born until the end of its neonate phase, four weeks after its emergence from the womb. For those four weeks it is still getting over the shock of being pushed out. Then, during the next twelve weeks, it begins to sit up and take notice. It develops enough strength to hold up its head and enough intelligence to look at things around it, stretch out for them and feel them, and also pay some attention to noises and, more significantly, voices around it.

Around sixteen-weeks-old it emerges from 'caterpillar' nullity into human consciousness. It begins to show some individuality, and by distinguishing father from mother shows that it is beginning to appreciate that it is a member of a group in which the others are man and woman. It begins to enjoy the smell and feel of life. Its pleasures are still primitively sensual, but now it welcomes these sensations with less passivity and more egocentric greed, and is aroused to passions of desire.

As the surrounding world and the objects in it became more recognisable and interesting the affair with mother loses some of its intensity, in the way that many love affairs do when other diversions are offered. Even so, when that time comes when we must be pushed out again, pushed out on this occasion not from the womb but from the encircling arms of the nursing mother whom we have sensually desired and sensually enjoyed, the expulsion comes as a shock to us.

Up to that moment we have had mother to ourselves. Father has been a shadowy figure hovering on the horizon, too far beyond our milk-besotted content for us to be aware of his masculine penis-equipped competition for mother's body and mother's love. We have enjoyed mother's enfolding love and generous feeding exclusively. Now she has kicked us out.

The weaning trauma is similar to the birth trauma in that it is another thrusting away. In the first we were thrust out of the womb; in the second we are thrust away from the breast. In the first we did not know what was happening, but by the time the second expulsion comes we have enough human individuality for a sense of resentment and loss to be imprinted on our dawning consciousness. We can, the psychologists warn us, carry that resentment and sorrow into our maturity, as well as the sense of longing for the denied breast.

When we are weaned and thrust away from the intimate sensual embrace of our mother we become more conscious of that other person in our lives, our father. It seems unfair to us that one who has appeared so late on the scene should be the favoured one and should enjoy freer access than ourselves to the mother who has thrust us away. Not until later do we become aware of his genital superiority, and it is even later that we subconsciously register the fact that he was on the scene before us, entering before we did the female body from which we emerged and which we had imagined to be our exclusive property.

We are exiled to a cot and father usurps our privileged

position in her bed. Slowly, still more subconsciously than consciously, we begin to appreciate the significance of the sexual difference; first the difference between father and mother, then the difference between man and woman. Through the bars of a cot we sense flavours of aggressive masculinity and compliant femininity. Between gurgles of pleasure and howls of indignation desires and jealousies take mental shape.

'Dadda! Mamma!' Of these early and significant words the first to be formed, most mothers report, is Dadda, often being uttered appreciably earlier than Mamma. One theory suggested is that the open-mouthed 'da' is the sound most likely to emerge from lips parted to attract attention and food, in which case the repeated 'ma' of mamma could also be seen as appropriate murmurings of appreciation issuing from a satisfied baby with its lips pressed against the breast.

Arnold Gesell records that at 16 weeks the baby reaches the stage of babbling, cooing, gurgling and laughing, by 28 weeks he is 'almost ready for defined duplicated utterance of mu, ma and da, which lead to his first words', and at 40 weeks the muscles controlling tongue and lips and chewing and swallowing begin to help in the forming of articulate vocalisation.

At this period of development the baby has enough mentality to recognise people, even to the extent of showing timidity when greeted by a stranger. One of the people he knows well enough to recognise has been introduced to him as Dadda, a title which nicely fits into the pattern of the noises he made earlier, and I prefer to believe that the uttering of 'Dadda' precedes the uttering of 'Mamma' because Dadda is usually the first person the baby actually sees and recognises as an individual. Mamma has, of course, always been present, but because she enfolds the baby so intimately and completely the baby has a sense of being part of the same body, enfolded in its comfort and warmth and odours, and thus Mamma is not seen as a separate individual in the way that father, beyond the horizon of breasts and softly-embracing arms, is seen. That gruff-voiced flat-chested hard-muscled figure becomes recognised as an individual called Dadda, and only later, when the baby has crawled or has been pushed over the horizon of nursing, can it look back and see in separate entirety another person called Mamma.

We have to accept the expulsion, but our subconscious so treasures the unity we enjoyed before weaning that at moments of critical danger we long for that unity and the protection it afforded. 'Mamma!' 'Mother!' In any part of the world, whatever the social structure and the role women occupy in it, any man, whatever his age, will call on his mother in moments of distress or fear.

Psychologists claim that when we copulate as adults we offset the weaning trauma with a subconscious analogy in which vagina and penis symbolise sucking mouth and mother's breast.

Up to the time of weaning we have been so unified with mother that our own sex has been of little importance. We have enjoyed the unity sensually, without concern with our masculinity or femininity. When we are parted from her we become a separate individual in the trio. The other two are father and mother, man and woman. Soon we must learn to which one we are sexually akin, learn to be sure whether we are male or female, and learn to act accordingly.

3 THE FIRST 'LOVE AFFAIR'

Whatever we have grown up into, man or woman, we share a common sensual memory from our past. The first body we desired physically was the body of a woman.

This applies whatever pattern our sexuality has assumed, whether we are heterosexual, homosexual, bisexual and transsexual. Whatever we now sexually prefer, man or woman, leather boots or stolen panties or beasts of the field, at the beginning of our lives our sensual desires were directed exclusively to the body of a female, our mother. The kind of man or woman we have become is to a considerable extent determined by how lovingly and wisely these sexual desires were gratified or how ignorantly or cruelly they were repulsed.

The root of our matured sexuality grows from that first sensual affair. The desire we felt in those early days was implanted long before we were capable of rationalising about things sexual and is therefore so susceptive within the fabric of our psychological being that it is something we scarcely ever think about. Indeed when our first love of a female body is dragged out it can come to us almost as a surprise, can even be somewhat distasteful like an inconsiderate reminder of some too intimate incident in the woodshed. It menaces that common concept of our babyhood which all of us stubbornly cherish, for despite all that Freud and his successors have revealed we still prefer to imagine that as babies we were bland innocents.

We are right. So far as sex was concerned we *were* innocents. On balance our concept of our babyhood is right: it is the Freudians who can so often fall into error. We must accept that term 'infant sexuality' with which Freud and the Freudians have made all of us conversant. It is, we admit, a convenient term. But it must be used with caution. As often happens to any attractive label it is frequently slapped on jars for which it was never printed. Reference to infant sexuality inevitably leads us into the tangled thickets of psychological controversy. There, just as inevitably, we meet Sigmund Freud.

The trip and the meeting are necessary, if only to find some path through the opinions and arguments that have sprouted so densely in the Freudian terrain. Many of them are out-of-date, dried up completely, and should have been hacked away. Many of them, still flourishing, have been distorted into shapes never intended by their original planter, for we find with Freud, as we so often find in the history of any genius, that those who do most disservice to the giant are not his detractors and critics but self-recruited disciples and self-styled successors.

Freud deserves high honour as an original thinker. A man of that stamp does not frame theories; he utters inspirations. A theory is merely an arguable speculation needing facts to buttress it: an inspiration is a flash of truth. Consequently one must accept as one must accept certain laws of life. If the laws do not seem to make sense, it is not the laws that are out of joint but our understanding of them that is awry.

In his *Freud and the Post-Freudians*, Doctor James A. C. Brown makes a point which should warn anyone against rushing into the ill-conceived criticism so easily made of an original and exploratory thinker. Doctor Brown justly claims that Freud 'revolutionised our way of looking at ourselves, and . . . may well come to be regarded rather as a moulder of thought than as a mere discoverer of facts'. A cogent point Doctor Brown makes is that Freud so 'changed the whole tenor of human thought that even those who most violently denounce his views attack them in Freudian clichés and with arguments which would have been incomprehensible had he never existed'.

It has been said of Freud 'there is no aspect of human life which his work has failed to illuminate'. Inspired, he embarked on a voyage of discovery into hitherto uncharted realms of the human mind. He is indeed a kind of Columbus figure, trailing behind him the glory of immense discoveries; though the very magnitude of those discoveries bequeathed to those who followed him an enormous and onerous duty of civilising whole new continents of thought and knocking them into some kind of scientific shape. But no one today can even so much as begin to discuss the different sexual psychology of men and women without taking Freud's theories into account, particularly his researches, dangerously intuitive but diligent, into the jungle of our buried, or suppressed childhood memories. From these researches into the birth of our male and female sexuality he returned with appalling treasures, with claims that he had not only discovered but had also mapped the source of human sexual-psychological behaviour. The turbulent and often subterranean river of our sexuality, he declared, began amid the swamps and miasmas of infancy. From that primitive source it flowed on through our lives, irrigating the jungles of our subconscious and leaving in its wake the debris of every sensual joy and every sensual shock we had experienced in our forgotten infancy.

Freud's natural eloquence was powerful enough to convince us. We were impressed. We were also titillated, some of us pretended to be shocked, by the revelation that our sex-life did not begin at puberty as doctors and educationalists and moralists had always told us, but begun years before pubic hair sprouted, before breasts grew, before voices broke, before sheets were stained with semen or menstrual blood. We now realised that consciousness of sex began at the breast. It stirred to expression in the mother's embrace. It rampaged in cradle and cot. It envied its father's access to the mother and competed with him for her sensual favours. It erupted in orgies of childish play and precocious sexual experiment. Every sexual gratification we experienced in babyhood, all the physical joys of sucking and excreting, all the ecstasies aroused by the caresses and kisses and nuzzlings of others as well as the self-induced ecstasies aroused by our own squirmings and thigh-thrashing, would determine the attitudes and desires of our adult sexuality, for from the early weeks of our life and through the months and years of our infancy not only were our bodies assuming male and female shape but our minds were being imprinted with sexual patterns of distinguishable masculinity and femininity, and some outrageous accident or some lack of love or excess of it could distort that pattern into perversity. Those infantile experiences could also lay the foundations for the mental and moral attitudes we would assume in adult life, sane and normal, or irrevocably off-balance. Sensual hungers, particularly sexual hungers, and all the appetites cultivated in infancy were the compost feeding our psychological growth, permeating every thought and every desire and every aspiration, guiding all our conduct and designing all our dreams.

Freud's theory, eloquently propounded, was too logical to be denied. It was also too tempting to reject. Here was a new concept of original sin. It neatly filled up the gaps caused by the expulsion of Adam and Eve, Satan and God. By only its boldness Freud's vocabulary was in itself sufficient to sluice away mountainous and stinking deposits of cant and superstition that had silted up during decades of nineteenth-century prudery and hypocrisy. The controversies he initiated encouraged later researchers to bring the light of scientific inquiry into dark corners of the mind where macabre fears and religious superstition had earlier waxed fat, crippling and deforming humans who but for those poisonous influences could have grown into normally virile sex-loving men and women. His great heave to the wheel of enlightenment hastened the advance of clinical psychiatry, one of the few scientific developments offering some measure of optimism in the threatening twentieth century.

But at the same time the rich and ample territory which Freud opened up for exploitation created a new race of adventurers. Freud's central theme of the human libido could all too easily be elaborated into ever wilder and ever more baroque curlicues of theory by self-styled Freudian psychologists, professional ones and drawing-room ones alike. Exploiting this saturnalia of social sexuality these entrepreneurs of psychology filled their waiting rooms and confessional couches with men and women tortured by doubts of their masculinity or femininity. We had never realised before what erotically exciting pasts we had enjoyed as boys and girls. For three guineas (or more or less, according to the address) we could enjoy those pasts again. We could learn just what repressed memory of what forgotten saucy adventure in the woodshed now made us tumescent at the very thought of knicker-elastic or corduroy; learn just what immodest caress in infancy had made us grow up biting our nails or obsessively cleaning away non-existent dust or allergic to *bisque d'homard*. Childish ailments such as measles, scarlet fever, whooping-cough or even diphtheria, which in any case were all being robbed of their terrors and subdued by modern medicine, now took second place to juicily-named sexual complexes.

These complexes are now accepted commonplaces in psychological vocabulary. Prominent on the list and much talked about because so descriptively named are 'penis-envy' and 'castration-fear'. But there are more exotic ones. The 'Diana complex' gives a woman, however buxom and curvaceously feminine she might look, masculine tendencies. The 'Electra complex' gives a daughter an erotic fixation on her father; the 'Jocasta complex' makes a woman libidinously attracted to her son, and the 'Lear complex' makes a father feel the same way to his daughter. Of complexes which upset relationship of father and mother and children the one most widely known because its legendary example has so often been exploited in drama, is the 'Oedipus complex' which makes a son compete with father for sexual possession of the mother. Oedipus, Jocasta and Lear in the same family suggest appallingly attractive permutations.

One example alone is sufficient to illustrate into what quagmires of gothic imagination Freudian theories have lured scholarly investigators. An eminent German psychologist reports in all seriousness that he knew a boy of less than three years old who 'tried to strangle his mother' with her necklace, thus showing he 'had death or castration wishes towards his mother in her pregnancy'. Can any sane person accept that an infant is capable of envisaging the act of murder? Can we even accept that a child of three could seize a necklace and draw it tight with conscious intent? In any case the only witness we have is the mother herself, and any court of law would throw out her evidence as the fevered imaginings of a woman in 'a certain condition'.

Most of us are, happily, unaware of having any predisposition, real or imagined, to incest, patricide or matricide. Consequently such complexes seem bizarre and are easily made fun of. They cannot, however, be laughed out of court entirely. When one probes deeply into psychological differences between man and woman they do evince themselves, much disguised, in the differing sexual attitudes of mature men and women.

For instance, according to Freud every male infant experiences the Oedipus complex, and he claimed that the attribute we recognise as the very signature of masculinity, the super ego of the male, is the result of our infant Oedipus complex. A boy, the argument goes, concentrates his mental and emotional energy on his genitals, and because the original source of his security and gratification has been his mother he seeks genital gratification from her as well. Pre-masturbatory playing with his genitals makes him aware of the sensual pleasures possible in this part of his body and occasionally he is also aware of the sexual pleasures his parents enjoy. From this knowledge springs envy of his father's sexual status; he tries to usurp the father's position and himself possess the mother. But overt acts to make this conquest are repressed because of his fear that the father might retaliate by castrating him. He compromises, and in doing so he identifies himself with his father, assumes the father's aggressive personality and proper masculine values, and consequently, according to Freud, develops the strong sense of justice and social interest characteristic of the male.

The baby girl also has Oedipal feelings, but, having no penis, she has no castration-fear. Consequently her Oedipal period is less intense. This, argues Freud, explains why 'for women the level of what is ethically normal is different from what it is in men'. The super-ego of women is never so inexorable, so impersonal, so independent of its emotional origins as we require it to be in men. A girl identifies herself with her mother and accepts her father's penis superiority and her own no-penis inferiority. With the result that women are less self-centred and less status-seeking than men. Melanie Klein, who makes a different analysis, argues that the girl, because of her biological lack of a penis, introjects identification with her parents into her body, whereas the boy, because he has his genitals outside and can show them and inspect them, can focus attention *from* his body instead of *into* it.

But whatever subtle corrections later psychologists have made to the Freudian canon we have to accept in broad terms his dogma that all our psychological sexual development has its roots in infant sexuality.

4   PENIS-ENVY

'How handy that is!' This, reports a psychologist, was the remark a little girl made when she watched a boy peeing and first saw a penis. Eager hunters for evidence of sexual complexes might argue that the words indicate the little girl was suffering penis-envy. A more commonplace explanation might be that she was revealing no more than typical feminine appreciation of domestic utility.

A vast pyramid of speculation has been erected on the theory that when a child first becomes consciously aware that it has a penis or lacks one it may suffer a shock so traumatic that, if the circumstances surrounding the discovery are not auspicious, its emotions can be scarred for life. Let us see how the discovery can affect boy with penis and girl without one.

The boy has something to show: a possession, a toy, a conspicuous decoration, a very practical instrument which he can flourish around, as he can also flourish a pistol, and with which he can at will create boastful arabesques of urine. In the last stage of a boy's sexual development, in what is called his phallic phase, all his sexuality is concentrated around this male organ. The boy delights in the adaptability and sensual activity of his penis until restrictions imposed upon him by his elders create the fears and sense of modesty which force him to relinquish such pleasures. Such childish tendencies must be suppressed when he begins the process of learning to be a socially acceptable being.

The girl has nothing so flamboyant. She sees her brother in possession of a kind of spigot which he can open or shut off when he pleases. As the little girl revealed, such a utensil seems admirably practicable to a feminine eye. All that she possesses is an opening much inferior in practical design and much more difficult to control. Therefore a girl approaching *her* phallic phase becomes conscious of lacking a boldly obvious organ upon which she can focus her sexual urges. The only possession that *she* has which is at all comparable to her brother's penis is a clitoris; a pitiable substitute by penis standards, being tucked out of sight and lacking the forceful, penetrating character of her brother's instrument.

For a boy his penis is a beautifully bold and undeniable symboy of his sex, a constant assurance of manhood. The girl, having nothing which she can strut around with and show off, feels that her sex symbol is a hidden and secret thing, something no one can see and which they must therefore accept on trust.

Because his genitals are outside his body the boy can take an interest in their growth and intensifying sexuality. Furthermore, because his penis has a double function, is an organ for use as well as for pleasure, he becomes familiar with it. It is an old acquaintance. The girl's clitoris, on the other hand, is not only hidden but is also in the nature of a secret luxury; it serves no practicable purpose and is concerned exclusively with sexual feelings.

The boy is proud of his possession. But there is danger in this pride: the prouder he is of his sex symbol the greater can be his fear of losing it, so that when he becomes aware that neither his mother nor his sister has such a possession he begins to ask himself, 'How did they lose it?' 'Was it cut off?' 'Why?'

Freud, in fact, came to the conclusion that every boy believes up to the age of six that all human beings have, or should have, a penis. A boy, said Freud, accepts that belief unquestioningly; either (a) he does not even see that his mother or sister lacks the appendage, or (b) if he does see this and has reached the age when he can reason about it, he will explain it away. He will explain away the lack of a penis on a small girl by telling himself that she is still too young to have grown one; he will explain away the lack on someone older, his mother or a sister, by telling himself that their penis must have been lost or cut off. The boy then goes on to ask why they have been castrated? Is it punishment for some misdemeanour? As at this time he is becoming conscious very often of feelings of guilt about his 'naughtiness', he asks himself if he might suffer the same punishment. That fear, insinuating itself into his childish and half-formed thoughts, takes root in his subconscious. He will never forget the fear. He will *appear* to forget it, *appear* to grow out of it, but it is always there, repressed and in danger of erupting in later life, distorting his sexuality and inhibiting his relationship with women and also with his fellows.

The girl collects and absorbs fears of a similar pattern. When *she* becomes conscious of lacking a visible outward sex decoration she begins to wonder what is wrong with her. She begins to ask what mistake at birth or what misdemeanour of hers has caused her body to have been formed without so attractive an embellishment. Or did she once have one? Did she, as her mother has obviously done, lose it?

Freud argued that lack of a penis gives women a sense of inferiority and they share the contempt felt by men for a sex which is lesser in so important a respect. Penis-envy, Freudians claim, can cause a girl to grow into a woman with a subconscious sense of deprivation so all-pervading that she will be plagued with feelings of inferiority. In abnormal cases such feelings can be so intense as to cause persecution mania. In less exaggerated form they might spur a woman into rebellion against the supposedly inferior status of the female in society; even stimulate some woman into such ambitious political activity that she might, as President Nixon has publicly speculated, become President of the United States. Similarly, it is argued, repressed fear of castration can create in a man a persecution mania which will make him timidly suspicious of his fellows. Such a man might over-compensate for these fears by aggression against his fellows to the extent of attempting to castrate, politically or actually, imagined enemies such as Jews or Negroes.

However, when we discuss sexual complexes we must take care. In the same way that some of Freud's valid observations have been over-simplified for popular consumption and carelessly used in fashionable conversation, so has the word complex been corrupted. Every other day, for instance, people talk about others or themselves as suffering from an 'inferiority complex'. Surely what they are really talking about is the *sense* of inferiority. A person might suffer from a sense of inferiority so persistently as to be depressively ill, but any such person could be cured by an improvement in circumstances or a change of scene, by a doctor's medicine or psychiatric advice, or even by winning a football pool. As for the person who suffers only occasionally from a sense of inferiority, he or she might be quite a wise person who is honest enough to recognise that on certain occasions anyone of us is inferior intellectually or physically to someone of superior intellect or skill. But *sense* of inferiority is not an inferiority *complex*. A complex, broadly speaking, means a condition of which we are consciously unaware. Consequently a person suffering from inferiority complex far from being *conscious* of being inferior compensates for his *subconscious* conviction of inferiority by assuming attitudes of superiority. Such a one could be, for instance, an over-pompous tycoon, an over-argumentative shop steward, a Hitler, or merely a school bully.

Failure to be exact in using the word 'complex' has led to careless distortions of Freudian arguments. The mis-use of his term 'penis-envy' is a case in point. Can anyone believe, for instance, that any woman describing her first sight of a penis, would come out with the phrase, 'No teapot without a spout felt so forlorn?' That woman's case, reported by Havelock Ellis, is retold by Simone de Beauvoir in *The Second Sex*. De Beauvoir can be excused for seizing on such a story because she is writing not as a psychologist but as a passionate woman who treads the Freudian path in her own feminist style. The writers who cannot be excused are those whose books purport to be scientific and reliable guides to psychology but, even though currently published, are lumbered with scores of similarly old-fashioned and loaded reports.

Woman's penis-envy and man's castration-fear are psychological states far too complicated to be illustrated in crude terms of a girlish teapot wanting a spout or a boyish teapot being frightened of losing one. It is an error as well as an insult to Freud to imagine that he was advancing ideas so elementary. He was not arguing that persons with such complexes were consciously envious of a penis or consciously fearful of losing it. What he was suggesting was that an adult suffering from these complexes had been confronted with the striking and disturbing penis-no-penis difference between the sexes at a time when the infant intellect was not capable of accounting for this difference, and the traumatic shock of the discovery has been repressed in the subconscious. If we do meet a woman who consciously expresses envy of a penis, a woman who can feel forlorn or remember that she felt forlorn because she did not possess such a spout, that woman is not suffering from penis-envy at all. All she is suffering from is a directly expressed conscious desire for a penis; admittedly a frustrating desire if she really does want one attached to her own body instead of wanting, as a normal woman does, occasional enfolding possession of the penis of her mate. But a woman suffering from penis-envy in the Freudian sense might never refer to penises at all. Her penis-envy could be detected in variations of thought and conduct and sexual activity having no relationship to penises at all, or in expressions and dreams in which the words spoken or objects dreamed of would be symbols as distant or more distant from penises as a giraffe's neck. Such a woman, like the woman politician compensating for her lack of a penis by forceful masculine behaviour, would reveal her penis-envy by her intellectual attitudes and habits, probably exhibiting a contradictory mixture of feminist argument and masculine behaviour in dress and manner. But she would no more confess to feeling forlorn without a spout than to an immoderate desire to possess the Speaker's Mace.

Similarly with the castration complex. An ambitious officer does not envy the Field Marshal his baton: he envies the Field Marshal the power and privileges implicit in possession of a baton. Only if the officer were grossly mentally disturbed, only if he suffered perhaps from some phobia of 'baton-envy', could he believe that if he got possession of the baton he would automatically become a Field Marshal, or that if he snapped the baton over his knees the Field Marshal would automatically be deprived of power and privilege. A normal man, when he eventually realises he has not got what it takes to become a Field Marshal, will sanely recognise his limitations and, although he might beef about his fate, accept the inevitability of a military future at a lower rank. A man suffering from castration-fear, however, would be convinced he was being unfairly treated by a society which blocked his opportunities to prove his greatness as a Field Marshal. He might resort to drink or women, or become a martinet major and sublimate his frustration by sadistically bullying anyone under his command.

Similarly no normal infant girl would think that by depriving her brother of his penis and attaching it to her body she could rise to first rank in her parents' affections. Instead she turns with extra fervour to her female pursuits, to the dollies' tea-parties of infancy. Or, if she is older, she cultivates her femininity more consciously, even to the extent of over-acting the part of mother, fussing maternally over baby and thus developing step by step towards the proud womanly maturity which her poor penis-hampered brother can never hope to achieve.

If girls suffer from penis-envy, why, it has been asked, do not boys suffer from 'breast-envy'? The breasts a baby boy first knows are his mother's, and at that time they are merely the source of gratification for his hunger. He does not notice other breasts until he has reached an age when he can to some extent reason about them and accept them as exclusively feminine. At such an age the sight of breasts does not therefore cause any bewildering shock and make him feel that his male body lacks something. Some psychologists do however go so far as to argue that boys can suffer from what one might call 'womb-envy'. They suggest that the boy's predilection to rob birds' nests of their eggs or stamp young plants into the ground are expressions of his revenge against his inability to give birth to life.

A baby girl, as any parent knows, can be disturbingly jealous of a newly arrived brother. In fact infant girls show jealousy towards younger siblings more often than do infant boys. The little girl's jealousy is easy to understand. Up to the time brother appeared on the scene she had been the beloved pet of mother and father: now she finds herself relegated to second place in favour of the male newcomer. It is therefore possible that brother's penis can assume some importance in her eyes. She notices that this symbol of masculinity is an appendage important enough to determine that the little boy will wear trousers instead of skirts etcetera. She might go further and see the penis as the adornment, the medal, worn by a competitor who has won greater favour with her parents.

All of us have our envies, and all of us can find symbols for them. Rational adults have enough intellect and experience to shrug away envies, but infants have emotional resilience also capable of relegating envy to its appropriate place. It is one of their processes of growing up.

Helene Deutsch relegates penis-envy to its proper position when she refuses to give it importance as a traumatic sex experience. She argued that whatever feeling a female has of lacking a penis is characterologic: that is, it is a factor in a structure so basic in feminine psychology that it exists *before* the reality of seeing a penis; and, presumably, can exist *without* the reality of seeing one. This characterologic sense of lacking a penis, as distinct from the trauma of envying one, is 'a component of the feminine soul that so regularly appears in analytic treatment that we must regard it as "normal". Only when it is excessive and has disturbing effect does it acquire an abnormal character.'

The freedom we enjoy nowadays to explain and discuss sex problems, to drag out and air sex complexes, is a precious one. In this eighth decade of the twentieth century there are many who criticise what they call 'sexual permissiveness' yet it is undeniable that we live in a saner climate than that of the clammy poisonously sex-obsessed nineteenth century. That century, notable for private debauchery and public moralising, might one day get its just deserts by being remembered, so far as morals and psychology are concerned, merely as the century when the 'limbs' of pianos had to be covered by 'unmentionables'. Sex in all its manifestations aroused feelings of guilt such as had surely never seen their like since Adam and Eve were expelled from Eden. There were doctors sufficiently concerned with the human plight to devote their talents to risky pioneering explorations in the realms of sex psychology. Yet even they seemed unable to make the final break with social prejudice. They could not shake themselves free of ingrained superstitions about sex of the kind one would expect to find only in the murky mediaeval minds of Protestant preachers and Catholic moralists.

A certain Doctor Gattel, for instance, visited Krafft-Ebing's clinic in Vienna and discovered that of 43 patients suffering from neurasthenia 42 confessed to being or were suspected of being masturbators. Ecco, said Doctor Gattel, this proves that masturbation causes neurasthenia! We should think little of any doctor's reasoning if, after visiting a sanatorium and observing that 42 of its 43 tubercular patients regularly ate carrots as a second vegetable, he rushed back to his study to tell the world that tuberculosis was caused by eating carrots. Obviously Gattel, sunk up to his medical eyebrows in the mud of nineteenth-century sex-phobia, could not distinguish cause from effect and was emotionally incapable of reaching the elementary conclusion that any 42 out of any 43 sufferers from neurasthenia might be expected to satisfy their lonely sexual urges by the same normal and convenient method that is used by convicts in a prison, by soldiers in a desert, or by boys and girls in segregated dormitories.

Some doctors could go to even greater idiocy: even to the extent of seriously stating that a person had died of 'masturbatory insanity'. Said Sir William Ellis, 'I have no hesitation in saying that, in a very large number of patients in all public asylums, the disease may be attributed to excessive masturbation . . . the true cause of dementia.'

Psychological inquiry is today more refined than was possible in Freud's day. Psychologists have access to techniques and instruments far more sophisticated than any that were available to him, their findings are more precisely analysed and documented, and measurements and observed data have taken the place of inspired theory and imaginative generalisations. What is more important research is not confined to one or two children but is extended to numbers of children who are studied in groups and studied more continuously.

For instance, the most interesting and revealing inquiry into infant concepts of male and female genitals that I have come across is one conducted recently in Israel by Hans and Shulamith Kreitler, who, at the moment of writing, are at the

Division of Psychological Studies at Princeton, U.S.A. Their study is probably unique. It is certainly, so far as I can ascertain, the first of its kind in recent years.

Questions were put by the Kreitlers to a group of children of Oriental and Western origin, 95 boys and 90 girls aged from four to five-and-a-half. Freud's theory that boys believed up to the age of six in the universality of the penis was one of the first to fall by the wayside. The children's answers revealed that on the contrary the overwhelming majority of the Western boys did *not* believe that all humans had a penis. Incidentally the inquiry also revealed that 'information boys have about the sexual organs of girls is more exact than that which girls have about the sexual organs of boys'. Not even *one* boy so much as hinted that he thought a girl had been castrated.

A question was framed to find out how girls would describe a boy's method of urinating. Fifteen per cent of the Oriental girls came up with the logical answer: 'From the trousers when he stands.' Which remark is very much in line with 'How handy that is!' as a characteristic appreciation of domestic utility. In fact psychologists nowadays report that many girls, far from having Freudian envy of the baby boy's penis, regard the tassel as an inferiority, looking upon it in the same way they would look upon a growth or a wart. Others have been known to say, 'Oh, I had one of those once.'

More significant even than the Kreitler findings is a case reported by Robert J. Stoller in *Sex and Gender*. It is a case which not only casts doubt on the theory of penis-envy but suggests that the penis is not necessarily important to a male's concept of his masculinity. Stoller tells of a boy who was born with no external penis and with a blind scrotum resembling the outer and inner labia of a vagina. The deformity had no apparent effect on the boy's masculinity. He was convincingly male in all his mental attitudes and habits. He enjoyed masculine activities and sports, including wrestling and boxing. Even his taste in clothes was uncompromisingly masculine. This suggests that a male can have an inbuilt tendency to masculinity that is strong enough to assert itself despite lack of or malformation of the genitals. Certainly this boy proved that he did not need so crude a symbol of maleness as a penis to assure himself of his essential masculinity.

In the Israel inquiry the Kreitlers showed the caution which psychologists now use in their researches. The questions they put to the children were designed with delicacy and cunning.

They had on the one hand to avoid shocking infant susceptibilities and on the other hand to use easily understood words which would evoke honest unhibited replies. I could not refrain, however, from asking the Kreitlers why they had not put to the children a blunt question asking the infants for their own explanations for the lack of a penis on girls. They pointed out, justifiably, that for psychological reasons questions so boldly worded were not desirable. 'Psychologists,' added Hans Kreitler, 'are *also* bound by professional ethics.'

Until quite recently psychologists, as greedy in their hunt for complexes as pigs for truffles, were by no means so scrupulous. That much can easily be discerned in the stories culled from their case-books and published again and again, often repeated, it seems, with no more reason than a lip-smacking relish for sexy stories. Some of the sexual confessions made by their patients are obviously the result of brutally direct questions. The answers also indicate that a great deal of what the subjects were guided to express as their own sexual thoughts were really thoughts which had been implanted in their minds by scientifically careless or too eager questioners.

For my own part I would argue confidently that whatever might be the cause for my own mixed-up psychology my subconscious bears no scars as a result of that session amid the cowslips, otherwise I should not recall it with such sentimental pleasure. Nor can I believe that my female collaborator has ever suffered from the least flicker of penis-envy. The last time I saw her she was an ample and most assuredly complacent matron attending the wedding of one of the many daughters born of two happy marriages, and although she still giggles overmuch it is unlikely that those convulsive ripplings are in any way a throwback to her infant giggles in the meadow. Instead I would rather believe that her first glimpse of my possession helped to put her on the road to making the fruitful use she eventually did make of at least two others.

Nor, when I line up in my memory all the women I have known well, those with whom I have had close and intimate acquaintance, domestically, socially and professionally, I cannot think of a single one of them who shows symptoms of penis-envy. In fact the only kind of penis-envy I have ever found has been among men. Male readers who went to boarding school will know what I mean, although my experience of living communally with males was in the more robust atmosphere of Army barracks. There I did find penis-envy, though it was not, of course, a repressed complex: it was frank and conscious envy felt by some members of our company for comrades who seemed to have been unfairly favoured by Nature.

Penis-envy is not all that distant from penis worship which has been a feature in ritual and beliefs since earliest times. The phalluses of Greece and India are best known because of their realism, but many religious decorations and ornaments used in the religions of other countries are symbolically phallic. There is, for instance, that phallic freak of Nature which lures pilgrims 13,000 feet up the Amarnath mountain in Kashmir: a five-foot high lingam of ice, worshipped as a symbol of Shiva, which waxes and wanes with the moon and reaches its greatest height on the day of the August full moon.

Like many neuroses, as well as many diseases, penis-envy and castration-fear must surely be listed among the by-products of civilisation. It is difficult to believe such complexes could ever exist among primitive peoples. Many primitive peoples, it must be admitted, live in circumstances of deplorable squalor and material and intellectual deprivation. They are often the helpless prey of diseases and victims of their own savagery. They also have their sexual superstitions, sexual taboos and horrific sexual rites. Though the reports of anthropologists do suggest that these latter seem to become more rigorous and ritualistic when people are emerging from natural primitive existence and attempting to impose forms of discipline and law on their community; when, in other words, they are making their first tentative steps in the direction of civilisation.

Yet it is observable and undeniable that among all primitive peoples infants enjoy more sexual communication, visual and tactile, than infants can enjoy in civilised society. Primitive adults naturally and unashamedly help both infant boy and infant girl to realise their sex and grow into consciousness of their sexual destiny.

In such communities a boy's elders will speak about his penis, tease him about it or admire it, as they would of any other part of his body. He is not nagged into the belief, nor is his sister, that there is a mysteriously indecent part of the body which must never be shown. With these infants there are no parts of the body which are 'secret' or, worse, 'dirty'; no parts which must be concealed by trousers and skirts and only peered at furtively away from adult eyes.

To a savage boy his penis is as much a part of him as are his hands or feet. So he can wear it frankly; without shame and, consequently, without fear. To him, as with an infant in a civilised society, his tassel is an assurance that he is male; but he has the advantage in that it is not buttoned up, and neither are the penises of others. His penis is small, of course, but he also is small. He will grow, as his elder brothers are growing, and his penis will grow like theirs. Someday he will have a penis as big as his father's. Then he will be a man. He is sure of that. He has no sex doubts; consequently no sex complexes.

Similarly with the infant girl. True enough, her brother, because of the exaggerated importance that might have been attached to his genitals by the virile males of a masculine-dominated society, probably struts around in postures of male pride. But she is not envious: she gets her own share of the admiration and petting suitable to a little girl. Her elders pat her pretty vagina with the same casually affectionate admiration with which they ruffle her curls or caress her arms and legs. For the moment her nipples are no bigger than those on her brother's chest. But she knows they will one day be much bigger because all around her, in the bodies of older playmates and sisters and her mother, she sees the pattern of her future feminine shape. Every moment of every day the growth of female bodies assures her that some day she too will have the breasts and figure of a woman. She too will be desired and chased by a man. She too will eventually lie in a hut and have a baby of her own.

Thus both boy and girl grow up in the certainty that they will become sexually mature as man and woman. Whatever kind of bed or mat they eventually lie on, one thing is certain, it will not be a psychologist's couch. Nor will either die of 'masturbatory insanity'.

5 HANDSOME BOY! PRETTY GIRL!

Stoller's report of the boy who showed masculine tendencies and tastes although he was born without a penis shows how powerfully we can be influenced to attitudes appropriate to our biological sex by genetic factors. It is noticeable that long before male and female babies can possibly be socially conditioned to masculinity or femininity they show sexual differences. Even in a baby's first months of life its masculinity or femininity is sufficiently defined as to be distinguishable. Each sex requires different treatment, evinces different patterns of thought, and makes different responses to illnesses.

The genetic influence can therefore be seen as basic in sexual determination, the foundation upon which a child's eventual sexual development is reared. Nevertheless that sexual development can be nourished or retarded by the influence of others. It is true that our sexual shape is biologically planned at the moment the egg is fertilised, but our sexual fortunes are enriched or impoverished by the influences and conditioning we experience at the hands of our parents and the society into which we are born.

Despite the genetical decision and its anatomical result, a boy's masculinity or a girl's femininity will be fortified or weakened by the sexual conditioning parents and society direct upon the child. Because development towards maturity in human life is so complicated, physically and mentally and also socially, because it is more subtle and intricate than the maturation of animals, and because humans have imposed upon themselves subtle and intricate complexities of social conduct, not weeks nor months but years of conditioning are necessary to train and educate human young to become acceptably male or female according to their society's concepts of masculinity and femininity.

At birth, the human baby is physically and mentally helpless. Despite a potential of intellect and skill immeasurably superior to that possessed by any other creature on earth, the human baby is completely dependent on its elders and incapable of surviving without the nursing and protection provided by a mother and a home. A foal totters to its feet within minutes of being born. Some young animals can survive away from their parents' lairs, track down and select the food suitable for them, avoid poison and danger, and very rarely fail to grow to physical perfection as adults. In lower species the young mature so quickly that they are able to procreate their own species within twelve weeks or days or less.

Not so the human baby. It is at the mercy of other humans more than any young animal is ever at the mercy of the pack; it can be moulded by its fellows into a perfect adult or distorted into an imperfect one as no animal is ever moulded or distorted by its fellows. The animal, as soon as it has finished suckling, can forage for itself and learns how to live. But the baby, after it is weaned, is still dependent; it must be helped and taught how to eat, how to walk, how to speak, how to clean and dress itself, and how to acquire the rudiments of human skills. It has also to be helped and taught how to become acceptably male or female.

During a baby's sexual education two processes happen simultaneously: it learns what sex is, and at the same time it is taught how to conduct itself in ways appropriate to that sex.

The first process, that of learning its own sex, happens more or less unconsciously, the information being absorbed by the baby through reflections of itself in the attitude and the eyes of others. Subtle variations in the way its mother and others handle it and caress it are compared or contrasted with the way others of the same sex or of different sex are handled and caressed. Before the meanings of names and words are fully understood the different tones of voice used for saying 'John' or 'Mary' confirm the child's conception of its own gender, and eventually one of the first consciously constructed sentences a child forms will be a declaration of its sexual identity, a proudly masculine 'I am a boy' or a primly feminine 'I am a girl' to any teasing adult who suggests the opposite.

At the same time adults are teaching the child by example and by precept to dress and play and act in male or female fashion. In this way a child becomes sexually oriented and identifies itself with male or female elders. Routine events in family life will train a child to the conduct appropriate to its sex, but its concept of masculinity and femininity will also be moulded by more subtle influences. The barely perceptible difference in the attitudes which parents adopt towards males and females will have a stronger and more pervasive influence on a child's concept of sex than any direct instruction.

In normal family life the example and influence of parents are the factors that are most decisive in teaching a boy to be male and a girl to be female. Not only the direct instruction which the parents give but also their own characters mould the child's concept of sex difference. For instance the uncertainties of gender that can be aroused in a boy with a weak, unmasculine father and a dominant mother is nowadays a truism in psychology. On the other hand in the archetypal family where the father's rule is dominant and the mother is obedient to him a boy will grow up believing that power and command are manly traits and will attempt to assume similar masculine status. In a Japanese family the older females assume postures of obedience and pretence of weakness to a boy when he is only four thus encouraging him to strut around in domineering masculine fashion.

The modern trend of supposedly enlightened parents to be sexually frank and attempt to guide children towards sexual maturation is well intended but is often far less successful than the sexual candour and seemingly cruel customs of sexual initiation common in primitive tribes. Margaret Mead tells of societies where a girl is dressed up with ear-rings and a floppy grass skirt when only six months old. 'Every man that comes along tickles her and flirts with her and plays with her until femininity is very highly emphasised.' In other societies small males have their pictures taken naked and 'there is a tremendous emphasis on maleness from the very early days so that masculinity is played up well beyond the point at which the child would biologically be prepared to exhibit it.'

Also from Margaret Mead come enchanting descriptions of childhood in Bali where enormous emphasis is laid on the difference between male and female genitals, boys and girls being teasingly and intimately caressed and admired as 'Handsome boy!' and 'Pretty girl!' In Bali, she reports, little girls of only two and three are so conscious of their femininity and what it entails that they walk around in postures that simulate pregnancy.

Margaret Mead says that if a society considers that a man should be stronger than a woman, then it will consider a child that is weak as less masculine and a child that is strong as more masculine. Similarly, she says, 'If to be a female is to burst into tears, then if you are a non-crier, you are that less female. Among the Iatmuls in New Guinea, for instance, not to be able to cry on demand is one of the most terrible things that can happen to a woman. It is far worse than having the wrong figure, because crying is something that is expected of every woman.'

Levine draws attention to an interesting attitude towards masculinity among the Ethiopians. The Amhara *wand nat*, masculinity, lays no stress on heterosexuality, and an Amhara male would consider it shameful to boast of his sexual achievements. His ideal of masculinity refers primarily to aggressive capacity, to exalting a man's ferocity in killing an enemy or a wild beast, to making little of physical hardship, to live for a long time in the wilds, to walk all day long with no food. 'In short, for the Amhara the virtues of the male are the virtues of a soldier,' and he quotes their exhortation, 'Kill a man! Kill a man! It is good to kill a man. One who has not killed a man moves around sleepily.' Crawley reported that the mammae of Ethiopian boys are amputated soon after birth in the belief that no warrior could possibly be brave who had them and that they should belong to woman only.

Civilised modes of life, although they add sophistication and grace to sexuality, create artificial impediments to sexual orientation. A child growing up in the candid atmosphere of a savage community is helped to sexual maturity by the intimate presence of males and females and the daylong presence of its parents as models of maleness and femaleness; but children in industrial societies spend most of their infancy only with their mothers, some of them seeing little of their fathers. This makes sexual identification more difficult for a boy than for a girl.

Using 2,650 women in a fascinatingly designed inquiry into the nature and origin of feeling feminine Benjamin Wright and Shirley Tuska found that 1,892 rated themselves as 'very feminine', 548 as 'rather feminine', and 210 as only 'slightly feminine' or 'masculine'. These 210 were identified in further questioning as the 'masculine group'. The feminine women considered themselves as more narcissistic, confident and comfortable in their femininity; the masculine women as more forceful, intelligent and responsive. Memories of parental attitudes had played a great part in their mental sexual development. Recollections of an emotionally satisfying mother and a successful father characterised the feminine women; recollections of an emotionally satisfying father but a frustratingly unsympathetic mother characterised the masculine woman. When asked the question 'Which parent did you feel was most closely attached to you?' the girls who felt passive (soft, lenient, light, weak and yielding) were more likely to answer 'Father!' than were the active girls who described their fathers as distant, cold and critical.

In their early years both male and female babies model themselves on their mothers. They can do the things she does, imitate her washing-up and cleaning the house. As such domestic duties are considered appropriate for a little girl she can continue the imitation of mother and find sexual orientation in becoming a 'little mother'. With a son it is different. Although the mother must nurse the boy through his infancy she knows that he will eventually escape from her control or, if needs be, must be expelled from it into a masculine future of manly independence. Therefore in a home where the father is rarely present the boy, who should not identify himself too closely with mother and will indeed be warned away from too closely imitating a female model, has to resort to constructing some imagined masculine model with whom he can identify himself. In that way the search, sometimes a vain one, for a father figure can begin in the nursery and continue throughout a man's life. This search for a father figure can often be detected in the tendency of adult males to adore even the shabbiest of demagogues and submit to most oppressive régimes whose poverty of reason and viciousness of policy they hardly notice because of their compelling hunger for authoritarian patriarchal guidance.

It has been recorded that the sons of sailor fathers who were absent from the home for long periods showed inhibition in normal boyish aggressiveness and some preferred to play with girls rather than boys.

The need for a boy to transfer identification from mother to father, or to imagined father, does cause boys to experience more psychological difficulties in early years. Boys find it harder than girls to settle down at school. The normal girl fits herself easily into a group of girls who are like herself because they still identify themselves with and therefore have not left their mother, a boy who has just left his mother finds it difficult to introduce himself into a group of stranger males.

Young boys have more behaviour problems than girls. 'Problem children' are nearly always boys. In this respect, however, available statistics are still somewhat deficient and are often compiled inconsistently by different authorities. However it does seem that school misdemeanours such as truancy, stealing, cruelty, laziness, masturbation and destructiveness are twice as common among boys as among girls. There is of course the possibility that the emphasis we put on a boy being courageous and adventurous and independent can account for some of those extra misdemeanours. It is also possible that misdemeanours of boys are more readily reported and those of girls more readily *not-reported*. Reporting or non-reporting can to some extent be determined by the idea that a 'bad boy' can best be restrained from further misdeeds by being reprimanded by authority outside the home whereas a 'bad girl' might be best dealt with by being sent home to mother. Three to four more boys than girls have to be referred to Child Guidance Clinics, and far more boys than girls are delinquents.

Very often delinquency is the result of a boy's desire to 'look big' in the eyes of his companions. This masculine tendency is often carried through to adult life, and it is significant that Newcastle, one of the last strongholds of typically working-class male supremacy where the tough hard-drinking Geordie is dictator of the life of his subservient wife and family, is also the area which recently headed the table of crime statistics with 5,005 crimes per 100,000 of population in ten years, with London far down with only 3,378.

In any case even in his earliest years a boy is more daring than a girl. This is shown in a boy's readiness to take risks, even with tasks in the classroom, as well as in sports and play, and when quite young a boy shows a masculine tendency for gambling. In an enlightening experiment by Paul Slovic at the Oregon Research Unit girls and boys were allowed to 'gamble' on a machine with 10 small switches, an unknown one of which was a 'disaster' switch. The safe switches paid awards of candies, but if the 'disaster' switch happened to be pressed the whole accumulated reward was lost. Girls proved to be much more cautious than boys, stopping more often than boys when they had won what they considered enough, whereas the boys showed a tendency to press on for bigger rewards at the risk of losing the lot. Incidentally feminine caution proved wiser: girls won on average 2.2 spoonfuls of candies, boys only 1.84 spoonfuls.

Whereas identifying with their mothers conditions girls to seek close and intimate relationships, boys are conditioned to life in groups. This results in the tendency for girls to have one special chosen friend, male or female, and boys to form gangs and enjoy group activities outside the home. Boys, because they are not expected to be tied for too long to apron strings, are expected to be rebels, mischievous and practical jokers, but girls are expected to be obedient and polite and not be rough with their playmates. When children are old enough to choose their own pursuits these tendencies become more apparent. The sexual difference can be seen even in reading: boys choose books with tales of adventure and exploration and war: girls choose stories of love and boarding schools and fantasy. Even parents who would prefer their children not to see films about war or crime tolerate their sons' preference for such films but would be worried if their daughters preferred them.

Parents are often unaware of how differently they treat boys and girls and of the different attitudes they have to the sexes. Most parents think they believe in equality of the sexes, but nearly always they treat baby boys with greater patience and give them more care and attention than girls. Dahlstrom reports a Swedish inquiry which showed that on average girls were breast-fed for only three months against six months for boys.

Boys 'are three times as interesting' as girls. 'They have got a lot of intellectual curiosity, whereas girls are, relatively speaking, just little bores. They have already taken on domestic attitudes, they talk just like their mothers, they have less freedom of the imagination of any sort.' This bold generalisation was thrown out by Margaret Mead at a World Health symposium on Child Development. One knows what she means. She is thinking of boys and girls as seen in an average family of a masculine-dominated society. In such a society, a boy, encouraged to be independent and adventurous, becomes the non-conformer of a family; a girl, drilled to be passively dependent, becomes the conformer. Naturally any non-conformer is more 'interesting' than a conformer. Even the boy's future seems more 'interesting'. The boy might become an engine-driver or a soldier, a policeman or a President or Prime Minister. In the world beyond the home he might achieve something in a blaze of glory. Even if he does something reprehensible, his future must always seem more 'interesting' than that of the girl. Her future will be a future of marriage and motherhood, a future no different from the life now being lived by her mother and therefore being neither so promising nor so problematical as the boy's. However, in our present society fewer families are so old-fashioned and socially restricted, and in the increasing number of families where daughters as well as sons are encouraged to train themselves for independent futures and careers it is unlikely that such girls are still 'just little bores'.

What is significant is that the majority of children of both sexes would prefer to be male. Some years ago in answer to a series of questions during school work 101 of 289 girls said they would rather be men than women, but only one of 302 boys said he would rather be a woman and 'live an easier life!' Of the girls who were content to be women half of them wished to serve their fellows in idealised feminine pursuits such as nursing, but the other half wanted 'to escape the responsibilities of men's lives and get more joy out of life'. The boys were much more selfish: 200 of them wanted to be men for merely selfish reasons. It would be interesting to extend this experiment and keep the statistics up to date to see if any significant shift in sex preferences occurs when more careers, as well as more responsibilities and cares, are available to women.

The family background will also strongly influence a child's sex preference. Some families will be overwhelmingly glad that they have borne a son, and their smiling praise and approval of masculinity will develop the boy's confident assurance that the male should by right enjoy a grander place in the scheme of things. Other families will lament when a girl is born, and their disappointment will condition a daughter to accept society's opinion that the female is inferior to the penis-embellished male. That feeling of inferiority might be eradicated only later in life when she enjoys the triumph of enfolding this masculine decoration in her vagina.

Some parents try to drill their children into the form they themselves once hoped to be. A father whose ambitions in the masculine world have been frustrated will try to make his son fulfil them; a woman whose narcissistic dreams have not been realised will try to enjoy their fulfilment vicariously by encouraging her daughter's feminine narcissism. The father has less hope of success than the mother. The boy, because he must be encouraged to be intellectually curious and adventurous and trained to become an independent male beyond the home, is more likely to rebel against his father's attempts to follow the same ambitions, particularly when the father's own failure becomes apparent. The girl, on the other hand, will willingly respond to her mother's encouragement to be narcissistic, because a girl is always much more in love with her own body than a boy is, luxuriates in any admiration of her femininity, and has a narcissistic compulsion to be prettier and more desirable than other girls, particularly girls whom she knows well and herself admires.

Freud's comment that parents' attempts to enlighten their children on sex usually come too late is still valid. Most parents are still locking the stable door after the mare has foaled, so any attempt to introduce sex education into schools or on to television is welcome not so much for the possibility that the child will get instruction which it would otherwise not get from its parents at home but that the instruction will be better.

Potted sex-instruction delivered ineptly can be more harmful to a child than any discoveries in school playground or under the bushes.

The most dangerous parents of all are often the ones who consider themselves progressive and enlightened. Many fathers and mothers believe they can train their children into casual and innocent acceptance of sex and sexual differences by parading around the home naked. They think that the infants will thus become accustomed to the sight of male and female bodies and be that much less prurient. After all, these well-intentioned parents argue, children of primitive societies enjoy that same daily sight of the bodies of father and mother. What the parents overlook is the fact that children in primitive societies have daily sight of all other bodies too, see sexual development at every stage and age, see the growth of pubic hair and penises and breasts as well as being witnesses of pregnancy and birth. But for a child in our society the sudden confrontation with father and mother equipped with mature sexual furniture which the child has never seen before is something like having a live elephant dumped into its bed instead of a cuddly velvet one. Far from being sexually enlightening and encouraging the spectacle of nude father and mother can be frighteningly traumatic, particularly at the time when the child's consciousness of sex is already confused enough by the social necessity of modestly covering its genitals when outside the home yet on the other hand being conscious that it must wear clothes of sexually different type to indicate the sexual difference secreted under trousers or skirts.

It is now accepted that many forms of sexual ambivalence have biological causes, often genetical, but it is still true that parents can be guilty of causing some. The emotional disturbances most common among children are those caused by parents who, at the same time that they are emphasising that a boy must train to be male and a girl must train to be female, are bullying those same children into the belief that the physical organs which symbolise the difference are shameful, or 'dirty', and must be kept secret.

Other emotional upsets often leading to complete deviation are caused by parents who, because they desired a son or a daughter, tend to treat a child according to the desired sex and not its real sex. Parents who desire a baby of one particular sex to such an extent should not play a game of Russian roulette with a child's future. They should use contraceptives and adopt a baby of the desired sex.

Bad management of love relationships by parents, sibling rivalry, coddling, rejection or sheer neglect can reactivate difficulties experienced earlier in childhood or even create a problem which never existed before.

Some peoples believe that effeminacy is transmissible. Crawley tells of an amusing custom among the Omahas. 'If a boy plays with a girl he is dubbed "hermaphrodite". In the Wiraijuri tribe boys are reproved for playing with girls—the culprit is taken aside by an old man who solemnly extracts from his legs some "strands of the women's apron" which have got in.'

The somewhat less primitive peasants of Germany always believed that a newly-born boy must be kissed first by its father and a newly-born girl by its mother; otherwise the boy would grow up without whiskers and the girl would have moustache and beard. The superstition does suggest some acceptance of the power of parental influence.

Henry quotes an interesting case of a sister who was as masculine as her brother was feminine. 'My father,' said the girl, 'used to hold up my brother to me and ask, "Which is the boy?" He wanted a boy when I came and a girl when my brother came. He would say that I should have been the boy and my brother the girl. My brother was constantly held up as an example. He was always so pedantic, and so careful and respectable. Once he said I would be good with a shave and a haircut. I hated him. I rode on garbage wagons and got along with bums and tramps. My brother is a weakling—just like a delicate woman. *He falls in love just like a woman.*'

I have italicised that last sentence because I consider it, innocent and instinctive though it was, as one of the most important observations ever made in sexual psychology. That simple sentence describes the subtle but powerfully significant difference between man and woman which is of far more significance than any difference in body, far more important than masculine, feminine and homosexual tastes. The emotional differences shown by man and woman in their different ways of making love or being in love emphasise the intellectual differences of man and woman. These emotional differences are moulded into final shape during the years of puberty.

6 YOUTH OR MAIDEN

We said earlier that when we think of the innumerable processes of biological engineering needed to fashion our bodies into proper male or female shape it does seem something of a miracle that we come off the conveyor-belt in only two sexual shapes. We can say something similar about our psychological sexual differences.

Considering how helpless we are at birth and how much our mental sexual attitudes have to be conditioned by the equally innumerable processes of our own sensual reactions and the nursing and training and education we suffer at the hands of others, it seems also something of a miracle that the vast majority of us do manage to finish up as more or less acceptably masculine or feminine.

Let us, as we did before, use our bodies as a diagram illustrating the forming of our mental sexual attitudes. Our physical development can indeed be seen as a working diagram of our psychological development. For instance, remember how our male or female genitals came into being. First, at the groin of our embryonic body, was that domed eminence called the genital tubercle, a sex bulb which showed no more indication of future maleness or femaleness than a bulb of a flower shows the pattern of the eventual bloom. Yet, by eventual blossoming into male or female genitals, the tubercle proved that all along it had had the potential to grow into a masculine or feminine trademark appropriate to the sex our chromosomes had designed for us.

That is a near to perfect diagram of our psychological sexuality. At birth we appear to be sexually neuter, but very soon in our lives we show that our psyche also has its inbuilt masculinity or femininity. But there is a crucial and perilous difference: our psychological sexuality can be deformed by outside influences as our physical sex can never be. Biology is stronger than parents or society: no amount of bad nursing, either intentionally bad or ignorantly bad, can ever distort the development of the genital tubercle, unless, of course, it is interfered with medically or surgically. But our sexual psyche can be perverted by careless or ignorant or cruel conditioning.

By the time we reach puberty most of that good or ill has

already been done. Through babyhood, infancy and childhood our masculinity or femininity has struggled to be loyal to our biological sex, but also it has had to adjust itself to the sexual concepts insisted on by our family and our society. At puberty we are on the threshold of physical sexual maturity, ripe for reproduction, fertile and capable of performing the necessary preliminary movements, and in this period of transition to manhood or womanhood the good or ill of our earlier conditioning becomes apparent. In primitive societies puberty is the time of life chosen for the candid initiation of boys and girls into male and female sexuality. But in civilised societies sexuality must, out of social necessity, be less overt. It can thus become an agonising personal secret.

Both boy and girl need to feel secure about their sex and to know that they are male or female according to the example set by their companions and elders. Sexual curiosity and some attempts to experiment sexually must be expected and tolerated in children during puberty. Boys tend to confine sexual expression primarily to their genitals, but girls, with other erogenous zones, including the breasts, can experience sexual excitement or even gratification without genital stimulation.

Henry argues that 'Preoccupation with sex during adolescence is so nearly universal that it must be assumed to be an important factor in the development of a healthy boy. If a boy is not interested in sex at this time it is almost certain that he is psychologically retarded.'

A boy's interest in the opposite sex during puberty can help his mental development. Because it is accepted in nearly all societies that the role of the male is to excel and be successful a boy attracted by a girl tends to work well to achieve masculine success.

Freud claimed that the development of a girl into a woman is more complicated than the development of a boy into a man. He saw the sexual life of a girl as split into two phases. Only the second is specifically feminine. During the first phase the girl feels much like a boy. In physical development she is a year or more ahead of a boy, and when pubertal desires are evinced she consequently chooses as male companions boys who are older, thus more physically developed and more sexually aware, than boys of her own age.

For the girl menstruation makes the transition a dramatic and sometimes frightening experience, but the boy also has physical preoccupations. His voice breaks; sometimes he suffers a slight swelling and painfulness of the breast. Although the age of puberty varies in different individuals, races and climates, it is usually earlier in girls than in boys, but the boy's sexual awareness is stronger than the girl's. He is conscious of an increasingly compelling desire for sexual gratification. The girl's sexual desire is dormant and awaits the arousal of courtship.

The feminine tendency to nag is traced to this aspect of a woman's development. As a girl she suffers excitements of the clitoris and other vaginal sensations. She cannot localise them, but feels them as irritating; so much so that even as a little girl she will sometimes be petulant and nag.

For both sexes puberty has profound effects mentally. The young of both sexes feel intensely the desire not only to be loved but also to love. Every emotion, every impression is now registered with greater sensitivity. But puberty is also the time when the hitherto protected seedlings must now be planted out in the world and hardened. The individual boy or girl begins to realise that a balance must be struck between the individual and society. The effort to strike this balance is repeatedly interfered with by waves of sexual desire. 'Puberty,' said Ploss, 'may be a time of religious conversion, of exquisite romantic devotion, of enthusiasm or idealism. It may also produce criminals, hooligans, prostitutes and procurers.' The young try to break free from the confines of the home and from the disciplines set by repressive elders. Boys form gangs and make mischievous attacks on parents and teachers. These masculine groups and actions are the precursors of political parties and revolts. Girls, more inward-looking, escape into close personal relationships with one or two chosen companions.

We know from experience that a boy's sexual desires are normally more active and aggressive than a girl's. That they should be so is surely in accord with the protrusive design and precocious development of his penis. But there are also considerable elements of activity and aggression in the unfulfilled desires and emotions of a girl's fantasy life. These would make her as active and aggressive sexually as a boy were they not bottled-up. This because her vagina does not provide her with an outlet as psychologically adequate as a penis is to a boy. Though Freud did maintain that the clitoris is the leading sexual organ of little girls and therefore the 'sexuality of little girls is of a wholly masculine character' and that 'a wave of repression at puberty' is required before the clitoris abandons its potential masculinity and the vagina establishes itself as wholly feminine.

This difference between boy and girl is noticed when the phallic phase of infancy is succeeded by what is known as the passive phase which comes before puberty. In the passive phase the boy's sexual urges cease to be concentrated exclusively on his penis, although the organ is still a prominently visible physical possession. For the girl, however, the fading out of the phallic (or clitoris) phase leaves her with the sensation of lacking a sexual organ. Her clitoris, no longer an active focus for her sexual urges, is a hidden organ, and it seems to her that all she now has is the vagina. Yet the vagina is not a lively active organ. It is fundamentally an organ whose main function is for reproduction and therefore it must wait for union with a penis before it can become sexually excitable. The psychological difference between aggressive attacking penis and passively waiting vagina is obvious and illustrates the essential difference between the sexuality of a man and a woman.

The aggressive content in male sexuality was emphasised by Krafft-Ebing who, reporting cases where sexual excitement was caused by the sight of battles or the paintings of them, quotes Schaeffer: 'The pleasure of battle and murder is so predominantly an attribute of the male sex throughout the animal kingdom that there can be no question about the close connection between this side of the masculine character and male sexuality.' The sadistic impulses of little boys when torturing their more sensitive fellows or mutilating animals, are often accompanied by an erection. As Wright points out parents regard a certain amount of aggression as normal for a boy just as they expect exhibitionism to be part of a girl's development towards sociability, and this parental acceptance encourages the development of these traits in men and women.

The modern trend for youngsters to resort to drugs is believed to be caused by attempts to overcome adolescent depressions. Dr Arnold Linken of the Student Health Service at University College claimed that with the new tolerance of sexual activity, young people were looking around for other ways of breaking out of the social pattern. He had found, in an exploration of coffee bars, university common rooms, and other places where young people went, that drugs were commonly taken. To prevent this, he argued, young people must be helped to understand the reason for their depression. He claimed that adolescent rebellion as a group philosophy was outdated. But parents who expected their teenage children to be in by 11 o'clock and who would not allow them to have long hair or wear teenage clothes must expect rebellion.

Mr. A. Chisnall, a sociologist who conducted a jazz club in London, claimed that young people who would be regarded as 'highly deviant' could become creative when they had learned to understand their problems. This, he said, applied even to delinquents.

The boy, however, is subject to more intense pubertal preoccupations than the girl. His penis is there to remind him constantly of his sexual purpose as a male. Unlike the concealed clitoris of the girl it is the always observable badge of his particular sex; its erection is a dramatically compelling phenomenon. Consequently if for any reason, real or imagined, he thinks he cannot perform the male role adequately his sense of sexual security is undermined.

The girl's clitoris presents her with no such challenge. There is no need for her to perform feats of physical skill to prove to herself or to others that she is feminine. Before puberty her sexual curiosities and anxieties induced fantasies of pregnancy and prostitution which she expressed in play-acting, putting a cushion under her dress or flirting with boys. These she now suppresses, trying to subdue sexual instinct in favour of romantic emotions. The boy's prepubertal fantasies give way to active masculine pursuits. But, like the girl, he shows a tendency to idealise the sexual instinct, choosing a love object in accord with this idealisation.

Discussing psychological consequences caused by anatomical differences between the sexes Freud argued that fantasies are an amalgam of two desires: the ambition desire which serves to elevate the individual's personality and the erotic desire which seeks sexual gratification. The youth's egoistic and ambitious wishes are clearly expressed alongside the erotic wish, but the young woman's erotic wish predominates almost exclusively, her ambitions being absorbed by her internal eroticism.

A cleverly designed observation made on boys and girls supports belief that outward-thrusting penis and indrawn vagina influence male and female physical and mental attitudes. At a World Health symposium Rene Zazzo reported an experiment at a cinema when, unknown to the children, photographs were taken of them in ultra-violet light. During moments of excitement in the film the boys made movements stretching out towards the screen whereas the girls made movements back towards their own bodies, touching their faces and chests. This outward-inward difference becomes psychologically apparent as children grow older. The boy, more active sexually, thrusts towards the outer world more adventurously than the inward-looking girl.

Anatomical differences must certainly account for the boy extending his interests more rapidly from himself to the outside world and for the girl internalising her interests. External penis anxieties remain with the male throughout all his maturity; internal anxieties of motherhood remain for the woman.

Girls are in general more 'knowing' than boys about sex, but if they do have doubts and worries they are, because of their identification with their mother, more ready to turn to her for information and advice.

A girl's compulsive eroticism makes her fall in love again and again much more rapidly than a boy does. The girl, however, is not so aware of the sexual nature of desire as a boy is. This makes her more dangerously precocious than a boy. Not fully understanding the sexual urge behind her love she has no sexual fears and will flirt provocatively, with the result that a pubescent girl, sexually ignorant, often seduces a much older and sexually sophisticated male. Once a girl has experienced sex with a male, her own sexual excitability is aroused and many girls become gluttons for sexual experience, and often feel that having been deflowered they have nothing more to lose. The potential Lolitas of the world are legion.

A pubescent boy can sometimes show the same tendency to flirt and seduce. If he has the feminine attitude of future homosexuality or if the sexual ambivalence of male puberty is more intense than normal a young boy is more often the seducer than the victim of a pederast.

In 1968 a disease known as 'Samaunda' erupted among schoolgirls in the North Celebese islands. It was characterised by 'laughing, dancing and screaming wildly'. A medical report stated, apparently quite seriously and without a cynical tongue in cheek, that the disease 'could easily be cured by teenage boys'. Just how 'the cure' was to be administered the report before me does not explain.

For both male and female the first co-operative copulation

is the 'passing-out' parade. Whatever their age, young or old, they have now graduated. They feel that now they know all there is to know. Actually they have much more to learn, and the lessons will be learned in ecstasies and agonies. Even so they are right in their claim that sexually they have arrived: they are now indisputably man and woman.

6 The Act of Sex

A man makes love to a woman; a woman makes love to a man. To be sexually attracted to only one sexual shape, the shape of the opposite sex, is considered orthodox sexuality by human society. It can be argued that the homosexual is also orthodox in so far as he or she is attracted to only one sexual shape although the desired shape is one of the same sex.

But there are others, and many more of them than is commonly supposed, whose erotic desires are not restricted to only one sex, nor for that matter restricted always to human beings.

To begin with there are the bisexuals, the men and women who enjoy sex with both male and female bodies. Most male bisexuals are unmarried sexual adventurers, but some are what one could call 'heavily married', have sexually lively and fruitful wives and often also a girl or two on the side. Nevertheless they enjoy sexual sessions with other males, usually with known homosexuals but quite often with men of their own stamp, bachelors or husbands, or even, as often happens, with the wife's male relatives. Naturally there are intricate psychological causes for the so-called deviation of bisexuality, but I am most attracted to the simple explanation made to me by one of those husbands: 'A man can give me something my wife can't give me.' The statement, crude though it might be, is anatomically undeniable. Were he to be psychoanalysed it might well be discovered that having seen his wife enjoying ecstatic pleasure during coitus he wanted to experience equal enjoyment himself. In this connection a hint of the latent physical bisexuality in all males is indicated by Boehm's observation that in boys and neurotic men one of the most excitable zones of the body is the region 'which, in biological evolution, corresponds to the vaginal aperture and the parts immediately around it in women', whereas, he adds, 'the sensitiveness of the penis, and especially of the glands, develops only gradually'.

It is more difficult to determine the prevalence of bisexuality among women. If an apparently normal girl or wife or mother does have an erotic attachment for a female friend or neighbour the association is camouflaged by the fact that feminine friendships are expected to be more intimate and demonstrative than masculine friendships and consequently even overt displays of affection between women do not arouse suspicions of deviation.

Whether one deplores bisexuals as depraved or envies them for being able 'to enjoy both worlds' depends entirely on one's moral outlook. So far as this book is concerned moral opinion has neither importance nor relevance.

But one thing which must be avoided is to treat this so-called deviation, bisexuality, as an oddity, a sexual joke. Bisexuality is actually part of the biological and psychological inheritance of every man and woman. Biologically it is a remnant of the beginnings of animal life; psychologically it is woven indestructibly into our mental development. Two generations of psychologists have failed in their scientific duty by attaching too little importance to it and devoting far too little time to specialised explanation of it. In the same way that the most talented doctors and surgeons are naturally more attracted, by virtue of that same high talent, to the study and cure of dramatically evident and extreme diseases to the neglect of the common aches and pains and sniffles of our daily life, psychologists tend to confine their researches and therapies to the more colourful and grosser sexual upsets in which any psychiatric success can have the same flavour of spectacular triumph as the transplanting of a heart or the isolating of a cancer virus. But compared with the psychological subtleties of bisexuality, a condition far more common than is generally supposed, the case histories reported by Freud and Krafft-Ebing and all who have followed their methods, appear brutally crude. So far as I can see the key to some of the more extreme and exaggerated disorders of sexuality could be found in deeper but delicate inquiry into the subject of bisexuality, a sexual condition plainly observable in some men and women but also apparently latent in us all. Such an inquiry must not, however, have as its purpose the object of what we call 'curing' these people, when, by 'curing' we really mean tampering with and distorting their personalities into patterns considered orthodox and socially acceptable. The purpose of the investigation should be an attempt to reach a better understanding of them and integrating and accepting them into society as men and women who, as they so often are, are as beautiful and valuably precious to their community as any so-called 'normals'.

From my own general observation in several countries and

among several different social classes, as well as by acutely personal encounters, I am convinced that a great number of men and women at present arbitrarily classified as homosexual are not really homosexual at all. They are actually persons who, because they have not been informed about such things, are bewildered by tendencies emanating from evolutionary traces of bisexuality which are common to us all but which in those persons, by reason of family circumstances or social conditioning or their own more febrile sensitivity have become more apparent. In this context I must confine my comments to men. My contacts with female bisexuals have been too frail and transient to allow me to use them as examples. But in my professional and social life I have met many men, some whom I have learned to admire for their personal integrity and achievements, who have been looked upon by society as homosexuals, and as such have to endure the social odium which, despite changes in the law, is not yet dispersed. Two of these acquaintances, both admirable and talented men, suffered legal punishment, one at the hands of an ignorant magistrate, and the other at the hands of a legally learned but psychologically myopic judge.

Among these men is one who to my mind is a classic example of how latent bisexual tendencies can lead to a man acting in a manner which will earn him the reputation of being homosexual. Actually his sexual desires are basically heterosexual. He is attracted to female bodies and enjoys using them sexually. On the other hand he is so misogynistic that he detests the mentality of women; or, it would be more true to say, detests certain attitudes of mind which he considers shallow, fickle and unformed, and all of which he sees, wrongly, as exclusively feminine. With the result that although he desires women's bodies sexually and finds pleasure in intercourse with them, when seeking emotional attachments he is attracted to men because he sees in them what he judges as peculiarly masculine attributes; deeper and more reliable interchange of ideas, more creative thought, and a stronger capacity for honest and undemanding attachment. He can feel this so intensely that with certain males his association can take the form of that same platonic romantic sexually-unconsummated love which is quite common between men and women. On occasions the attraction he finds in a male friend can take him further, leading him to submitting to or initiating sexual love-making with a homosexual or other bisexual male whom he admires to the extent of suppressing his basic heterosexual preferences. His deviant sexual experiences, becoming known, have led him to be considered homosexual and on one occasion to a humiliating appearance in court.

Another pattern of sexuality commonly considered as non-orthodox is sexual fetishism. Actually there is some element of fetishism in all of us. Most lovers, for instance, can find erotic stimulation in the garments put on by a lover; or by the garments a lover takes off. Many men and women can experience, during a lover's absence, sensual pleasure at the sight of or the handling of clothes or other articles intimately associated with the lover. The holiday snapshot on the mantelpiece or in the wallet is not all that removed from a fetish.

Further along the road to more exaggerated fetishism proper we find such cases as that of the young plumber reported on in the *British Journal of Psychiatry* of 1965. This man obsessively collected all the pin-up pictures he could find and hid them throughout the house under furniture and carpets.

Some fetishists go further than that. Or perhaps it is more psychologically exact to say not that they have *gone* further but that their tendencies have *taken* them further. These are fetishists whose erotic desires have been transferred completely to objects. The sexual desires of fetishists who have reached that stage are no longer directed exclusively to bodies, male or female. They can obtain erotic gratification from the mere sight or feel of garments, not necessarily by dressing-up in them or dressing anyone else in them, but even at the sight of them hanging empty in a wardrobe or lying empty on a bed.

What strange forms fetishism may develop is instanced in the case of a talented artist who has told me that he is erotically stimulated to the point of erection whenever he catches sight of one of those old-fashioned ribbed radiators. In most cases the original cause for fetishist fixation on a certain object is buried in the subconscious of the fetishist, but this artist can remember the actual event which launched him on his bizarre central-heating sex life. He had a crush on a schoolmate, but the boy had refused to indulge in the mutual masturbation normal among boys of that age. Probably the lad was already too sexually sophisticated to be satisfied with such elementary childhood pleasures. Instead, he showed the young artist the trick of achieving ejaculation into a sponge wedged between the ribs of the dormitory radiator. The case of this artist showed how sexual initiation can often determine the sexual direction of mature sexuality. That was his first orgasm, and consequently radiators remain compellingly nostalgic sexually for him.

In the same line of country is the case of the American woman reported on by Dr. R. T. Morris of New York in the 1892 *Transactions of the American Association of Obstetricians*. The woman 'had never allowed herself to entertain sexual thoughts referring to men, but she masturbated every morning when standing before the mirror and rubbing herself against a key in the bureau-drawer. A man never excited her passions, but the sight of a key in any bureau-drawer aroused erotic desires.'

There are many other variations of sexual non-orthodoxy. There are the voyeurs, the exhibitionists, the masochists and the sadists. Much more rare are those whose sexual libido has been transferred from humans to animals. However, this summary list of a few sexual unorthodoxies is sufficient for our purpose here. It has been presented merely to remind readers that the range of human sexuality is vast and imaginative. Some people will find the practices mentioned odious. Others will smile at them. But before we condemn too fiercely or smile too broadly we should take stock of our own sexuality. If we are honest enough to face up to the truth, we have to confess that the forms of sexual gratification which we condemn or find ludicrous are usually the forms which we do not like and in which we do not indulge. One man's meat is another man's poison; so with one man's sex.

All the sexual deviations which have accreted around our human sexuality as a result of our peculiarly human febrile imagination, all those so-called perversions, should not be viewed as indication of human degeneracy but as expressions of the infinite intellectual inventiveness of which the sexual human being is capable. Most of us believe, and it is a belief held not only by those who consider themselves sexually orthodox but also by those who know they are sexually deviant, that there exists what might be called normal man-woman sexuality. We imagine it expressing itself in the ideal, almost chaste, way of a man and woman in love performing coitus in a simple manner without ingenious 'positions' or any extraneous physical embellishments. Actually such sexuality is rare. Most of us would probably find it eventually positively boring. In every sexual relationship there are times when we feel variations on the theme of coitus are necessary. Sometimes we may surprise ourselves with an unexpected spontaneous ability for devising such variations. We should not be all that surprised. We are human. We are imaginative creatures. In our sexual imagination may lurk some of the dangers of being human, but also many of its joys.

Even our so-called normal sex has been censured on occasions. Theologians and philosophers and other spoil-sports have railed against it. Nearly 2,300 years ago even so kindly a schoolmaster as Epicurus said flatly, 'Sexual intercourse has never done a man good and he is lucky if it has not harmed him'; though perhaps it was his chronic gout and dropsy which caused him to fear any form of physical exercise. Some two centuries later his successor, Lucretius, was a little more lenient. There was, he said, no harm in sexual intercourse provided it was divorced from passion.

Obsession with sex permeated the Judaic religion. Sex is the *leit motif* of the Old Testament. Love in its ideal sense hardly gets a look in but sex is hardly ever off the page. The Bible's most beautiful 'love poem', the *Song of Solomon*, is an ecstatic inventory of physical enchantments. Any mind or wit or intellectual charm which the beloved might have had is not so much as hinted at. The pious Jew was exhorted to overcome the sins of the flesh. But those sins were sins of incest and adultery and sodomy: it was no sin, in fact it was a Jew's stern duty, to copulate freely, to be fruitful and multiply. However, of the few love stories in the Bible the most moving is the story of David's affair with Jonathan. It was not until he had acquired three wives that David learned the 'love of women'. After that he found five more. But it does seem that David considered all eight wives as merely instruments for adding to the population: his emotional love was still directed to beautiful young men.

Christianity, smelted in the same cultural crucible as Judaism, inherited Judaic sex phobias and Judaic fears of the sexual organs and the sexual act. It also accepted that Judaic belief that Jehovah had created the earth and 'desired it to be filled with living beings'. From that it is only a short step to condemning the enjoyment of sexual intercourse without conception and banning the pill.

The Christian Church had to accept that sexual intercourse was necessary for God's purpose, but could not free itself from the feeling that the operation was basically sinful: anything so enjoyable must be. One could be granted indulgence for it only if one produced a child. Christian theologians even suspected the virtue of women who had been raped. The victims could be forgiven only if they could swear or prove that they had not enjoyed the experience: if they had enjoyed it, they were sinful.

Paradoxically there is, as Doctor Norman Haire remarks, a certain logic in the Christian church's orthodoxy. 'Once we admit that sexual intercourse is justifiable as an end in itself —merely for the production of sexual pleasure and with the intention that it shall not result in reproduction—it becomes difficult or impossible to draw ethical distinctions between one sort of sexual intercourse and another ... The Roman Catholic Church has realised this clearly, and has therefore maintained a quite uncompromising attitude, regarding sexual intercourse between husband and wife with the use of a contraceptive, as just as "unnatural" and "sinful" as masturbation, sodomy, incest, bestiality, etc. While I do not agree with the Roman Catholic attitude, it does seem to be a logical one.'

When the Christian churches and their commercial and political allies carried to the far corners of the expanding world their message of enlightenment and built their missions and schools and hospitals, they took with them also their Biblical concept of the original sin of sex, often with traumatic results to the inhabitants of the invaded Edens. Guyon speculates, for instance, that the importation of the Judaic-Christian theory of sin to the Polynesian people might have caused the deadly neuroses 'which have decimated these races'.

But any religious and political creed which needs to impose authority is forced to consider as suspect what it recognises as the essentially subversive element in sex. After all the sex act is a so secret and so personal affair. Indeed in our increasingly authoritarian era it is about the only true liberty left to the individual; and those scientists who are now making tentative steps towards genetical control of birth, even though they might be fabricating their mysteries of sperm-banks and breeding-chambers out of honourable and genuine hope of ensuring a healthier genetic future, can be seen as the first sappers undermining the wall which protects humanity's last exquisitely personal freedom.

Authoritarian abhorrence of sexual freedom is shown in the way in which Communist states, after an initial saturnalia during their revolutionary beginnings, become sexually buttoned-up. In Soviet Russia, for example, everything which we in our as yet free societies now regard as pathetically or amusingly 'Victorian' is expressed in an increasingly puritanical attitude to sex. The Soviet has not yet got around to covering up the legs of its pianos, but its earnest propagation of the idea that sport and other physical activities are 'effective safety valves' for pent-up libido cannot fail to remind us of Arnold of Rugby and cold baths. Characteristically the theories of Freud are anathema to Communist moralists and are condemned in Russia as 'squalid and degrading'. Naturally Communists dare not tolerate the teaching of a man who declared, 'We can demonstrate with ease that what the world calls its code of morals demands more sacrifices than it is worth, and that its behaviour is neither dictated by honesty nor instructed by wisdom.'

As medical science widened its scope and purged clinics and laboratories of superstition, doctors, particularly those confronted daily with the ills and upsets caused by sex fears and sex ignorance, opposed the repressive tendencies of church and state. But in their revolutionary fervour they also went too far. Their physical and anatomical explorations encouraged them to argue that the sex act was a biological need, and this theory resulted in some of them actually declaring that sexual abstinence in a man could result in an 'over-loading of spermatozoa'. This, they said, stimulated the nerve impulses to sexual urges, and, they warned that, unless the damned up flood could be relieved by ejaculation, it would become embarrassing and painful. Many people still have this misconception, although medical men discarded the idea half-a-century ago, as is shown by a candid question asked in a questionnaire circulated among members of the Y.M.C.A. in the United States in 1915. 'Has anyone ever tried to give you the mistaken idea that sex intercourse is necessary for the heath of the young male?'

Research into the psycho-somatic structure of the human has finally dispelled the 'biological necessity' myth. Modern evidence, says Professor F. A. Beach, shows that our sexual appetites are formed by our experiences, actual or vicarious, and are more mental than physical. The adolescent boy's sexual urges, for instance, are stimulated not so much by his newly acquired reproductive glands as from psychological stimuli.

In other words sex in human beings is a mentally cultivated habit. It is a very pleasant habit, but no more essential to us than any other acquired human tastes. As with other tastes, once we have cultivated it we come back for more. It is indeed a case of the appetite growing by what it feeds on. We can become gourmets, as choosy as devotees of wine in our demands for the best vintages and appropriate room temperature, or gourmands, satisfying our greed to the point of satiation.

This modern opinion that erotic urges arise more from socio-cultural conditioning than from biological need is in accord with Freud's insistence on the important role of sexual factors in individual and social psychology. He argued convincingly that sexual emotions and desires play an important and continuous role in the individual mind, even in the case of children. We censor our sexual desires, driving all ideas associated with them into the subconscious, because of the anti-sexual bias imposed on the growing mind by our social system. Such repressions can be responsible for symptoms revealing the presence of neuroses, and, said Freud, we become neurotic when we are prevented from satisfying our libido. When for any reason, while we are sleeping or not in conscious control of our thoughts, the censorship is relaxed and our sexual repressions reveal themselves in more or less coherent dreams or deliriums and anxieties.

Hirschfeld, when he spoke in Berlin on the historic occasion of the first congress of the World League for Sexual Reform, emphasised the importance of sexual fulfilment. 'The sexual needs of the majority of human beings have just as imperative a demand for occasional fulfilment as the needs for food or sleep. The mind and will may inhibit, excite or considerably repress sexual needs as they do other needs. But such repression is not possible for any length of time without serious bodily and mental results. As in all bodily and mental functions, so here, the best way of living is to avoid either starvation or surfeit and to keep the *via media* between a necessary medium (of activity and experience) and a maximum which shall not prove intolerable to the powers and the balance of the personality. The significance of sexual love is not limited to its biological result of reproduction. Adequate sexual fulfilment is one of the conditions of a good life, both in external efficiency and mental health and poise.'

A similar attitude permeated the cogitations of a working party set up by Lord Goodman, chairman of Britain's Arts Council, to review the inept clumsy and out-moded Obscene Publications Acts of 1959 and 1964. The working party came to these concusions: The so-called permissive society may have its casualties, but the repressive society almost certainly has a great deal more. Repressed sexuality can be toxic both to the individual and to society. Repression can deprave and corrupt. And the working party derided the illusion common among moralists today that fifty years ago sources of titillation were lacking. 'Indeed they were probably more plentiful, though scarcely recognisable as such today. The first line of chorus girls to appear bare-legged was a natural aphrodisiac spectacle, and ceased to be so within a year. Custom and acceptance are the great anti-aphrodisiacs. Nothing could be more antiseptic sexually than a nudist colony. There the almost essential peep-show has been eliminated, with predictable results.'

However, true ascetics, individuals who can forgo sex without suffering mental torments, are rare. For although sex is not a biological necessity it does seem to be a psychological necessity. So, not the pressure of our glands but the pressure of our emotional desires forces us to seek sexual gratification and express ourselves sexually. Let us see how men and women engage in that human activity; first how they learn the technique, and then how they use it.

1 LEARNING HOW TO MAKE LOVE

Nearly five hundred years ago King James IV of Scotland initiated an experiment with two babies, a boy and a girl. He placed them in charge of a dumb nurse on the rocky island of Inchkeith in the Firth of Forth. His ambition was to find out what language children would develop if they grew up without hearing human speech. Unfortunately the result of the experiment has not been recorded, though a commentator of a later period (obviously a pious Bible-reading Scot) claimed that when the children grew up 'they spak very guid Ebrew'. A psychiatrist with whom I discussed this experiment expressed the opinion that almost certainly the children would grow up as idiots because they lacked human communication. Might that be why the result of the experiment was not recorded at the Scottish court?

Ever since I read about the experiment and tried, unavailingly, to discover more facts about it, another problem has teased me. I have wondered less about the speech development of two isolated children than about their sexual development. If there was no society to guide them and set sexual examples, would they, when they became sexually mature as male and female, become distinctively masculine and feminine in their behaviour? Would they appreciate their sexual difference and be erotically stimulated by it and eventually, in their Eden, consummate an Adam and Eve union?

The answer is undoubtedly yes. But with a reservation. Their sexuality would be untutored and primitive. Their courtship would be an affair of grabbings and grunts and instinctual fumblings ending in a brutish copulation. For their masculine and feminine attitudes would lack that mingling of sexual display and sexual restraint and all other imaginings and curiosities and mental flavourings which children absorb as they grow to puberty and maturity in society.

A distinguished psychologist, writing very carelessly, has remarked that 'human beings have no need to be taught how to use their sexual organs'. As a popular radio personality of years ago might have said in such a context. 'It all depends on what one means by "*taught*".' True enough we humans do possess many organs which we never need to be taught how to use. For example we do not need to be taught how to use our hearts for circulating our blood, nor how to use our lungs for oxygenating the blood and for breathing. The psychologist's careless statement can really be applied only to such organs as heart and lungs and all other automatically functioning organs such as liver and kidneys and sphincter muscles and suchlike. Our sexual organs do not come into that category at all. Like our eyes and ears they do need intellectual control. We do not need to be taught how to see or hear, but we do need to be taught how to look and listen. Similarly our sexual organs need educating. Although they are capable of operating instinctually, their operation needs mental direction. Admittedly they do have the characteristic, like eyes and ears, of appearing to do their required job without any thought or skill on our part. Instinctual manipulation and friction can stimulate them even to the point of giving us the sensations of orgasm, and on occasions they can even appear to express what they want before our mental processes have quite caught up with their physical desire: the involuntary erection of the penis is as good an example as any of that. So far, but only so far, we could agree that human beings have no need to be *taught* how to use their sexual organs. That is, there is no need to teach us how to use them in an animal way. But the human is not an animal. In the same way that even in the most primitive society the human has to be *taught*, by precept or by social example, how to look with his eyes and listen with his ears and then intelligently evaluate sights and sounds, so must he learn to use his sexual organs emotionally and intellectually in accordance with the complexities of human sexuality, and also legally in accordance with the customs and proscriptions of society. If we humans had been able to keep our sexual organs operating at the 'no need to be taught' level of our heart and lungs, we would certainly have avoided a lot of our human psychological upsets, but the upsets human society would have suffered would have had effects on human social developments far worse than individual psychological upsets.

Nor is one initiatory lesson in using our sexual organs sufficient. In one lesson we can be taught how to keep afloat in water: we need many more lessons to learn how to swim with speed or grace of style. It is the same with sex. As human society has become increasingly complex and as its laws and religions and its terms of social conduct have enforced their discipline we have had to drill our mental desires, passionate and romantic and spiritual desires, to accord with the conventions of our era and and our race. Similarly we have had to drill our sexual organs to perform their functions only at times or in circumstances when genital performances are considered decent or practicable or acceptable.

We are still learning. We can leave our heart and lungs etcetera to get along with their primitive functions, but we still, whether we like it or not, need to be taught how to use our sexual organs. We are not, of course, referring to the kind of tuition offered in those earnest manuals which instruct men and women how to use their sexual parts in the most attractive and agile ways and thus extract most joy from copulation, fruitful or unfruitful as desired. We are referring to the necessity of being taught, or conditioned, to use our sexual organs as part of our whole human thinking being.

It is not the fashion in civilised society to teach boys and girls how to copulate. In primitive less-inhibited societies sexual initiation rites often have, in addition to superstitious and religious significance, some element of practical information which will guide the pubescent young along the sometimes difficult steps to sexual maturity. Our society, however, considers initiation rites uncivilised. We leave it to the youngsters to fabricate their own: on the campus or in factory basements or at teenage petting parties. But those are sporadic outbursts, neither engineered nor condoned by society, and although nowadays there is a great deal of instruction on sex morals there is still no practical sex tuition. Henry suggests that the 'candid teaching and wider knowledge of sex, even to the extent of some physical experimentation and/or assistance in youth, is necessary not only to the well-being of the individual, but the whole of society'.

The mating of man and woman means much more, physically and psychologically, than a flurry of feathers in a farmyard, far more than a momentary orgasmic spurt of semen from penis to vagina. The mating of humans involves not only the mutual operation of sexual organs but also the mutual fusing of the sensitive and exquisitely fashioned psyches of man and woman. We can happily and successfully achieve that physical and psychological fusion only when we have reached sexual maturity in mind as well as in body, and to reach such maturity each of us has to go through the lengthy and often mentally agonizing apprenticeship of puberty. Perhaps the strangest indictment of indifference to human needs which can be levelled against modern society is not its indifference to hunger and terror and aggression but its failure to enlighten its young on the fundamentals of sexuality.

A reforming step could be that of freeing the sex act from the 'forbidden fruit' proscriptions which, like barbed wire around an orchard, make it so challengingly attractive to the young. An even more progressive reform would be to emphasise that coitus is not necessarily an act of love, not at all essential to proving one's dedication to the love-object. Robbed of that glory premarital coitus would be less tempting, or, if it happened, less traumatic.

But as Krich remarks, 'much in sex remains "unique and unexplainable" even after taxonomic analysis. *After we know what we do, we still need to know WHY.*' It is useful for anyone learning to drive a car to know why certain movements have to be made, and, in fact, the licensing authorities in some countries insist that drivers must prove they possess such knowledge. The damage which can be done by uneducated sex is usually more socially destructive than that inflicted by an untrained motorist.

For centuries the young have been taught how to read and write, how to learn languages and algebra and science and play pianos, even how to play games and how to eat and be good-mannered, but only now are we coming round to the realisation that a human also needs some guidance on how to perform the function which is at the very root of our being and is in fact responsible in the first place for us being here at all. Probably we are still a long way from the stage of recruiting men and women experts qualified by wisdom and experience to demonstrate the sexual act and initiate us into the proper performance of it in the same way in which, for instance, a sergeant teaches a recruit how to oil his rifle and fire it.

Even the mild attempts now being made to educate the young are facing a backlash of outraged public opinion, particularly in America where the American Education Lobby recently launched a nation-wide campaign against sex-education, claiming that it would lead to the destruction of traditional American moral values. In some States, including Maryland and New York, sex education was already compulsory in public schools, but in the majority of States there was organised opposition to existing programmes. In Louisiana, for instance, there was a complete moratorium on sex education.

Boys have traditionally enjoyed some advantages over girls in sexual education. In some societies it still is an accepted practice for fathers who can afford the expense to send their sons to some amiable matron. This serves a dual purpose: the boy gratifies the insistent sexual urges that have preoccupied him, and he also learns valuable lessons in sexual performance. Apparently such relieving of adolescent sexual tensions can sometimes have therapeutic effect, for Stekel tells of a schoolboy who was a miserable and preoccupied dullard until the age of fourteen; then he began visiting prostitutes and developed into a brilliant student, among the best in his class.

Even the most liberally enlightened parents of our society would hesitate to extend sexual education to their daughters. It is taken for granted that girls will learn all that is necessary when they become the brides of young men coming home from their 'finishing schools'. Primitive peoples are wiser in a more 'down to earth' manner. One example will suffice. One of the first European explorers into central Africa, H. Crawford Angus, described how girls of the Chensamwali tribe were initiated into sexual intercourse. At the harvest festival a boy and girl were allowed to 'keep house' and attempt to act the parts of man and woman. But if, during this process, the girl's vagina had not become sufficiently enlarged for normal sexual intercourse a horn or a corn-cob was used to stretch it to the desired size. In a later ceremony, one barred to the menfolk, the girl was instructed in the movements she must make to enhance the pleasure of sexual intercourse for herself and her mate. Our physiologists and psychologists have only recently come round to realising that many cases of frigidity and even of supposed sterility of male and female are the result of the lack of that very primitive knowledge of really enjoying the affair to the full. Buttock-squirming thigh-pressing lessons given to maidens in primitive tribes throughout the world are probably the main reason for the apparent absence of sexually frustrated wives and husbands in such communities.

Angus tells how, 'the girl is then stripped and made to go through the mimic performance of sexual intercourse, and if the movements are not enacted properly, as is often the case when the girl is timid and bashful, one of the older women will take her place and show her how she is to perform.'

The nearest our children get to demonstrative sexual education is in the seats of a cinema where the sexual act is suggested in an ambience of deceptive and dangerous romanticism, chocolate wrappings and deodorants.

Parents in our western society are usually appalled at any idea of helping their sons and daughters towards sexual initiation. Every time the boy or girl stays out late, every time father or mother surprises a young couple in a darkened room, they imagine 'the worst'. Yet even then stop short of putting their fears into words. They 'hope for the best' and leave their young to the mercy of the sexual accidents which happen when they begin to mingle socially with others and rub up, literally as well as metaphorically, against their fellows. Inevitably one of those fellows will become a sexual instructor, and it is only a matter of luck whether or not the teacher is desirable and the instruction healthy. We leave it to youths and maidens to 'find their own feet'. Well, they might do that very thing: there are also foot-fetishists.

Our prudish attitude to sex puts our young at hazard, for our fear of being frank about bodily sex and the sex act prevents us from coming out into the open and fighting the insidious sexual corruption of our children. In mentioning sexual corruption of children I am not referring to anything so trivial as fiddling with their genitals. The corruption children suffer nowadays is the tampering with their minds. Taking advantage of parental inhibitions commerce by using sex as an advertising slogan is blatantly seducing youth. This is worse than prostitution. At least prostitution does not necessarily deny the natural sexuality of the human in the way that the investing of every product from sports cars to cigarettes with meretricious sex imagery debases sexuality. In this 'sell by sex' climate sex is no longer a proud and lovely affair of manhood and womanhood: it is merely the use of the furniture of male and female bodies for sales appeal, and results in what Margaret Mead pungently describes as 'a series of pin-up girls whose breasts, tailored for love, are explicitly *not* meant for the love and nourishment of their children'. A female nude draped over a limousine at a motor show is far more dishonest and psychologically unhealthy than those objects a chemist keeps discreetly under his counter. All the education our children receive on the truths and beauties of art and science is in danger of being submerged in that 'sell by sex' market in which they are coaxed into believing that mere sexuality means 'love' when it would certainly be more honest and undoubtedly more healthy for them to realise that what the marketeers are offering is only sensual fun.

Primitive peoples, despite their wise approach to the sex act, are surprisingly ignorant about the procreative consequences of it. Some primitives cannot understand that the part the man plays with penis and ejaculation has any connection at all with the procreation of children. Some think that babies are born as a result of ancestral spirits which hover around rocks and trees and enter the bodies of women to be reincarnated as children. Some, a little more advanced, believe that a man must penetrate a woman with his penis and rupture her hymen. But not to give her a baby; only to make an opening through which the fecundating spirits can enter. Rossel Islanders, one step more advanced, believed that it was the father who laid the egg in the mother.

Haire reports that 'Even advanced primitive tribes do not clearly link the two phenomena. The natives of British New Guinea believe that conception takes place through the breasts and that later the child moves down into the abdomen; the Australian aborigines believe that the fecundating spirit "Ratapa" introduces itself into the woman's body and that impregnation follows the eating of certain fruits; the Queenslanders imagine that the children are inserted ready-made into the mother's entrails; the Eskimos believe that children are of supernatural origin and that the man's ejaculation is only intended to feed the foetus.'

It is easy enough to understand children entertaining unformed and imaginative ideas of how a baby comes into being. In the Kreitler inquiry in Israel 44 per cent of the Oriental boys believed that the father's part in creating the baby had been performed by such masculine habits as reading the newspaper, going for a walk, or 'beating the mother'. Many western children dream up comparable ideas. They think the baby is the result of something which Mummy has eaten, or that the doctor, with or without daddy's help, has performed a babyplanting operation. But we find it harder to believe that adults, however primitive, could believe similar fictions. Surely, we ask, when a man and woman copulate and a baby appears, they must put two and two together? But putting two and two together is as difficult to the savage mind as it is to a child's mind, especially when the sum of the two and two emerges only nine months after the event of copulation. The visible process of birth makes the relationship between *mother* and child obvious to the primitive mind, but the causative relationship of the *father* is not always understood.

Among primitives, however, sexual ignorance is not likely to lead to personal worries and social disaster. But in civilised society any ignorance of sexuality, even mere doubts, can be held as largely responsible for many sexual malformations among men and women.

'Of all the obstacles standing in the way of sexual harmony by far the commonest is ignorance,' says Kenneth Walker. 'This word is used in its widest sense, to include not only the absence of knowledge, but also the existence of wrong ideas. It is, indeed, the latter type of ignorance that is at the root of most sexual difficulties, and it is better to approach marriage completely ignorant of all that it means than with wrong ideas incubated by faulty upbringing. There is a deep-seated aversion on the part of many people to the idea that by knowledge and art, sexual union can be converted from a crude physical experience into an act which expresses to the full the strong emotional ties that bind two people together.'

We persist in a complacent belief that the young will follow their sexual instincts and blunder on the truth. Blunder they certainly can, often disastrously. 'Love will find a way', is a common enough expression, but what we are really thinking behind the words is 'Sex will find a way'. As indeed it will.

For animals, instinctual blundering is all that is necessary, but with humans the difference between the sexuality of male and female is more delicately and dangerously complicated than the mere triviality of a difference in genitals. There are far more buttons to undo.

2 HYMEN AND VIRGINITY

Once upon a time boys began having sexual intercourse before their genitals were fully developed. In order to clasp these immature penises firmly the female had to make the entry of her vagina smaller, so she developed that 'membranous fold which partially or wholly occludes the external orifice of the vagina'. We call it the hymen.

That engaging theory has been seriously advanced to account for the presence of the vaginal obstruction. The argument apparently suggests that the hymen was designed solely for the increase of male pleasure. Even if there were a shred of fact, evolutionary or anatomical, in the theory, even if the hymen had anything at all to do with those small penises, the theory is still awry. It puts the cart before the horse.

Nature's primary concern is to encourage the procreation of a species. If small penises did have anything to do with the matter at all, then the hymen's primary function would be to make sure the vaginal grip would be sufficiently firmly enfolding as to excite the small penis and inflame it to the necessary ejaculation of semen. If such extra grip gave extra pleasure to the precocious boys, then it could be accepted as a bonus bestowed by Nature on youngsters who had performed a man's job so early in life.

It is, however, inconceivable that Nature was being so accommodating. The hymen, nevertheless, is something of a mystery: an even more peculiarly human attribute than woman's menstruation. In certain female mammals there can be found something which zoologists can just describe as analogous to the female human hymen, but actually the hymen is a distinctively human characteristic, non-existent even in anthropoid apes.

Hymens vary much in shape. In the majority of women the hymen, when stretched, forms a ring, but sometimes a half-moon shape. Occasionally it is cribriform (perforated like a sieve), or its free margin forms a membranous fringe. Sometimes there may be no hymen at all; sometimes it can form a complete septum across the lower end of the vagina. The normal hymen partially blocks the entrance to the vagina and makes the opening smaller than the diameter of the male penis. The penis, to achieve its desired penetration, must 'pierce the veil', must tear the obstruction. In a vagina, after the hymen has been ruptured, are found small rounded elevations known as the *carunculae hymenales*. These, like stumps of walls of a ravaged castle, are the remains of a virgin's maidenhead.

The whole story of the rupturing of a girl's hymen on her first experience of coitus and the accompanying spasm of pain and exuding of blood is like a parable illustrating the popular idea of the thrusting dominating male's sexual initiation of the submissive pliant female. The bloody event must have played its part in forming or encouraging sexual masochism in women. It represents symbolically that actual or imagined seduction integral to 'the bedroom scene': frail and innocent virgin at the mercy of man the violator, man the ravager.

Helene Deutsch characteristically argues that 'A painful bodily injury—the breaking of the hymen and the forcible stretching and enlargement of the vagina by the penis—are the prelude to woman's first complete sexual enjoyment.' She points out that although surgical defloration is possible, 'Whenever I have had opportunity of studying the woman's subsequent (conscious or unconscious) reactions to artificial defloration, I have found that she felt a contempt, hard to overcome, for the man who lacked the courage to violate the taboo. This contempt seemed to me more dangerous for the marriage and love relations than the possible reaction of anger and revenge to the conjugal rape. The husband, while possibly achieving protection against his wife's aggressive reactions, failed to gratify her deeply feminine need to be overpowered.'

Many of the words we use in relation to ceremonial and solemn mysteries can be illustrated by the hymen. Veil, mantle, curtain, screen, shroud. Tear any one of them apart and a secret is revealed, a sanctity violated. Thus the hymen has become integral to our concept of a state which is near to sacred. Just as the word 'virgin' also represents to us untouched unsullied unexplored and untilled territories or thoughts or materials, virginity has assumed also an aura of sanctity. The Virgin's 'immaculate conception' is one of the most treasured legends of all time. Trystan, the perfect Knight, and Ysault lying side by side with a sword between them represent an ideal of noble chastity.

We all use phrases such as 'taking' a girl's virginity, 'breaking' her maidenhead, 'deflowering' her. These phrases have a flavour of sacrificial ceremonial. In ancient times, and even today among primitive peoples, the rupture of the hymen was a ceremonial, religious, tribal or conjugal.

We put the hymen to practical use socially and conjugally, employing it as a kind of litmus-paper test of virginity. Bloody evidence of the ruptured hymen has always been considered as proof that the man has conquered virgin property. Like the cellophane wrapping on a candy bar or the seal on a letter it shows he has received goods 'untouched by hand' or knowledge unknown to others. Man's virgin bride thus becomes an individual possession, and consequently enhances his status as a select and unique individual.

On the other hand women are happier, though they might think otherwise, with a man who is not a virgin. Freud's famous 'South Russian' claimed that 'every woman in turn would like to be the first to initiate her young partner', but Freud himself admits that 'Complete abstinence during youth is not the best preparation for marriage in a young man. Women divine this and prefer those of their wooers who have already proved themselves to be men with other women.' Many young girls recognise this instinctively, surrendering themselves to older men and finding in their talented embraces greater pleasure than they can in the fumblings of youths of their own age group.

Women have been ingenious enough to perfect methods of simulating virginity after they have lost it. Women in one province of France are reported to have done this by concealing a fish bladder filled with pigeon's blood in their vagina. As the stain on the sheet was the same colour the deceit could have been revealed only by a forensic scientist. Earlier in history we find Nero's wife Poppaea advising: 'In order to pass for a virgin, bathe your genitals with a solution of benzoin, which has a milky appearance; dry them with a linen cloth and powder with ground starch.'

Nowadays it is even simpler. The 'virginity' of mutilated maidenheads can be restored by plastic surgery. No statistics are available, but a few months ago a consultant gynaecologist in Britain was asked by a 20-year-old girl who was about to be married, 'Please make me a virgin again.' He took legal advice and was assured that the necessary plastic surgery would not be a breach of the law, though the operation would have to be done privately: it could not be performed under the National Health Service.

The earliest age of lost virginity seriously recorded, except in cases of infant rape, is confessed by the notorious Marquise de Brinvilliers who claims she was deflowered at the age of seven.

Fluegel is very harsh on the hymen-virginity subject. He considers a woman has no more right to boast about her intact hymen and her proved chastity than she would have to boast about never having used her eyes or her ears. In other words, he is saying that being blind or deaf to sex is as bad as being blind or deaf to the sights and sounds of life.

'The most charitable thing we can say about chastity,' he says, 'is that it is useless: and that, if we look at the matter closely, those who lead chaste lives appear to be the victims of an illusion. Chastity . . . merits neither admiration, praise nor criticism. There are people who have a large appetite, others who have a moderate one, still others who have no appetite at all; it is a strictly personal affair. To turn it into a question of right or wrong . . . is surely a most lamentable outcome of false reasoning.'

Nevertheless the presence of an unruptured hymen is not a fool-proof guarantee that its possessor is a virgin. Pregnant women have been found to have intact hymens. Semen although emitted only at the entrance of the vagina has found its tail-flaying vigorous way to its desired destination, or the hymen might have allowed penetration by extending without rupturing. The criminologist Wachholtz is quoted by Haire to have reported finding 70 unruptured hymens in 102 cases of raped women.

Yet modern psychologists endow the hymen with almost as much psychological importance as the physical importance primitives attached to it. They see it as a protective device which shields the vagina from precocious sexual assault until a female has reached that stage of physical and emotional development when she is sufficiently mature, anatomically and mentally, to perform sexual intercourse and bear and nurse children.

In some societies kings or priests performed the act. The hymenal blood was considered, probably as menstrual blood was, as unclean or poisonous, but kings and priests were immune from such hazards and could therefore perform the initial penetration and protect the intended bridegroom from danger; an antique version of the *droit de seigneur*.

Crawley reports a comparable ritual among tribes in Central Australia. The ceremony was brutally practical, but was obviously considered solemnly sacred by all the participants. The bride's hymen was first artificially ruptured, sometimes by her sister, and then the men assisting at the ceremony penetrated her in turn according to some rota dictated by their status or relationship. This is somewhat akin to the 'gang rape' resorted to in certain tribes supposedly to make a woman submit to man's authority but almost certainly resulting in her becoming more easily 'available' for sexual intercourse. Among tribes of the Celebes the defloration was performed by the father. Among the Todas, where 'a man of strong physique' did it before puberty, a man might refuse to marry a girl if the ceremony had not been performed at the proper time. Greenlanders, Crawley says, paid an Angekok, a priest, to have connection with their wives in the belief that the child of a holy man was bound to be better than others.

In our society we supposedly leave the rupturing to be performed more or less haphazardly in the alien atmosphere of the honeymoon hotel, but in cases where the hymen resists penetration it can be dilated surgically, and Ploss remarks, 'If the doctor can get some idea of the thickness of the husband's erect penis, it will guide him to deciding to what extent he should dilate.'

Ceremonial defloration might appear savage and immodest, but the fact that it is a ceremony does invest it with a certain dignity and purpose, and consequently probably robs the process of those agonising shames and shynesses which so often make a western bride's first night with her husband, and sometimes all her subsequent nights, a painful and unsatisfying experience, physically and psychologically. The bridegroom, if not too full of wedding alcohol or, even more inhibiting, the fear that he might not perform his male function adequately, finishes his initiation of his bride before she has got anywhere near her climax. He turns away to sleep; she lies awake asking, 'Is that all it is?'

3 THE DIFFERENT ORGASM

'Orgasms for Women!' The campaign has become as strident as 'Votes for Women!' ever was. Having established their right to 'equal pay for an equal job' women are now demanding equality of reward for the job performed between the sheets. Among women in the U.S.A. the conviction that they are being deprived of full sexual pleasure has become a fashionable health obsession second only to worries about over-weight and deficient bosoms. The demand gets so much sympathetic publicity and so much informed support from marriage-guidance sexologists that vigorous and impatient males are now becoming afflicted with acute feelings of guilt when their hasty ecstasy reaches the winning post while their female mates are still under starter's orders.

But there is a dilemma. It does seem that those women who are clever enough and educated enough and intellectually independent enough to know what they are missing are the very women who are least likely to get it. The orgasm ratio seems to be: the higher the education the lower the orgasm. At least so it appears from the Kinsey Report which claims that whereas nearly 100 per cent of uneducated Negro women had experienced orgasm in sexual intercourse only some 80 per cent of high school graduates could say the same. Higher up the scholarly scale, among the women college graduates, 50 to 80 per cent had never experienced orgasm. Statistics like these might be quoted to support Nietzsche's wild statement that 'when a woman has scholarly inclinations there is generally something wrong with her sexual nature'. No rational person would go so far as that, but Lundberg and Farnham do argue that lack of orgasm might be the punishment women suffer for avoiding their natural feminine duties. No children, no nursing, no cooking and dishwashing, no looking after their menfolk: therefore no orgasm. Lundberg and Farnham also found that the percentage of women described as 'frigid' tended to be higher among the more educated and ego-striving career women.

The man is usually blamed. Selfishly pursuing his own pleasure, he races towards it without bothering to carry the more slowly progressing woman with him. Having got what he was after, he is usually in no condition physically and may have little inclination mentally to go back along the road and help her.

Ejaculatio praecox it not all that uncommon among males. It is medically described as 'ejaculation of the semen immediately after the beginning of the sexual act', though I know one young man who ejaculated at the mere sight of his partner unscrewing the cap of a tube of lubricant. He has got over that. Eager youths usually do. Young males, sometimes too ardent or sometimes preoccupied about their masculine ability, often experience ejaculatio praecox during early attempts at sexual intercourse. When copulation becomes less of an exciting novelty they overcome the tendency. Despite Stekel's statement 'I have never seen a couple who were really in love complain of ejaculatio praecox' the truth is that man, by his sexual nature and construction, is 'quicker on the draw' than woman. No equivalent to ejaculatio praecox is found in women.

An observation in a recent BBC television programme that a male has an 'erection usually a little faster than the female lubricates' fairly sums up the different m.p.h. of man and woman in coitus. According to Kinsey three-quarters of the average male population reach orgasm within two minutes. At detumescence man has 'had it': he is satisfied. Woman, often by then not even sexually aroused, is left, in every sense of the word, flat.

Dunlap argues that in sexual intercourse the average woman often attains neither the mental pride nor physical satisfaction attained by the man. He, by primitive instinct and ancient tradition, regards himself as the active partner in matters of love and thinks that his own pleasure is legitimately the prime motive for sexual activity. The average wife 'falls into the complementary position, regards herself as the passive partner and her pleasure as negligible, if not indeed as a thing to be rather ashamed of should she by chance experience it'.

Hammond doubts whether in as little as ten per cent of the instances of intercourse women experience the slightest pleasurable sensation from first to last. Walker compares the difference between the rapid ejaculation of man 'occurring within a few minutes of the beginning of active coitus' and the tardy arrival of woman's orgasm which is linked with 'less well understood genital phenomena'. He says that a woman might experience it only once or twice in the whole of her married life. In fact, he says, even some mothers of large families have never known it.

Until nearly 300 years ago doctors went along with the theory advanced by the ancients that man got more intense pleasure from coitus than women but that the pleasure of women lasted longer. It is just that 'lasting longer', the sexual pleasure Freud described as Nature's 'premium' for doing her work, which women are now demanding.

Public discussion of the subject is a striking and not unhealthy contrast to the prudish avoidance of it in the past. In the Middle Ages, when Christian dogma had made people conscious of the 'original sin' in sexual intercourse, the Church was at least charitable enough to say that if the woman did not experience orgasm her sin was thereby somewhat lessened. But right into the nineteenth century it was commonly accepted that it was hardly proper for women to enjoy the sexual act, and defenders of women described suggestions that they had sexual feelings as 'a vile aspersion'. Even feminine lubrication was suspect. *Rees's Cyclopedia* said 'that a mucous fluid is sometimes found in coition from the internal organs and vagina is undoubted; but this only happens in lascivious women, or such as live luxuriously'.

The modern approach is welcome, and I take advantage here, in dealing with the so intimately feminine subject of woman's orgasm, to quote *in extenso* the admirably written non-clinical description of the female orgasm by Ruth Martin in *Woman's Own*. I have not seen it better described in a pile of impressive volumes written by immensely authoritative sexologists. Ruth Martin says that in basic terms the physical satisfaction of sexual intercourse is the orgasm. 'But I believe many women have only a hazy idea of what the word orgasm actually means. During intercourse, a sexually-aroused woman experiences a gradual build-up of sensation in the vagina (the front passage), the clitoris (the peak of sensitive tissue at the front of the vulva, which is the part of the sex organs on the surface of the body), and the lower part of the abdomen.

'These sensations are enjoyable, and go on increasing in intensity until they reach a climax of feeling. The muscles of the vaginal wall start to rhythmically contract and relax, and the pleasurable sensations spread to encompass almost the entire body, making the heart beat faster and breathing become more rapid.

'This uprush of feeling is followed by a sense of great peace and relaxation, and an overwhelming desire to sleep, which is why so often people prefer to make love in bed, at night, so that sleep can follow naturally, and why "sleeping together" is so commonly used as a synonym for sexual intercourse. Recent research shows that the degree of feeling experienced is a very variable thing, both from woman to woman, and from time to time in the same woman.

'To expect orgasm to be the same every time is absurd, any more than one expects every meal to be equally enjoyable. Sometimes it is a little more than a "sneeze in the loins", as one writer described it, sometimes an uprush of intense feeling. In early married life, during pregnancy, after childbirth, just before or just after menstruation, and at the time of ovulation there are bound to be variations. And all of them are probably perfectly normal.'

Actually, most writers on the subject agree that Nature's 'premium' is nearly always obtained by false pretences. Nelson Foote claims that it is an empirical fact that less than one in a thousand human coital acts result in pregnancy *and fewer are intended to do so.*

Positions supposed to be best suited for enjoying the pleasure 'premium' to the full have been written about and sketched in every century and every culture, as well as in every style from the imaginatively erotic to the clinically informative. Now they are also being photographed. It is a popular supposition, almost a superstition, that there are the same number of coital 'positions' as there are Articles of Religion in the Church of England, although it is certain that human sexuality is inventive enough and the human body dexterous enough for there to be many permutations on the basic thirty-nine. Apart from beautifully executed sculptures and paintings, those of the ancients and the Indians for example, and the intrinsically humorous comments of Beardsley and the surprises of John Lennon, there is no aesthetic quality in pictures of the sexual act. Human capacity for sexual imagery and symbolism being what it is, a painting of a pair of downcast eyes or the photograph of an enigmatic smile can have far more compelling erotic content than any detailed representation of gymnastically entangled limbs and a smudgy fuzz of pubic hair. It is encouraging to know that fundamentally all of us, even the less intellectually sophisticated, do treasure a conception of the sexual act more elegant than the brutally anatomical facts illustrated in coital textbooks. We reveal that concept in our vocabulary when we refer to two bodies in sexual conjunction as being in 'harmony' or in 'concert'. Rob the sex act of its music and it does indeed become nothing but a squalid 'fiddle'.

Which reminds us of Simone de Beauvoir's description of the normal male-female 'position'. She says, 'It is the man who decides what position is to be used in love-making, especially when the woman is new at the game, and he determines the duration and frequency of the act. She feels that she is an instrument: liberty rests wholly with the other. This is what has been expressed poetically by saying that woman is the violin, man the bow that makes her vibrate.'

Romantic indeed, almost sentimental, but Simone de Beauvoir is here on the right track, the track so often missed by the sexologist obsessed with the penis-vagina appurtenances. Romance and sentiment are really what sex, for the human, is all about. We ignore in this context, of course, the brutal physical act of quick and near-to-accidental orgasm in a back alley. Admittedly the physical part of the business, the 'position' chosen and the emission of male semen and female secretions, is of considerable physiological importance, apart from being occasionally procreative. But, because we are human, the psychology of the sex act, the ingredients of time and place, the sense of occasion and the essential condiment of intellectual emotion, model our sexual performance more significantly than our bodies do. In other words, 'making love' is not merely a gymnastic enterprise begun only with physical limbering up between the sheets and ending with an orgasm, solitary or mutual. Those demands for feminine equality in the share-out of the premium can sound shrill and funny, but actually their source is emotional, and they are additional proof that the sexual gratifications sought by men and women are more psychological than the merely physical ones sought instinctually by animals or sexually brutish humans.

At this point we come to the really essential difference in the orgasms of man and woman. The difference is more than the difference in actions of penis and vagina. It is not only a matter of 'positions', of who is physically on top or underneath, of who enters and who receives.

Embedded in the difference of penis and vagina and the difference in the physical sexual urges of man and woman are profoundly different mental attitudes to the sexual act. The man's compulsive desire is to relieve himself of accumulated secretions: in vulgarly descriptive terms he wants 'to shoot his load'. The secretions which the woman discharges have not the same quality of being burdens which she must get rid of; they are essentially lubricants for the continuance of sexual pleasure. So, although sex for the sake of it can satisfy a man, it cannot for long satisfy a woman. The different psychosomatic balance of male and female in performing the sex act can be summed up in this way: man's sexuality is primarily physical with psychological colorations; woman's is primarily psychological and expresses itself with physical responses.

This difference can be seen at its most emphatic in pre-coital love-play. The male plays the part of the aggressor, the woman that of the attacked. The man is saying 'Let's get at it', but the woman wants to delay 'it'. Incidentally the woman can be much more cunning, show much more acting talent in this comedy than the man. She can convincingly assume a defensive role as the seduced, but she is quite often the seducer. Even her supposed passivity is, in Marro's words, 'the passivity of a magnet which in its apparent immobility is drawing the iron towards it'.

Westermarck says that 'Woman by being coy prolongs pre-coital excitement and thus increases the secretions of the sexual glands. This is hinted at by Tillier, who pointed out that the excitement might therefore render the chances of fecundation more numerous. . . . Or, more generally and vaguely speaking, the prolonged excitement may be supposed to serve the same object as that enormous production of spermatozoa.'

But perhaps the greatest physical difference in the sexuality of man and woman, and here again it is a physical difference which intensifies the emotional difference, is woman's superabundance of erogenous zones. These zones are those parts of the body which are peculiarly sensitive to the caresses and titillations which arouse sexual desire. When a man is vibrantly in love with a woman the mere meeting of their fingers can be sufficient to inflame his sexual desire, but apart from such ecstatic circumstances, a man has far fewer locations where excitation arouses sexual urges than a woman has. In most men the erogenous zones are for the most part crowded into the expected region: his genitals and anus. In some more sexually sensitive men the nipples are erogenous and, to a lesser extent, the thighs and buttocks. But rarely are a man's non-genital erogenous zones excitable to the intensity that is normal in nearly all women.

The mouth is an erogenous zone and is sexually important from earliest infancy. Consequently kissing is a great arouser of sexual excitement, though even here it would seem that the mouth of a man of normal sexual tendencies is not of itself erogenous: the sexual excitement a man derives from kissing a woman's mouth or any part of her body seems often to be the transference to himself of the excitement which the woman is experiencing.

Man can reach orgasm by the manipulation of his penis by masturbation or other means apart from coitus, and similarly the caressing or manipulation of vagina, clitoris or uterus can lead to orgasm in a woman. Those are her vitally erogenous zones, but it is true to say that generally every part of a woman's body and every organ of it is in same measure erogenous. That intense current of sexuality which links her breasts and genitals in sexual sympathy seems to be diffused over the entire surface of her finer and more delicate skin, from the top of her head to the soles of her feet. Particularly the soles of her feet. That imperial expert in matters sexual, Catherine the Great, employed foot-ticklers to excite her. The custom had been imported from the courts of Byzantium where for generations a coveted post was that of 'Sole-tickler'.

For a final word on erogenous zones we turn not to the scientists or sexologists but, unexpectedly, to Raquel Welch who recently said perceptively 'Woman's most erogenous zone is her mind'. She is right. And the same might be said of men. For when we explore human sexuality we find that every path leads ultimately to our minds. Every sexual physical joy is an amalgam of impressions received by all our sensory organs and passed on to our minds.

Of prime importance sexually is our sense of touch. Only slightly less important, though sometimes equally important, is our sense of sight. Like earth-worms, who come out for sexual intercourse only when it is dark, most men and women prefer to perform the act hidden from daylight, but by then sight has nearly always already played its part in selecting the love-object, with the result that the human lover will see in the darkness that which his eyes saw as so desirable in light.

Smell, which is one of our most memory-stimulating senses, is also important. Henry III of France is said to have been inflamed to a paroxysm of desire by the mere smell of the sweaty shift of Marie de Clèves, and a similar eroticism might be responsible for Tyrolean peasants believing that an infallible way of conquering a girl was to bunch a handkerchief under their armpits while dancing and then present it to the sweetheart of their choice.

Hearing is less important, though the sound of a lover's voice, even when it comes over hundreds of miles of telephone wire, can be erotic; and words of love or sexual content whispered or gasped can increase sexual excitement.

The sense of taste is perhaps the least important in sexuality; though such expressions as 'the fragrance of her lips' suggests that we do imagine ourselves tasting the love-object as much as feeling, seeing, smelling and hearing it.

Nearly 200 years ago Dr. Francis Gall, who discovered a new technique for dissecting the brain, came to the conclusion that the sexual instinct must reside in the brain and not in the sexual organs. Strenuously he opposed the medical opinion of his day that the seat of 'erotic mania' was to be found in the genitals. He observed that sexual instincts developed in children before their sexual glands matured, and saw how sexual instincts survived into old age or even when sex glands had been castrated or were congenitally absent. But Gall was another who was too far ahead of his time, and up to less than half-a-century ago doctors were still arguing that the theory that any part of our brain could control our sexuality was 'purely hypothetical'.

But Gall was right. The break-through has now been made. The 'sex area' of the brain has been located. It has been signposted.

The region of the brain recognised as the 'sex area' is the hypothalamic-hypophysical region. The hypothalamus is closely connected with, among other things, the control of fat and carbohydrate metabolism, heat regulation, sleep *and* sexual activities. Sexual impotence can be associated with cerebral tumours in close relation to this area. Delicate probing into the thalamus and clinical lesions of it, as well as tumours or disease in the area, have been found to cause various forms of adiposity, increased sugar in the blood, abnormally high body temperature, disturbance of the sleep rhythm *and* sexual disturbance.

Therefore it seems that our real mother, or father, or guardian, or call it what you will, is the hypothalamus. The organisation of sex is under the control of the hypothalamus; and when copulation has succeeded and the next generation appears the hypothalamus enforces maternal and paternal behaviour.

It influences the structure as well as the functioning of the body to carry out those many acts. Nathan says that the 'total act of copulation is organised in the hypothalamus and the neighbouring parts of the forebrain' adding that 'when bosoms heaved as they did in Victorian novels' it was probably the hypothalamus which was taking over control.

The sexual appetites of human patients, says Dr. Nathan, can sometimes be increased because of lesions in the region between the forebrain and the hypothalamus. 'This region is either near to the region or it *is* the region of sexual pleasure-rewarding centre of the rat, rabbit, cat or monkey.'

A clot of blood on the brain can make a woman ungovernably amorous. Dr. Nathan quotes the case of a 48-year-old woman who had a blood-clot in the region between the forebrain and the hypothalamus. 'When she was in hospital waiting for an operation she would ask any man who was visiting to come to bed with her, there and then, in the ward. After the operation to remove the clot had been performed and the lady was again behaving normally, she was most embarrassed when questioned about this unusual behaviour.'

Cats prove to be of special interest in the inquiry into the 'sex area' of the brain. It has been experimentally demonstrated that a cat's hypothalamus has a mechanism which integrates the animal's reflexes into a complex pattern of sexual behaviour. After pointing out that women may continue to have sexual desire after they have lost their ovaries, surgically or naturally, Dr. Nathan says, 'Cats, as we can all observe, are different. The gonads gone, many aspects of the feline world lose their interest. Female cats who have had their ovaries removed respond to propositions made to them by tom-cats with hate and not with love. But if a minute pellet of oestrogen is injected into the correct part of the hypothalamus, their behaviour changes and they accept proposals.'

Professor F. Roeder of Goettingen has actually tried the effect of destroying this sex behaviour centre. After experimenting on cats and monkeys he operated on a 52-year-old business man who had served three prison sentences for sexual assaults on teenage boys. Professor Roeder's target was about one-tenth of an inch wide, three inches behind the eyes, close to the optic nerves and to those centres controlling appetite and body temperature. With an electric probe he destroyed the sex centre on one side of the brain. The operation was spectacularly successful. The man no longer had dreams or fantasies about boys and began to have relationships with women.

Anatomically the sexual organisation of our bodies is a spider-web of sensation, its centre the brain and its strands stretching, vibrant and expectant, from brain to genitals, from brain to erogenous zones, from brain to hands and feet, nose, eyes, ears and mouth. Our sexuality is so dispersed that we can find physical evidence of it in parts of our body which we would not associate with the sexual act. Somewhat imaginatively but not unreasonably Ploss refers to parts of the nose as 'genital' areas, not only because these regions inside the nose so strongly resemble the erectile tissues of the genitals, but also because there is a 'certain functional interaction' which, he claimed, was proved 'by the frequent and severe attacks of nose-bleeding in the years just before and during puberty and menopause, and by the dilation and congestion of the nasal passages during menstruation'. Not without reason Helena Wright likens a sneeze to an orgasm; both are short and explosive, both follow a sensation of tension building up.

Accompanying the campaign for equality for women in orgasm has been a great deal of loose talk about women suffering from sexual frustration. What is really being referred to is deprivation of physical sexual pleasure. But real sexual frustration is emotional, not physical. Man, because of his belief, erroneous, that his accumulation of semen must somehow be discharged, can be said to be prone to a type of sexual physical frustration, but a woman's sexual frustration is basically emotional, caused by the deprivation of love, disappointment with it, or being brutally used without love. Such frustration can be suffered by a woman who is indulging in sexual intercourse all hours of day or night. That Queen of Aragon who royally decreed that cohabitation six times a day was the correct amount was probably a typical emotionally frustrated woman. In sexual intercourse or orgasm the criterion is, as in most good things, not quantity but quality: in sexuality *quality* is love. The Platonic concept of love is elegantly summarised by W. Hamilton in his introduction to his translation of *The Symposium*. 'Physical procreation is only one, and that the lowest, of the forms which Eros can take. Far nobler is spiritual procreation, the activity of the soul to which we owe not only the products of art but all progress in civilisation and the ordering of society. All such advances are apparently to be attributed to the marriage of noble minds; when a man's soul is pregnant with some creation or discovery he looks for a partner in association with whom he may bring his spiritual offspring to birth. Physical beauty will influence his choice of such a partner, but the marriage will not be fertile unless there is also beauty of soul.'

Even the most knowledgeable of sexologists can go wildly astray when, ignoring that ideal quality love, they plunge into analysis of human sexual desire. Guyon says, 'A man always looks, thinks and compares, before choosing even the companion of an hour; and when he takes one woman rather than another, it is because the one selected answers to some idea of his as to what is desirable in a woman and possesses certain physical characteristics which appeal to him.' That is not untrue: it is merely inadequate. It lays too little stress on the emotional appeal which can attract man to woman as compulsively as physical desirability can. Emotional desire, usually the product of past experiences on traumatic occasions, can impel a man or woman to abnormal preferences. Norman Haire says, 'There are women who like men to wear spectacles, men who have a passion for drooping breasts, and hunchbacks are highly rated on the love mart,' and draws attention of Descartes' passion for cross-eyed women. I recently read the case-history of a man who could sexually desire only a woman with a wart who would pull his hair and shake him violently. These are oddities, but it is true that a lover can be overwhelmingly attracted to a man or a woman emotionally and hardly notice whether spectacles are worn or breasts droop.

The importance of emotional attraction even in the full enjoyment of the 'premium' is substantiated by the fact that men and women who are of themselves especially sensitive emotionally are usually most vigorous sexually. The greatest, the most vibrantly poetic of writers and musicians and artists are notorious as 'great lovers'. Powerfully muscled labourers and physically splendid athletes are equally notorious as inadequate ones.

Maeder classified women into two fundamental sexual types: the uterine or maternal type, and the cliteroid or sexy type. The uterine craves the tranquillity and assurance of one man's love and marriage; if she fails to find them she loses her appetite for sex and becomes a staid old maid. The cliteroid loves a man for sex, she takes great care of her body for that purpose, and is always ready for a sexual tourney. Guyon made a parallel classification of men. His 'orchitic' man corresponds to Maeder's uterine woman. The orchitic is the type who, after marital orgasm, is content to wait for the next, feeling no need for sexual adventures outside the family life he enjoys. He is a good husband, a born administrator, a perfect Civil Servant. Guyon's masculine version of Maeder's cliteroid woman is 'phallic' man. Phallic and cliteroid often meet up. You can see that happen at many a cocktail party. The 'phallic' wants not just one woman, he wants them all, and even when enjoyably engaged with the present one he is dreaming of the next.

There is one type of love which rarely wins the prize of the 'premium'. It is a love which does not demand, often actually avoids, the messy finale of orgasm. It is a love indifferent to erogenous zones, sometimes even indifferent to emotional response from the love-object. This is romantic love, an ecstasy or an exquisite agony of adoration. The literature and songs of the Middle Ages are permeated with it. In romantic love the woman does not lie in bed; she stands enchantingly and inspiringly out of reach on a pedestal. She is worshipped. She can become spiritual. Indeed the fabric of a religion is often supported by such love. It finds its highest expression in the cult of the Madonna.

Many of the processes of sex seem miracles to the simple mind. So some of them did to us before Freud pulled aside the curtain, and scientists showed us the route to the hypothalamus. To primitive man sex was a religious mystery, and throughout the span of civilisation we see how sexual eroticism and religious fervour are commingled. One classic example can suffice: the meeting of St. Teresa and her Angel. 'When he withdrew his long golden dart it was as if he was going to tear out my entrails and he left me all inflamed with love. I am certain that the pain penetrated my deepest entrails, and it seemed as if I was torn when my spiritual spouse withdrew the arrow with which he had penetrated me.' Freud, Nathan and the most devout theologian cannot fail to meet in recognising how the symbol of orgasm is implicit in such ecstasy.

4 CHANGE OF LIFE: WOMAN'S AND MAN'S

Before demands for orgasm usurped the headlines, the female problem most prominently and persistently discussed was the menopause. Like menstruation the menopause is a feminine peculiarity. Indeed it is so especially feminine and comes so late in life that it hardly merits much attention in a discussion on the *difference* between a man and a woman. It might seem harsh, or even incompetent, to dismiss so brusquely a phenomenon which does often have disturbing, sometimes disastrous, effects, at least for a few years, on a woman's life. Women might protest that their climacteric deserves as detailed consideration in this book as was given to their menstrual processes which, after all, are exclusively feminine. But the sad truth is that whereas menstruation is a vital factor in the formation of the difference between men and women and at its onset lifts the curtain on the full drama of woman's so different life, the menopause is no more than a fading out of her maternal importance. The big difference, the essential difference in the drama of sperm-carrier and egg-breeder has lost its importance. The menopause is merely a last act, and not all that well written either.

The only question of interest to us before the curtain falls is whether man also experiences what can be called a 'change of life'. Quite a lot of people believe that man also has a climacteric, and physiologists have actually speculated on the possibility that male sex glands and sex secretions undergo changes comparable with the changes happening in the female body during the menopause. But all evidence available up to now indicates that this is not so. Nor is there any reason why it should be.

Nature's prime concern is the preservation of a species. To that end woman is constructed to be the egg-breeder, to gestate and give birth to children, and to suckle and nurse them. With splendid biological precision Nature organises things so that, when the woman reaches the age at which she no longer has the physical stamina for the job she is given her cards and is pensioned off. Her ovaries no longer produce eggs. But whereas it is vitally necessary for the well-being of the species to eliminate any possibility of ageing and physically inadequate females bearing young, there is no equal necessity to turn off the masculine tap. Why not let the male go on producing those armies of spermatozoa? He can still be quite useful on the production belt. His anatomy does not have to endure the strain of gestating young or producing milk or suckling babies. All he has to do is ejaculate 180 to 260 million spermatozoa into the right place: the right place, however, is not the uterus of an ageing woman; at least not so far as procreation is concerned. But so long as a man is capable of erection and ejaculation Nature can find him plenty of young females with years of potential lusty maternity ahead of them waiting round the corner for impregnation. It is as simple as that.

That explains why the most intricate biological explorations of middle-aged males has discovered in them no trace of gonadal and hormonal changes analogous to those taking place during a middle-aged woman's menopause.

Clinically minded readers can turn to Horowitz's summing up for concise medical opinion on this subject. 'Does the average male have to expect to experience the climacteric?' he asks. 'I believe not. All research and experiments on the secretion of gonadotrophic hormones in normal males, examinations of testicular tissue removed at orchidectomy for carcinoma of the prostate in aged men, the sexual history of elderly normal men and their physical examination indicate that both the germinal and the hormonal function of the testes is preserved well into senility in the average man.'

However, if we drop the precise term 'menopause' and turn to the popular all-embracing words 'change of life', we do find that in middle-age a man can suffer symptoms which superficially resemble those shown by woman in menopause. Seeley and his colleagues describe the 'change of life' as being as critical a period for the male as it is for the female. 'Surrounded by more secrecy than is puberty, except when it is the subject of not too gentle joking, this period threatens, sobers and frightens.'

Like a woman in menopause a man too can be irritable and nervous, suffer sweats and fears and sleeplessness. Like a woman a man can also feel a sudden increase in sexual desire, sometimes so intense that he can be tempted into murky adventures which, to everyone's surprise can bring a previously highly respected colleague or neighbour into the police court in humiliating circumstances. In many cases, as Horowitz points out, the persistence of the libido combined with the decline or loss of potency brings a man miserably to his doctor.

A man, like a woman, can be saddened to the stage of worry and despair by the thought that all the lovely juicy sex-life which he had so much enjoyed is now coming to an end. The man is as wrong there in the same way that woman in menopause can be wrong. In neither sex does the 'change of life' necessarily put an end to the pleasures of sex.

At menopause woman must face up to the fact that she is

out of a job. Nature has terminated her employment. It is no good her kicking her heels in the outer office: the only reply she will get is, 'You are no longer any use to the firm as a mother. Why not be content with a quiet comfy job as a Granny?'

If the woman is unwise and feels that life has finished for her, Nature will do no more than shrug and leave her to wallow in her 'change-of-life' frustrations, among which frustrations is sometimes a sense of grievance that man is still on the payroll. If, on the other hand, the woman is wise and physically aware, she will find that retirement from the procreation factory has freed her to exercise her femininity in ways more assured and mature. As with a man, the 'change of life' can be for a woman a period of achievement richer because of a maturity of middle-age.

Sexually the 'change of life' can be a kind of Indian Summer with lots of the 'premiums' of sexual joy. No contraceptives, no pills, and no nagging jealousies either. And wiser and more tolerant minds, wiser and more tolerant bodies into the bargain. Many women in middle-age are more attractive emotionally, and often physically so, than they were in their earlier sex-conscious years. Or, even if not more attractive, they ought by this time to have learned the skills of making them appear to be so.

It is on record that women of seventy and two decades after menopause can enjoy sexual intercourse. Of course it is easier for a woman. Her anatomy gives her at least that bonus. The vagina can to the end of its days always entertain a guest: the penis inevitably reaches the time when, however appealing and insistent the invitation, it has not the strength to cross the threshold.

5 MAN'S BIGGEST FEAR

In 1968 a bizarre 'epidemic' struck the men of Hong Kong. Among the sufferers was a young seaman who had recently married. He rushed to his doctor in a state of acute anxiety and reported that he had contracted the 'disease' of *Koro*, or, as it is known among the South Chinese, *suk-yeong*. His penis was getting smaller. Not only that, he said, but he was convinced that it would eventually disappear into his lower stomach.

The 'disease' spread rapidly. The hysteria was infectious, and other men rushed to their doctors. Those who did not seek medical advice resorted to homely remedies. A popular therapy was to tie a length of string or tape round the penis. At least this ensured, it was argued, that if the penis did retract into the body one could pull it out again. Others thought the only way was to hold on to it all the time, though this must have been inconvenient as it would leave only one hand free for the daily needs of life and work.

Reviewing the cases the Hong Kong Psychiatrists' Association reported that most patients said the malady usually struck at night, during sexual intercourse, or in a cold bath. Some of the patients were plagued with feelings of guilt and worried over imagined sexual excesses. Perhaps, they thought, they had been overdoing things. One patient believed that his attack had been brought on as a result of being involuntarily sexually stimulated on a moving bus. A hairdresser ascribed his to the debilitating effects of being constantly aroused sexually when he handled women's hair during his work. Another said the attacks resulted from his exposing his genitals to the cold in winter either during coitus or while urinating; a belief almost akin to the popular notion in southern Europe that urinating against the wind can cause a person to 'catch a cold' and suffer resultant gonorrhoea.

All the attacks, doctors found, were accompanied by panic, faintness, or a sense of impending death. Psychiatrists found cases of sexual anxiety caused by sexual deprivation and a few of constitutionally determined hyper-eroticism. Under psychoanalysis most of the men revealed subconscious lack of confidence in their virility. In other words it was an eruption of that old Freudian complex, castration fear, evidencing itself first with one or two men and then infecting other hysterics.

It serves as a classic demonstration of man's biggest fear: his dread of impotence. It is a basic masculine fear. However great a man's reputation may be, whether he is a powerful business tycoon, a renowned athlete, or an acclaimed hero, he can be ashamed, or worse, if he lacks sexual potency. Great wealth or power, victories in the boxing ring, or the highest honours of war glittering on the chest count for nothing when the portfolio and take-over bids are locked in the desk, the boxing shorts and bemedalled tunic removed, and, naked between the sheets, the man cannot rise to the occasion.

Women are immeasurably lucky in this respect. A woman

can never suffer this humiliating failure, can never really be in a state of being incapable of performing at least the movements of love. She can, of course, be accused of frigidity, a condition which does exist, though it is far less common than is commonly believed. In most cases frigidity is, as of course male impotence often is, the result of a lack of mutual desire or the incompetence of the partner. Often it is as unfair to blame a woman for being frigid as it would be to blame a violin for wrong notes uttered by it when the bow is wielded by an unskilled or insensitive performer. If a woman is cold or unresponsive in the arms of a man, or in the arms of several men, it might be the fault of the men, not the result of her inability to be sexually aroused.

Woman does have that advantage over a man in that she can always 'go through the motions'. Even if not sexually aroused she can still receive the thrust of love: man can give that thrust only if he has an erection.

Failure to achieve that erection has nearly always a psychological cause. There are, of course, some physical causes for partial or complete impotence: certain diseases, intoxication induced by alcohol or the intoxicants encountered in certain industrial occupations, or over-dosing with drugs, particularly narcotics. Even heavy smoking has been suggested as a probable cause of impotence, for it has been found that nicotine does affect genital secretions. Physical reasons more subtle than all these can be found, as would be expected, in the brain where that dynamo of sexuality, the hypothalamus, has its residence. Nathan describes how experiments on the brains of animals and operations on the brains of humans have resulted in amazing changes in sexuality, in a voracious and unashamed increase in the appetite for sexual activity.

Impotence is, however, nearly always the result of psychological upsets and fears. The fears are the most common. In their grosser and more understandable form they can be fears of contracting venereal disease or of causing unwanted pregnancy. But the most common fear of all is the fear of impotence itself. Here we have what can be described as the most 'vicious circle' of sexuality.

Few men are reduced to a state of obsessive anxiety when, in any attempt to acquire a skill at work or in sport or in any other activity, they fail to do it right the first time. We take it for granted that we have to learn how to do anything requiring skill. It is a pity we do not take it for granted that sexual intercourse also requires intellectual and manual dexterity. Most men think they ought to be able to perform such a natural act by virtue only of their masculinity, and feel ashamed if at their very first trial at the nets they fail to put up a good show.

What is worse, the shame of failure can stick in a man's mind. He is afraid he will fail at the next trial. Thinking so makes it very probable that he will fail. With the young male the fear of failure often results in ejaculatio praecox. That he usually grows out of. But with the ageing male the result is impotence and he feels he can never overcome that. Fearing the humiliation of repeated failure he retreats into hypochondria and takes sad refuge in persuading himself that he is 'past it'. Where the monk or the ascetic says, 'I *will* not do it,' the saddened impotent says, 'I *cannot* do it.' 'Only he becomes impotent who gives up his potency,' says Stekel.

The condition described an anticipatory anxiety, fear of possible failure when it comes to the crunch, is a common cause of a husband's impotence and a bride's frigidity on the honeymoon. Fortunately, human anatomy being what it is and the sexual urge being as strong as it is, two young people usually surmount that hurdle.

Excessive respect or excessive disgust for the partner can also cause impotence. Certain kinky prejudices can cause it. I know a man who is incapable of erection *between* the sheets: he must always have that rough male kiss of blankets. Another common cause of impotency is the sense of guilt, the feeling that 'I should not be doing this'. In cases where the man *should* not be doing it this can be a foolproof contraceptive: when the feeling invades the marital bed it is unfortunate.

By preventing the achievement of sexual gratification impotence is harrowing enough when it happens only occasionally. Much worse is the feeling that one will never achieve sexual ecstacy again. Gyurkovechky claimed that 'a man's entire energy, his courage, his pleasure for work and life, depends almost without exception upon his sexual powers'.

Stekel, whose book on impotency has established him as the most-quoted authority on the subject, declared, 'I have never seen an impotent man who was happy.' He sums up our social attitude to impotence when he says, 'Among civilised people the sexual athlete is a rarity; while the sexual weakling and the semi-impotent individual are almost the rule. And yet impotence is perceived as a severe blow to the feeling of self-regard. The individual who is impotent does not consider himself a man. And while a frigid woman does not look upon her condition as humiliation, considers herself in full possession of womanhood, and under the circumstances is proud of her coldness, a man suffers when he is impotent. . . . Public opinion even elevates her infirmity to the rank of a virtue, and gives it a heroic varnish, whereas the virtuous impotent man succumbs to the curse of ridicule.'

The point made by Stekel is underlined in macabre fashion by the fact that whereas it is near to impossible to imagine any woman committing suicide because she was frigid, a significant percentage of men do commit suicide because they are impotent or think they are. Inevitably fears of impotence grow in the man when he reaches his 'change of life' in middle-age, despite the fact that Kinsey reported a fifty per cent incidence of impotence in men was reached only after the age of 75. Stekel mentions some men whom one suspects must surely be legendary, but their prodigious sexual feats at advanced age might hearten any man fearful of the passing of sexual pleasure. One of these men, a certain Thomas Parre, is reputed to have 'committed an immoral act' at the age of 102. Apparently he lived down this disgrace because eighteen years later he married a widow. Then there is a Peter Albrecht who married when he was 80, begot seven children, and unlike many old men who drop dead after marriage in old age, lived to be 123. A Monsieur Longville had ten wives. He courted the last one at the age of 99, and when he was 101 she bore him a son.

Those men of higher intellect and emotional sensitivity whom we mentioned as being less affected by change-of-life worries are naturally less subject to impotence. Artists and writers seem singularly free from worries about their erections and their hypothalamuses. In fact it is believed by many psychologists that retention of sexual vigour in old age can actually be a sign of emotional and intellectual vigour.

Nietzsche, in one of his rare moments of unprejudiced clarity on such subjects, wrote that, 'Artists when they are worth anything at all are men of such propensities (even physically), with surplus energy, powerful animals, sensual. Without a certain overheating of the sexual system a man like Raphael is unthinkable. To produce music is also in a sense to produce children; chastity is merely the economy of the artist, and in all creative artists productiveness certainly ceases with sexual potency.'

Freud argued, 'The sexual conduct of a man is often symbolic of his whole method of reaction in the world. The man who energetically grasps the object of his sexual desire may be trusted to show a similarly relentless energy in the pursuit of other aims.' One thinks that Freud's use of the word 'grasp' in that context might have been a 'Freudian slip' by Freud himself; anyway it is right.

Even men who are not impotent can have their doubts about the quality of their potency. It has been estimated that some 55 men out of every 100 are inclined to consider their potency as being below par. What is worse, about 38 wives out of a 100 think the same about their husbands.

Perhaps many of those wives are themselves to blame. A husband can be reduced to impotence by a nagging or domineering wife. No wife who really loves her husband will ever reduce him to impotence. Not even the sexually hungry wife who occasionally exhausts her husband. Given an interval for recovery that husband will be up and willing again.

In fact nearly all cases of imagined impotence can be cured by an understanding and inventive lover. Just as that young seaman in Hong Kong was cured of his attack of *Koro*. He was cured at home. Not by tying string to his penis or holding it daylong in his hand. His resourceful bride cured him. The Hong Kong Psychiatrists' Association reported: 'A cure of biting used in Malaysia and Singapore was applied by the upset bride, and the seaman today says he is back to normal.'

PART THREE

The Difference in Mind

These are no women of genius: women of genius are all men

GONCOURT

7 No Women Beethoven

Why has there never been a woman Beethoven?

Admittedly the question is a resounding cliché, but it would be difficult to think of any other question pointing more directly at the most remarkable of all sex differences: the difference in male and female intellect which prevents any woman from being a creative genius.

The Beethoven question is usually posed in this context because the history of music does so especially illustrate the absence of women in a sublime territory of creative art where, in the words of Lévi-Strauss, the creator of music is 'a being like the gods' and makes music 'the supreme mystery of human knowledge'.

In a recent discussion I had on this point one distinguished feminist, casting around for the name of a woman composer, trying to find any woman of any note at all, did venture the name of Dame Ethel Smyth. A poor trophy, with all respect to a talented lady, to lay beside the name of Beethoven, or Bach or Mozart or . . . Yet a glance at Dame Ethel, at the person rather than the composer, is relevant. Most revealing are scraps picked from Virginia Woolf's entranced description of Dame Ethel rehearsing: a short skirt and a workmanlike jersey, a battered felt hat and a flat chest, a drop on the end of her nose and a powerful baritone voice resounding through a vast cold room in Portland Place. A Dame Ethel built up from such oddments is not what Concourt had in mind, though the picture does mischievously fit his aphorism.

After that pen-portrait of Dame Ethel, Virginia Woolf asks the characteristically naïve question: 'What if she *should* be a great composer?' The only answer to that one is *The Oxford Companion to Music*'s dry comment about the composer. 'It is the opinion of some that had she been a man she would have been more quick to make her mark as a composer, and of others that she would with difficulty have made it at all. It is perhaps fair to consider that these views cancel out, leaving sex as no important factor in the sum.'

No important factor? A search through the pages of the *Companion* shows that even if sex is or is not an 'important factor' in assessing Dame Ethel's talent in particular, it certainly seems to be a most important factor in assessing the contribution made to music by women composers in general.

Look, for example, at Cecile Chaminade. At the age of eight the girl's talent moved Bizet to prophesy an illustrious future for her. Ten years later Ambroise Thomas was so impressed with Cécile that he declared, 'This is not a woman composer, but a composer-woman', whatever that might mean. Yet the promise petered out, and Cécile became a woman who, to quote the *Oxford Companion* again, 'is known to most people as the writer of tuneful and graceful short piano compositions, with no intricacy of texture, no elaboration of form, and no depth of feeling, but pleasant to hear and play, and so tasteful in conception and execution as to disarm the highbrow critic'.

The faint praise of Cécile Chaminade's compositions can be applied to all compositions by women. Woman's contribution to music has been a quite pleasant but so minute a tinkle. We do not here ignore the array of highly talented women pianists, violinists, harpsichordists, and other instrumentalists; even critics; and, above all, singers. But those women are not composers: they are executants, translators of music, and however much a composition is embellished and improved by brilliance of interpretation, the interpreter remains only subsidiary to the creator of the composition.

Attention is often drawn to the fact that no woman has ever invented any well-known musical instrument. The comment might seem trivial until one realises that it encapsulates not one but two examples of woman's restricted intellectual range: it indicates not only that woman is not a musician but also that neither is she an inventor.

It is true that no great inventions have ever been made by women. By *great* inventions we mean those that are creatively great; inventions that have been of generative importance in human development. In that sense the word 'invention' includes mental creations as well as physical ones: philosophies, religions, political concepts, and such products of creative thought as the laws of gravity and relativity, as well as scientific and mechanical inventions and the harnessing of the forces of water, steam, internal combustion and nuclear fission.

There have been women whose discoveries and achievements are of such brilliance that they have the aura of genius. The name of Madame Curie comes immediately to all minds; and there comes to my mind, because I had to write about her, the name of Rosalind Franklin, the crystallographer who inspired work was of tremendous importance in the exploration of the DNA genetic code. There are women of similar high calibre in many of the arts and nearly all the sciences. But any truly objective appreciation of their achievements reveals that all these women, vastly important though they are, were fundamentally not creators but were actually the exploiters and improvers of earlier inventions. In the same way that women singers interpret music created by man, these women were the interpreters and improvers of thoughts or inventions primarily created by a masculine intellect.

It must be stated boldly that conceptual thought is exclusive to the masculine intellect. Indeed the intellectual disparity between the sexes is so constant and universal throughout all the world and throughout all known history that it must be accepted as a distinctive sexual characteristic. Obviously the case must be that woman lacks some intellectual attribute or intellectual strength which man possesses.

Let it be clearly understood that this is not a question of superiority or inferiority. Man and woman are so complementary to each other, not only physically but also mentally complementary, than any attempt to argue that either is superior or inferior to the other is as pointless as arguing whether the key or the lock is inferior or superior in the job of securing a door. Though it is difficult to steer away from the sterile superiority-inferiority argument, because as soon as one attempts any comparison of the differing abilities, physical as well as mental, of men and women there is usually an outcry. Sometimes the protests and prejudices take absurdly strident form. As they did, for instance, in the rowdy attacks made on an American author, Lionel Tiger, after the publication in 1969 of his book *Men in Groups*. When he appeared on television in New York a group of feminists (Mr. Tiger alleges they were 'goaded by David Frost') walked out of the show. A band of militants paraded with banners outside the offices of a Canadian magazine which printed an article of his. Undoubtedly this storm was blown up around Mr. Tiger because a reviewer had described him as 'a sociologist who says men are superior to women', although Mr. Tiger claimed that his hypothesis 'that women are biologically suited to different things than men does not mean that they are inferior, merely different. I have tried to show that for women to take up arms against the powerful in-groups which men seem biologically bound to form is not only difficult but a waste of time.'

But it is essential that we should not concern ourselves with such petty uproars. The whole superiority-inferiority argument is elegantly dismissed by Kenneth Walker when he says, 'In order that she may succeed in the world to which she rightly belongs woman has been equipped with a greater sensitiveness to affective stimulus than has a man. The fact that in the sphere of intellectual abstraction she is at a disadvantage is no sign of inferiority, for it is no exaggeration to say that a man's judgment is as warped as it is helped by his intellect. "A woman judge," is has been said, "would always deliver her sentences in accordance with the dictates of her heart". But, as Maranon has asked, "what better method could there be of judging the action of others than season tempered by feeling?" It is therefore no deprecation of a woman to state that she is more sensitive in her emotions and less ruled by her intellect. We are merely stating a difference, a difference which equips her for the special part for which she was cast.

'All discussions on the subject of which is superior, a man or a woman, are senseless and void. There is neither superior nor inferior, only a difference. The rivalry of the sexes is based on an error, for men and women rule in separate and complementary spheres.'

Let us leave it at that. Let us agree that the mental deficiencies of men and women must be examined as dispassionately and objectively as we have examined their physical differences. When, for instance, we made the anatomical observation that man has larger muscles than woman we reached the conclusion that man is consequently stronger muscularly than woman, and we accepted that conclusion without any emotive undertones about superiority or inferiority. The observation that apparently man's 'mental muscles' are also larger and stronger than woman's must be treated just as coolly.

Another point must be emphasised. The possession of genius does not necessarily imply that its possessor is 'better'. Despite the names mentioned above genius is not always noble. There can be 'evil geniuses' as well as beneficial ones. Hitler, for example. Although Hitler's intelligence was petty and his mentality perverted he showed a genius for evil that was characteristically masculine in that its creativity, creativity of a malevolent type, was far more powerful and gross than any woman could possibly possess. So, it can also be said with equal truth that neither has there ever been a woman Hitler.

1 WOMAN'S HIGHER I.Q.

The fact that woman has not the genius to become a Beethoven or a Shakespeare does not mean that women are less *intelligent* than men. In fact there are indications that in general women are more intelligent than men. But genius is not necessarily the outcome of intelligence: it is the outcome of creative intellect.

This is demonstrated most clearly by those geniuses, particularly creative artists, whose trained human intelligence has been no more than average and who have in fact sometimes shown what seemed to their contemporaries to be lack of ability in normal intelligent behaviour and the conduct of their lives. In fact, the drive and force of genius very often disregards the censorships and cautions of intelligence. Conversely men and women of the highest intelligence and scholastic attainment are often intellectually sterile and utterly lack the vital spark of creative genius.

The essential difference between *intelligence* and *intellect* is that one, intelligence, can be injected from outside and developed and trained by tuition, but the other, intellect, although it can be enriched by outside influence, originates from within, emanates from the whole individual, from what we call character or personality or temperament.

Thus intelligence, being a commodity that can be passed from individual to individual, or from society or teacher to individual or pupil, can differ in male or female recipients according to the circumstances or attitudes of society, teacher and pupil. But intellect, because it is the product of individual character, must be different in a man than in a woman. This cannot be disputed. The point at issue is not why woman's intellect is *different* from a man's but why it should be *less*.

One of my researchers, after collating findings from psychological and sociological studies of comparative male and female intelligence, has reached the conclusion that in general women are more intelligent than men; or, at least, that more women than men achieve average I.Q. He suggests that his findings can be illustrated by a diagram.

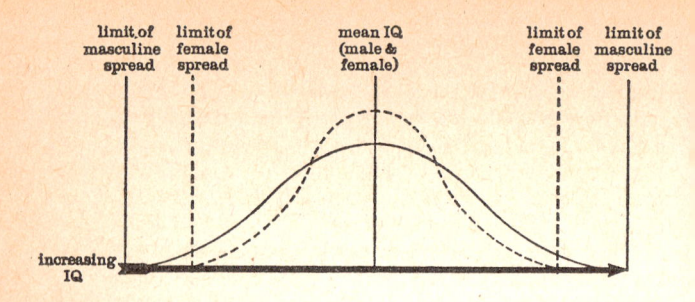

[Diagram labels: limit of masculine spread | limit of female spread | mean IQ (male & female) | limit of female spread | limit of masculine spread; y-axis: increasing IQ]

The diagram, not drawn to scale, is merely illustrative of the general trend of the findings. It will be seen that in the range of mean I.Q. women outnumber men, but that the 'spread' through the whole range from sub-normal intelligence to super-normal intelligence, is far greater in men. That is to say, more men than women reach highest intelligence, but also more men than women suffer sub-normal intelligence.

That 'greater spread' is of outstanding significance. It confirms observations that were made long before intelligence was measured by I.Q. tests. Darwin, for example, came to the conclusion that 'there is a great variability in the male sex', and Burdach reported 'wider variations in men, more genius and more idiocy, more virtue and more vice'. Both geniuses and criminals are probably more prevalent among men than among women, and it can be reasonably supposed that many of the geniuses will be found at the highest I.Q. level and many of criminals and men of 'more vice' will be found at the lowest.

The diagram also confirms findings arrived at in research among children; findings which on balance do suggest that in certain respects girls are more intelligent than boys. The 'greater variability' of boys is confirmed in Eysenck's summary of a 25-year follow-up study made at Stanford University by Professor L. M. Terman and associates. The aim of that study was to discover what physical, mental and personality traits were characteristic of intellectually superior children and what kind of adult a typically gifted child might become. Says Eysenck: 'By means of various procedures, almost 1500 children out of a school population of about one quarter of a million were found whose I.Q.'s placed them in the top 1 per cent of the population. Although both sexes had an equal chance of being chosen, boys exceeded girls in the ratio of

115:100. Terman convincingly rules out the possibility of bias in the selection of subjects for testing. The probability that there exists a true average superiority of boys in the intellectual functions tested is fairly reliably excluded by the large amount of comparative work that has been done, and the most likely possibility is that boys are more variable with respect to intelligence than girls, producing more very bright and more very dull specimens.

'This hypothesis is supported by investigations carried out by Thomson in Scotland, embracing whole age groups. Consistently the boys there showed greater variability than the girls. The well-known fact that more geniuses and more mental defectives are male than female might also be supposed to support this argument, although there are obvious historical and social reasons which might explain these facts equally well.'

A footnote in D. O. Hebb's *A Textbook of Psychology*, says that 'girls do better with verbal tests, boys with mechanical, spatial and quantitative ones. Males, who are inclined to think that verbal skill is due simply to talking too much, may be reminded that language is man's distinguishing mark as a species. The lower animals also do better with non-verbal tasks.'

That footnote is of particular significance. Sex difference in the formation of language has been observed for some generations. One early report maintained that among normal children baby girls used words with understanding and in appropriate context one month earlier than boys, and that among feeble-minded children the girls were *two* months ahead of the boys. A psychologist of Minnesota University found girls were superior in sentence formation from the age of eighteen months. Another American child-psychologist found that girls had more patience in situations demanding analysis, the manipulation of an object or the understanding of a subject. They showed more alert attention to details, and above all more rapidity in extracting meaning from any situation and expressing that meaning in words. Though he did find that boys tended to be more methodical, more critical, more logical, less wordy, and, as one might have expected, more resistant to suggestion. Research in Sheffield, England, produced concordant results.

Contemporary research confirms those findings. Dr. Arnold Gesell, reporting on a study of language formation in infants, writes: 'The sex differences are not striking, but it may be observed that the four largest vocabularies are reported in girls. While extensive data on sex differences in language development have not been reported at the 18-month level, most investigators have agreed that girls have accelerated over boys in language development during the first two or three years of life. Responses to the picture cards at this stage show the girls identifying a greater number of pictures correctly than boys, but the boys very much more likely to name at least one picture.'

During a wide-ranging discussion on 'the childhood genesis of sex difference in behaviour' organised by the Tavistock Clinic, Dr. Rene Zazzo, commenting on Gesell's 'baby tests', said that when applying them to a French population it was discovered that boys from the age of two years, perhaps even before, were more advanced than girls in the tests of motor-co-ordination. Boys from the age of two or three years were more advanced than girls in all the tests of spatial organisation. On the other hand, as soon as language developed girls showed superiority over the boys in several aspects of spoken or written language.

There is, of course, a great overlap in the sexes in infant development of language formation, but on average the girl does start speaking earlier than the boy, and one reason advanced to explain this is that whereas the boy, as soon as he is independently mobile, tends to be eager to go out of the home and explore the world, the girl tends to stay at home and talk to mother. Biological demands might account for this. The female is designed to rear children and look after them. That job will require ability in human relationships and a capacity to be conscious of human emotions and intentions. Her earlier formation of speech can thus be seen as the laying of the foundations necessary for her future as wife and mother.

Because of her earlier grasp of the fundamentals of speech a girl develops linguistic skills such as reading and sentence-forming sooner than a boy does. For example, at the age of eight the average girl can frame longer sentences than a boy can, and at that age some 59 out of a hundred girls compared with 43 out of a hundred boys can frame complex sentences.

These findings are of utmost significance in any discussion of the suggested higher I.Q. of women. The use of language is essentially a human attribute. Consequently its development must be accepted as a reliable measurement of development of human intelligence. Therefore superior language-development in female children must be considered as significant. It supports that I.Q. diagram which shows more women than men achieving average intelligence.

Havelock Ellis reports a reading test conducted by G. J. Romanes in which women were found to be usually more successful than men: not only able to read more quickly but able to give a better account of the test paragraph. One woman could read exactly four times as fast as her husband and even give a better account than he could of the small portion of the paragraph he had been able to read.

Such tests might be considered comparable to present-day I.Q. tests. They measure intelligence, but they have no validity as an assessment of intellect. Imagine that a woman has just read the last twenty lines of this text in ten seconds or less. She is called upon to repeat it and does so successfully. This shows that she has an aptitude for quick-seeing and a good memory. A Shakespeare might have been unable to pass such a test. His mind might have been arrested by one word, by the word 'woman' for example. His thoughts might hover around that one group of five letters and extract from it vast treasures of association and imagery. This observation is not fanciful. Romanes does report that in his tests 'some highly distinguished men were among the slowest readers'.

The diagram does suggest that woman's range is more restricted than man's: she is less able to move up the scale to high I.Q., and is also less likely to fall down the scale. Something debars her from being as variable as the male, as extravagant in either genius or idiocy. The same thing that happens to the young female mind, early promise and then a slowing up, does seem to be analogous to what happens to the female body which, after early growth, is suddenly halted at puberty.

We must not disregard the fact that social factors can to some extent intensify sex difference in intelligence. Margaret Mead rightly points out that social attitudes can sometimes cause certain aptitudes to be more developed in one sex than in the other. Social custom can lead to these aptitudes being accepted as more appropriate to a man or to a woman. 'It may be,' she says, 'that the most gifted mathematician will always be a man, that the real mathematical gift might occur in one-tenth of one per cent of the female sex, but always in males. . . . Or it may be that a larger percentage of men than of women deal well with mathematics, and the stereotype is set up and communicated to children that way. Or it may be that historically men have dealt with mathematics to such a degree that mathematics is thought of as male.'

This social attitude, which does undoubtedly exist, is reflected in those warnings educationalists used in the past when they insisted that there were dangers in trying to educate girls to too high a level. They feared that the strain was too onerous for the feminine mind, and they reported that girls often failed to develop beyond 'crammed' knowledge. In the light of recent startling academic successes now regularly being achieved by women at our universities such views seem rather threadbare, yet Helene Deutsch hints that those old-fashioned fears might have some justification. 'Only exceptionally talented girls,' she says, 'can carry a surplus of intellect without injuring their affective lives,' and she argues that 'woman's intellect, her capacity for objectively understanding life, thrives at the expense of her subjective, emotional qualities.'

Until recently such psychological comments were no more than theories, but the theories are now being proved as facts by the more disciplined and exact probes performed by biologists and geneticists. In her *Histoire et Sociologie du Travail Féminin* Evelyne Sullerot refers to studies by the gerontologist Dr. Denard-Toulet which shows that it is possible to plot the intellectual performances of men and women in quite different growth curves. Whereas a man reaches his intellectual peak between 20 and 30, a woman reaches it in middle-age. More significantly, a woman's intellectual performance is at its lowest during the years she is marrying and having children. In other words, Dr. Denard-Toulet is suggesting that woman's intellectual performance is adversely affected during the time of her greatest hormonal activity.

Surely, therefore, it is reasonable to argue that the linked phenomena of woman's arrested growth at puberty and her retarded intellectual development during the time of hormonal stress have a common cause. Such common cause must be biological. Any later intensifying, by social conditioning or education, of different male and female mental aptitude has its roots in the fundamental difference between male and female biology.

For more than two hundred years, ever since Claude Arien Helvetius declared that all children were born with equal intellectual potential, educationists and environmentalists have argued that good or bad social conditions and expert or inept tuition were the determinant factors in developing or retarding the growth of intelligence in any individual. This belief seemed logical because apparent examples could be produced from different social classes and different races. But the belief is losing ground in face of the new discoveries being made about genetical inheritance. It is becoming increasingly clear that it is not the *conditions* of class or race which determine intelligence but the *genes* of those classes or races. Sir Cyril Burt has gone so far as to suggest that nearly 90 per cent of the variations in intelligence is due to inheritance. Already geneticists have proved that any imbalance of the sex chromosomes can cause demonstrable deficiencies in intelligence and character. Claims and discoveries of this kind support the argument that the male and female intelligence-and-intellect difference must arise from differences, genetical and chromosomical or hormonal, in the construction of male and female bodies.

Intellect is the product of the whole human. A human being is the sum total of human body and human mind. The human body has become what it physically is today by genetic mutation, and we must realise that the human mind has also become what it is today by genetic mutation, though admittedly allied to another process of mutation, the cultural mutation in ideas and attitudes and imagination. We carry within us not only the genetic strains of our primitive ancestors but also the acquired wisdom, and follies, of all generations of mankind. We must not attempt to separate these influences. We must not say 'Here is the human body' and 'Here is the human mind'. Neither can exist, neither can be considered human without the other. But Julian Huxley is right when he castigates 'ethologists and students of behaviour, especially in America' who still stick to the point of view of 'the old-fashioned behaviourists' who denied any genetical influence in behaviour. 'They forget,' he says, 'that even the *capacity* to learn, to learn at all, to learn only at a definite stage in development, to learn one kind of thing rather than another, to learn more or less quickly, must have some genetic basis.'

Therefore, the point to bear in mind is that not one of those girls whom Helene Deutsch describes as 'exceptionally talented' could ever be a genius in the full sense of the word.

'Byron produced his finest works just as women produce beautiful children—without thought, without knowing how it was done.' In that provocative analogy Goethe sums up not only the intellectual difference between man and woman but also the basic difference between genius and intelligence.

Genius is the life-force, a creative urge that might be uncontrolled and unplanned. On the other hand the exercise of intelligence is a planned and cautious operation and within the competence of the decently educated.

Undoubtedly the greatest manifestation of human intellect is that moment of imaginative creativity when a genius sees the earthly scene and circumstances from a sublime and commanding angle of vision and portrays what he sees in the language of his unique creative powers. The leap from controlled and intelligent intellectualisation of scene and subject to imaginative creating in the abstract is the leap that only genius can make. The history of intellectual achievement proves universally and constantly that this leap is beyond the capacity of feminine intellect. Proves it so conclusively that we must accept the intellectual incapacity of the female as a basic law in human evolution. So much a law, in fact, that I shall attempt to present it diagrammatically, using the same plan that my colleague used earlier to illustrate the disposition of I.Q. scores among males and females.

Although no one has found means of scientifically establishing that creativity, divergent thinking, is something distinct from intelligence, most of us do feel that there are two such distinct attributes. Recent tests performed in Dublin by J. Dacey and others support the belief that there does exist a clearly distinct trait which we can call creativity and which is unaffected by culture, age or education. Such findings make valid some attempt to plot *creativity* in the same way that we can plot *I.Q. scorings*. The resulting diagram is not scientific and it has no statistical support but it seems a reasonable thing to offer as a basis for discussion.

It will be noticed that I have used the same masculine and feminine curves as those in the I.Q. diagram. Merely casual personal observation can lead to those curves being accepted as valid, for it is easily demonstrable that more women than men reach what one could describe as a 'mean-level of creativity' in interpretation or exploitation of the arts or the sciences, but that there is a wider 'spread' of creativity, for good or ill, in the male. Definite findings by authorities do support the hypothesis that in creative intellect there is greater variability in man than in woman, that the masculine intellect ranges from greater extremes of vice and virtue both intel-

```
limit of      limit of          mean IQ              limit of    limit of
masculine     female            (male &              female      masculine
spread        spread            female)              spread      spread
```

← war, murder, criminality, delinquency

domestic & social cultures, science, mathematics, interpretative arts

creative arts: (fine arts & literature; music)

conceptual thought & creative genius

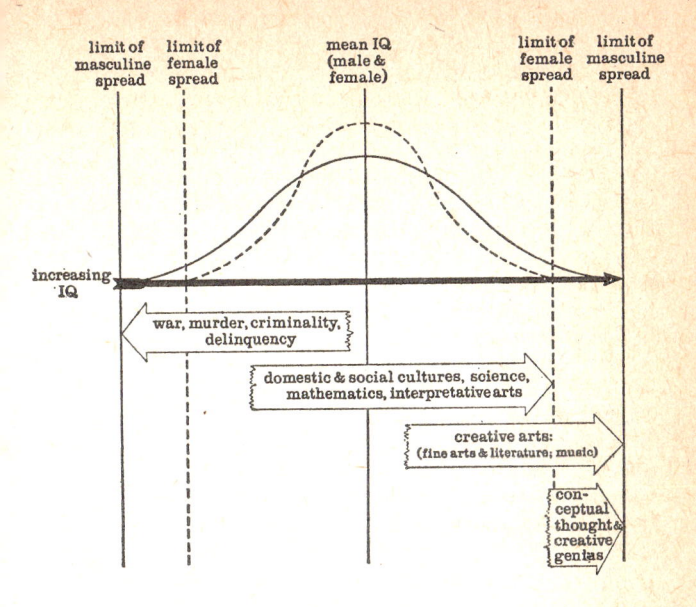

increasing IQ →

lectually and morally. Thus we find those lowest levels where intellect is non-existent inhabited almost exclusively by men with a proclivity to ingenious criminality and sophisticated violence; the individual violence of murder as well as the communal violence of hunting or war. At the other end of the scale we see man's greater variability expressed by the creative geniuses of music and philosophy.

It will be seen that whereas science, mathematics and literature fall within woman's intellectual range music remains stubbornly just beyond it. Because of the outstanding successes achieved by women mathematicians it might have been expected that music, because its intellectual subtleties can be seen as related to mathematics, would be within woman's grasp. The mathematics of music are certainly within her range: what persistently eludes her is the abstract creative ability to compose great music. Music's affinity to mathematics is at the level of construction and orchestration; great music is the product of a mind that has made the leap from intellectualisation to creative imagination.

Rubinstein expresses the bewilderment felt by many people in the fact that woman, although she is so sensitive to the passions and loves of life, has not been moved by these emotions to express them in music. 'It is a mystery,' he says, 'why it should just be music, the noblest, most beautiful, refined, spiritual, and emotional product of the human mind, that is so inaccessible to woman, who is a compound of all those qualities. . . . The two things most peculiar to woman—love of a man and tender feeling for a child—have found no echo from them in music. I know no love duet or cradle song composed by a woman. I do not say there are none, but only that not one composed by a woman has the artistic value that could make it typical.'

It is no mystery at all. The translation of felt emotion into art requires not only sensitivity to emotion itself but also creative intellect, and the creative intellect demanded for the creating of great music obviously lies in spheres beyond woman's attainment. The diagram does show that some of the arts are just within her reach. Literature and painting and sculpture, for example; though always below the Shakespeare and Rembrandt and Donatello class.

2 WOMEN WRITERS, AND OTHERS

Not only in music, but in all spheres of intellectual achievement, even in those spheres where women have won some renown, the genius at the summit is always a man. For not only has there never been a woman Beethoven, neither has there ever been a woman Leonardo, or a woman Plato, Newton or Einstein. Our vocabulary of artistic appreciation and criticism reveals our instinctive acceptance that creative art of the highest quality is masculine. What do we say of any work if it lacks intellectual vigour or creative power? We call it 'effeminate'.

One of the arts in which women have achieved some notable success is literature. There women can lay claims to great and resounding names. In our own language we have such brilliant writers as the Brontës and Jane Austen and that most majestic George Eliot whom Herbert Spencer was, in an extravagant moment, moved to describe as 'a woman Shakespeare!' She, who herself wrote scathingly enough of 'silly women novelists' would have been among the first to reject such unbalanced praise, but she is undeniably one of the 'greats' in literature.

And today we have a regiment of talented women writers producing work that is eloquent and charming; sometimes even of literary importance. So much so, in fact, that there does in the realm of literature seem evidence of a progressive 'improvement' (using the word in the Darwinian sense) in woman's intellectual range. Already we do have and have had women writers of equal stature and even similar literary style to Thackeray and Bernard Shaw, or, at a lower level, Maugham; and although a woman Shakespeare seems, despite Herbert Spencer, impossible, there might, if the 'improvement' continues, someday be women writers of the calibre of Henry James or Flaubert or other masters whose high talent falls just short of creative genius in the highest sense. Obviously that high intelligence which gives a writer or any other artist the power to observe the human scene and the talent to see and select which objects should be selected and perceptively recorded is within woman's range. But, equally obviously, what is beyond her range is the power of the genius who, using that same material, transmutes it with the breath of his unique creative imagination. Standing back from the world, the genius creates his own world of universal significance: the lesser writer, the Thackeray and the Shaw, or even the James and the Flaubert, cannot stand so far back.

A woman usually cannot stand back at all. The reasons why are self-evident. A woman is by virtue of her feminine nature too personally involved in sensations and emotions to be objectively creative. The difference between the masculine artist's attitude to his work and the feminine artist's to hers is analogous to the difference in the attitudes of a father and a mother to a child. A father sees a child as his, but as something created *outside* his body. A mother sees the child as hers, but as something created *inside* her body and still part of her.

This explains what seemed so mysterious to Rubinstein. Why, he asked, was woman, although she was so sensitive to love, incapable of writing music which is fully and artistically expressive of love? The answer is because woman is so involved, not only psychologically but also biologically and anatomically involved, in the emotions and physical processes of love that she cannot stand back from it with the objective intellectualism with which a man of genius can stand back even at those moments when he might be distilling the very essence of his own ecstasies and agonies.

Helene Deutsch records as 'personal' her impression 'that women whose literary achievements are brilliant as long as they confine themselves to a field in which they can make use of their psychological gifts, often prove inadequate when for political or other reasons they switch to intellectual fields in which the objective approach is paramount. Their intellect is not on a level with their innate feminine intuition.'

Within the confines set by their subjective involvement women writers can be exquisitely observant. Jane Austen displays this feminine intelligence at its most acute sensibility and sensitivity. It was not merely gentle irony which made her say that '3 or 4 Families in a Country Village is the very thing to work on'. In that comment she was showing her awareness of feminine range, of woman's talent to observe, to pick up and handle the objects and moods of the human scene, and her work demonstrates superbly the feminine talent for domestic economy, the conserving of the observations and their utilisation as ferments for artistic creativity. Similarly with the talented but flawed Virginia Woolf whose attitude to life and quality as a writer is brilliantly described by Patrick Anderson as having 'a little too much the flash and froth and jewelled sparkle of surfaces, a feminine attention to the polish of things, and their embroidered details, with here and there deeper threads and crispings and concentrations of verse, of scholarship . . .'

We are admittedly on dangerous ground when we talk of women writers. In some quarters it is considered almost offensive to refer to *women* writers, *women* poets and the like. To do so is judged as indecent as to notice that a writer's slip is showing, or, for that matter to pay undue attention to the colour of a person's skin. Art, it is said reproachfully, should transcend gender. In a work of art the sex of the creator should be neither apparent nor of the slightest critical importance. Mary Ellman, for instance, considers it insulting to call Marianne Moore 'the best *woman* poet in English'. But, May Sullivan retorts 'like it or not, the encomium is meaningful. Whatever the reason, there aren't many excellent women poets . . . A poet's sex may finally be irrelevant, but for the time being and among the generality it is of interest, though it chokes me to say so.'

Actually it is difficult to imagine any work of art worthy of the name which is so lacking in the individuality of its creator that the sex of the creator is not apparent and meaningful. In literature the psychology in general and the true sex in particular of the writer are undoubtedly of supreme importance to any work worthy of critical appreciation. One of the most interesting oddments I have come across in this respect is a psychoanalytical study of a short story by J. D. Salinger. This study to some extent established that underlying the story's conscious composition there was detectable in the phraseology and symbolism the subconscious desire of a young man to demonstrate his masculinity. This finding makes one think that a psychoanalytical search for hidden masculine or feminine symbols in the works of both male and female writers might give results analogous to those provided by the biological tracking of both masculine and feminine hormones in male and female bodies. Any work of art might well have male and female elements. But it is undeniable that the greater the work of art the more apparent is the thumb-print of masculine creative genius. No one could ever imagine the verse of Shakespeare, the painting of Rembrandt or the statues of Donatello to be any but the products of masculine intellect.

On the other hand the iridescent femininity shown by the best women writers is the particular beauty and value of their work. Colette, for instance. Despite her personal sexual ambivalence her works are feminine in the richest sense. When we read the work of writers of this level we enjoy knowing the writer's sex. We welcome that knowledge as added flavour to our appreciation of a work. We like a woman to speak as a woman, and a man to speak as a man. We are disturbed by neuters or transvestites, or by those entertainers of the Gore Vidal class who have the brilliant but ambivalent talent of being interpreters of a scene instead of the creators of it.

This does not mean that we want a woman writer to be constantly declaring suffragette-fashion 'I am a woman!' and forcing her tortured femininity down our throats in de Beauvoir or Leduc fashion. Such agitated feminism makes a bore of a woman. She is the kind who arouses the sigh of weariness in Sacha Guitry's 'I would gladly concede that women are our superiors, if only they would stop trying to be our equals.' The Virginia Woolfs and Mary Ellmans of this world wrongly and sadly believe that a woman writer faces hostility because she is a woman and that her work is in consequence unfairly judged, yet the law in the appreciation and enjoyment of creative art would seem to be that if the creation is a true expression of its creator's genius everyone will be aware of and concerned with the sex of the creator. Only in the creator must art transcend sex and be of no account. All artists who attach undue importance to their sex produce flawed work. This is particularly so with those male artists who are impelled by nagging uncertainties about their own gender to over-compensate their image of he-man masculinity. Like Ernest Hemingway and Henry Miller, who do it bluntly and openly; and D. H. Lawrence and Bernard Shaw, who do it more deviously and with greater art.

On planes lower than genius there are styles of writing which can be diagnosed as 'masculine' and 'feminine'. Like male and female hormones both styles can be seen in the hands of both male and female writers. Take for example my own writing. Without suggesting that it merits even the slightest critical analysis I present it merely for clinical examination. I am acutely aware that one of the major faults of what we arbitrarily describe as 'feminine writing' is discernible in mine: preoccupied attention with detail; an inability, however much one is aware of the fault, to sweep from mind or desk the housewifely, or spinsterish, hoard of unselective trivia, to stand back from the subject and really create.

This trait is observable even in writers of higher than ordinary calibre. There was, for instance, not a little of the 'mind-and-millinery' quality in Arnold Bennett. Compare his piling up of domestic minutiae with the writing of Balzac, a writer who likewise drew vast collections of the details of daily life into his writing but did so with much masculine power. Or compare Bennett with Jane Austen, who observed as only a woman could observe, but selected and presented with an objective intellect that transcended Bennett's feminine subjectivity.

Such comparisons show clearly that in its highest manifestations literary creation, like all artistic creation, depends on intellect rather than on intelligence. Consequently, the higher we climb in our exploration of creative genius we find fewer and fewer women and more and more men, until we reach the supreme heights where there are only Shakespeares and Dantes and Miltons *et al*.

In our social subconscious we know this is true. We reflect that knowledge in our everyday vocabulary, for at the moment we still refer to the 'man writer' and the 'woman writer' and have not yet moved on to 'writer' and 'writeress'. We do now have 'actresses' and 'hostesses' and, some of us 'mistresses'. But we do not have 'paintresses' or 'doctresses' or 'farmeresses'. Similarly we still need to say 'woman conductor', unless we are referring to the lady who wields the ticket-punch and not a baton. An eminent woman sculptor tartly corrected me when I referred to her as a sculptress. 'I am a sculptor!' she retorted. But despite her objection the word 'sculptress' still survives. For how long? Until such time when it is taken for granted that a sculptor need not be a man. But see what has happened in the theatre. There having been near to equal numbers and near to equal quality between men and women on the stage it was found convenient and necessary to coin the sex-differentiated words 'actors' and 'actresses'. At the moment there is a roughly similar equality in numbers and performance between the males and females who punch your tickets. So in transport vocabulary we have accepted 'conductor' and 'conductress'. We resist 'conductor' and 'conductress' in music vocabulary because the woman conductor is still a rarity and it is still taken for granted that when we refer to an orchestral conductor we are referring to a man.

These inconsistencies in vocabulary are a key to our social doubt of woman's ability to execute arts or tackle jobs which our social subconscious judges as arts and jobs that are intrinsically masculine. In the artefacts of all societies we see masculine creative intellect taking over where feminine domestic intelligence leaves off. In primitive societies, past and present, woman is usually the labourer, so it is the woman who has in her hands most of the materials needed in human industry. She uses these materials with feminine practicability and moulds them adeptly and intelligently into the utensils of daily life. When, however, a society is intellectually advanced enough to feel the desire for its utensils to be decorative or stylised, when in other words art becomes first as important and eventually more important than utility, it is the man who takes over the creative job.

At domestic level this can be seen in cooking. Here is a craft in which one would expect mothers and housewives to be more competent than men, and indeed at a certain level of domestic need they are usually more competent cooks than men. They can also cook prettily and write about it excellently. Yet when cooking becomes more creative it is the man who elevates the craft into art and becomes the imaginative chef, so that we might add to our question about Beethoven 'And why is there no woman Escoffier?' without, of course, going to the absurd lengths of Nietzsche who in one of his many inane passages declared 'Through bad female cooks—through the entire lack of reason in the kitchen—the development of mankind has been longest retarded and most interfered with.'

One of the arts in which women have been said not merely to rival but actually to excel men is the art of acting. A reasoned appreciation of great actors and actresses forces us to question the word 'excel', for in general it would seem that great actors and great actresses have shown equal brilliance. However in considering acting we have to realise that it is not a true art. It is not creative in its own right, it is the representation, or at best the embellishment, of a work of art already created. In the theatre, just as in music, there are creator and executant. There must be a composer before there can be singer or instrumentalist; there must be a playwright before there can be an actor. Certainly in that fundamental creative role of playwright no woman has equalled, let alone excelled, the great men. When the play is transferred to the stage a great actor or actress can give to it some measure of creative intelligence as well as executant intelligence, and at that level it is undeniable that great actresses have equalled men, have enriched the playwright's original characters as much as women singers have enriched the arias of Mozart or the songs of Schumann. Dame Judith Anderson, who has recently had the opportunity of satisfying her lifelong ambition to act Hamlet and thus follow in the tradition of Sarah Bernhardt, Eleanora Duse and Siobhan McKenna, says: 'The majority of great parts are written for men. The minds of men are more exciting than the minds of women. They have greater scope of power, imagination, kindness and brutality.'

Women have also of course exploited their physical charms on the stage. The universally erotic appeal of the female body has been a profitable sideline in entertainment since classic times. This 'bring on the dancing girls' mentality reached its commercial peak in this century when film moguls sold their so-called 'stars' in cattle-market style by retailing their 'vital statistics'. The measurements referred to were, of course, those of breast and waist and hips, and not that most vital statistic of all, the measurement of the skull. Obsessed by the box-office potential of female curves, film producers affixed not only on bosomy beauties but even on actresses of high talent the label 'sex appeal'. They even tried to find somewhere to pin it on the frame of Garbo, failing to appreciate that Garbo's appeal to her adoring millions was the more alluring mystery of a rare personality emanating neither from breast nor hip nor even from facial beauty but from the source of truly creative art, her mind.

Perhaps some reference is necessary to the prevalence of homosexuals on the stage; though the fact that homosexuality does seem more prevalent in the theatre than elsewhere might be an illusion fostered by the demonstrative nature of acting which projects homosexuality, as it projects any other personal trait, forcibly. A reasonable explanation why so many homosexual men and quite a number of homosexual women have achieved resounding triumphs on the stage might be that a homosexual is possibly the ideal blend, both biochemically and psychologically, for acting. Perhaps a homosexual actor or actress does have attributes of both playwright and player, does have in one skin some measure of both creative masculine intellect and interpretive feminine sensitivity.

Another sphere of entertainment in which woman has also equalled men is in dancing, including the ballet. This is one of the instances where woman can compete with man on equal terms in sheer physical strength, for her thigh muscles are of equal proportionate strength. But in this art also she is merely the interpreter of music composed usually by man and nearly always the performer of steps plotted by male choreographers. Even in dancing of a more common type man is usually the creator and woman is usually the interpreter of the dance. Any Greek boy dancing under the pepper trees at a taverna shows a wealth of virile creativity in translating bouzouki music into dance. In the comparatively rare event of a girl joining him she has to follow steps dictated by the male. Even at the local palais or in the more sterile ambience of a fashionable ballroom it is usually the male who guides and determines the pattern of the dance.

'In any of the arts, creative or executant, women *may* be equals of men.' This declaration by Brigid Brophy, herself a doughty equal of many of the finest men writers on the scene today, is not so bold as it at first appears. It is saved by that '*may*', and so far we must agree with her, for there is, of course, no way of proving that women *may* not be equal. The sad truth is that they never *have* been. However, Brigid Brophy did not write those words to begin an argument: she wrote them as a springboard from which to jump to the statement: 'There is only one respect in which physiology insists they must be not merely equal but dominant: they have more interesting singing voices.'

We will make the effort to ignore the reproachful ghost of Caruso. We will try to forget Gigli and Schipa and Fischer-Dieskau and try to accept as 'more interesting' the voices of Price and Sutherland and Los Angeles and Schwarzkopf. We will even hazard the opinion that women have achieved greater triumphs as singers, particularly in opera, than men have. But where does that agreement bring us? Back to the realisation that all the songs and arias so exquisitely interpreted by women's enchantingly interesting voices are songs and arias written by men.

And to finalise the argument we must make an observation which, although it might appear brutally unfair, is, if considered objectively, critically and philosophically sound. The greatest of women writers, even the George Eliots and Jane Austens, and all the greatest of women in any field of art have had to write about or portray a world and a society which has been invented and created by that special attribute of the masculine mind, creative conceptual intellect. The fact that this creative force is exclusively masculine is not the result of male tyranny: it is the result of chromosomes and genes and hormones; the result, in short, of Nature's designing the difference between man and woman.

3 'SHE HAS NEVER HAD THE CHANCE'

That observation brings us face to face with a popular but erroneous explanation for there never having been women geniuses of the stature of Beethoven. Women, it is said, have never been given the chance to compete on intellectually equal terms with men. Through all human progress, it is argued, the social conditions of masculine-dominated societies have denied women the intellectual outlets enjoyed by men. Man, the husband and tyrant, has imprisoned woman in the kitchen, in the nursery and in bed, and has denied her the opportunity of marching beside him as his equal on his ascent to intellectual heights.

It is staggering that this explanation always finds facile

acceptance. To begin with it is untrue. The idea that woman has always been enslaved by man is a romantic fiction. There have been many periods in history and there have been many societies throughout the world in which women have enjoyed equal status with men and exercised decisive power in affairs. There were powerful female agitators in ancient Greece, for instance; luxuriously wealthy ladies in Imperial Rome; empresses in Byzantium; talented queens and poetesses in the Middle Ages and in the Renaissance; and banker mothers-in-law in China. In our own era female tractor engineers in Soviet Russia and stock-encrusted widows in the United States enjoy equality of opportunity and wealth with their menfolk.

But the 'never had a chance' argument is worse than untrue. It is also damnably derogatory to women. Embedded in it is the slanderous suggestion that throughout the thousands of years of man's intellectual evolution woman has been his miserably deluded dolt. For if it could be proved that woman has always been man's slave, then it could be argued that she has submitted to the role because she has not the wit to be anything better, has been exploited and cheated by man because man has been too clever for her.

It is diverting to see how ardent feminists fall slap into this morass. Betty Friedan, for instance, revealing what wicked things man has done to woman's 'image', says that whereas in the 1930's the published 'image' of the American woman was that of an adventurous intelligent career woman, now 'young and frivolous, almost childlike' women are being presented to the public as ideally feminine. Cunning man, says Betty Friedan, has engineered that shift of opinion. Unable in this day and age to exploit physical strength to keep woman in subjection, man has now resorted to guile. 'The experiences of feminine fulfilment that are fed to women by magazines and movies, and by parents, teachers and counsellors who accept the feminine mystique, operate as a kind of youth serum, keeping most women in the state of sexual larvae, preventing them from achieving the maturity of which they are capable.' The more one reads that sentence the more apparent becomes the low opinion of woman's intelligence expressed in it; and that by a woman.

In any case, the 'never had a chance' argument ignores the very nature of genius. Genius does not ask for chances, it takes them. To suggest that women could become geniuses if they were not oppressed and enslaved suggests that men have become geniuses because their talents were caressed and cultivated by societies which favoured and encouraged the male. It is true that genius does occasionally flourish in the high noon of public favour and generous patronage, but it seems equally often to be born of neglect and agony and to flourish most magnificently when defying interdicts and proscriptions immeasurably more onerous than any endured in kitchen or in bed. Masculine genius has achieved some of its greatest triumphs in execution on the cross or at the stake. Works of immortal grandeur have been created in the dark and pain of prison. Nothing in the least comparable has ever come from a harem.

Feminists leap, at the merest chance of a game, to dealing out court cards, each one displaying a great name, as proof that throughout the story of human life women have gloriously demonstrated genius in every sphere of endeavour. In but a moment they can deal a whole hand, a jostling glitter of beauty and wisdom from Cleopatra of Egypt to Elizabeth of England, from Mary of Nazareth to Madame Curie, from Sappho of Lesbos to Elizabeth Barrett Browning, from Joan of Arc and Catherine the Great to any contemporary Barbara Castle. We must halt here. Beginning with Eve of Eden we could fill the rest of the pages of this book with nothing but female names, names of great women. And by 'great' we mean great in the sense of decisively influencing political history or enriching the artistic and scientific and social fabric of human society. If, however, we dare to point out that no table is big enough to hold the court cards, nor even any nation's telephone directory big enough to hold the names of great men who have done the same and to a greater degree, the feminist will argue that we are cheating, or taking advantage of rules that have been fabricated by masculine chicanery. Abandoning the game the feminist argues that women could have won more tricks if they had not been enslaved by man.

Women, says the feminist, have always been unfairly restricted with maternal burdens. And, the feminist continues, the emergence of greater numbers of women on the intellectual scene nowadays shows how women are reaping the advantage of the freedoms resulting from birth-control and emancipation and the like. I suspect that this idea that the proportion of women achieving intellectual success is increasing is illusory. Admittedly there do seem to be more women writers and women artists around, as well as more women politicians and lawyers, scientists and doctors and the like. But, after all, there are vastly more people around in any case, both men and women, and also a greater variety of media hourly drawing attention to a greater number of increasingly mediocre triumphs. Women are indeed becoming barristers and judges, ministers of government and premiers and high executives in business. But a large and increasing number of men are doing the same without being accorded the extra attention a woman gets as soon as she achieves a position considered out of the norm for a woman.

In any case birth-control is hardly new. They were using a mixture of crocodile dung, honey and soda with some contraceptive success in ancient Egypt. And in all societies and in all eras there has always been a goodly proportion of women who, either because they so desired it or because circumstances compelled it, had neither kitchens, nurseries nor husbands to occupy their minds. Even so, none of the women of those societies either was a genius.

In all civilisations and in all societies it is always the men who are inevitably the creators and initiators, the builders and fabricators, the inventors of new techniques and new arts. Probably in the earliest domestic societies, as in many primitive societies today, it was woman's domestic duty to scoop out from wood or mould from clay the drinking vessels and bowls needed for the home; but in those early societies, as in present day societies, whenever new utensils had to be designed or new decorations applied, it was the man's job to do that designing or decorating. Man has always been the one expected to give creative gloss to human artefacts.

Margaret Mead suggests that because the cultural inventions in civilisations have always been in the hands of men, because it has always been men who have built the temples, roads, boats, aeroplanes, supreme courts and parliaments, boys and girls grow up to accept that what men do is important and what girls do is unimportant. There is some validity in her suggestion that in the course of cultural evolution the human mind has probably become imprinted with an acceptance of masculine superiority, and that the result has been that women tend to assume an inferior role instinctively and do not dare to venture into any creative activity which is thought to be man's prerogative. This theory that woman has of herself become subconsciously submissive is certainly more acceptable than the theory that man consciously enslaved her.

But whichever of the two theories we explore they bring us eventually to the same point, the point where we ask how this masculine-feminine division of duties was first established. It must have happened long before any concept, let alone a discipline, of social conduct had been glimpsed. Long before there was a sense of human community the physical differences between man and woman, the physical difference in strength and size, determined different masculine and feminine duties in the pack. Another physical difference determined different roles. The difference between father and mother made man more independent and more free of tribal chores and made woman more dependent and bound to a cycle of maternal duties. Notice, however, that it was not the other way about, as some people confusingly seem to think. It was not because man assumed independence and freedom and because woman assumed dependence and bound herself to maternal duties that he became masculine and she became feminine in habits and competence. It was because they were masculine and feminine in the first place, because they were man and woman, father and mother, each differently endowed with the strengths and weaknesses, physical and mental, appropriate to masculinity and femininity, that they found different levels of intelligence and intellect and creativity. The diagram best designed to illustrate the creative and intellectual difference between man and woman is still that diagram of male and female bodies which shows the projecting creative penis which a man calls his 'tool' and the retiring secretive vagina which represents so exactly the self-sufficient self-absorbed inward creativity of woman.

Increasingly popular with sexologists is a theory that the urge which drives the male to creativity, manual and intellectual, arises from the sense of frustration he suffers in boyhood at his inability to perform the fascinating creative function of having a baby. The conclusion that man invented fire and wheel, built temples and laws, wrote verse and painted pictures because he could not have a baby and woman was satisfied to do none of those things merely because she could have one, seems a rather brusque and summary explanation of creativity, but that forward-thrusting penis and that receptive indrawn vagina illustrating the differences between father and mother do also illustrate the fact that man creates *outside* himself and woman creates *inside* herself; mentally as well as physically.

Man always creates for a reason, for what can be called 'an ulterior motive', for status and, in its widest sense, profit. And he creates competitively; in competition either with his fellows or against the natural forces he must use or conquer with his creative science. Man's creativity is always fundamentally objective.

Woman, on the other hand, creates for herself, out of personal joy in the act of creation and out of personal joy in being subjective to her creation. To become a mother is woman's destiny; maternity is her ultimate creative fulfilment. Man feels no biological compulsion to be a father; but he also does have a compulsion to perform a creative self-identifying act, to create something which proves his individual existence. In its highest manifestation this compulsion is expressed in masculine intellectual creativity. Whereas any woman can enjoy creativity in secret biological fulfilment, man can produce evidence of his creative power only by producing some artefact, a painting, a sculpture, a poem, a symphony.

In short, man spills out his art. He ejaculates his symphonies, dramas, statues, paintings, cathedrals, mosques and palaces. He fathers them. Woman, unless she is one of those who is trying to compete with man in the market-place of art, absorbs man's creations, gestates and nurses them, interprets them. This, the ultimate manifestation of the complementary nature of man and woman, is seen in the placid everyday sense of the ideal partnership between husband and wife. Many a creative genius has needed a woman to stand as midwife to his labour of creation, and although we do always refer to '*man* the inventor' and '*man* the builder' we admit that without woman to aid him, to 'drive him mad' to do it, man might sometimes neither have invented nor built.

Apart, however, from the domestic co-operation of individual husband and wife, all men and all women are partners in human intellectual evolution. In this essential human partnership we can see woman as the patron. She is the one who, having brought the prodigy to life out of her body, can sit back indulgently, knowing that if he does get the glory he also provides the glamour. Instead of conquering enemies or hewing marble or writing scores woman produces a baby and, in effect, says to her man child 'Win battles!' or 'Sculpt statues!' or 'Write music!' Man, like an actor on a stage, does get the honour of star-billing; but woman is not all that discontented that her name is less emblazoned, for, as sophisticates know, the producer behind the scenes is usually more important than the one who gets the limelight.

No, there never was a woman Beethoven. But there was a woman of equal importance to music. Maria Magdalena Kerewich was the daughter of a cook who married a drunkard musician at the Court of the Elector of Cologne and gave birth to three sons. The eldest was Ludwig van Beethoven. So, after all, if we want another Beethoven, we have to wait for another woman like Maria Magdalena Kerewich.

8 Woman's Smaller Brain

Why is woman's intellect inferior to man's?

If you go around asking that question, you soon find yourself unpopular. It causes offence: not only to women, which could be expected, but also to men. Either through some sense of chivalry or for fear of their wives in particular and their women-folk in general, the most learned of men brush all evidence of women's lesser intellectual achievements rapidly under the carpet or try to explain it away with generalisations about woman's sociological suppression and the like.

If you suggest that the difference in intellect must have some physical origin, you are given the impression that you have transgressed all codes of decent discussion. To argue that woman is intellectually weaker than man because of some physical 'handicap' is akin to mocking a sufferer from some abominable affliction of body or mind, or even akin to arguing that an individual has more or less ability or importance because of the colour of his skin or the shape of his nose or the curls of his hair. In short, to say that the physical fact of being a woman bars a woman from intellectual heights attainable by man is, in this egalitarian age, a kind of 'racialism'.

However, if we can dodge such irrational attitudes and sentimental prejudices, we shall find that it is easier to face up to the question nowadays than it would have been only a few years ago. In the light of modern research we are more prepared to accept that differences in mind and intelligence and intellect can be caused by physical differences in the body. We should therefore be more prepared to accept as probable that differences in male and female intellect might be traced to physical differences in male and female bodies. Discoveries now being made in anatomy and biology and neurology certainly seem to indicate that there can be a physical explanation for woman's weaker intellect; that the difference in her mental powers and the way she uses them is caused by differences in her body, by things that can be seen, can be measured or weighed or chemically assayed.

In these discoveries can be found one theory which suggests a basic reason why woman is intellectually weaker than man.

This reason, expressed in brutally simplified terms, is that woman is more infantile than man.

The word 'infantile' is used here in its evolutionary sense, in the sense which means that woman is some steps nearer our ape-cousin ancestors than man is. Certain anatomical observations support this view. For example, woman's body is less developed than man's in the evolutionary sense. Her skull has less defined corrugations and brow ridges, and must therefore be described as more infantile. Her skull is also smaller than man's; and so, of course, is her brain.

In other words woman has 'come down from the trees' more slowly than man has.

No one must blame women for this. Her slower arrival is not the result of feminine procrastination or of any capricious delay in keeping appointments. Neither is it the result of any influences outside woman. Her slower development has not been caused by exterior circumstances or domination by man. It is the inevitable result of unavoidable circumstances in the evolution of the human female. Woman's physical growth, and in consequence her mental growth, has been retarded out of biological necessity; by the special loads, physical and psychological, imposed on her in her role as egg-breeder and mother.

This is the theory we shall examine in this chapter. Doubts will be cast on some of the assumptions we shall make, and it must be candidly admitted that some of these doubts will be supported by formidable scientific authority. But this must not deter us. We have now reached the stage which we foresaw when we referred to the 'mystery' of menstruation. A detective who fails to find decisive evidence of the trajectory of a bullet or traces of poison can nevertheless prove by deduction that murder has been done. Like him we must also rely on what can be called 'circumstantial evidence'. We shall unearth a wealth of it, and incidentally in doing so we shall meet a formidable body of scientists whose findings encourage belief in the theory.

1 THE SUBTLE KNOT

In earlier chapters we discussed some of the easily observed differences of a woman's body: smaller frame and shorter legs, smaller head and lower brow. All these are features which are to us the very trade-marks of femininity. So much so that if a woman has longer legs or higher brows or is more than usually muscular she seems to us that less bit feminine. Science bears us out there: such deviations in woman's anatomy are described as 'masculine characteristics'. In those earlier chapters we also examined more subtle differences in anatomical details of men and women as well as those important biological and biochemical differences which determine a man's masculinity and a woman's femininity. Now we are going to develop our theme and show how those differences result in the minds of man and woman also being different.

From all these differences, anatomical, biological and biochemical, we choose one clinical specimen best fitted to illustrate the theme: we choose the brain: woman's smaller brain and man's larger brain. In any discussion dealing with mental capacity the brain might seem a fairly obvious choice. But the choice has its dangers. During centuries of arguing whether woman's smaller brain resulted in her having less intellect some passionate and crazy opinions have been expressed. By the German Max Funke, for instance, writing under the offensive title, *Are Women Human?* He declared that by virtue of her smaller brain woman should be considered as a sort of 'missing link', halfway between man and anthropoid ape.

That kind of argument carries no weight nowadays. We know now that the brain is not the only organ we 'think' with. When Michael Polanyi declared 'Mind is the meaning of the body', he rightly argued that *knowing* is an activity which involves the whole man. This concept of a human being as a total of human body and human mind is one we readily accept nowadays, for we know that neither brain nor body can live, in the sense of having meaningful existence, without each other. All that we are going to write about the brain must be read in the light of that. We have chosen the brain as a 'symptom'. It is only *one* symptom of woman's retarded evolution, but it is the one which illustrates our argument in most vivid and understandable form.

Fortunately nowadays enough is known about the physical composition and processes of the brain for our discussion about it to be free of the emotions and passions which would have clouded such a discussion in the past. Not so very long ago it would have been considered indecent, even sacrilegious, to suggest that human thought had an anatomical source. As recently as the middle of the last century Francis Lord

Jeffrey could solemnly declare: 'There is not the slightest reason for supposing that the mind operates through the agency of any material organ.' Admittedly Lord Jeffrey was an opinionated and arrogant man, and a Scot into the bargain, but his statement did sum up the belief commonly held by brilliant and educated people of his day and even later. They genuinely believed that human intellect did have its origin in a mysterious or even divine source outside human anatomy. We know better now. We know that Lord Jeffrey was wrong. We know that the human mind does operate through the agency of a 'material organ'. That material organ is the brain.

The brain is a wondrous instrument: the knot *is* indeed infinitely and beautifully subtle. But it is a physical knot, a clump of grey and white matter. And it is ours. It is not some spiritual endowment handed to us in a bony box already wound up and ticking like a magical toy given to us by some genial or sacred uncle. We created it and we perfected it. It is so much our own creation and so much our own possession that we must not allow it to overawe us.

All of us are nowadays more or less familiar with the physical appearance of the human brain. Countless photographs and diagrams have presented it to us as a mass of grey and white matter, intricately folded and cunningly tucked into a protective bony casing we call the skull. Yet, despite this familiarity, we are at all times so aware of its magnificent and terrifying potentiality that we find it difficult to free ourselves from the habit of seeing it as something sacred and paying homage to it as, in Donne's beautiful words, 'that subtle knot which makes us men'. However we shall make no progress at all in our attempt to study the difference between the brains of man and woman unless we study the brain clinically and objectively as what it actually is: one organ of the body, a mass of tissue occupying a suitably dignified elevated position in the cranium at the upper end of the central nervous system for the purpose of receiving and interpreting information from the body and formulating and initiating responses to that information. In addition, it has the capacity of storing information. It creates a memory-bank so that the information it receives or transmits can be compared, and then our thoughts and actions can be adjusted in accord with information received and actions taken in earlier experiences. Having thus appreciated its functions we can take the further steps of measuring it and weighing it and smoothing out those involuted folds to examine those particular areas of the cortex, the 'rind' of the grey and white mass, where the brain registers and responds to the sensory impressions sent to it. Having got so far we can also examine those other areas of the brain that are even more important to us as human beings; those areas in which our peculiarly human talents of calculation and thought and judgment and imagination and intellectual creativity are located.

If, under so clinical an examination, the brain loses its aura of superstition, it nevertheless gains immeasurably in physical wonder. For to my mind the fact that all the attributes that 'make us man', all our ability to think and calculate, to dream and create, and all the passions that move man and woman to face each other and dream of love, are all performed by electrical processes ticking through fifteen-thousand-million intercommunicating nerve cells is far more wondrous than the banal primitive concept that human thought is some miraculous essence breathed into us by a superhuman agency. There is marvel in the thought that from this fatty mass radiates everything that has raised the human being to supreme intellectual heights dazzlingly far above all other living creatures. Here is the repository of all the secrets of human evolution, every human desire, every human aspiration, and all human vision. This clump of grey and white matter tamed fire. It fashioned the wheel and the boat. It charted the earth and framed laws. It weighed the universe and measured routes to the stars. It wrote the verse of Shakespeare and the music of Beethoven, carved statues and painted pictures, built cities and cathedrals and mosques. It has created (or, if you prefer, recognised) God himself. And today it is within reach of the ultimate power of being able to destroy its own mystery. For the human brain is the instrument which the human being has perfected to such a stage of intellectual power that now it can be used as an instrument to investigate and explain the workings of the instrument itself. So we are now too knowledgeable, too grown up from primitive human infancy, to romanticise the brain in superstitious religious terms as some kind of 'soul'.

As we have remarked, the brain is not by any means lord and master of our beings. It is very dependent on other organs in our bodies. On our liver for instance. The healthy functioning of the brain depends on the chemical state of the blood which keeps it alive and working. In fact the chemical state of that blood depends in its turn so much on the efficient working of the liver that at least one eminent investigator has been moved to say 'the future of brain research lies in the liver'. And we show how aware we are of the effect of the liver on the brain every time we use the phrase 'feeling liverish'. It is reasonable to speculate that future discoveries in biochemistry might well disclose differences in the biochemical processes in the livers of men and women. If there are such differences then they most probably have differing influences on the brains of men and women.

When I recall some of the experiments I have witnessed I cannot feel that any speculation, in biology in general or on brain research in particular, can be ruled out. Let me describe one of these personal experiences, for it is the one that impressed upon me more vividly than anything else I have seen a realisation of the essentially physical nature of the brain.

Some years ago when I was writing a work on mental disease my research led me to a group of buildings, half laboratory and half hospital, a few miles from Bristol. This is the Burden Neurological Institute, an establishment which deserves far greater fame throughout the world than has yet been accorded it. What I saw at Burden made a greater impact on my thoughts and beliefs than anything I had seen earlier or have seen since in the great and famous hospitals of Europe. It was also my first meeting with that scientist and visionary W. Grey Walter.

I shall take it for granted that many of my readers will have read Grey Walter's masterpiece of a book, *The Living Brain*, which for now eighteen years has been at the forefront of all books on the subject 'intended for general reading'. Having mentioned Grey Walter, however, I feel that I must emphasise that I have not slipped that distinguished name into my text to support all the way-out opinions I am expressing in this chapter. To underline that disclaimer I draw particular attention to the fact that my visit to Burden was on an assignment not at all related to this present book.

At Burden I *saw* thought. I agree that this might seem a sensational way of expressing myself, a straining after effect. But I can think of no better way of describing my experience. I did *see* thought in Burden's laboratories. I also saw the intellectual processes of the brain being *physically* manipulated. I watched neurologists, using electrodes of the infinitesimal power of one ten millionth of a volt as their 'torches', peer into the recesses of a living brain to examine those billions of neurons performing the electrical operations that are necessary in the process of thinking. On charts which those neurologists could read as musicians read orchestral scores I was shown records of the effort a brain had made as it switched on to anticipate an event or to foresee the possible consequences of that event. In other words I was seeing that most abstract of all abstractions, human imagination, translated into physical terms. I was also shown how electro-surgery, employed with delicate precision within that mass of grey and white matter, could manipulate and mould mental processes and how errors in these processes could be corrected: *physically* manipulated, *physically* corrected. After Burden even Lord Jeffrey would find it difficult to doubt the source of intelligence.

Any last stubborn doubts would almost certainly be dissipated by recent physiological experiments in which brains have been 'grown from buds' in other parts of the body than the head. It has been convincingly demonstrated that, just as a tooth grows from a bud, a brain also develops from a scrap of tissue embryonically destined to become brain. In our prenatal life there is, between our gut and our central nervous system, a flexible embryonic rod called the notochord. The notochord defines the axis of our pre-natal body and out of it grows our brain and our spinal column. If a piece of notochord is transplanted to the underside of an amphibian creature a brain will grow there on the skin of the creature's belly.

Our primitive ancestors apparently considered the brain as no more than a tasty tit-bit for their cannibalistic cuisine, for excavated human skulls of their day appear to have been emptied of their succulent contents in the same way that the skulls of calves and lambs are emptied by present-day butchers to provide material for delicately digestible dishes.

A brain does look easily digestible. It also looks softly vulnerable. Indeed it is. Those fatty folds are so soft that only the slightest pressure is needed to push one's finger deep into them: though if one did do this to a living brain one would annihilate a few thousand units of human thought as one pressed to useless pulp thousands of the nerve cells and dendrites which form the grey matter and thousands of the nerve fibres of which the white part is chiefly composed. Fortunately that tender mass of fatty folds is protectively lodged in a strong bony case, the skull. A skull is tailored with anatomical precision to cover the brain it has to protect. It grows to the exact size required: a small bony box for the woman's brain and a large bony box for the man's brain. Those differences in size of skull and brain we must now examine.

2 A TEN-PER-CENT DIFFERENCE

On average a woman's brain is somewhat more than ten-per-cent smaller than a man's. According to Sir Henry Morris's *Human Anatomy* 'The average length of the brain is about 165 mm . . . It is slightly longer in the male . . . than in the female . . . Its average weight is 1,360 grammes (48 ounces) in males and 1,250 grammes (44 ounces) in female.' *Gray's Anatomy* claims a greater diversity. Quoting maximum and minimum weights for samples of approximately 200 males and 200 females it gives maximum weights as 1,840 grammes for men and 1,585 grammes for women, and minimum weights as low as 964 grammes and 879 grammes respectively.

It can of course be argued that in a way a woman's brain is not really smaller than a man's; that it is smaller only absolutely, not relatively. That is to say, in proportion to the overall size of her body a woman's brain is as big as a man's. This is true. In *relative* terms the brain of the average woman is about the same weight as a man's is in proportion to his bodyweight. In quite a lot of instances it is actually relatively heavier.

It will also be argued that it does not follow that because a woman's brain is absolutely smaller her mental powers will be less, and, admittedly, there is as yet no proof at all of any correlation between size of brain and 'size' of intellect. Indeed, on occasions when the brains of men of great intellect have been weighed and measured they have been found to be no larger and no heavier than the brains of men of merely average intellect. One brain often referred to in this respect is the brain of Anatole France, which weighed only 1,000 grammes. Reference is usually also made to the fact that the biggest human brain on record, it weighed no less than 2,850 grammes, was the brain of an idiot; though it is surely self-evident that this idiot's brain must have been a diseased and bloated organ. As for Anatole France's small brain, we will for the moment do no more than remark that he obviously made good use of small equipment. How and why he did so is the very point we shall be soon discussing.

Attempts have been made by physiologists, psychologists, anthropologists and sociologists to collect statistics over wide ranges of humans to find any possible correlation between brain size and intellect, but none of the findings which I have examined seem to be in any degree conclusive. The scientific problem faced in such an inquiry is concisely stated by Michael H. Day, Reader in Physical Anatomy at the Middlesex Hospital Medical School, in his imaginatively concise *Fossil Man*.

'During the known evolutionary history of man, an overall increase in brain size from 600–700 cubic centimetres to 1,200–1,300 cubic centimetres can be discerned. It is easy to speculate that this increase in overall brain size must correlate with greater intelligence and capacity for thought, but in modern human populations normally intelligent people may have brains ranging in size from 1,000–2,000 cubic centimetres, and with this range there is no convincing evidence that intelligence is related to volume. *Clearly other factors are involved, such as number of brain nerve cells and the complexity of their connections with one another.*'

Precisely. I have italicised that last sentence because it puts us straight on the road to a crucial point in insisting that the size of the brain is important. The point is this: possession of a larger brain does not automatically ensure possession of greater intelligence and intellectual power, but it does ensure *greater potentiality* for the development of that power. This seems implicit in Day's reference to the number of brain nerve cells and the complexity of their connections.

To clarify the point let us choose a simple mechanical analogy. Let us liken a brain to a telephone switchboard. We will consider the switchboard as the nerve-centre, as the central intelligence of an organisation in the same way that a brain is the 'central intelligence' of a body. A switchboard handles incoming and outgoing calls. A brain, as we have described, also receives incoming calls which relay communications received from the sensory organs of the body and also sends out outgoing calls which transmit instructions. A switchboard handles inter-communicating calls between departments: a brain also has its 'complexity' of 'communications' within itself when it taps calculating and assessing information of its memory bank.

A small switchboard with a small number of lines and housed in a small office will be adequate for a small organisation. But if increasing demands are made on that organisation, or if, and this is even more analogous to the human brain, the organisation itself feels a desire to extend its operations, the organisation must increase the size of that switchboard so that it can install more lines of communication with the outer world and also more lines for use between its own expanding departments. The organisation's evolutionary development will, for example, require that its 600–700 lines shall be increased to 1,000–2,000. This will be necessary not only to give more lines for more incoming calls (like the sensory impressions *received* by the brain) and more outgoing calls (like the instructions *sent out* by the brain), but also for intercommunication. Thus there will be a vast increase in the 'complexity of their connections with one another'. As the switchboard increases in size the room containing it must also increase in size: just as the human brain and human skull had to be larger to allow for man's evolutionary development; or just as the baby's skull grows over the baby's rapidly expanding brain to provide a casing exactly ample enough to house that brain. Thus a big and complex organisation will eventually have a big switchboard in a big room.

It will be argued that often a big organisation with a big switchboard is less efficient and less agile in keeping up with daily demands than is a small organisation. The small organisation will often be more adventurously productive, more creative, than the big one. The big organisation can be lazy and unadventurous, and many of its switchboard lines will become rusty with disuse. In other words a big organisation can be less 'intelligent' than a small alert organisation possessing only a minimal switchboard. Even so it would be ridiculous to argue that the small switchboard's potentiality equals that of the big switchboard. What does happen to the smaller and more intelligent organisation is that when its desires for expansion exceed its switchboard's capacity it instals a bigger switchboard to increase the number of lines of communication. Or it makes a take-over bid, acquires its giant moribund competitor, cleans the rusty lines of the big unexploited switchboard and employs them to their full potential.

Neither of these procedures is possible with the human brain. We cannot increase our switchboard: we have to make use of the one we have got. Fortunately its billions of lines are capable of so many billion-billion permutations of thought that they are adequate to deal with any as yet conceivable human mental requirements. And although we have developed computers to help us by speeding up the mediocre labour of addition and subtraction and the like, it is unlikely that even in the distant future any human mental effort will exceed the potential switchboard at our command in our skulls. Nor can we 'taker-over' a competitor brain. We can use another brain, we can employ it, but we cannot absorb it into our own. In another respect the switchboard has a mechanical adaptability denied to the human brain.

Miniaturisation has made it possible to increase the potentiality of switchboards and other instruments without increasing the size of the instruments, so an organisation that needs to expand its lines of communication can still pack its potential into the same small room. But no miniaturisation is possible in the human brain. A neuron is a neuron is a neuron. Neurons vary in size from about 1 mu or so to 20 mu diameter, but the neurons of a woman's brain are the same size as the neuron's of a man's brain. Therefore a man's ten-per-cent larger brain must have ten per cent more neurons than a woman's brain; and it seems that therefore a man must possess ten per cent more 'lines of communication' than a woman. As neurons are numbered in thousands of millions, a ten-per-cent superiority suggests the possibility of hundreds of millions more 'lines of communication'.

The existence of so many extra hundreds of millions of nerve cells suggests that there can exist in man's brain that greater 'complexity' of connections described by Day. If this is so, then the permutations of thought possible in a man's brain are hundreds of millions more than are possible in a woman's brain, with the result that the processes of thought could be correspondingly that much more complex.

Up to now we have restricted this speculative calculation to a supposed difference of only ten per cent because of the proved ten-per-cent difference in the size of brain. But the difference of potential could possibly be much more than ten per cent. Which brings us to a difference probably of far greater significance than the difference in overall size.

To explore this difference we must examine the cortex, that part of the brain which we have described as the rind of the brain. It is known that of the processes performed by the brain those which relate to the highest mental activities are performed in the cortex. This has been decisively demonstrated by experiments on living brains.

Parts of the cerebral cortex were removed from the brains of rats who had earlier been taught to find their way through intricate mazes. The parts taken away were small; too small, in fact, to interfere with their stored-up maze-learning. But the removal had serious effects on the reasoning capacity of the rats. In succeeding experiments more of the cortex was taken away, and it was eventually discovered that up to eighteen per cent of the cortex could be taken away without having more than a negligible effect on *learning*, but it entirely destroyed *reasoning*.

The inference is clear. The cortex is particularly important for *reasoning* and less important for *learning*. Therefore the cortex is especially important for the *intellect* and less important for mere *intelligence*. Bearing that point in mind, let us turn from the brains of rats to the brains of humans and look again at the cortex of a human brain.

From those familiar pictures of brains we know what a cortex looks like: a bunched-up arrangement of tucked-in folds. Those folds are what we must now particularly examine. Brain research has established that the greater the extent and number of those folds and therefore the greater the area of the cortex, the greater is the intellectual effectiveness of the brain. Those recent experiments with rats have more than confirmed this; they have also alerted us to notice with particular attention the emphatic use of the word 'intellectual' in that observation. The suggestion that the cortex is the abode of reasoning, that the larger the cortex the larger must be the reasoning power of the brain, raises an exciting new possibility in our comparison between man's larger brain and woman's smaller brain. If a brain is ten per cent larger overall, it can be surmised that it possesses at least ten-per-cent more folds. What happens then if we smooth out these folds and measure the whole cortical area? It could be found that the smoothed-out folds make the total cortical area of a larger brain *more* than ten-per-cent greater. If so, then the effective reasoning area is also *more* than ten-per-cent greater.

Having gone this far into mathematical argument let us go a step further. In doing so we shall find reasons to suggest why woman's intellectual capacity may be even more restricted than we have as yet indicated.

Consider the possibility that any human being, either male or female, needs to have a certain number of 'lines of communication' in constant operation for the routine departmental processes of keeping alive. Walking could be taken as an example of one of these processes. After we have mastered very elementary lessons in the aptitude, we walk without conscious mental effort. We delegate entirely to the brain the job of controlling our legs and feet, of seeing to it that one foot is put before the other to move us along in an orderly way. If we take too much to drink we are soon painfully aware of how completely we have delegated 'walking instructions' to the brain. Bemused by alcohol the brain cannot attend to the process properly, and we, unaccustomed to thinking out the process for ourselves, finish up flat on our face or in the arms of a policeman. But, unless it is incommoded by alcohol or by drugs or injury or disease, the brain takes over our walking operation without us needing to tell ourselves 'I am walking; I must keep upright; I must move my left leg to put my left foot in front of my right' and so on.

Among other necessary departmental processes that the brain undertakes are many of which we are even less conscious than we are of walking. Breathing, for instance. We don't have to think, except when purposefully exercising, or purposefully inflating and deflating our lungs. The brain sees to that. As it does to our digesting of food and our circulating of blood.

How much of the brain is continuously occupied, 24-hours of the day non-stop, with such necessary maintenance work? How many lines of communication, how many neurons, are occupied with these regular calls.

Dr. Grey Walter also argues the importance of the 'complexity of communications' on our switchboard. The significant factor in brain function, he says, is not the vast number of neurons. 'It is the enormously greater number of ways in which these elements can interact with one another that indicates the scale of cerebral capacity.'

During his research into cybernetics he built a machine which he christened *Machina Speculatrix* because it was 'primarily designed to illustrate a living creature's tendency to explore its surroundings', but it soon became known as an 'electronic tortoise'. Unaided it could wander around the house, could avoid and circumnavigate obstacles, and when it became 'conscious' of how much energy it needed for its return journey it returned to base and recharged itself. It even, when it came face to face with a mirror and became confused with the contradictions of reflected signals, suffered electronic hysterics. And all this the result of a 'thinking equipment' of only *two* neurons.

As Grey Walter points out *two* neurons makes mathematically a huge leap in potentiality from *one*. 'A single cell with only one function is trivial and inert unless stimulated' but when two 'can interact freely, the whole system is transformed . . . The single-element system has only two modes of existence: on and off; the two-element system has seven.' These are: on, off, A by itself, B by itself, A acting on B, B acting on A, and A and B acting together. One sees now that if only two neurons are sufficient for a walking-about life, a few more neurons could endow even an 'electronic tortoise' with vast 'complexities of communication'.

We humans need brains and central nervous systems powered by billions of neurons to make the permutations possible for thinking out the millions of necessary functions our bodies have to perform. The movements of walking and breathing and the like make demands on our nervous system, but probably even those demands are less than other demands made on our brains by the processes concerned with growing and replenishing the structures of all the organs of our body. For we need to be constantly fabricating bones and tissue, producing blood and salts, manufacturing chemicals to convert our food and liquid into life-giving protein, and executing many other complicated procedures demanding care and precision and energy to keep our bodies alive. All this before we even begin making those bodies do anything, physical or mental, of normal human purpose. To cope, therefore, merely with living, quite apart from thinking or studying, must surely occupy the cerebral and nervous energies of billions of intercommunicating neurons. How many we cannot calculate, let alone count. But what can be suggested is that the number of neurons employed for these purposes might be in the region of the number contained in the brain of our closest existing genetic relative, the ape. This seems a logical suggestion, because the ape does not do very much more mentally than keep alive. Apart from a very rudimentary capacity to learn primitive imitative tricks from humans the ape has progressed neither mentally nor culturally. To me it seems self-evident that it has not done so because its smaller brain has been occupied to the limit of its capacity with the job of keeping alive. It just did not have any extra brain-potential free for intellectual development. The ape-size brain is apparently just big enough to attend to all the 'departmental processes' of keeping alive and nothing more.

The size of brain in the most intelligent apes, the gorillas and chimpanzees, can be around 650 cubic centimetres. That is about half the size of the average human brain. On this basis, therefore, we shall assume that if around 650 cubic centimetres of brain is enough to attend to the routine processes of keeping a gorilla or a chimpanzee alive, it should be enough to do the same for a human. This leaves the human with another 650 cubic centimetres of brain to spare: six hundred and fifty cubic centimetres apparently available for 'other business'.

If we accept this, then we can also accept a beautifully simple but wondrously dramatic explanation for all man's cultural and intellectual progress. That extra 650 cubic centimetres of the 'switchboard' was what gave man the power to begin his progress upward to civilisation and leave his ape-cousins gibbering in their dark ignorance. Man had 650 cubic centimetres of extra brain available for human thought; for imagination, for creative activity, for intellect.

If we can accept this assumption as valid, if we assume that an 'extra part of the brain' is free for intellectual development, then the disparity between the intellectual potential of man and woman is actually doubled. For if both man and woman use around 650 cubic centimetres of brain for living purposes, the balance woman has left for intellectual use is twenty per cent less, not ten per cent less, than the balance man has. However, it could be argued that man's larger body will make a correspondingly larger demand on his brain for its living processes. For instance, the parietal area of the brain, that area which is the general area of sensorimotor representation and is concerned with muscular activities, is larger in a man's brain than in a woman's. This, in view of man's larger muscles, could be expected.

Pay particular attention to the fact. It is of supreme importance to all we are saying, for it does prove that differences in the size and make-up of male and female brains can be caused by differences in male and female bodies.

But however big are the extra demands man's larger body might make on his brain resources, it is doubtful if they exceed the demands made on woman's brain by her particular feminine processes. Woman has a great deal more to do biologically than man has. All such jobs as creating ova, gestating babies and producing milk surely demand more procedural effort than merely producing sperm. A woman probably has to keep many extra lines of communication open for receiving calls and transmitting urgent information necessary for menstruation, egg-breeding and gestation, as well as booking orders for milk and making arrangements for it to be delivered at the right address at the right time.

Thus woman's smaller brain and the heavier biological demands made upon it must leave the feminine switchboard with far less potential for the production of intellectual byproducts. Even if all the available extra lines in the brain of a talented woman are humming with intellectual effort her optimum product must be less than the product of a masculine genius working at full output and using his potential of billions more lines of intellectual communication. So it would indeed seem that the only hope a feminine organisation has of competing with a male organisation is for it to do a 'take-over'; for the woman genius, as Goncourt hints, to become a man.

This does not mean, of course, that *any* man is automatically and inherently a potential genius. The average man can be as intellectually lazy as one of those big organisations with a rusty switchboard. Few men make any use of their extra potential. On the other hand, a woman can be as energetic as one of those small competitive ambitious organisations, and can outstrip the intellectual efforts of thousands of male contemporaries because she is using her smaller potential to better effect.

There are many women who have exercised their smaller brains to much greater intellectual creative effect than that achieved by men with larger brains. Scores of women of my personal acquaintance have developed in their smaller brains an intellectual ability astronomically outstripping any intellectual ability I have managed to develop in my nearly-five-ounce-heavier brain. Just as there are men with smaller bodies who have developed those smaller bodies to be far stronger than my larger body. After all, it is demonstrated daily on any sportsfield that with exercise and training smaller arms can be stronger and smaller legs can run faster than larger untrained arms and legs.

Let us consider one phenomenon of human development which most of us know something about. A baby's brain is immensely greater, relative to body-size, than an adult's brain. A baby's brain is some fifteen per cent of baby's body-size as compared with the adult brain's two-and-a-half-per-cent of body-size. By the sixth year of life an infant's brain has reached 90 per cent of the weight it will have in the adult. The size of a baby's brain, however, is no indication of the baby's intellectual powers. At that stage of life the brain is an unexercised organ: it has to be trained to perform its functions, just as limbs and other organs have to be taught to perform theirs. Yet the possibilities of that brain are enormous. That clump of grey and white matter has a vast potential of intellectual development. Given propitious circumstances of favourably combined inherited tendencies as well as ideal opportunities for learning, that untrained organ can become the brain of a genius. Of an Einstein for instance. Or, for that matter, though humanity has not yet produced such a prodigy, of a Mrs. Einstein.

Although these speculative attempts to assess male and female brain potential do seem logical and reasonable, we have to admit that scientifically they pose a dilemma. Scientists become every day more agile and more imaginative in their research. We have mentioned some of the discoveries they are making in this field. Those experiments on the cortical area of the brains of rats for instance are particularly significant to our argument in that they prove that the destruction of part of the cortical area can reduce reasoning. In other words, a brain made smaller by surgical interference will have less intellectual power, just as would a brain made smaller if injury or disease incapacitated an area of the brain. But even such elegant and enlightening experiments are only a minute contribution to answering the biggest question of all. No one has as yet devised a mechanistic method of proving, or disproving, that a complete healthy larger brain has larger intellectual potential than a complete healthy smaller brain in another body.

Although intelligence can be to some extent 'measured' by such methods as I.Q. tests, it still cannot be measured or weighed mechanistically. Even more abstract is intellect, or, to use the more emotive word, genius. Genius, as we have said, is not necessarily the product of spectacularly high intelligence. It is a product of individual intelligence combined with, or inspired by, individual character and expressing itself in a favourable cultural climate. Beethoven, for example, needs more than the intelligence to read and write music, needs more than the mental and manual dexterity necessary for translating themes by musical notation and marshalling the intricacies of chords and crushed seconds and the like. Beethoven must also have the character and the intellectual genius to invest his compositions with his peculiar grandeur, as well as the peculiar sensitivity of a genius to his cultural landscape, a sensitivity which gives him the cunning to bring his vision to his contemporaries or, on the other hand, create a vision which will survive the ages until a future and more enlightened people are capable of listening to and appreciating his compositions.

Unless he were engaged in speculative philosophising, no scientist would suggest there could be any discernible correlation between such an abstraction as human intellect and the physical facts of the human body. Yet, some day some scientist may crack the code and find some means of measuring human intellect quantitatively and qualitatively in relation to the human body. It will need someone of the stature of a Newton or an Einstein, some such visionary as Julian Huxley had in mind when, writing of Darwin, he said, 'sudden intuition was responsible for some of his most important discoveries of principle . . . a valuable reminder of the fact that imagination as well as hard work is essential for scientific comprehension'.

Nevertheless we do already possess apparatus which can measure and record the efforts and impulses of a brain at work. Using such an apparatus, we might even watch the brains of a Shakespeare or an Elizabeth Barrett Browning actually at work. We could even, at such a place as Burden, measure and record the effort made by these two brains while they composed a sonnet. We could go further: we could locate and measure the precise areas of the brain employed in the process of imagining and composing the sonnet. But it is as yet beyond scientific comprehension to devise any method of explaining why the larger masculine brain did produce sonnets of such greater intellectual grandeur than those produced by the smaller feminine brain. This apart from the scientist's justifiable refusal to assess (in scientific terms as distinct from criteria of personal taste) whether one sonnet really is better than the other.

There is the crux of the problem. We appreciate the impossibility of scientifically linking the abstract with the physical. Any observer of the human scene knows, just knows without necessity of proof, than the intellectual creations of great men are of higher calibre than those of great women. But no proof that this is so can be encapsulated in a scientific theorem. Even a scientist should know that work by Donatello is a greater and more universal achievement artistically than even the most magnificent creations of our own great Barbara Hepworth. But the scientist cannot *prove* this is so. Therefore even the most sophisticated investigation of the brain of sculptor and sculptress would be to no purpose. Questions of judgment and taste can be debated only in the realms of intellectual criticism, never decided in the laboratories of science.

That the reason for the difference in male and female intellect and the difference between the sonnets of Shakespeare and Elizabeth Barrett Browning might be caused by the difference in male and female biology was imaginatively expressed by the poetess Ruth Pitter in a recent broadcast.

'I'm very firmly of the opinion,' she said, 'that there is a great genetic difference between poets and poetesses, just as there is between man and woman. After all, we have extra chromosomes, and these extra chromosomes often rattle with indignation or other emotions. We've got to remember, too, that emotionally women's habits are different from men's. In spite of all our emancipations we have a tendency to hide our deepest feelings, and men, on the whole, like to advertise them: there is that difference, and I like to mark it.'

That observation also hints at another difference in the mentalities of man and woman, the difference in masculine and feminine emotions. But before we discuss that difference, we must now do something we promised to do. We must turn to the 'circumstantial evidence' produced by a body of scientists whose discoveries and arguments do support the theory that a larger brain indicates greater intelligence and greater intellectual potential.

3 THE DESCENT FROM THE TREES

In 1933 near the banks of the River Murr in Southern Germany a skull was found. The men who unearthed the brain box knew that they had discovered something very old because the ground in which it had been embedded was a gravel deposit that had been left in the valley by melting glaciers before the last Ice Age or even earlier.

Nevertheless they knew the skull was human. There was no doubt about that. Its rounded back, its low vault and narrow forehead, and its low eye-sockets and proud straight profile were similar to those in the skull of a modern human. Here, then, was the skull of a human being who had presumably once walked upright in the valley of the Murr, and died there. A very long time ago. In fact, some 115,000 years ago, give and take a score of thousand years either way.

Who was this ancient Murrian? A hunter killed in the chase? Or a warrior buried by his fellows? Not at all, said the experts. It was a woman. How did they know that? They knew it in the same way that palaeontologists examining the skull of another Ice Age human, this one found on Gibraltar, could confidently label it 'Gibraltar woman'. The palaeontologists, discoverers and investigators of fossils of the past, particularly of our human past, are the scientists to whom we now turn to prepare our dossier of circumstantial evidence.

'The skull of a female from Gibraltar; the contours are more rounded, brow ridges less exaggerated.' Those words, loaded with significance, occur in the caption of a photograph in Professor Alfred Sherwood Romer's book *Man and the Vertebrates*. From hundreds of books and reports by palaeontologists and zoologists and physiologists it would be easy to gather up thousands of phrases equally valuable to our argument as that 'Gibraltar woman' caption, but we favour any quotation from Romer because this brilliant Harvard Professor of Zoology is an ideal counsel to brief for our argument. Romer devoted the major part of his career to the study of the vertebrates, the back-boned animals, but his particular value to us is hinted in the biographical note printed in a recent edition of his great work. 'Although not disdaining living vertebrates, he is especially interested in the tantalising problem presented by the study of fossil forms, and therefore is as much a palaeontologist as an anatomist.' The last words are the ones we seize upon. Palaeontologist *and* anatomist. This means we have conscripted to our aid a scientist with a foot in both camps.

Palaeontological research inevitably lures scientists further and further back towards the beginnings of life on earth. The way in which first man and first women evolved from the animal background and eventually became twentieth-century models familiar to us today can be explained by Romer and his fellow scientists only if they can discover how (and, an even more absorbing study, why) every part of our bodies, their minutest tissues and structures as well as their bones great and small, and all our digesting, breathing, blood-circulating and reproductive organs, were first fabricated and then, through hundreds of thousands of years, adapted to and modified by changing circumstances of life on earth. To my taste no one has ever described that process more eloquently and excitingly than Romer has done in his scientifically exact but evocative style of writing. His entrancing book guides us through tens of thousands, through hundreds of thousands, and through millions of years. Romer describes how life emerged on earth and how the vertebrates were born and fashioned. Until during, as he puts it in his magnificent throw-away phraseology, 'the last three hundred million years or so', humans appeared on the scene.

From the 'circumstantial evidence' provided by Romer and his fellow scientists we are going to abstract points which indicate woman's evolutionary development was slower than man's.

One thing pleases us about the palaeontologists. They do not pull their punches; they tell us facts without fear or favour. When they come to discussing and comparing the cranial capacity of men and women palaeontologists seem to be neither as timid nor as discreet as neurologists and psychologists, and are certainly boldly free of the conventions which seem to inhibit doctors of medicine. They have, of course, an advantage over doctors. After all, the palaeontologists are making comments not about present-day patients but about women who passed from the scene hundreds of thousands of years ago, women too long dead to protest, too long dead to file suits for libel or chain themselves to railings. Thus the palaeontologists state without fear of reprisal from outraged females, and without any of those cautionary reservations about relative size, the bleak uncompromising truth established by the fossilised bones they have unearthed: woman's skull has always been, for hundreds of thousands of years, not only smaller than man's but also more evolutionarily 'infantile' than man's. These prehistoric skulls prove, therefore, that woman's brain has been smaller than man's for hundreds of thousands of years, so we can assume that for all time also her nervous system, the whole complex of her sensory and thinking organisation, has been smaller to a corresponding degree.

It is true, of course, that those human skulls, both male and female, found by the palaeontologists, had developed considerably in capacity and in beauty from the skulls worn by our arboreal ancestors before they stopped capering amid the branches and came down to earth. It took hundreds of thousands of years for the small low-browed brain-boxes of our Tertiary ancestors to develop into the domed and handsome brain-boxes of modern man. But it is also true, as revealed by twentieth-century woman's skull, that the female skull has been just that bit slower than the male skull in progressing towards high-brow human dignity. With the result that just as the skull of the Gibraltar woman was that bit smaller and less developed than the skull of her savage mate, so the skull of twentieth-century woman is smaller and less developed than that of twentieth-century man. This difference in brain size between the sexes is seen in all early humans. Neanderthal woman's brain was smaller than her mate's, so was Cromagnon woman's, so was Upper Palaeolithic woman's.

Not only her skull of course, but her whole anatomy reveals the slower evolutionary development of woman. Her shorter stature, for instance. Throughout all ages, and throughout all races it seems, woman has always been shorter than man. Woman's larger median incisors, the extra vertebrae in her coccyx, the less frequent fusion of the vertebrae at the base of her spine, the extra gluteal tuberosity of the thigh bone, even the greater frequency in women of excessive growth of hair and their corresponding infrequency of baldness; all these are features instanced as 'proofs that the female is more persistently true to ancestral type'. That is, woman is a stage nearer to our savage forbears than man is.

These anatomical differences are factors we must bear in mind even when concentrating our attention on the skull and brain. Combined with the marked difference in the brain those other anatomical differences add up to an overall anatomical difference. That anatomical difference must be the result of an overall biological difference. Equally obviously it must have had an overall effect upon woman's life and mentality.

For the sake of simplicity, however, we shall confine ourselves as much as possible to that most striking anatomical difference in the seat of intelligence, the brain.

In bone formation woman's skull is both more like the baby's skull and more like the skull of our primitive ancestors. The prominent overhanging brows which are almost invariably a marked characteristic of a man's face are very rarely seen in a woman. When they are, the woman is nearly always one with marked masculine characteristics. Such brows are never seen in a normal baby.

This difference in size and development of the skull cannot

and should not be discussed as a mere oddity, a capricious variation in evolution. So significant a symptom must hold some clue to the difference in male and female intellect. For unless we do take the plunge and accept the theory that a smaller brain does indicate smaller intellect, then everything Romer and his fellow paleontologists have told us about the evolution of *homo sapiens* seems worthless.

For why do scientists excavating the sites of early human life exclaim with joy when they unearth a skull with a larger braincase than usual? They do so because that larger skull proves that they have discovered yet one more fossil trace of ancestor man. To them that human skull by being bigger than the skull of ape or monkey is evidence of greater brain-power; more room for brain, more room for intelligence. That bigger skull shows that the human had the extra brain space, the extra potential, to become the thinking intelligent and intellectual being he is today. Thus, at least to the palaeontologists, bigger brain is accepted as decisive proof of greater intelligence.

When and how did that human brain potential begin? Way way back, millions of years back in fact, our arboreal ancestors, the ones who darted gibbering through the trees, needed dexterous grasping hands and agile feet to leap from branch to branch. Such a method of locomotion demanded development of brain centres capable of coping with such intricate muscular coordination. Even to this day we carry in our brain traces of this cerebral inheritance: our higher mental facilities are sited alongside those parts of the brain known as the motor centres. Of tremendous importance in human evolution was the development of a grasping hand. The hand, in itself the endproduct of hundreds of millions of years of evolutionary progress, became a sensory appliance. It first felt objects, then it grasped them, and then it picked them up. Objects felt and picked up were then turned over and examined, by touch, by smell and sight. All the messages aroused by this examination, tactile and visual messages, were sent to the brain. When it received these messages the brain had to sort them out, had to think about them, calculate and to assess them, and then to store them as information in the memory bank. By such means the object was 'grasped' not only physically but mentally. It became an object evocative of thought. It could be seen as similar to or different from a neighbouring object.

A bigger intellectual advance however was when the human became capable of 'seeing' objects when they were not actually before him, when he became capable of visualising them, thinking about them, seeing them in his 'mind's eye'. The acquisition of this capacity signalled the birth of an attribute exclusive to human intelligence, the power of constructive imagination. It was the first stirring of human intellect, the first minute step towards the genius of man.

Swinging from trees demanded something more than dexterous grasping hands and feet. It demanded good sight as well. The development of visual acuity gave another thrust to the evolutionary growth of intelligence. Before their sight improved the tree dwellers had been forced to rely heavily upon their sense of smell, but improved sight provided far richer possibilities for acquiring intelligent knowledge than ever smell could have done. So, by learning to use their eyes to more and more advantage the arboreals added another treasure to the foundation of human intelligence. Today, millions of years since our ancestors in the trees learned to do that very thing, when we meet fellows who are slow in the uptake, we snap them out of their mental blundering by telling them to do what our tree-swinging forbears learned to do: 'Use your eyes!'

Incidentally, by that reference to the human development of sight we have touched the tip of an iceberg of vast sexual significance. Using our eyes has been of crucial importance in the evolution of human love and in making men and women different from all other living creatures in enjoying visual delight in sexual shape. I shall enlarge on that in my last chapter.

It is the palaeontologists and zoologists who have made it possible for us to see how human intelligence evolved and developed from the days of the far distant hominids to the days of modern man. In this context the term 'modern man' must include Murrian, Gibraltar and Swanscombe humans, for they, as humans, are almost our contemporaries, standing alongside us at the present end of a vast time scale going back millions of years. Before their day the proportions of the human skull had been changing for hundreds of thousands of years. The beetling ape-like brows had receded. The human forehead had come proudly into sight and the world saw the first 'high-brows'.

That descriptive term 'high-brow' is not a misnomer for a haughtier intelligence. It is often used in a snide manner; yet the fact is that the high dome of the scholar is not a fiction. For instance, what do we do when we want to portray brutality or ignorance or savagery, a 'Mr. Hyde'? We sketch a face with a low primitive brow. As Romer points out, the facial effect of a relatively small size of brain 'is in great measure responsible for the rather ferocious appearance of such a form as the gorilla with its low forehead and beetling brow ridges'. Look instead at a face expressing intellect. Let us choose a face with which most of us are familiar: the face of Voltaire as sculptured by Houdon for the bust in the foyer of the *Comédie Française*. Even if we did not recognise that face, even if we did not know the name and were not able to say 'Ah, Monsieur Voltaire!' we would know we were confronting a person of the highest intelligence. If we measure it we see how 'high-brow' its proportions are. That immense brow actually represents half the whole visage, for its height equals the length from eye to chin. As a feminine contrast, one that exaggerates the difference in brows, I should choose practically any one of Titian's women; the ones in *Diana and Actaeon*, for instance. Titian was undoubtedly desirous of painting women of intense, adorable and sensual femininity. Their low and pretty brows give the requisite femininity to their faces. Or one can look at the women of our own acquaintance. If we ignore the effect of different hair-styles, hair drawn back and emphasising the brow or falling over it and concealing it, we find that the faces which impress us at first glance as being particularly feminine have brows which are nearly always quite low and certainly never have the slightest suggestion of the strong ridges seen in a masculine brow. In fact from personal observation I should say that any woman who has noticeably high brows or strongly delineated features or any other characteristic approaching masculinity in her face will invariably show other masculine characteristics in her body, and also possibly some masculine mental attitudes, even if only slightly.

But high dome of skull and greater size of brain are scientifically even more important than clues in the evolutionary development of primates and the emergence of man. They are now recognised as vitally significant in the classification of species, and even when zoological or biological definitions have to be expressed in as few words as possible an editor must include some reference to brain size. For instance, if you turn to even so concise and pocket-size an encyclopaedia as the *Penguin Dictionary of Biology* for a definition of 'Primates', you read: 'Order of placental mammals containing man, apes and monkeys', and then the significant phrase 'relatively larger brain'. If you want to know a bit more about these placental mammals, turn to the entry which tells you that the 'characteristic of placentals is that the embryo develops in the maternal uterus, attached to the maternal tissues by a highly organised placenta', and then you come to words which I italicise because of their particular importance to us here: *'The cerebral cortex is larger and more complex than in other mammals.'*

Take another scientific quotation, this one from Romer himself: 'A constantly increasing brain size has been a characteristic feature of primate development. The cerebral hemispheres have grown in size, and in all the higher Anthropoidea completely cover the cerebellum. Among the smaller monkeys are to be found the highest relative weights of brain to body in any mammals.'

Still keeping to Romer we find in his accounts of the unearthing of skulls in South Africa these two remarks. 'The creature was certainly below human standards, for estimates of the brain size indicate that it was of ape rather than human volume', and 'Brain capacity has been estimated in two specimens at 450 cubic centimetres and 650 cubic centimetres. The latter figure exceeds the largest capacity recorded in any known ape.'

As we have mentioned earlier the brains of gorillas and chimpanzees can be as large as 650 cubic centimetres. This is about half the capacity of the brain of the average twentieth-century human, which, differing from race to race, has capacities from some 1,200 cubic centimetres to 1,500 cubic centimetres. It is freely accepted that the higher intelligence of gorillas and chimpanzees over other apes is the result of their brains being bigger. So apparently it is accepted by zoologists that there is some correlation between size of brain and relative intelligence in apes. Then what forbids us from extending the comparative argument to humans?

To do so we return to the palaeontologists for some more circumstantial evidence. In 1936 and 1937 two bones were unearthed in the Thames Valley at Swanscombe. The two bones were from a skull but were not sufficient to tell what kind of a face the Swanscombe inhabitant had had, how big the jaws had been or how developed the ridges of the brow. One thing which could be determined however was the size and shape of the cranium. That brain-box had a capacity of 1,350 cubic centimetres. A skull of that size, the scientists said without hesitation, must have been that of intelligent man.

We are going to enlist Swanscombe man to help us. The palaeontologists have shown that he had a brain twice as big as the apes of his day and the apes of today. In their ape-size brains the apes had apparently lines of communication only sufficient to go on living their ape lives. But with his twice as big human-size brain Swanscombe man had that glorious human potential for intellectual development.

Before we jump to too many conclusions, however, we must turn to the cautionary words of another scientist, Doctor Cedric Carter, and quote from his elegantly argued *Human Heredity*, a book which lights the layman's path through some of the difficult mazes of eugenics.

'Taking the view over hundreds of thousands of years,' says Carter, 'it is obvious that in the evolution of man there has been a steady selection for intelligence. The two main indications are an increase in brain size, shown by the internal cubic capacity of fossil skulls, and the improvements in technique of making tools and weapons.

'The relationship between brain size and intelligence is not close, but there is a relationship,' he goes on. 'The relationship between culture and intelligence is also, perhaps, not very close, because even under primitive conditions one group of men could learn techniques from another and perhaps improve on them without necessarily being more intelligent.

'But taking both brain size and culture together it seems likely that the intelligence of man's ancestors improved steadily between the times of the earliest Australopithecine apemen, perhaps 2,000,000 years ago, and the earliest men who were undoubtedly of our own species appearing in the second half of the fourth and last Ice Age about 25,000 years ago.'

Carter points out that although the Australopithecines had only 600 cubic centimetre brains, about the same capacity as that of present-day gorillas, some of them were tool-makers. The later Java and Pekin *Homo erectus* of about 25,000 years ago had brains of 900 to 1,300 cubic centimetres, and the Neanderthaloids, among whom are our Murrian, Swanscombe and Gibraltar friends and 'who were dominant in Europe and Asia at the end of the third inter-glacial and the first half of the fourth Ice Age up to about 50,000 years ago, had brains of modern size. The men of our own species who replaced them, perhaps with some admixture, also had brains of full modern size.'

From this Carter can argue, and with justice, that there are no '*anatomical indications*' of any increase in intelligence since the middle of the last Ice Age.

Yet the more we ponder over these words the more encouraging support we find for our speculation on the 'potential' of a larger brain. Indeed let us be bold enough to claim that the argument that we are making, the argument that larger brain equals larger intellectual potential, is the foundation for the whole magificent theory of human evolution.

The principle of natural selection insists that we accept that in determining whether a species will survive and evolve environment is a stronger force than the desire of that species to survive. Only a species capable of arriving by genetical mutation at a form capable of survival can continue to exist. What enabled man to survive? What else but his brain. Only because man was in possession of a brain capable of advising him to protect himself, devise cunning methods of protection from predators and no less cunning methods of hunting and attack, was he able to survive, and every lesson learned in every exercise of that art of human survival added to human knowledge and accumulated to the great total of human wisdom which finally gave him intellectual dominance over all other living creatures. The bigger human brain, and that alone, made all this possible.

In those Murrian, Gibraltar and Swanscombe days that brain was already there. The skulls prove it. It was a big brain, but untrained and waiting. Just as the big untrained brain of today's baby waits, that Neanderthal brain waited for experience and training and knowledge. Swanscombe life was a restricted savage life. The same 650 cubic centimetres of brain an ape possesses would probably have been quite enough for Swanscombe man to cope with such a life, to blunder dully and unimaginatively through the primitive grunting routine of a savage's day in the Thames Valley. Perhaps Swanscombe man would have been quite content to use no more than those 650 cubic centimetres. But he did have those 650 cubic centimetres more. Those 650 cubic centimetres presumably contained tens of millions of more lines of communication, and therein lay his superior intellectual potential. So, whether he liked it or not, whether he willed it or not, each time he grasped an object, lifted it, turned it over, assessed its shape and value and fashioned it into a tool, he brought into use some more of those lines of communication, used some bit more of that extra territory of brain which the ape does not possess.

We twentieth-century humans might properly feel humble when we see ourselves in evolutionary perspective; when we accept the fact that in our brains, as also in our limbs and bones and flesh and skin and in every part of our anatomy, we are, again to use Romer's words, only the 'product of primate evolutionary trends'; and when we accept the truth that man 'owes in his high state much to his arboreal ancestry, to features developed by his Tertiary forefathers' life in the trees'. Yet also can we be proud, as sons of any noble and distinguished line should in filial duty be proud, of our ancestor, our Swanscombe forbear who, although so much weaker in physical power to battle with his environment, so much more naked to attack by tooth and claw, nevertheless nurtured his precious humanity and used to such magnificent effect the potentiality of his extra brain, coaxing to ever strengthening power the human intelligence which protected him from jungle hazards and gave him first the cunning to evade and defeat animal enemies and then the more thoughtful human skills of taming and using them.

Those fossil evidences of human skulls exquisitely reinforce the rejection of superstitious beliefs that human intellect is bequeathed to us from some beneficent source outside human anatomy. They do far more. They sustain, equally exquisitely, our speculation that the unexploited area in a larger brain represents a greater potential of intelligence waiting to be used.

The skulls of Swanscombe and Murrian man and the smaller feminine skull of the woman from Gibraltar excite us to a vision of how the human has exploited that potential. Not through mere centuries nor through mere millennia, but through hundreds of thousands of years of human blood and sweat and toil the human has learned to perfect new skills of hand and foot and eye. Every scrap of experience reaching the human brain through the sensory organs, every lesson learned in every creative action performed, the use of fire and the incalculably more wonderful use of words, the fashioning of wheel and boat and home and loincloth, demanded extra space for extra thoughts, extra employment for hitherto unused lines in the human's vastly greater number of reserve lines of communication. The human brain and human nervous system had that extra space; twice as much 'thinking space' as the brain of the ape.

And the human male had just that bit more extra space than the human female. For she, the woman, as well as learning alongside man to think and speak, to build and create and imagine, had an additional task imposed upon her: the biologically retarding task of bearing man's big-brained babies. To illustrate how motherhood has made particular biological and anatomical demands on woman we can choose no more vivid example than the female pelvis, which we have already described as a part of woman's skeleton so obviously modified to give her the required shape for motherhood.

The female pelvis had to be designed on especially ample lines, wider and shallower than a man's, to allow for the birth of the baby. More particularly the exit has to be big enough to facilitate the passage of the part of the baby that is most important, the baby's head.

Because of that factor it has been seriously suggested that the size of woman's pelvis might have had some effect on the evolution of human intelligence. Carter refers to the supposition that brain size of humans might 'be limited by the size of the outlet of the mother's pelvis through which the baby's head must pass'. Though he quickly adds the cautionary comment that if this were so, one might have expected in the course of human evolution the size of the female pelvis would have been 'capable of responding further to selective forces by further increase in size'. And, he argues, there are 'no clear indications of a rise of average intelligence in historical times'. He points out that 9,000 to 6,000 years ago men and women of great natural intelligence in the Near East 'invented all the main elements of our present-day culture, agriculture, stock-keeping, building in stone, weaving, pottery and writing'. However, we had better leave Dr. Carter's thought-provoking arguments on hereditary intelligence there. Otherwise we could find ourselves discussing not only the intellectual potentiality of the brain but also the intellectual potentiality of the pelvis.

Let us stick to the physical differences in the pelvis. Apart from the sexual difference in overall size and shape there are many less noticeable and refined differences. The bones of the female pelvis are more delicate, and its muscular impressions are not so well marked. The scetabula, the cup-shaped cavities in which the head of the thigh-bone articulates, are smaller than a man's, are wider apart and face more definitely forwards. The obturator foramen, the large opening between the anterior inferior part of the hip bone and the inferior dorsal part of the hip bone, is shorter in the female and tends to be triangular in shape; in the male it is more heavily oval in outline. Enough. There are other differences which would involve us in even more refined and precise anatomical vocabulary. Those just mentioned were detailed in medical terms merely to illustrate the subtle differences in engineering which we find when we examine only one part of woman's body.

Any and every examination we make proves that woman's biology, woman's metabolism, woman's genetical pattern determine both big and minute differences in female structure. For what purpose? Certainly not just to create a different female shape for the sake of appearances, or for the sake of giving men sexual pleasure, visual and tactile. No; the only purpose for all these feminine differences is to create the body of a mother.

As those differences have persisted through hundreds of thousands of years of human life it is surely inevitable that they have had their cumulative effect on women. Her destiny as a mother has been dictated by her metabolism. Metabolism is the sum of all the physical and chemical processes by which living organised substance is produced and maintained, as well as the transformation by which energy is made available for the uses of the organism, and woman's metabolism had to be geared to the creating and maintenance of a body capable of breeding eggs and gestating and bearing children.

The 'circumstantial evidence' that we have produced seems to prove that the extra load on woman's metabolism has retarded her throughout the history of evolution. Neanderthal woman was four to six inches shorter than her man. So is twentieth-century woman. Both male and female humans have grown taller since Neanderthal days. The average height of adult men of all races is now between 62 and 70 inches; the average height of adult women is still uniformly four to six inches shorter. Woman's lesser height, shorter limbs, her infantile skull and smaller brain, all seem to add up to proof of the theory that woman has 'come down from the trees' more slowly than man.

4 AGAIN, THE MYSTERY OF MENSTRUATION

What a pity that the calcium-loss menstruation theory cannot be substantiated. We can imagine the joy with which Havelock Ellis seized upon it and enlarged on it. In his eyes it must have seemed a Rosetta Stone with which he could decipher the biological text of sexual differences and explain why menstruating woman could never reach the physical maturity attained by man. Such hopes of finding any self-contained key to a biological riddle are destroyed when Ellis's convincing eloquence is traced to its condemned source.

Even so, the theory nags. What if, despite everything, Ellis was on to something? Since the days of Bell and Ellis many discoveries have been made during research into menstruation. Fortunately most of the old superstitions and fears attached to it have been swept away, but its importance, both physical and psychological, is recognised. It cannot be claimed that a single finding in recent research gives any support to the Bell-Ellis theory, but the cumulative effect of present-day findings forces us to ask whether after all it is possible that Bell and Ellis were, at least in believing menstruation had profound and lasting effects on the female, moving in the right direction. They were, we now know, moving wrongly, moving without due scientific caution, moving from the standpoint of a false premise. And yet? Is it possible that they were blundering, mistakenly and without proof but intuitively, at least in the direction of a truth?

After all that kind of thing has happened often enough before. The history of science is rich in men, not all of them even scientists, who were fired with that inspired 'imagination' Julian Huxley recognises in Darwin. Such men propounded theories which were merely intuitive and could be disputed scientifically, and yet held a truth which would be found, often centuries later, to be a basic truth of life. Indeed any outline of science through the ages reads like romance, so full is it of stories of despised ugly ducklings who became revered swans, dreamers whose dreams were scoffed at and then came true. Consider, for instance, Xenophanes of Ionia. He had a theory (an inspiration, a dream, call it what you like) about the origin of human life. It was a theory which he could not establish mechanistically. He had none of the instruments and techniques available to later scientists. All he had in the way of what we might call scientific evidence was a collection of fossils. Even so, 2,600 years ago, Xenophanes had the wit to suggest that man had emerged from the sea. An inspired guess? Perhaps. Modern scientists justifiably warn us that Xenophanes must not be glorified into a prodigy, an ancient forerunner of today's evolutionists, because his theory was based upon and permeated with the mysticism and pantheism of his time. Another Greek, Anaximander, declared that worlds were not created but evolved, and that the human, like animals, was descended from the fishes. Then there were Democritus and Leucippus, contemporaries of Socrates. We can call them 'atomists' because they, 2,400 years ago, expressed the belief (only the belief; how on earth could they prove it in those days?) that everything was composed of atoms in motion and physically, though not geometrically, indivisible. In fact Democritus, going as far as many scientists dare go even today, declared there was 'no purpose in the universe; only atoms governed by mechanical laws', and denied that anything could happen by chance.

Something else that Democritus said makes him even more apposite to this chapter: he was one of the first, if not *the* first, to say that 'thought is a physical process'.

This evidence that dreamers had the vision to *imagine* theories which could not be accepted as scientific fact until 2,000 years later should restrain us from scoffing at Ellis or Bell or any sincere theorist. Bertrand Russell has said: 'As a rule, the man who first thinks of a new idea is so much ahead of his time that everyone thinks him silly, so that he remains obscure and is soon forgotten. Then, gradually, the world becomes ready for the idea, and the man who proclaims it at the fortunate moment gets all the credit. So it was, for example, with Darwin; poor Lord Monboddo was a laughing stock.' And the fact remains that Xenophanes of Ionia, and Democritus· and Leucippus and Anaximander, by whatever wrong paths they blundered towards scientific truth, were right, whereas all the accepted authorities of their day, all those learned contemporaries of theirs who explained the origin of mankind with legends of mating gods and bestial miracles, were wrong, as wrong as all our own authorities throughout centuries of the Christian era are now proved to have been wrong on the self-same subject.

Indeed religion and science are often alike in their tendency to intellectual sclerosis. In all religions, Christianity included, there comes a time when legends and myths and peasant folklore ossify into dogma. The same thing happens in science. When it seems that finality has been reached in some particular field of scientific inquiry the tendency is for science to become dogmatic and to resist ideas or even facts which threaten to render current generalisations untenable. The archpriests of science can be as jealous and fierce as the archpriests of religion in guarding their mysteries, in suppressing heresies among their fellows, and suppressing curiosity among laymen.

The scientists who chart the path to the future are usually the heretics of their day. However, heresy is, as Professor John Ziman argues, essential to scientific progress. 'In the Christian religion the idea of heresy forces people to criticise the accepted ideas. And out of that has grown one of the key principles of scientific tradition—the idea of falsification. When somebody puts up an idea that you don't agree with, it is one of your duties to say: "Let me see in how many ways I can prove he is wrong." And that, of course, turns out to be very creative.'

Proving Ellis wrong might in fact work in that very way. The process of refuting his theory, uncovering mistakes and producing evidence to show he was wrong might lead inquirers to the study of significant facts about female biology. Actually the basic mistake Ellis made was not actually in believing the calcium-deficiency theory but in jumping to the conclusion that any *one* cause could be responsible for woman's anatomical differences. His was the error often made by enthusiasts: that of creating a vast generalisation out of one particular. And, as we know, even that one particular was wrong. Yet, considered objectively, the mistake was far from stupid. There can be no other reason for woman's different shape than biological evolutionary reasons. Ellis's mistake was to believe optimistically that he could pinpoint a single reason, to believe that the one physical oddity of menstruation and a deficiency of only one chemical could account for everything. Incidentally it was a mistake very much in tune with his time, for it was an era when research was uncovering all kinds of single simplicities to account for natural mysteries. In an age when minute chemical secretions called sex hormones had been revealed as the essential biological essences of masculinity or femininity it was easy for an enthusiast like Ellis to be tempted into the belief that one factor like calcium deficiency could have a drastic overall anatomic effect. The problem of woman's anatomy is obviously more complex than that.

In what way, biologically, does woman differ most from men? In that she is a mother. The needs of motherhood, as we have seen, have determined her bodily shape. One of the processes associated with human maternity is menstruation. Therefore menstruation is one process which must be taken into account when we are discussing the human female's evolutionary development.

We must take into account the known somatic and psychic effects of menstruation, and also the accepted psychological fact that bodily functions have a stronger effect on the mentality of a woman than they do on that of a man. The female mechanism, its physical and psychic inter-relation, is more complex and delicately contrived than the masculine mechanism. With the result that the stresses and strains of living, as well as the joys of living, impose greater stress and strain on a woman's brain. This is inevitable, because of the demands of her maternal role. Thus the character of a woman reflects the fluctuations of emotional pressures such as are never experienced by a man and, because they make no demands on masculine mentality and no imprint on his intellect, leave him that much freer for intellectual adventuring.

So, although we dare not go as far out on a theoretical limb as Ellis did, we are forced to speculate on the possibility that the almost exclusively human phenomenon of menstruation must have had, in ways yet to be discovered, a retarding effect on woman's physical and intellectual development. Calcium deficiency or not, we have to admit that menstruation every lunar month for up to five hundred thousand years adds up to a formidable flow.

It is obviously not without significance that the onset of puberty is, as we have reported earlier, the period of life when the otherwise more durable female is at hazard in physical health. There are indications that the beginning of menstruation might also affect the general level of intelligence, for although girls during childhood tend to show on average some superiority over boys in mental aptitude this feminine superiority tends to decrease on the onset of puberty.

The majority of educationalists and psychologists agree that it is not until after the age of sixteen that the intellectual superiority of boys, the non-menstruating sex, asserts itself.

A cumulative effect of this disparity through hundreds of thousands of years of human evolution must surely be considered as a factor possibly responsible for retarding female intellectual development.

Dr. Katherine Dalton, a doctor who has specially studied menstrual problems, analysed the results obtained by 125 girls in 'A' and 'O' level examinations in relation to the phase of the menstrual cycle when the examinations were taken. Before she made her survey she had reached the considered opinion that during menstruation school-girls were 'naughtier', more unpunctual, untidy and forgetful. Prefects, she found, were stricter and showed increased tendencies to administer punishment when they were menstruating.

Dr. Dalton's analyses, published in *The Lancet* in December 1968, showed that during the premenstruum (the four days preceding menstruation) the pass rate of girls taking 'A' levels was 13 per cent lower and the distinction rate 9 per cent lower than during the inter-menstruum (the days between menstruation and the pre-menstruum). Similarly the average mark they obtained was 3 per cent lower during the para-menstruum (the eight days of the pre-menstruum and menstruation), although in 11 of the 162 examinations in this study the para-menstrual drop was between 30 per cent and 60 per cent.

Menstruation's effect on intelligence is demonstrated even more emphatically in the fact that while the para-menstrual failure rate in 'O' level candidates was 17 per cent for girls whose menstrual loss lasted up to four days, the rate increased progressively until it reached 50 per cent for those whose loss lasted a week. Moreover, the para-menstrual failure rate was 29 per cent for those with short menstrual cycles of 25 days or less and those with normal cycles of 26–30 days. But it rose to 40 per cent where the cycles were unduly prolonged. Dr. Dalton suggested two ways of defeating the menstruation 'examination block'. Examiners should space examinations to avoid girls being wholly in the para-menstruum during an examination. Or girls facing examinations should be given medicines containing oestrogenic substances to bring on menstruation early and get it out of the way *before* the examination, or balanced doses of an oestrogen and a progestogen to defer it until *after* the examination.

In *The Menstrual Cycle* Dr. Dalton says that at four London hospitals half of all female accident cases were admitted during their para-menstruum. 'Some admissions were the result of accidents at home, some on the road, some in factories, some women were passengers and some were drivers, but the influence of the para-menstruum was the same. It seems to be a slower reaction time which accounts for the injuries.'

Dr. Dalton's findings confirm a report made by the Industrial Fatigue Research Board as long ago as 1927 that 'a periodic heightening of functional activity occurs late in the intermenstrual phase of the monthly cycle, and that a corresponding reduction below the average is found shortly before or at the onset of menstruation'.

In *The Second Sex*, Simone de Beauvoir, after a positively frightening summary of all the pains and glandular upsets which a woman suffers during menstruation, sums up: 'The woman is more emotional, more nervous, more irritable than usual, and may manifest serious psychic disturbance. It is during her periods that she feels her body most painfully as an obscure, alien thing; it is, indeed, the prey of a stubborn and foreign life that each month constructs and then tears down a cradle within it; each month all things are made ready for a child and then aborted in the crimson flow. Woman, like man, *is* her body; but her body is something other than herself.'

We shall not introduce the more macabre and often merely imaginative statements of writers on the subject; for instance, such claims as women being more inclined to violence, crime and suicide during menstruation. In 1900 one doctor declared in *The Lancet* that in all the 107 cases of suicide in women that he had examined the act had been committed during menstruation! Such exaggerated myths have been largely discounted by the saner attitude to menstruation prevailing today, and can be relegated to the realm of superstition and taboo.

Nor, tempting though it is, will we give much attention to the theory that infantilism is linked with neurosis. This theory of Freud's, as paraphrased by Schwarz, suggested that 'neurotic symptoms show a great resemblance to the rites and customs of primitive people, so that neurotics are not only infantile, which means retarded in their individual development, but might be looked upon as throwbacks to earlier stages of civilisation.' Nevertheless in this context it is pertinent to mention that some anthropologists do venture the opinion that primitive racial elements in a population are preserved more distinctly by the women than by the men, and we must not overlook the possibility that the psychic effect of menstruation has been intensified through ages of superstition and taboo, nor ignore the stultifying effect on women of having been for some days of every lunar month for tens of thousands of years 'out of the running'.

The fact that menstruation, although it is a natural and inevitable process, can nevertheless have the aspect of a recurrent 'illness', psychologically as well as physiologically, could cause menstruation to have a cumulative effect on mental development. The relationship between good health and high intelligence, the eugenic importance of that relationship and, consequently, its evolutionary importance, is discussed by Dr. Cedric Carter in *Human Heredity*. He claims that 'the man or woman of average intelligence is intrinsically biologically fitter and has more surviving children than either the dull or the clever . . . It is . . . a widely-held popular belief that clever children tend to be inferior in health and strength to the average child. But studies on this point have shown that this is not the case and that clever children are, in general, healthier and stronger than the average.'

It seems logical to link this observation with Kenneth Walker's statement that 'Not only in her physical but also in her psychological make-up everything in a woman is sacrificed to the function of motherhood'. In summing up the physiological effects of that 'sacrifice' Walker uses a most significant quotation from Maranon which I have italicised in my extract from Walker's *The Physiology of Sex*.

'The female body may therefore be regarded as a body that has undergone no further development through the stimulating action of the male hormone. Biologically, therefore, a woman may be regarded as "*an organism arrested so far as her general evolution is concerned in the borderland of adolescence by the necessity of specialising a large part of her activity to the transcendental function of maternity*". For this reason her aptitude for physical and intellectual exertion in the primitive struggle for existence is less than that of a man.'

In other words the burden of motherhood has made woman weaker not only *physically* but also *intellectually*. This difference must have existed in the earliest stages of the emergence of humans on the evolutionary scene, although we can speculate that it became more marked at that stage of evolution when our primal ancestors first stood erect and walked on two legs instead of four. We can imagine that it might have been during that 'walking erect stage', a traumatic moment of change from animal to human, that the process of monthly menstruation began. So although we have, with no small regret, to dismiss Bell and Ellis from the dossier, we can persist in our belief that the process of motherhood in general, including the process of menstruation in particular, has determined for woman a physical shape and strength which must have some effect upon her intellectual 'shape' and strength.

At this point it seems necessary to refer to a popular misconception regarding women who are described as 'career women', those women who, out of personal desire or because circumstances force them to do so, refuse to accept the role of motherhood, and do not marry or at least do not devote their lives to husband, home and children. It is frequently asked why women who have escaped the demands of maternity and often risen to eminence and renown in their chosen careers could not become intellectual equals of the men at the very top. This question is easily disposed of. Although a woman can opt out of maternity, she cannot opt out of being a woman. Whatever she might choose as a career, her body and her mind are still governed and restricted by the biological processes of being feminine, by the secretions and glands which demand that at puberty she must begin producing the eggs which, if not fertilised, must be expelled by menstruation. In fact it could surely be suggested, though very speculatively indeed, that by denying fertilisation of the eggs and the bearing of children a woman could be denying her feminine body and also her feminine mind the fulfilment essential to her as a woman, and that the consequent necessary menstruation to rid herself of the abortive eggs could probably be subjecting her to a physical and mental effort more insidiously debilitating, physical and mental, than that of bearing and nursing children. That thought comes to my mind because among the women of considerable intellectual achievement that I have known all but two have been married and nearly all of those have been mothers; though against such a personal and unscientific observation one must balance the medical and clinical findings that maternity makes heavy demands on women.

Nearly 50 years ago Dr. Crichton Miller boldly declared in the *British Medical Journal* that it was impossible for woman's 'thyroidal storehouse of energy to cope with both child-bearing and artistic creation at the same time'. That was in 1922, and since then we have learned very much more about the effect of glandular secretions not only on our physical growth but on our minds and mental attitudes. We have, in fact, learned enough to believe that the 1922 doctor was probably right. It does indeed seem more than likely that research into hormones might uncover the crucial clue to the mental difference between the sexes.

One thing however that can be said with confidence even at the present level of research is that throughout her life and in either condition, in virginity or in maternity, woman suffers greater stresses, physical and mental, than man. It seems self-evident that she cannot suffer those complex and demanding stresses without her physical development being affected, and also, we argue, her intellectual development being affected. Therefore we are forced to the conclusion that woman's intellect has not been retarded by social tyranny. It has not been retarded by masculine tyranny. It has been retarded by the inescapable tyranny of her own feminine biology.

9 Woman's Intuition

'Of course there is no intellectual difference between the sexes. Speaking as a woman . . .' The voice interrupted me when I was tidying my desk to begin this chapter. The interruption was not entirely fortuitous, for I was keeping my ear cocked in case one member of a symposium of learned broadcasters might say something new on the old subject of women's rights. I switched off.

The eminent lady's vocabulary is slovenly. Or, worse, her logic is. Almost certainly she was not talking about 'difference' in intellect at all. What she had in mind was 'superiority' or 'inferiority'. If she did mean 'difference', then she contradicted herself in the next breath when she said that she was *speaking as a woman*, for with those words she acknowledged that a woman does speak differently. As speech is one of the attributes of intellect, difference in speech must therefore prove difference in intellect.

However, the eminent lady's howler is no worse than is usually made when men and women are striking attitudes in those perpetual male-versus-female arguments. When not engaged in such disputes we take it for granted that there is an intellectual difference. We do so, for instance, whenever we use such words as 'from a man's point of view' or 'from a woman's point of view'.

Let us seize on that phrase 'point of view'. It is very useful for our argument. Just as the laws of relativity and time depend in their way on 'point of view', so does the irreversible natural law of the difference between masculine and feminine intellect. See how it operates at one of the crudest levels of intellectual expression, the physical desire of male for female. Woman's point of view is from behind breasts: man's point of view is from behind a penis. From such differing points of view masculine and feminine mental attitudes must inevitably be different. If they were not, there would be that agonising mental confusion which, as we know, is suffered by certain psychologically disturbed deviants.

At higher levels of sexuality, at levels where sexual desire is intellectualised with emotion and imagery, this difference in point of view is not lessened by the intellectual content: it is intensified. At that stage the behind-breasts behind-penis points of view are impregnated with personal and social concepts of masculinity and femininity.

But quite apart from sexuality any confrontation between any human beings is coloured by male and female points of view. There is a wealth of psychoanalytical observation on this subject, but even without that we know and can see for ourselves that men and women do react differently and do assume different attitudes when coming face to face with members of their own sex or the opposite sex. This is not surprising: indeed only if the reactions were *not* different would it seem surprising.

Different points of view are expressed also in the processes of everyday life. That men and women wear different clothes, and that they attach differing values to the instruments and utensils of life and handle them and use them differently, are manifestations of their differing mental attitudes.

Let us illustrate the different 'point of view' simply. Imagine a man and a woman listening together to that radio broadcast on women's rights. The broadcaster uses the word 'woman'. Immediately the thoughts of the two listeners are on a different course. To the man it means someone of the other sex, one of 'them'. To the woman it means someone of the same sex, one of 'us'. The sentence of which the word 'woman' is the subject is therefore heard from a masculine or feminine point of view. Whereas the man's 'point of view' is from outside and he is watching what 'woman' is doing, the woman's 'point of view' is from inside and she is identifying herself with what 'woman' is doing. If the sex of the broadcaster is relevant to the statement being made, then there are even more permutations in 'points of view'. Indeed, every moment of our lives, sometimes consciously but far more often subconsciously, we are looking at things and evaluating them from masculine or feminine 'points of view'.

As a final example, and because you have it in your hands at the moment, take this book. However objective the writer has tried to be, however much the writer has tried to present both masculine and feminine points of view by retailing the opinions of both men and women, the fact remains that the writer is a male. He can never completely isolate himself from his maleness or from a masculine point of view of the subject of the book. Still less can he hope to isolate himself from a point of view that is far more pervasive because it is largely subconscious, his male point of view of life in general. It is impossible for him to eunuchise his thoughts so completely as to eliminate all traces of that point of view. But even if he had done so, even if he had made the impossible possible, the book has now finished up in the hands of a man reader or a woman reader. Like the man or woman listening to the broadcast this reader is now translating the words 'men' and 'women' into 'them' or 'us'.

All the mental and psychological differences we discuss elsewhere in this book have relation to male and female points of view, but in this chapter we shall restrict our investigation to two striking intellectual differences: sense of humour and intuition.

1 SENSE OF HUMOUR

It is only oneself who has a sense of humour: the other fellow rarely has. Broadly speaking that is also how the sexes think about each other. Or the best that one sex can say about the other is that its sense of humour is strangely different. Which is true. How and why it is different is revealing.

Freud demonstrated that an analysis of a person's sense of humour could provide a penetrating insight into that person's subconscious. Indeed he is so convincing on the subject that we almost begin to believe that what we laugh about might be more revealing than what we cry about. Freudian subtleties are profound, and we shall not attempt to plumb their depths. As what we are searching for is the sex difference in sense of humour we shall use the shortest route. We shall go straight to 'sex', and examine the different attitudes of men and women to the sex joke, to what is known as the 'dirty story'.

During our childhood quite a lot of what we learn about sex comes to us by way of the dirty story. Which is not as unfortunate for us as some moralists and educationalists think. It does seem preferable to learn the facts of life with laughter rather than with tears, and one hopes that even when sex-education is being handed out in hygienic untouched-by-hand television packages the young pupils will still find opportunities for the occasional giggle.

We begin to understand the sex joke at the same time that we are beginning to understand more about life in general, at the time when we are becoming aware that beyond the cosy horizon of family and school is an immense and exciting world. As we become conscious that we have a personal future in that outside world we begin to realise that life is big, full of joys and adventures and gratifications. Because this is also the time when we are becoming aware of sex, our own sex and the sex of others, it is inevitable that all the joys and adventures and gratifications we expect in life become infused in some measure with sexual flavours. We learn to restrain our sexual appetites. We learn to restrict them to appropriate time and place, and our wilder sexual imaginings sink into the subconscious. But because all our hopes of what we are going to get out of life always have that infusion of sexual flavour adhering to them our gender, our masculinity or femininity, becomes important to us as an essential feature of personal fulfilment. The importance we attach to our masculinity or femininity is revealed by the mental attitudes we adopt to confirm or assert our gender. We reveal it, as Freud shows, in our sense of humour, and, as one would expect, we reveal it most recognisably in the sex joke.

Asserting gender is a more strenuous task for a man than for a woman. A woman can prove her femininity merely by being passive, merely by *being*. But to prove his masculinity man must be active, must strut around with an erection. This is seen in the attitudes men and women adopt to the sex joke.

A man's sex jokes reveal the importance he attaches to gender. He identifies himself with his sex jokes. Like a boy reading a cowboys-and-Indians yarn he wants to act the part of the hero, especially a virile hero. It is a part of his fantasy life of masculine sexual conquest, just as a war story or a golfing story is part of a fantasy life of masculine courage or superiority. Man's self-identification with his sex joke can sometimes be a sublimation of sexual frustration. It is significant that the man most prone to telling sex jokes is often the man who has subconscious uncertainties about his gender: he has the infantile belief that real masculinity can be symbolised only by an erect penis.

For a man the sex joke can also be a catharsis. With a guffaw he can purge away all those sexual repressions that have been nagging away deep down in his subconscious, and that is undoubtedly preferable to having to purge them away on a psychiatrist's couch.

A woman, because she is not under the same compulsive necessity of asserting her gender, is naturally less interested in the sex joke; certainly never as interested as she sometimes pretends to be. Women do make risqué jokes, but usually as a kind of social gesture when they feel the circumstances demand they should be 'one of the boys'. They will put on a show of being amused, but they obviously get far less fun out of the stories than their menfolk. They are not necessarily shocked, though out of social convention they might pretend to be, because, by and large, the 'point' of the joke seems to them to have little importance: they have not identified themselves with it.

Woman's comparative indifference to the sex joke, her near contempt of it, is surely the cause of her being notoriously less alert than man to the *double entendre*. A woman is not, as most men constantly are, aware that the bawdiest double meaning can lurk in the most innocuous of words. During my own newspaper experience I have seen visible effects of this feminine blindness to the hazards of the *double entendre*, and Hugh Cudlipp has recorded how a female writer on a very proper woman's newspaper, without a suspicion of a blush, headlined her Paris column with the words 'Our French Letter'. And another woman journalist, editor of a very prim household magazine, might have asked what on earth was wrong in putting below the picture of a pretty Netherlands girl in a knitted bonnet the inspiring exhortation 'Knit Yourself a Pretty Dutch Cap'. It was also a woman, brilliant editor of an elegant journal, who, after spending some time trying to cut down the number of words in a caption so that it would fit above a fashion photograph of a hat, decided, so logically, that after all the word 'hat' was not necessary. With the result that the printers received a page-proof bearing the teasing invitation 'Spend Your Weekend Under a Big Black Sailor'. Obviously it is only man who is always 'thinking of sex'.

When she is in company or, for instance, watching entertainment in which the *double entendre* can be expected, then a woman will recognise it and be duly amused. Otherwise she remains sublimely unaware. A man can hardly restrain a smile when he hears a building described as an erection: for a woman the word means either a building or a tumescent penis according to the context, not both at the same time.

Feminine disregard, amounting to distaste, of the sex joke is fundamental in female psychology and is not an attitude peculiar to our society or to our time. The same attitude has been repeatedly observed among primitive peoples. A most pleasing example is provided by that eighteenth-century traveller J. R. Forster when he describes women of a South Sea island. 'Virtuous women bear a joke without emotion, which, among us, might put some men to the blush. Neither austerity and anger, nor joy and ecstasy is the consequence, but sometimes a modest, dignified, serene smile spreads itself over their faces, and seems gently to rebuke the uncouth jester.' Any man who has ever gone that 'bit too far' at a dinner table can recall embarrassing memories of that gentle rebuke, that serene but devastating smile which tells him that the lady hospitably forgives him for his liberties but is not amused.

Dr. Gesell remarks that girls of eleven 'are not as interested in "smutty" stories or in observing animal intercourse as boys are. At that age they are interested in knowing more about human intercourse, though they are becoming more reticent in talking about it.'

It is true that during puberty girls are sometimes prone to make coarser jokes than boys, but this outburst is psychologically diagnosed as a denial of, or protection against, the awakening sexuality of which menstruation is making them aware, and not an enjoyment of sexuality. Coarse jokes fade away as the girl matures. By the time she has become a woman she has, as it were, 'had it'. In fact from personal observation I would say that the woman who has not 'had it', whose sexuality has been frustrated or unsatisfied, is the woman more inclined to attach importance to 'verbal' sex, to smirk or bridle coyly at actual or imagined suggestiveness in conversation, whereas the woman who has had sex early in life without inhibitions and has had her fill of it is quite openly bored with sex talk or sex jokes. She knows what she needs to know about sex: it is not all that funny.

There, I think, we have it. The girl on the verge of puberty does of necessity feel, as she becomes conscious of sex and her sexual destiny, that she must know more about the *facts* of life than about the *fun* of it. As she gets older that attitude strengthens, and it is reflected in the sense of humour of a mature woman. To her sex cannot seem funny. Indeed it is a thing of high seriousness. The man's smoking-room jokes are thick with invented pictures of male conquest and bizarre modes of coitus, but woman, who is on the receiving end of coitus and has the eventual result to bear and nurse, is less likely to see the act as highly hilarious.

Though women do have their sex jokes, just as men have,

and Zippin maintains that each sex has a whole repertoire of jokes 'too subtly bound up with sex role for members of the opposite sex to be understood or be amused by them'. But he reports also Edith Jacobson's theory that woman's tendency to react to humour 'with inner amusement rather than overt laughter' is because by so doing woman expresses the superiority of her inner penis (her clitoris) over the male's external genitals and his more showy demonstration. Which observation confirms in psychoanalytical terminology what we said more crudely above: that woman feels no necessity to assert her gender, but man must show off his erection.

Man is more usually the collector of pornography than woman. Woman will evince interest in pornography when it can be used to arouse sexuality in a man or will enhance the sexuality of a scene, but man has an almost masturbatory love of pornography for its own sake. Witness those rich collections of pornography amassed by frock-coated Victorian gentlemen. Admittedly a woman, Beate Uhse, has in Germany become one of permissive society's tycoons of pornography, but she is an exception, and we can imagine few female counterparts to that Pisanus Fraxi of London who spent £100,000 on sex books nor imagine many women contributing towards the £200,000 paid for his library after his death.

But although a woman is less responsive to the sex joke than man and her reaction to all types of humour less overt than his, it must not be thought that the feminine sense of humour is deficient. Woman's 'inner amusement' indicates that to her humour is something personal and private. Because of that it can be more subtle, more finely shaded, something not easy to transmit to an audience but capable of being appreciated inwardly. Several writers have made too much of the fact that in the world of entertainment there are many more comedians than comediennes. This might also be explained by woman's capacity for inner amusement. Humour is something she can enjoy herself; she does not need others to laugh either *with* her or *at* her. The work of many women writers and the speeches and conversation of many women in public life, in politics and the arts for example, prove that a woman can be as responsive to humour and as quick-witted in the use of it as a man.

2 'WOMAN'S INTUITION'

'A man is ruled by his head, a woman by her heart.' We hear that often enough, and although we know that it is merely poetically imaginative to think of the head as the abode of reason and the heart as the abode of emotion, it is commonly accepted that what we call 'reason' is substantially masculine and what we call 'emotion' is substantially feminine. Man, we say, 'reasons things out', woman 'jumps to conclusions'. A spot check among our acquaintances will show that this is not true in all cases. Any one of us knows men whose opinions and actions erupt from irrational angers or impulsive sentimentality; any one of us knows women whose words and deeds are sweetly reasonable or even downright calculating. Even if we persuade ourselves that such men and women are freakish exceptions and even if we persist in our belief in the existence of some kind of mental spectrum in which man, coldly analytical, is at one pole, and woman, warmly emotional, is at the other, even so we are forced to admit that there are infinite variations in the reason-emotion prescription between the two extremes.

Therefore, we might ask, is it possible that these psychological variations are analogous to the physical variations in male and female bodies? Is there, for instance, something like those mixups that are caused by the sex hormones? We know that the bodies of both men and women have masculine and feminine hormones, and we knew that if the mixture is not quite what it should be males can be a bit too feminine and females a bit too masculine. Can it therefore be that masculine reason is sometimes tinged with too much feminine emotion, and vice versa?

That pretty analogy is founded on error. The error is in thinking that reason and emotion are individual and separable attributes. They are not. Hormones can be separated and isolated and confidently labelled masculine or feminine. But reason and emotion cannot be separated and isolated because they have no separate existence. They are merely colorations in a complete and indivisible entity, the mind. A sphere constructed of pieces of mirror-glass suspended and revolving in a ballroom reflects the brilliance and colour of the lights that are beamed upon it. Switch off the lights and the sphere makes no response. A mind is analogous to that sphere in so far as it also is an individual unity and cannot operate unless impressions are beamed upon it. The mind's responses will be bright or dim according to the brilliance or dullness of the impressions and according to the sensitivity and educated clarity of its 'mirrors'. The response is the response of the entire mind: it is only the observer who evaluates a response as reasoned or emotional, and then only according to his point of view.

We must therefore disregard that imaginative separating of reason and emotion. We must examine masculine and feminine minds as entities. We have already agreed that they are different. But then *all* minds are different. That is one of the felicities, as well as one of the problems, of being human. Each of us inhabits mentally a unique world. To any situation we react in terms of our own personality, differently in some degree from the way the next person, man or woman, reacts. To the observer it might appear that we are reacting in the same way as another person. We might, for instance, both be voting for the same candidate at an election, looking at the same scene, listening to the same music, reading the same book or newspaper, even loving the same woman or man. But in all those things and at every second of our life our reactions are individual, unique to ourselves.

But is there, in all these so differing and so individual minds, a common sexual denominator? Is there something so distinctive and exclusive to one of the sexes that its existence permits us to say that one type of mind is masculine and another type is feminine?

It seems that there is such a sex distinction and that it is the one responsible for woman 'jumping to conclusions'. Psychoanalytical research supports the view that women are more sensitive mentally than men. They are more suggestible, and this gives them a capacity for 'weighing up' a situation of a person quickly as though by sensory instinct. In other words the suggestion is that there really is something we can call 'woman's intuition'.

Most people put intuition in the same category as telepathy, considering both either as superstitions believed in only by gullible folk or as inexplicable phenomena which cannot be proved but can be taken on trust. It is true that both intuition and telepathy can be defined as phenomena which operate outside the recognised channels of sense. But beyond that generalised definition the similarity ends. Intuition is the immediate apprehension of an object by *one mind* without the intervention of any reasoning process: telepathy is the communication of impressions between *minds* without the employment of recognised channels of sense. The basic difference is that one is a demonstrable reality and the other is a myth. In short, intuition exists and telepathy does not exist.

I am accused of being too dogmatic in stating that telepathy does not exist, and I am told that the most I should dare to say is that telepathy has not yet been *proved* to exist. But our knowledge of the physical processes of thought is already sufficient to assure us that the concept of telepathy defies all natural laws. Of course it often happens that two people simultaneously experience the same thought, but it is erroneous to consider coincidence as proof of telepathic communication. That 'parallel thought' is not being communicated from person to person but is reaching each from some common source either in their memories or in their genetically inherited human consciousness.

Research into telepathy, spiritualism, extra-sensory perception and other so-called psychic-phenomena has taken me to some very odd places; among them, for instance, a physics laboratory in the hinterland of Czechoslovakia, and, even stranger, a secluded building in Germany bearing the almost sinister name of Institute of Borderland Psychology. At the former I met the team who were investigating a man's claim that he could influence the movements of a physical object by mental force alone. At the latter I met a distinguished scientist who was analysing the convincingly prophetic dreams of a film actress and tracing the roots of those dreams to her extra-sensory perception of future probabilities. These are serious scientists, and their research must not be scoffed at as bizarre. To a large extent what they are really exploring is the human mind and how it works. They are not trying to prove the existence of that mysterious power which their subjects believed they possessed.

Elsewhere I have met the men and women who call themselves para-psychologists. Engaged in research into psychic-phenomena of all kinds some of these do attempt to conduct their inquiries and experiments in accord with scientific discipline and are cautious in their claims. But there are others, more 'committed' to their beliefs, whose experiments are fabricated, without regard for the clinical objectivity necessary in scientific research, to prove merely what the experimenters have decided in advance, consciously or unconsciously, the result should be. None of all these have proved under really scientific conditions that minds can communicate telepathically with other minds.

However, my explorations into these borderlands of science made me certain of one thing. If telepathy or communication with departed 'spirits' were possible, they would more likely be demonstrated by a woman than by a man. This because woman can be seen to have a mental sensitivity which would surely be the first prerequisite in such communication systems. Which brings us to the subject of woman's extra-sensory perception.

Extra-sensory perception is in a different class from telepathy and spiritualism. Here we are dealing with something demonstrable. I believe that the memory-banks of our brains do contain memories and knowledge of which we are unaware in the sense that we have not yet developed the facility of tapping them in a consciously controlled manner. Some memories and knowledge are part of our genetical inheritance. Others are sensory impressions we have picked up without knowing that we were doing so. As Polanyi says, 'We know more than we can tell.' But there are occasions when memories or knowledge, stimulated by some other sensory impression, can pop out like a card from a card-index, showing that, unknown to us, our memory-bank has all the time been steadily at work calculating and computerising probabilities.

In this respect I believe that a woman can be more sensorily-perceptive than a man. Her female biology hints that this is possible. That extra female sensitivity which, for instance, disperses a woman's erogenous zones over the whole surface of her body can be seen as an illustration of the way in which a woman's mental sensitivity might also be dispersed throughout her whole being, and consequently she is more vibrantly receptive of sensory impressions than a man. Kenneth Walker says, 'Woman has been equipped with a greater sensitiveness to affective stimulus than has a man. She sees life through her feelings, and emotionally reaches many a truth to which man, working laboriously through the medium of his reason, remains permanently blind.'

Spiritualists and other archpriests of mysticism realise this and take advantage of it. Most of the hierarchy are men, but nearly all the subjects they use in their experiments or demonstrations are women, as are also the majority of their disciples and audiences and the members of their associations or 'churches'. Spiritualism provides a striking example of this. Its hierarchy is principally male, its most popularly successful faith-healers are men, but in the lower ranks women predominate. Women who can be persuaded to believe in spiritualism make ideal mediums and fervent followers. The intuitive quality of a woman's mind, her capacity for immediate response can result in a woman medium's performance being dramatically convincing to an audience prepared or desiring to believe that the medium is controlled by departed spirits, particularly when the medium also believes, as most of them sincerely do, that she is so controlled.

Women are easy 'believers'. So are some men, of course, but practically all women are more susceptible than men to superstition and less critical in accepting creeds and beliefs. It is noticeable that in advanced societies, where religions have lost much of their power and credibility, women worshippers far outnumber the men. The sociological factors which have conditioned women to be more docile than men in obedience to beliefs are obvious and need not be categorised, but equally determinant has been the psychological factor of feminine suggestibility.

How passively obedient women can be was demonstrated in an experiment conducted at, of all places, a pedestrian crossing. Eysenck tells how a test made by a Road Research Laboratory showed that more women than men used the crossing. Even the women who did not use it crossed the road nearer to it. Then a policeman was stationed at the crossing, not to control the pedestrians but just to stand there as a symbol of authority. The effect, says Eysenck, was dramatic. Nearly all the men now conformed and used the crossing, but as soon as the policeman went away they went back to the former habit of not using it. But the presence of the policeman made no effect on the women at all: the same proportion used it whether he was there or not. Eysenck rightly remarks that it would need a psychologist to work out whether the observations are psychologically meaningful, but to the non-psychologist it does seem that having been conditioned into obedience to a rule most women tend to continue to obey irrespective of whether the eye of authority is on them or not.

Anyhow, if to be exploited or submissive are the penalties woman must suffer because she is suggestible and impressionable, those same attributes are also responsible for her gift of intuition. That capacity for immediate apprehension is so uniformly observed in women that some psychologists are prepared to accept it as a feminine characteristic: so much so that if it is observed in a man, the man can be expected to have some femininity in his personality.

Woman's facility to 'jump to conclusions', and very often the right ones, and her often demonstrated capacity to weigh up a person or a situation is not the result of speeded-up thinking, nothing so crude as a computer-type intelligence capable of comparing received impressions at the flick of a switch. Nor is her capacity to sense what another person is feeling the result of any transference of thoughts from the other person. It must be remembered that intuition is defined as operating 'without the intervention of any reasoning processes', so it is not something a woman switches on as demanded. It is suggested that the operation takes place at subconscious level, at which level a woman subjectively experiences what the other person is experiencing. She can, as it were, put herself in the other person's shoes without reasoning about it. Psychologists arguing in orthodox Freudian terms suggest that a woman is able to do this because she has retained into later life the awareness of her own mental processes which was one of the traits of her adolescence. In adolescence such self-study is sometimes near to obsessive and is always more intense in girls than in boys. The masculine tendency is to grow out of it, or suppress it, but woman retains it and, being subjectively sensitive to her own mental processes, is more sensitively aware of the mental processes of others and subconsciously identifies with others.

I favour another reason, blunter and more matter of fact. The different roles and positions of men and women in society can surely be responsible for woman retaining her preoccupation with her mental processes and man being forced to abandon them. It seems self-evident that whenever a situation demands conscious reasoning, some 'intervention' of mental processes, subconscious promptings, are censored out and suppressed by conscious calculation.

In civilised societies man has had to assume positions of authority and responsibility in family and in government and engage in occupations and pursuits in which reason and calculation have had to be employed forcibly and purposefully. In the process his subconscious sensitivities have had to be censored, with the result that his sensitivity to the feelings of others is dulled.

It would be interesting to psychoanalyse women who have adopted careers and see whether under the necessity of using reason and calculation they have lost some of their feminine subjective sensitivity. I hazard the opinion that they have; and I base that opinion on personal observation of women mediums and the like. The lower the intelligence of these women, the less inhibited they are by reason, the more their utterances and actions are controlled by their subconscious, and consequently the more dramatic are their performances and the more convincing to the gullible.

There are 'pedestrian crossings' in social conduct as well as in the streets, and woman has always had to be more circumspect and obedient in using them than man has. Her social position imposes on her the necessity of being more sensitively observant of what people are thinking of her, particularly what men are thinking of her. Preserving her adolescent self-awareness gives her the capacity of adjusting herself instinctively to the moods of others in social encounters, to assume, as it were, protective colouring. But this is not necessarily a submissive posture. Just as a woman singer interprets a man's music and can embellish it by her interpretation, a woman can similarly interpret man's feelings and mould them to a desired emotional shape.

A feminine facility for assuming the 'colour' appropriate to the circumstances is woman's high diplomacy in relationships. Indeed many a woman seems to have brought this adjusting to such an art that she can be suspected of being as subtle, or as dishonest, as the most devious diplomat. But she is not consciously acting a part. When, for instance, she assumes a mental attitude flattering to a man's sense of his masculinity, she is not deliberately calculating which word or which mood will best do that: she is merely following the promptings of the intuitive sensitivity which is second nature to her.

Here we have a hint of what we can call woman's 'tact', the facility to adapt herself to the personalities and moods of others, the attribute which, for instance, makes it easier for the wife of a self-made man often better able to adapt to changed circumstances than her husband. In fact woman suffers less from nostalgia than a man, because her suggestibility, although it can induce fears and phobias and obsessions in her, helps her to adapt herself more easily to new surroundings and different modes of life.

Many instances when woman's intuition seems to lead her astray into wrong judgments are very often instances where she has not trusted her intuition. The errors she makes are because she did not have the courage to follow her hunch. She has made the mistake of letting reason intervene. Later she finds out that she knew well enough what the situation was and what would happen but she did not use her intuitive capacity.

It is claimed that very often women of outstanding talent are unsure of their opinions and ideas until they are confirmed by someone they respect or, a greater danger, by someone they love. A woman will often all too easily accept the opinions and statements of anyone she loves. Havelock Ellis, agreeing with the Freudian concept of woman as passive and receptive with a desire 'to be seeded from outside', claimed that 'Even in trivial matters the average woman more easily accepts statements and opinions than a man, and in more serious matters she may even be prepared to die for a statement or an opinion, provided it is uttered with such authority and unction that her emotional nature is sufficiently thrilled'.

Man has always been somewhat suspicious, even somewhat frightened, of woman's intuition. At the dawn of civilisation women prophets were held in awe by men. Their demonstration of feminine intuition gave them a supernatural aura. 'More ancient than the male prophet is feminine prophecy', said Bachofen. 'More constant in loyalty and firmer in faith is the feminine soul. Woman, weaker than man, is nevertheless occasionally capable of rising far above him. She is more conservative, particularly in cults and when it comes to the preservation of the ceremonial element.' These attributes, he said, could be 'traced back to the prototype of Demeter. The earthly mother becomes, as it were, the mortal representative of the telluric primitive mother.'

From such mystic veneration of woman's origin it was only a step for woman to be seen by men as a witch, and for her uncanny intuition to result in her being burned or drowned or disembowelled. The Christian Church, easily superstitious and easily frightened, spent several centuries gorily executing women whose intuitive powers made frightened men believe that the women had the devil in them. With typical masculine logic they decided the issue by such means as the test by water: if a woman could swim she was a witch, if she drowned then she was innocent.

There we have a pretty example of what happens when

man's reasoning suppresses utterly his human sensitivity, of how fierce masculine reason lacking the humanity of subjectivity, can drive man to such masculine pursuits as persecution, capital punishment, massacre, totalitarian dictatorship and war.

The realms of abstract thought and metaphysics are inhabited solely by chill and scholarly men, not merely because woman is less capable of abstract thought but because the essentially intellectual process of analysis is alien to her mind. To a woman life is essentially human and sensual; she abhors the attempt to freeze it into a frame of logic and abstract propositions. She believes, and is so often right, that the just and proper deed is more likely to be performed on impulse, by intuition, and most often is corrupted and distorted by the arguments of reason. She feels that any attempt to make a chart for moral decisions and moral acts according to rigid intellectual rules inhibits that instinctively emotional response to life which is her special feminine attribute. That is the reason why although women can be more devoted and pious than men in observing the rites of man-designed religions and dogmas they are so only because they are extracting from them emotional guidance and solace, and they willingly assign the arid questions of intellectual structure and metaphysical politics to the men, to the cardinals and popes.

Seen in that context intuition can be defined as a subconscious awareness of truth. To a woman truth is something known; to a man it is something he must prove. Intuition endows a woman with the capacity of feeling the existence of a truth even when that truth is beyond intellectualism. Man, having abandoned or suppressed that sensitivity, must resort to forging truth on the anvil of logic. History shows us in appalling paradox how often this intellectual effort to rationalise truth impels man to re-enact his original role of predator. Bigger-muscled and bigger-brained than woman, he is superbly designed to protect his mate, to conquer enemies both natural and chosen, and gloriously to survive. But he is designed also to be intellectually the Cain, the male architect of homicidal history all the way from the day prehensile man first took into his hands a lump of rock and bashed in another human head to this day when twentieth-century man, in all his learned and dangerous grandeur, has taken into his hands another lump of mineral and threatens every human head on earth.

PART FOUR

The Difference in Life

And the eyes of them both were opened, and they knew that they were naked; and they sewed fig leaves together and made themselves aprons.

GENESIS

10 The Laws of Sex

Look at the boy and girl walking ahead of us along the street: both in jeans, both wearing frilled and flower-patterned shirts, both with hair falling at about the same length into the napes of their necks. If the girl is young and has not yet accumulated on hips and buttocks the fatty deposits of feminine maturity, and if the boy is plump and has not yet lost all his puppy fat, it is difficult at first glance to distinguish which is male and which is female.

Look at clerks in offices and workers in factories. Here difference in dress often distinguishes male from female, but if we examine the work being done, the calculations and decisions being made at the desks or the objects being constructed and packaged in the workshops, we find no differences in the products or working habits of male and female.

Go further afield. Look, as I did some months ago, at a squad of Israeli soldiers in an armoured truck along a road in occupied Jordan. When you catch up with them you think at first they must be the prettiest soldiers you have ever seen. Then it dawns on you that they are girls.

Or imagine yourself watching hordes of youngsters swarming in political demonstration through the Gate of Heavenly Peace at Peking. In that mass of blue-smocked figures, most of them slim and dainty of build, it is not easy to distinguish boys from girls.

Sights like these, common in all countries of big population and industrial development, give the impression that men and women are becoming increasingly alike, and it might indeed seem that by wearing similar clothes, by doing the same jobs and facing the same duties and hazards in war or politics, men and women are eroding the difference between the sexes. Indeed, some people, referring to the title of this book, have asked, 'But *what* difference? Isn't it getting less and less?'; while others have expressed the opinion that we are witnessing today the first indications of that distant bisexual future envisaged by physiologists and zoologists when life on earth will come full circle to its hermaphrodite beginnings.

It is not so. Those similarities in clothes and conduct are only surface similarities. The essential difference between man and woman persists at deeper levels than outward trappings of dress or way of life. Just as different male and female genitals and body-shape are merely secondary sexual characteristics, our clothes and customs can be considered as only secondary to our real sex.

In fact we can formulate a fundamental law on the difference between man and woman. We can base this law upon the proved fact that in the lowest species of life (both the species existing in the earliest stages of life on earth and primitive species still existing today) sexual differences hardly exist, and male and female are merged into one body. But the higher a species is in the scale of evolution the more defined is the difference between male and female. Therefore, the more mature human beings have become in the evolutionary sense, the more distinct from other species and the less brutish they have become, the more emphatic has become the difference between man and woman, not in the physical sense but intellectually and psychologically. In other words, the more *human* we are, the more refined and beautiful and agile we are in body and in intellect, the more marked is the difference between man and woman. At the same time, the difference becomes ever more essential to our physical, intellectual and psychological evolution as human beings.

Indeed we can go so far as to say that the difference between man and woman has been the vital factor in human evolution. For the sexual urge which that difference has aroused, along with the increasingly sophisticated emotions and imagery with which men and women embellish their sexuality, is the driving force behind every human endeavour, the inspiration of every human achievement, from the building of the first home to the noblest creations in thought and art and science.

When we apply this fundamental law of sexual difference to all forms of life we see it established with almost mathematical precision. Generally speaking it can be said that the lowest forms of life are hermaphrodite in character, and, as we have said, the sexual difference intensifies at each step up the evolutionary ladder. We must not accept any contradictions to this rule. If we do find any species to which we have allocated a lowly position in the evolutionary league table but which shows outstanding male-female sex differences, it is not an exception to the rule. Rather it is our scale of values that is awry. We should change that scale of values. Instead of classifying any species as low or high according to its general anatomical development we must classify it on the criterion of how little or how much its sexual difference has developed. Seen in this light the story of human evolution beautifully proves our argument that the intensifying of the physical and psychological difference between man and woman has resulted in human beings becoming the highest form of life on earth.

Just as we must accept that we can no longer run amid the treetops because we had to come down and eventually use our hands for human purposes, so must we accept that for at least as many hundreds of thousands of years as our imagination can conceive man and woman will be of different shapes; as they now are, emotionally different as well as physically different.

That difference is a vital human distinction which we must jealously preserve: socially and politically it ensures the continued freedom and dignity of mankind. For there are many who welcome the whittling away of differences in human beings. Tycoons, the tycoons of politics as well as of commerce, would sit more comfortably, the former more securely and the latter more profitably, in their seats of power and wealth, if people were more alike. The dictators, not only the gross ones of Stalin or Hitler brand but also the faceless bureaucrats of supposedly democratic governments, are aware that any individual of any shape or colour differing from the mediocre norm is a potential rebel. The dictators of politics and commerce can collect votes and profits more easily from a populace ironed into uniformity, drilled into card-index communities of voting or purchasing units, their bodies housed in similar boxes and their minds conditioned to the lowest common denominator. To such dictators the ultimate ideal could be for the last human difference, the difference between men and women, to be abolished in a mass-minded mass-produced 1984 Brave New World of voters and drones. Fortunately that sinister ambition can never be achieved if we hang on to our awareness of being individual men and women. Other species of life have submitted to laws enforcing conformity, have toed the biological and zoological line until they became extinct or reached the drab cul-de-sac of their restricted evolutionary destiny. Only man, because human aspirations make him at heart a rebel, has defied such laws and, as will be shown in the last chapter of this book, has had the courage and also the intellect to design his own evolutionary future.

1 FIRST MAN AND FIRST WOMAN

Life emerged from the sea hundreds of millions of years ago. Primitive creatures stranded on land by the changing pattern of the oceans, slithered through coastal swamps into the undergrowth of primeval jungles. In a changing world only those who possessed the biological equipment capable of change could survive. Through ages of ice or heat, through sudden convulsions of earthquake and volcano, through slow erosions of continents and the rise and fall of oceans, those creatures hung on and lived. Primitive sea-living creatures became primitive land-living creatures. Gills that had filtered water became lungs to breathe air. Fins and paddles that had propelled them through sea became legs and feet for crawling over land. Through millions of years minute changes in bone and limbs and skin and fur and sensory organs brought these creatures step by step nearer to the forms of life which we know today.

Through the slow ticking of millions of years, through vast ages of changing landscape and changing climate, every living creature had to adapt itself, had to change each and every organ of its body in order to survive or, failing to adapt and change, to die. From those millions of evolutionary changes let us choose just one example. It tells us how we got our teeth. We inherited them from the skins of sea creatures. Sherwood Romer tells the story:

'Teeth were, of course, absent in the oldest jawless vertebrates. They take their origin from small pointed structures found all over the skin of a shark and found frequently on the surface of bony plates and scales in primitive fishes. These superficial denticles ("toothlets") are in structure very similar to teeth, having a root and hollow pulp cavity, a main portion of dentine, and usually a shiny enamel-like surface covering. Presumably teeth arose from denticles which lay over the developing jaws at the margin of the teeth.'

Somewhere among those creatures who inhabited sea and land in the dawn of life and in whose skins were the buds of human teeth was our ancestor. It was not an ancestor we could recognise as such. There were no visible human characteristics in its primitive shape, for this creature, by spawning innumerable mutants through thousands of generations, was to become ancestor also of our very varied cousins; ancestor of our near cousins the apes, in whom we can see some remote 'family likeness', and ancestor also of our half-cousins, the hyena and the crocodile and, even more surprising, the minnow, the pretty tom-tit and our most unhuman relation, the cobra. But, although unrecognisable as a forbear, that creature was our ancestor in a genetic sense. He was the destined mutant, a changer, and in his primitive body were the basic genes which in millions of years of mutation and conditioning would build the teeth, the limbs, the observant eyes and agile hands, and the brain of the human of the future. Let us turn to Romer again.

'In a primitive amphibian there was already established the essential pattern of the limbs found in man. Bone for bone, almost every human element was present in those primitive swamp dwellers, which, first of all back-boned animals, gained the power of leaving the water to walk on four stout limbs. Most of the changes that have occurred in the last three hundred million years or so have been changes in proportions rather than the addition of new elements.'

Again our attention is arrested by Romer's beautifully casual throwaway phrase 'three hundred million years *or so*'. It jolts us into an appreciation of the immense span of time that must be envisaged when we study the emergence of man's genetic ancestors from the sea and man's eventual evolution from his animal background.

Among the survivors, among the creatures who adapted themselves, were those supreme changers, those arch-mutants our forbears. Those were the ones who climbed up from swamp and undergrowth. They took to the trees, swinging and shrieking through shadowy canyons of interlaced branches, scrabbling for insects and grubs, and, in seasons of heat, copulating.

A few of us living today take pride in providing our direct descent from kings and queens or other personages of great renown. But every one of us, all those men and women of so-called 'royal blood' as well as men and women who cannot be sure who their grandparents were, can claim as common ancestors those creatures who gibbered in the trees and who, each time they bore their young, came one generation nearer to us.

Their methods of coitus would be abrupt, brutal and casual. For them copulation was merely a response to sexual instincts at their most primitive level. Coitus was utterly devoid of thought or imagery. Nevertheless in their way of producing their young they had come a long way from egg-laying and egg-hatching. They were like us in so far as male mounted female and male sperm fertilised female ova. They were also like us in that their young were gestated inside the body of the female and, when born, fed at female teats, grew into adults and, in their turn, copulated and created the next generation.

Already they had climbed the scale of sexual law. Already the difference between male and female was emphatic and rich with the future potential of desire.

The time at last arrived when those forbears of ours came down from the trees. It was a decisive moment in human evolution. Those creatures with the 'royal blood' of future man in their veins had begun the first exploration of the world. They were on their way to becoming the human conquerors of earth. They crossed the vast savannahs. They travelled in packs. They made lairs in caves. They became tribes. For scores of thousands of years the earth with its changing continents and climates was their master. But the time was to come when these creatures would become men and women, and then, instead of being pushed around by the earth, they would turn on it and master it, would mould it into the shape they wanted it to be, until ultimately it would become the populous city-studded machine-enriched electrically powered world we have today. This home we have inherited from our arboreal ancestors who, leaving the trees, became adventurers and explorers, and staked man's claim to the whole earth and all things on it.

How different was first man from first woman? Far less different than is twentieth-century man from twentieth-century woman. The procreative sexual difference was, as we have said, emphatic; but little else. Man had his testicles to produce sperm, and a penis suitably designed to transmit the sperm to its right place. Woman had ovaries to produce eggs, a uterus in which to gestate the baby, and hormones to instruct her body for milk production. But in all other respects, in the attitudes of unlearned minds and the habits of the brutish communal life of a savage herd, the difference between early man and woman would be no more than the difference between a present-day male and female chimpanzee.

One can imagine that those early humans would hardly be

aware of being male and female. Man would mount any woman who was at hand when he had the sexual urge; woman would offer herself in a sexually accessible posture whenever she wanted intercourse. At that primitive level of existence copulation and birth and puberty and sexual maturing were devoid of thought or sentiment. Early humans would also be free of any of the traumas which surround these events today. For not until humans began to think and to reason could sexual events assume individual significance.

In this way the difference between man and woman has had and always will have decisive influence on human thought and conduct. In superficial outward appearance the difference might in certain ages or in certain conditions seem to be submerged below a camouflage of unisex clothes and work and habits. But like anything submerged it can, because it is less consciously apparent, become subconsciously more persistent and influential.

2 SEX TABOOS

If a woman steps over a sleeping Bantu man he will be unable to run. A husband of the Barea tribe of East Africa seldom shares a bed with his wife 'because her breath will make him weak'. In South Africa a man in bed must not touch his wife's body with his right hand for 'if he did so he would have no strength in war and would surely be slain'. In Siam it is considered unlucky to pass under a woman's clothes hung out to dry.

Those are just four of the hundreds of sexual superstitions reported by Ernest Crawley. The books of innumerable anthropologists are packed with similar evidence of sexual taboos among primitive tribes. Outstanding among recent works of this nature is Margaret Mead's *Male and Female*, which, based upon her devoted studies of the peoples of the South Seas, brilliantly argues the universality of sexual taboo. At the moment, however, there is a tendency to denigrate the theories of the anthropologists. It is now being argued that studying remote and primitive tribes does not help us to understand the sexual behaviour of our more advanced society because the very fact that those tribes are primitive is the result of their having been cut off from the mainstream of human evolution; consequently their customs and beliefs are eccentric individual survivals and, therefore, unrepresentative of mankind in general. The argument seems illogical. It seems to ignore the almost certain possibility that the taboos of these stranded societies, bizarre and unique though they might appear to us, are the outcome of superstitions which all humans could have entertained at the dawn of human intelligence. In fact, we should look upon those primitive peoples as laboratory specimens of our common human memory, and, in the same way in which a psychoanalyst must probe and bring to the surface buried childhood memories when he attempts to explain the conduct of an individual adult, so we, by probing the minds and studying the customs of these 'children of the world', might find explanations for many aspects in the behaviour of adult civilised society.

Psychologists have had to accept that atavistic memories of our primeval ancestors are implanted in the subconscious of every twentieth-century human being, in the subconscious of an Einstein and a Russell no less than in the subconscious of any unschooled labourer in the most primitive corner of the world. Surely then it is self-evident that society as a whole must also have a subconscious and that in the same way that suppressed and repressed childhood memories mould an individual's mental attitude and influence his individual conduct, primeval communal memories subconsciously influence twentieth-century social behaviour.

What is history all about but a record of our conscious social memory? Just as each individual consciously makes decisions according to his past individual experience, so does society confront the events of today with the knowledge of what happened in other ages and in other places. But, like the individual, society also has a subconscious; a subconscious that is pervaded with forgotten or suppressed memories of unrecorded traumatic experiences, built up of layer upon layer of communal experiences suffered by societies that existed before recorded history and, below these, deeper and darker layers of the experiences encountered by those earliest of all humans when they emerged from jungles and caves to scratch upon the face of the earth the outlines of those tribal settlements and earthworks of which our cities are the descendants and within which cities the desire for the protective cocoon of home and city wall is as subconsciously insistent as is the psychological desire of the human individual for the enfolding womb.

There must be, in that social subconscious, traces of the first wondering experiments and exploratory achievements of our ancestors who came down from the trees. About half a million years ago, some twenty thousand generations distant from us, there lived on earth *pithecanthropos erectus*. It is suggested that this early human was perhaps the real Prometheus, perhaps the first human to twirl the stick or strike the flint which created fire. We inherited that discovery from him; along with all its attendant comforts of warmth in our homes and cooked food on our plates. But at a deeper level in our social memory lurk those wonderings and fears which disturbed even earlier packs of humans; the humans who, before they had learned how to make fire, must have seen it as a natural destructive terror, the flaming rage of some mysterious supernatural power which their primitive minds were as yet incapable of conceiving as god. Those fears still stir in our social subconscious. Indeed a reflection of them might be seen in our almost masochistic reverence of the terrors of nuclear-fission and the mushroom cloud awfully rising from its sacrificial pyre.

So it is with sex. During half a million years of evolution the human being has ennobled that fundamental and essential animal desire and embellished it with idealism and romance, painting it in hues of glory or of sin. But however sexually understanding and knowledgeable society becomes, our social subconscious still retains memories of the sexual desires and fears of primal man, communal memories of lust and rape and incestuous couplings in the cave.

Human society is the sum of its parts, is the total of all its men and women. Therefore the sexual development of society should be seen as analogous to the sexual development of the individual man and woman. Just as at birth each of us is born with sexual instincts of no defined direction but has later to mature physically and psychologically into male or female with masculine or feminine integrity, so society has had to mature from a state of sexual infantility into the civilised sexual maturity it displays today.

We now know that within the subconscious of each one of us are memories of incestuous love of and sexual rivalry with father or mother. When we reach sexual and intellectual maturity such memories are repressed, and we resolve earlier sexual conflicts into modes of sexual conduct that are socially acceptable. In the same way it was necessary for society to grow to sexual maturity. The primeval love-hate of matriarch and father-figure had to be rationalised into the enthronement or adoration of those parental figures as symbols of goddess or king. There are times when society can, like an individual, be mentally retarded or deranged, and then the repressed love-hate rises to the surface to erupt into the incest of rebellion or the castration of assassination.

We can however imagine that earliest man and earliest woman would be as inhibited in their sexual habits as were their animal neighbours. A man and a woman would probably seek out secret crannies for copulation. But they would do so not out of any sense of modesty, only because animal instinct would impel them to choose a private and protected rendezvous in which to perform an operation which made them for a time so defenceless to attack by predatory enemies or sexual rivals.

Primitive laws about sex and superstitions and taboos came later when man and woman became more intelligently conscious of sexuality and began to think about it and to appreciate its family and racial consequences. In communities in which homes were being built and tribal disciplines were taking shape, sexual taboos became a social necessity. As society became more complex, even at primitive tribal level, sexuality had to be disciplined, had to become less the overt promiscuous copulating of male and female in a herd and more the selective contract between a husband and a wife.

The menstruating and the pregnant had to be isolated; incest had to be proscribed and virginity had to be treasured; children had to be protected against precocious sexual assault; and young males and females had to be initiated into masculine and feminine sexuality. For such reasons sexual taboos were woven into the fabric of social life. Our argument that they could eventually become part of the social subconscious is sustained by Helene Deutsch's observation that 'primitive taboos, like the fantasies of civilised people, are reflections of processes in that part of the mind that seems impervious to the influence of civilisation'.

As tribes became multi-family communities and became aware of racial needs and racial purpose the sexual code and its accumulated taboos were fashioned into tribal rules for families and child-rearing and hygiene. Such rules became laws, and as those sexual events in individual lives assumed significant importance to the community the events had to be marked by ceremony. To enforce the sexual laws and to endow the sexual ceremonies with compelling awe some power greater than the community itself had to be invoked. The desire for and need of fertility, the need for women to bear children, domestic animals to bear young, the land to grow crops, led inevitably to the concept of the Earth-Goddess and her phallic consort. Civil tribal ceremonies became mysterious and symbolic. Magical powers became divine, witch doctors became priests, and religion was born.

The survival of the community was essential. To provide hunters for food and guardians against enemies and predators the community had to breed more hands. The women had to be fertile. Fertility, argues Leo Schneiderman, 'is what primitive religion is all about'. Because of that we find not only in highly intellectualised dogmas such as that of the Catholic Church but also in archaic religions that sex must be indulged in only for fertility and that sex 'for the fun of it' is a sin. Through Jesus of Nazareth the Christian Church inherited Judaic sexual beliefs and laws which had been founded on the obsessive preoccupation with the necessity of increasing the population and ensuring the survival of a small and threatened race. The concept of sex without procreation being sinful impressed Christian theologians so acutely that they could even upset the Biblical legend of Eden's innocence. John the Scot, for instance, could argue that it was only as the result of sin that human beings were divided into male and female. Woman, he argued, embodied man's sensual and 'fallen' nature. He looked forward to a salvation of humanity almost akin to the physiological destiny prophesied by zoologists, for he declared that in the end distinction of sex would disappear and man would again have an asexual spiritual body. To the ascetic Christians even the thought of sex, let alone the act of it, could be sinful, and Jesus of Nazareth himself declared 'I say unto you that whosoever looketh upon a woman to lust after her hath committed adultery with her already in his heart'.

The elders and wise men began to spin legends which could give sacred power to communal law and also explain the difference between humans and all other creatures. Man and woman were a special and unique creation of the imagined divinity. In nearly all ancient societies and in most primitive societies today we find an entrancing similarity in the myths of creation. Nearly always a 'Garden of Eden' legend depicts nostalgically an age of primal innocence when man and woman lived in bliss and were free of the sexual torments which later beset them in community life. This universal Eden myth has many pretty and ingenious variations. One Negro tribe tells how the Creator, Nzambi, left lying about, as the 'forbidden fruit' of his Eden, a Koala nut. The Eve of that Eden was wiser than the Eve of ours: she warned her Adam not to eat it. Although Nzambi admired the woman's obedience he was not pleased that she should show herself as stronger than her man so he cut her open and took out some of her bones, thus making woman smaller and softer to the touch. When he came to sewing her up again he found he was short of thread, with the result that a part of woman remains open to this day.

The myth is compellingly self-identifying. Just as each one of us looks back upon an imagined roseate childhood of gentle innocence, despite the psychologist's assurance that our childhood was neither gentle nor innocent, mankind as a whole prefers to imagine an Eden of innocent tranquillity. But just as the twentieth-century baby suffers its birth-trauma and lives its early years of infant sexuality, so did the whole of human society suffer a collective 'birth trauma' as it emerged from animal existence into conscious appreciation of its sexuality and the difference between man and woman. It became aware, as the baby becomes aware of father and mother, of male and female and the purpose and sensual attractiveness of each. The earliest artefacts of man demonstrate a surprised awakening to the erotic delights of the difference. Ancient graffiti and crudely modelled figures of clay betray a primitive preoccupation with the sexual shapes of man and woman, with phallus and vagina. Grossly erected penis and burgeoning breasts which were first symbols of only brutish pleasures became symbols of fertility, then of magic, then of religious worship. Woven into the fabric of every religion, even the most austere, are the early superstitions and fears engendered in the human beings who began to *think* about, as distinct from merely performing, the sexual act. Sexuality permeates every known creed ancient and modern; either glorified unashamedly in erotic rites or repressed and denounced as a sin of the flesh. From those earliest beliefs in gods and goddesses, in male and female spirits of woods and seas and fields, come also all our laws, our customs and our arts. Primitive attempts to understand sex and discipline it were the first steps to endowing it with intellectual and imaginative purpose. Once the difference between man and woman was intelligently appreciated mankind had begun its climb to the heights.

The capacity to intellectualise sexuality has made the human the most beautifully complex of all living creatures. This exclusively human capacity has its hazards and its evils of course. It has made men and women peculiarly vulnerable. Psychologically it has made them subject to torments and doubts and a whole catalogue of neuroses which are suffered only by human beings. But these disadvantages are overwhelmingly outweighed by the joys and glories of human sensuality, and we repeat emphatically our argument that human sexuality has been the vital driving force in mankind's intellectual evolution. Every single thing that mankind has achieved, all human imagination and aspiration, has its sexual *leit motif*. Just as we can trace man's anatomical shape back to a primitive sea creature unrecognisable as our genetic ancestor, so can we trace everything man has created, the most magnificent of his creations as well as the most repugnant, to the sexual urge of his primitive forbears.

Latent in first man's realisation of sexual difference were all those differences between men and women which we now accept as appropriate masculine and feminine attitudes mentally and sociologically. Different biological demands of male and female fashioned different roles for man and woman as inevitably as genes fashioned their shape and colouring. When the difference between man the father and woman the mother became apparent to early human tribal communities it became necessary to clarify and codify differing roles in society for male and female. Social chores had to be divided between man the hunter and warrior, and woman the egg-breeder and child-rearer. In this partnership man had, of necessity, to be the dominant and decisive partner. Consequently the control and eventually the government of the community devolved on him. The man, therefore, had to become the one who framed laws, the one who enforced them, and the one who would fight to impose them on other communities subjected to his conquests.

Sexual taboos evolved into sexual codes and eventually these became moral codes, designed by and enforced by man. Woman was man's mate and man's delight. But she was also his obsession and his temptress. She was at once the lover of and the betrayer of his manhood, mysteriously powerful in seduction. This mingling of desire *for* and dread *of* woman is rooted in man's earliest instinctive fears; in his fear of losing his penile joys and strengths and in his fear of castration, physical and mental and sociological. This is established by the fact that these fears, which can be detected in some form in all our laws and in all our religions, are seen at their strongest in communities fighting for racial survival. The Israelites for instance. From the Garden of Eden legend right through to the time when the Israelites became a sophisticated civilised nation under David and Solomon fear of woman's mysterious power permeates Judaic belief.

A vivid illustration is seen in the taboo that an Israelite warrior was forbidden to sleep with his wife when he was on active service. This explains King David's dilemma after he had seduced Bath-sheba. He recalled her husband, Uriah, from the siege of Rabbah with the obvious intention of giving a marital alibi to any pregnancy that might result from his adulterous copulation with Bath-sheba. But Uriah, even though David made him drunk, was too observant of sexual taboo to sleep with his wife, and David had to send the warrior back bearing sealed orders which would send him into a battle where he would be certain to meet his death. After even a nocturnal emission an Israelite soldier had to undergo ceremonial purification before he could be considered restored to martial vigour.

Such taboos have survived to this day in primitive communities. In the Admiralty Islands, for instance, no man can sleep with his wife for five days before he goes fishing. Lumholtz in *Unknown Mexico* reports that the Huichols of Mexico abstained from women during hunting. 'The deer would never enter a snare put up by a man who is in love: it would just look at it, snort "pooh pooh", and then turn back the way it came.' Crawley, to whom I am indebted for that quotation, says that in the Marquesas Islands if a woman happened to sit upon or even pass near an object which had become taboo by contact with a man, it could never be used again and the woman was put to death. Among the evil spirits which surround primitive societies the one most feared by men of the South Celebes is the one that can make a man incapable of copulating; and the natives of Amboina believe in a witch called Pontianak who steals children but, more terrifying also steals the genital organs of men.

Such anthropological reports seem at first glance divertingly bizarre, yet when we examine some of the beliefs of our own sophisticated society we can unearth vestiges of similar primitive sexual fears and taboos, although some of them are so woven into the fabric of our customs that society is unaware of their existence as an individual is of his own subconscious repressions.

Fear of woman's sexual power can be found in the most intellectually civilised of men. That arch anti-feminist Nietzsche, despite the attitude of lordly masculinity which he attempts, reveals, just as so many ostensibly 'he-men' novelists similarly reveal, a subconscious fear of women. That fear probably explains why his actual experience of women seems to have been confined almost entirely to his sister. 'We take pleasure in woman as in a perhaps daintier, more delicate, and more ethereal kind of creature,' he writes. 'What a treat it is to meet creatures who have only dancing and nonsense and finery in their minds! They have always been the delight of every tense and profound male soul. However, even these graces are only to be found in women so long as they are kept in order by manly men; as soon as they achieve any independence they become intolerable.' It needs no profound psychological insight to see in those words the revelation that Nietzsche is just plain scared of the 'dainty' creatures of 'delight'. He is trying to give sociological import to his private masculine fears.

Man does collectively what Nietzsche did individually. The philosopher tries to suppress his fear of women by convincing himself that they are weak and contemptible creatures. Similarly masculine-designed society has always attempted by taboo and law and marital customs to deprive the dangerous daughters of the all-powerful earth-goddess of their power and keep them in their place by encouraging the concept that they are merely 'creatures who have only dancing and nonsense and finery in their minds'.

Basic to a man's sexuality are: (i) his desire *to* seduce, and (ii) his fear of *being* seduced. Seducing a woman establishes his male dominance; being seduced by her makes him subject to her. He must be active and she must be passive. Woman is more adaptable. She can enjoy at one and the same time the passive role of being seduced as well as, often without the man being aware of it, the active role of temptress and seducer. It is primarily because of his fear of being emasculated by seduction that man tries to subdue woman to the role of mate and housewife and plaything. That his masculine ego is inflated by this partnership is merely a secondary result. In other words, the moral and social codes of sexuality that man has designed were not designed as an attack on women but in self-defence.

Crawley argues that in all societies, primitive and civilised alike, 'Man and woman are as ignorant of each other as if they were different species; they are constantly tending to become what they never can become, two divided castes; every woman and every man are, as men and women, potentially taboo to each other.' There is some truth in the observation, but it falls into error by implying that taboos have been designed and enforced by both men and women, for the primitive social pattern of early packs of humans would make it inevitable that it would be the dominant male who initiated and enforced taboo and the female who accepted and became obedient to taboo. There are instances in later civilised societies which might appear as exceptions to this, when a taboo or a law has been promulgated or enforced by a female ruler or priestess or oracle or witch. But close examination will reveal that only the voice is female and that the taboo or law is merely reinforcing codes primarily designed by a masculine-dominated society. Just as in this century of so-called female emancipation the suffragettes in their clamant demand for equal rights were not creating a new concept of government but merely elaborating the ideal of democracy inherent in masculine-dominated political philosophy. But the best illustration of how the masculine view of sexuality controls the social subconscious is the often quoted one of society's attitude towards prostitution. However enlightened and emancipated any society considers itself and however liberal and permissive its laws, the female prostitute is always held in greater disrepute than her male customer.

It is usually argued that sexual taboos and the sexual laws arising from them have caused the separation of the sexes in communal life. Such separation can be seen not only in primitive societies with their 'men's houses' and 'women's houses' but also in civilised societies with men's and women's clubs. It is more logical to imagine that the separation of the sexes came before the taboos. In early tribes of humans the different pursuits of man and the necessary maternal duties of woman would lead to the sexes congregating separately; taboos would come later to enforce a separation which was recognised as practicable and sexually safe. In every part of the world and at every level of civilisation it is seen that in communal life men do prefer to be with men and women with women. Although the 'men's houses' of savage tribes, the places where men only gather for their ceremonies and gossip and games, are a subject of constant comment by anthropologists, our own Athenaeum is different only in degree, notably in the dress and conversation of its members.

Taboo intensified and gave the force of law to the separation of the sexes. So much so that it has led in some primitive tribes to such extreme taboos as a man being forbidden to sleep under the same roof as his wife, or, as in Fiji, forbidding even brothers and sisters to speak to each other or eat together.

Nearly always such codes have a pro-masculine bias imposing the greater restriction on the freedom of women in a 'men only' society. The more primitive the society, the more subjected are women to exclusion from male society. Not only 'men's houses' but even areas of ground are forbidden territory for woman in some savage communities. In some parts of the Moslem world women are denied any religious instruction at all and they are excluded from the mosque.

This taboo separation of the sexes can be seen in modern and supposedly advanced societies. For instance the sexes are still kept apart in many Roman Catholic churches and in all Orthodox synagogues. Quite recently a most 'emancipated' and world-travelled woman journalist whom I had arranged to meet in a certain bar in Edinburgh was allowed into the bar reluctantly and even so only if she would agree to sit behind a curtain drawn across the corner of the bar. For in Scotland, as in certain other backward corners of Europe, it is still considered improper if not dangerous for a woman to circulate among male company alone. This view is strongest in working-class communities. In those communities the separation of the sexes is most marked. Adolescents congregate in their sexual groups, even perform a kind of courting in groups. After marriage the woman returns to her feminine companions and the man goes out to his pub or club.

3 WHO PROPOSES?

A man is more sexually restricted than a woman. A woman can have sexual intercourse at any time with any man; a man must choose his woman or his time or both.

This statement is a fundamental biological contradiction of the generally accepted concept of man as the free promiscuous adventurer and woman as dutifully monogamous. A woman can perform the act of copulation, even if her part in it amounts to no more than passive acceptance, with a man for whom she feels no desire, even with a man who is repugnant to her. Or she can be raped. But a man cannot perform the act unless he has an erection, and this necessitates that his desires must be aroused, either by his partner or some attendant stimulation.

This near-to animal pattern of sexuality would be about all that humans demanded. The male would copulate with the females of the pack more or less indiscriminately. If his brutish attempts to arouse a woman to desire proved unavailing, he would rape her. When the pack became a settled and more ordered community, sexual taboos and codes became necessary. Taboos against incest made it necessary for male and female to seek sexual gratification outside the family pack and to choose their mates from neighbouring packs. Such seeking would lead to selection of a desired mate, and this selection introduced into sexuality an intellectual element which had not been present in previous spontaneous couplings of male and female. Early men and women had thus made the first steps towards intellectualising sex. That act of making a choice between one mate or another was the birth of the complex of sexual desire and emotion and imagery which we today call love.

Choosing the most desirable mate would also lead to a process of natural selection and would encourage survival of the healthier and more physically perfect in a tribe. Among women the crippled or misshapen, the diseased or deficient, if they had been allowed to live at all, would not attract suitors and would have no progeny. Among men the strongest and most courageous or cunning would have power to choose the best wife or wives. To that success of the cunning ones we owe our genetically inherited intelligence. Though as soon as concepts of property and status permeated tribal attitudes, the deficiencies of a less favoured bride could be outweighed by the bridegroom's ambition for a share of her father's status as chieftain or his bigger herd of cattle. There would also be cases when a man's desire for a certain woman could not be gratified for reasons of taboo or wealth and caste. He would see her on the horizon of desire, would have to look on her from afar, and his desire would become imaginative and intellectualised. That was the birth of romance.

Despite these sophisticated variations on the theme, however, it was accepted that the basic difference between man and woman in courtship and marriage was that man should be the seeker and chooser and therefore the master of his mate, whereas woman should be the awaiter and docile receiver of the man who had chosen her. This concept still persists. 'Some day my prince will come' is still the theme song of courtship and marriage not only romantically but even sociologically.

Practically all customs and ceremonies of courtship throughout the whole world from ancient times to the present day are formulated on this basic concept that man should be the proposer and woman should be the one who awaits the proposal or at least makes the pretence of awaiting it. Furthermore, when we examine our own social attitudes to courtship, and when we examine also our philosophies, our art and our romance, even our economics, whenever they touch on the subject of male and female courtship and sexuality, we find that we accept without question that primarily it is the female who should be the one who is erotically attractive to the male. Even in those instances where romance or history tells the story of a woman yearning for her handsome prince or suitor, the description 'handsome' applies not so much to his physical erotic charm but rather to the courage or gentleness or purity of the perfect knight and lover.

In this we accept that basic law dictated by sexual biology which decrees that it is the man's desire which must be stimulated because otherwise sexual union would neither be possible nor productive. In his *Utopia* More suggests that bride and bridegroom should have the chance of seeing each other naked before marriage. 'No one,' he argues, 'would buy a horse without first taking off the saddle and bridle.' From the wording it does seem that More is concerned principally with the male point of view. Is the woman attractive enough to be a desirable sexual partner?

Nevertheless the very fact that a woman does passively await proposals can result in her having the chance of choosing from a pack of suitors, like the waiting female moth who attracts a swarm of males from as much as an hour's flight away. The more primitive the human community, the less chance there is of the woman having any choice. The more sophisticated the community, the more opportunity she has of choice, and although with feminine tact she retains her semblance of passive waiting she can express her choice by making it apparent to which suitor she will surrender her hand.

For the human capacity to elevate sexuality above mere physical instinct, to intellectualise it with visual and emotional factors, has led to subtle variations of the masculine and feminine roles in courtship. Taboos and codes have controlled and restricted the choice of sexual partners, but even more influential have been the sophistications of civilisation. Romantic imagery, status ambitions, alcohol and drugs, soft lights and sweet music can stimulate man to extend his erotic desires to women who in more primitive circumstances would not have attracted him. The same influences have conditioned woman to make herself less available to promiscuous suitors and be more selective in her acceptance of sexual attentions.

Even among animals it can be observed that the female will show preference between one male and another. It would seem that for a female animal on heat any male should be acceptable in gratifying her sexual urge, but she will repulse one and accept another. Zuckerman argues that 'it is possible that in all lower animals the attitude of the female is, in some way or other, a necessary factor in eliciting the full sexual response of the male'. The human being has intensified that *necessary* factor into the *essential* factor in copulation. Human intelligence has done that.

The animal's choice can have no really intellectual content and must be the result of certain physical preferences. Of the competing males the one preferred by the female on heat is apparently more desirable for physical reasons such as smell or familiarity, or perhaps his superior sexual strength and insistence makes his invitation to coitus more compelling. The earliest most primitive woman had something more to guide her to preference. She had human intelligence, visual power to compare one man with another, and glimmerings of imagination. So even in her position of passively awaiting the courting males she could go some way to indicate which one she would prefer and could in some way make courtship easier for the one she desired.

Man's role as chooser is underlined by the gifts he conventionally bestows upon the desired mate. Early man would enhance his position as suitor by displaying trophies which provided evidence of his prowess as a hunter or courage as a warrior. Later man would present gifts that indicated superior status or greater wealth. The pattern persists. The modern suitor woos his woman with gifts, a box of chocolates or an island, a posy of flowers or the largest diamond in the world according to his wealth.

Even in the lowest form of life we can find males who bribe their way into female favour. Most ingenious is the empid fly. When courting the female this cunning wooer catches a smaller insect and parcels it up to present to the female. The parcel is so cunningly folded that the opening of it engages all her attention, and before she has finished the operation and consumed the delicacy the male fly has got what he wanted.

Even in societies where woman is protected from promiscuous sexual assault and has some freedom of choice the ritual of courtship retains vestiges of primal rape. Among the Koryaks the girl puts on a combination suit and her friends tie up the sleeves and trousers. The suitor must then go through the ceremony of pursuing and overpowering her. When he has cut the bindings and touched her sexual organs she allows him into her tent and the marriage is consummated.

However, whatever independence of sexual choice a woman enjoys before and during courtship she loses in marriage. Marriage binds a woman sexually to her husband more exclusively than marriage binds a man to his wife. This is biologically inevitable. By marriage a woman becomes the breeder and nurser of a man's children; individually and socially her adherence to marriage vows is therefore more important than man's. A man can have other women, mistresses or wives, without destroying the concept of family so much as a woman does if she has other men as lovers or husbands.

Some form of marriage exists among all human communities and must have always existed from the beginning of human intelligence. The most common form of marriage is the simple union of one man and one woman as husband and wife. Variations are polygamy, where one man has several wives or concubines, and the rarer polyandry, where one woman has several husbands. More exotic variations include the levirate, in which a widow has the right to continue the family by cohabiting with the male relatives of her deceased husband. Although polygamy has been accepted as rational by vast numbers of humans, polyandry has been an unnatural eccentricity, usually the result of a shortage of marriageable females in the community. The instinctive acceptance of polygamy as biologically natural and polyandry as unnatural and even distasteful is neatly summed up in the Chinese observation that 'one sees many cups with only one teapot, but never many teapots with only one cup'.

Helene Deutsch says that psychological inquiry suggests that 'the feminine woman in an overwhelming majority of cases is fundamentally monogamous', and argues that 'Human society created monogamy to meet the needs of a definite social order and economic organisation. Monogamy was imposed for the sake of preserving the species, because the human child, in contrast to other living creatures, needs help and protection for a long time after birth.' On the other hand Margaret Mead does point out that 'there are many societies in which a woman feels very put upon if she has to conduct a monogamous marriage and will nag her husband into getting her another wife, either to share the onerous duties of sex or bring in the firewood and look after the children or go fishing or whatever'.

Throughout most civilised history the wife, the chosen one, was considered as man's property: not only sexually but also commercially and financially. Her property became his, and any legal rights a wife retained were of lesser importance than the legal rights the husband had over her person and her possessions. In England even into the nineteenth century a wife was considered so much her husband's personal 'property' that in 1823 one Halifax man was able to bring his wife to market and extol her charms so eloquently that the price of twenty shillings paid for her was thought so unexpectedly high as to merit comment in *The Times*. The usual price was five shillings, but a husband in Essex took his wife to Ongar with a halter round her neck and sold her to the local smith at the bargain price of two shillings 'plus the usual market tolls' imposed on sales of livestock.

During this century marriage and property laws have rapidly reformed in Western society towards giving a wife equal status, legally and financially, with her husband, but it is undeniable that in our moral social attitudes we still think of a wife as being the personal sexual property of her husband, and greater odium is felt for any wife who transgresses this taboo than is felt for a husband who consorts with other women.

As we mentioned earlier there is nowadays an outspoken

demand that women should get as much sexual joy out of marriage as a man does. A century ago it was considered improper to the point of indecency to suggest that women should demand satisfaction for their erotic desires; it was even doubted whether a woman should have them. As Kenneth Walker remarks, nineteenth-century wives 'accepted physical maladjustment with resignation, and would no more have thought of demanding sexual satisfaction than they would have thought of claiming the right to wear trousers or enter the Houses of Parliament'. Nowadays it is generally accepted that a woman is entitled to sexual satisfaction in marriage. The modern view that marriage should be a contract founded on mutual affection and assent is in accord with the view expressed by Freud that marriage is a 'group of two', a concept of love essential not only for human survival but also for the full enjoyment of life. In this context the wording of the laws of divorce is even more illustrative than anything in the laws of marriage. 'The restoration of conjugal rights' is a significant phrase, implying as it does a command for two adults to live together, for both man and woman to surrender their bodies to each other.

It is now accepted that a wife should no longer be treated merely as the passive acceptor of her husband's attentions at any moment of his choice, but should enjoy equally with him the delicate ecstasies of preliminary love-play. It is argued that this concept of equal partnership should pervade not only the sexual aspects but all other aspects of marriage; so that just as husband and wife should have equal share in the sexual crises of their marriage they should also equally share the burdens and responsibilities of family crises, the wife's judgments and opinions having equal importance with the husband's.

Even so there is still a profound difference between man and woman in their concept of marriage. It is an ineradicable difference, for it springs from that basic biological difference mentioned above: the ability of a woman to have intercourse with any man, and the inability of man to have intercourse unless his sexual desires are aroused.

For most men the idea of having a privately owned and constantly available sexual partner is subconsciously, even sometimes candidly consciously, the compelling lure of marriage. His chosen woman might have many non-sexual attainments which make her desirable as a wife. She can show latent ability as a housewife and bearer of children; can 'cook as well as mother' and desire a family. She may have amiabilities and intellectual attributes, shared interests and hobbies, and a whole catalogue of virtues which enhance her value in his eyes. But a woman's sexual promise is nearly always what first attracted him to her and is a compelling factor in his desire to make her his partner.

It is not so with the woman. Subconsciously she is aware of that biological fact that any man, physically attractive or not, can serve her maternal purpose. Because of that awareness the physical attraction of a man or even his sexual prowess is a less important criterion in her acceptance of his courtship. To a woman *marriage* is as important as *love*. If love and sexual passion are there, well and good, but for full feminine happiness in its broadest sense marriage must primarily provide her with a home, a position in the world as a wife, and the gratification of her peculiarly feminine creative desire, the bearing of children. Although the breakdown of many marriages can be attributed to some form of sexual maladjustment it can be imagined that wives are more able than husbands to endure sexual disappointment or even sexual deprivation in its crudest sense of lack of sexual intercourse or satisfaction in coitus. As was emphasised in the chapter on sexuality woman can enjoy the physical ecstasies and stimulations of love in far more parts of her body than man, and her capacity for the enjoyment of love is similarly diffused through her entire psyche. There are moments when man is nothing more than an instrument awaking love but woman is love in its entirety.

11 Why Trousers? Why Skirts?

Why trousers and skirts? Why indeed? To begin with, from a practical sexual point of view we seem to have got our priorities all wrong in our western fashion of trousers for the man and skirts for the woman. Surely it would be far safer and far handier the other way round: safer for the woman to be securely buttoned up against sexual assault in trousers; handier for man, who is supposedly always lusting for sex, to have freedom for instant exposure provided by a skirt. As we know, there are societies where this is so; where it is the women who are sheathed in decorous pantaloons and the men who wear robes.

The basic question, however, is why men and women should wear different clothes at all. There is actually no functional reason why they should; certainly not in our western society where men and women live such similar lives and do such similar jobs. For instance, what practical reason is there for half the clerks in a bank to wear jackets and trousers and the other half to wear floral dresses? In fact it is near to impossible to think of any circumstances in modern life where there is a practical need for different male and female clothing.

The truth is, of course, that practical need has nothing to do with it. Neither has law, nor fashion, nor propriety. Men and women's clothes are different because we sexually desire them to be so. In a sexually mature society difference in male and female costume is psychologically essential.

It was not so in the Garden of Eden. Those fig-leaf aprons, the earliest garments on record, would almost certainly be unisex. Adam and Eve had only just become sexually aware. They were not yet sophisticated enough to think of stitching fig leaves into distinctively sexy 'him' and 'her' styles. Similar unisex aprons are still worn in some remote corners of the world. But only by the most primitive peoples, for unisex clothing is basically primitive. In fact it is as primitive, sartorially and culturally speaking, as, biologically speaking, hermaphroditism. For in the same way that the hermaphoditism seen in the lowest forms of life indicates biological primitivism, among humans a failure to be sufficiently conscious that sexual difference demands sexually different clothes indicates social primitivism. The more culturally mature a society is, the more highly civilised its life and politics and art, the more intellectual is its attitude to sex, the greater importance it attaches to sex distinctions and the more pronounced are the differences between male and female costume.

This fundamental law is not refuted by any sporadic flurries of unisex fashion. Those are transitory, and although they might be symbolic of profoundly passionate revolt against the social order they are nevertheless only outward symptoms. Rebels, particularly the impatient and candid young who have become bored or disgusted with the mistakes of a reactionary and inept ruling generation, seek ways to demonstrate their revolutionary camaraderie and also their open contempt for the conventional order of things. They choose a uniform to express their unity in opposition of the establishment. As such unisex costume is agreeably egalitarian and good fun. The revolt expressed in the uniform might be significant and have profound and decisive consequences, but the outward trappings soon lose importance. As soon as unisex fashion has lost its novelty and capacity to shock it has no purpose and drifts away on the ebb of fashion. At the time of writing, for instance, unisex garments have become so universally accepted that they are being energetically advertised and marketed by clothing manufacturers. But by being commercially accepted the innate rebellious character of the fashion is destroyed. Before long, probably before these words reach print, these same unisex garments will be subtly restyled, or less subtly embellished, to emphasise the male and female sexuality which they at the moment pretend to ignore. For there is a great deal of pretence in it all. By their very ambiguity unisex clothes encourage male and female exhibitionism. In other words, in a sophisticated society unisex, while pretending to be sexually indifferent, is actually sexually emphatic.

We are all to some extent clothes fetishists. Only a few of us steal panties from clothes-lines, but all of us attach some erotic significance to the garments worn by our love object or to the way in which our love object wears those garments. For unless we are primitive in the primevally savage way difference in male and female costume is part of our sexual consciousness, rooted in our sexual past and developed throughout our sexual evolution. To understand how it has developed we will first study the teasing question of the different attitudes men and women adopt to nudity and modesty.

1 WHO CHOSE THE FIG LEAF?

The Garden of Eden legend tells us that in the beginning man and woman lived in naked and happy innocence, but then, having eaten and enjoyed the forbidden fruit of sexual delight, they found their different bodies so unbearably shameful that they covered their genitals with aprons. The lovely story does not stand up to examination. All our evidence, anthropological and psychological, shows that it is the other way round: dressing-up comes first and modesty comes later.

Earliest men and women of the primeval world, living in savage packs in their natural state, would not find total nudity erotically attractive. In primitive societies today there are still Adams and Eves who are brutishly unconscious of their nudity and make no attempt to cover their genitals.

From people who are less primitive and who have adopted clothing we can learn what men and women first wore: such things as aprons made of bark or fig leaves and other leaves, scraps of animal skin, and cords and tassels. But these coverings were not originally put on, as in the Garden of Eden story, out of a sense of shame. There could be no shame at first. Only when bodies had been covered could nudity be considered immodest. The first clothes were not put on to hide something: they were put on to protect something; to protect it physically against natural hazards. And it was later, when that something was covered up and less often seen, that it became erotically attractive. In other words, it could not be until Adam and Eve had fabricated fig-leaf aprons and dressed up in them that they would begin to attach so much importance to what was under the aprons and experience erotic thrills by taking fig-leaf aprons off.

As the Adams and Eves of the world became more clothes-conscious, those originally protective coverings became decorated and ornamented, often in sexually significant fashion, with the result that although something was covered it was also being shown off.

From the desire to decorate those primitive coverings come all the clothes we know; all that vast and variegated wardrobe worn by men and women of different races and different eras; all the loincloths, togas, kilts, sarongs, tunics, bodices, tights, sumptuous robes of state and emblazoned uniforms, necklaces, amulets and public tassels, as well as provocative bustles designed to exaggerate woman's behind and boastful codpieces designed to exaggerate man's sexual promise.

In one way the narrator of Genesis shows sound psychology. He makes it clear that Adam was more shocked by his nakedness than Eve was by hers. He would be. A man is more modest than a woman.

Saint Augustine would have us believe that what actually frightened Adam was the 'shameless novelty' of his erect penis. Such a thing, Augustine declared, had never occurred until the Fall of Man! It has, however, occurred often enough since, and perhaps on occasions it can alarm particularly innocent adolescents.

But notice that although it is Eve who first tastes the fruit and tempts Adam to join her in her forbidden delight; it is Adam who says to God, 'I was afraid because I was naked.' Not a word from Eve.

The whole situation is psychologically accurate. Eve, having dropped her feminine pretence of modesty and inveigled Adam into gratifying her sexual desires, will from now on have no silly girlish shames about being nude in his presence. Adam cannot entirely lose his modesty: it is his nature as a man to be more modest.

We can see these different male and female attitudes even in children. The infant girl is nearly always more aggressive and adventurous sexually than the infant boy, coquettish with her clothing and enraptured by her nakedness. Not until the onset of puberty does her modesty appear. A young virgin, becoming conscious of her feminine sexuality and her changing body, is usually more shy than is a youth of her age. But once woman has experienced sexual gratification she loses that shyness. Modesty now becomes merely a posture, a pretence with which she cloaks herself to become more teasingly desirable. In fact most men find that a woman who does not act modestly is sexually less attractive. Prostitutes often simulate postures of modesty to make themselves more desirable. Any experienced married woman is usually far less shy in sexual matters than her husband is. However modest she was or pretended to be during courtship she need no longer act the part. She has got her man.

This different attitude is certainly caused by the fact that a man is often more acutely conscious than a woman of some sexual content in nakedness. Whereas a woman can retain an attitude of modesty even when totally nude, a man finds it difficult to consider complete exposure as harmless. For to a man nakedness is a direct incitement to sexual contact. This is why men often accuse women of being immodest. It seems so to them because female nudity does arouse excitement in a man.

Women retort, with some truth, that their attitude to the body is more natural and healthy than man's: they can enjoy the pleasures of nudity without fearing or even intending genital desire. Man, says woman, sees sexuality where none is intended. All the dingy little strip clubs of London's Soho and similar regions in any great city bear this out. Man is the eternal voyeur. It is man who sneaks in to peep at female nudity; it is man who buys magazines full of curvaceous breasts and hips. One finds it difficult to imagine any woman queuing up, let alone paying, to see male strippers, or any woman drooling over photographs of nude musclemen.

Man experiences so much pleasure in gazing on female nudity that he finds it difficult to understand woman's indifference to nakedness. How can woman be, as he sees it, so brazen? The answer lies in that Garden of Eden legend. Adam is more afraid of being 'caught with his trousers down' than Eve is. After puberty a woman's body becomes less of a secret. There is no point, and even less possibility, of hiding her femininity. Although a spinster might retain her modesty, an attitude of shrinking timidity and old-maidish fear, the woman who has performed her feminine functions becomes of necessity unmistakably and consequently unashamedly female, and in pregnancy and motherhood she has to surrender her body to the eyes and hands of others. Being a father does not impose any such surrender on a man's part. His body remains secret: his nakedness is still something he is afraid of. Most men would be reluctant to go to a woman doctor for intimate examination: few women show similar reluctance in consulting a male doctor.

Of course, one crude anatomical reason for the different attitude of man and woman to nakedness is that man does have more to hide. When he is naked his protrusive genitals are more obvious than a woman's. They can also be more expressive: always there is danger of that 'shameless novelty'.

Female fashions demonstrate how bold Eve can be in displaying her body. She delights in showing off her feminine parts, exposing different erogenous zones to the caress of appreciative eyes, or, if she cannot expose them, exaggerating them with tricks of fashion. When her breasts, almost bare during the Empire period, had to disappear behind high-necked bodices, she nipped in her waist and emphasised her hips and buttocks with draperies and bustles. When bosoms came back into fashion brassières were cunningly designed to shape and lift the breasts, and 'falsies' were inserted to give the wearer the appearance of possessing particularly ample female charms. When the emphasis shifted to legs skirts became shorter, and ultimately became mini-skirts, and it is notable that to ensure that legs would get full visual attention arms and necks were covered with long sleeves and high necklines.

A man does not indulge in sexual exhibitionism so brazenly. In his youth he goes through a period of narcissistic display, a cockerel phase of strutting around and showing off his masculinity, but as he matures what becomes important to him in his dress is not its sexual significance but its social significance, the wealth and status it represents.

There have been occasional outbursts of male exhibitionism in dress. A notable one was the codpiece. This decoration to man's crotch, often fashioned in a violently contrasting colour to the breeches from which it impudently protruded, was deliberately designed to draw attention to the male genital area, and on occasions was even pushed upward and padded to simulate perpetual erection. Similarly in the Middle Ages long-pointed shoes, *poulaines*, were shamelessly shaped like phalluses and, despite indignant protests by moralists, enjoyed fashionable popularity for a long time. Modern shoes by having a longer point than is warranted by the shape of the human foot retain some of that phallic character. In fact in civilised societies that is what happens to any sexual expression in male costume. It sinks to what one could describe as a subconscious level, and is then so embedded in normal fashion that the wearer is unconscious of there being any sexual significance at all. For example, the padded shoulders of a man's jacket and the epaulets of military uniforms have sexual significance in that they are designed to make the wearer appear broad-shouldered and broad shoulders indicate masculine muscular strength.

However, any man who makes deliberate and conscious

attempts to emphasise his masculinity is looked upon as an exhibitionist. In fact such a man is usually laying claim to more masculinity than he possesses; just as during the era of the codpiece the size of the adornment expressed the wearer's hopes more often than it registered reality.

Apart from such outcrops of sexual exhibitionism the civilised male normally dresses in styles designed not to emphasise his masculine *parts* but his masculine status. Instead of emphasising sexual characteristics his dress emphasises his dignity or wealth, his high position in the social order, his fierceness as a warrior, his power as a judge or ruler, his success as a merchant, as in past ages man's costume was designed to show his occupation; farmer or fisherman, craftsman or tradesman, mariner or trader, priest or clerk. The clothes of the wives of such men did not vary in style, only in richness according to the poverty and wealth of their husbands, just as today.

Whereas we criticise sexual exhibitionism in a man, we accept exhibitionism as natural to a woman. In fact we welcome it. We consider it normal and desirable that a woman should spend more energy and thought as well as more time on choosing her dress and arranging it to draw attention to her sexual attractions.

But although man's dress is in general not sexually exhibitionist, this is not to say man is not narcissistic. After all Narcissus was a male. A man has an equally strong desire as a woman to dress up, to embellish his image and present himself in the best possible light. He probably spends less time and energy and money in the process than a woman does; though there are areas of the world and have been whole eras of civilisation, as well as notable personal exceptions like the Duke of Buckingham with his 1,625 suits, where men have been more prodigal in dress than women. But even in our western society, where the emphasis of fashion is still on what woman wears despite a resurgence of interest and inventiveness in male attire, a man nevertheless attaches much importance to his clothes and the impression he creates by them. Although a man might be unconscious of sexual exhibitionism it is psychologically accepted that a man who does not care how he dresses is usually feeble in phallic eroticism. We can confirm this observation for ourselves anywhere at any time. For example we can compare shabby professors or effete aristocrats in bedraggled tweeds with lusty young workers who strut around proud as cockerels, and often as erotically, in spanking new suits. Also by personal observation we can see how declining eroticism in an ageing male is nearly always signalled by growing indifference to dress.

Nevertheless the essential difference is that sexual exhibitionism in dress is largely subconscious in a man but deliberately conscious in a woman. At the root of woman's exhibitionism is her biological need to draw attention to her feminine sexual characteristics by arousing the sexual desires of the male. If in the process she competes with and excels other women in display, that is merely incidental, for her main purpose is always that of attracting a mate or maintaining her attractiveness to the mate she has.

The role that Narcissus must play is the opposite. However attractive he may make himself to a female by his manners or by his manliness or by any masculine attributes such as courage or strength or success, when it comes to dress he must primarily compete with his own fellows rather than try to attract the women. For he knows that it is little use drawing female attention to his male parts. That codpiece was not a bait for sexually hungry ladies: it was actually a boast among his fellows; like infant boys showing off their larger genitals or men telling smoking-room stories of sexual triumphs.

But Narcissus knows well enough that his sexual characteristics are never as erotically exciting to a woman as a woman's are to him. So, instead of exhibiting his masculinity to the female, he adorns and displays it in fashions calculated not to show off his sexual parts but to demonstrate the superiority of his status to that of his competitors.

He can enjoy woman's exhibitionism in a vicarious way. He will adorn his woman as richly as his purse will allow, or as richly as *she* demands, and find pleasure in showing her off as the jewelled and desirable prize won by his superior masculinity. The more his mate enhances her sexual charms, the more envious of him are his fellows and the more his pride is inflated.

But what sparked off the difference? When did the centuries-long pageant of male and female fashion begin? Not, we have to admit, in the Garden of Eden. Nor is it very likely that the first breeches were made of fig-leaves.

There have been learned battles about those fig-leaves. That great Arabist and Biblical scholar, Friedrich Heinrich Wilhelm Gesenius, is only one of the many eminent scholars who bent his mind to studying the problem Adam and Eve must have faced when they tried to cover their nakedness with fig-leaves. He came solemnly to the decision that it was near to impossible to make breeches from fig leaves because of 'the softness of the leaves and the difficulty of sewing them together into a continuous covering'. He decided that Adam and Eve must have used the leaves of the banana, for this plant is called 'fig' by the natives of Malabar. Certainly the banana's ten-foot leaves would furnish more decently ample covering than fig leaves. In opposition to Gesensius other scholars retorted that the Hebrew narrator of Genesis could not conceivably have had in mind a Malayan plant which at that time was unknown even to the Egyptians. They maintained that it was natural for the narrator of Genesis to write of fig leaves because fig leaves were the largest leaves to be found on any indigenous Palestinian plant.

Some authorities have found significance in the strong relationship between fig leaves and sex. The fig leaf has been associated with fertility from ancient times. At their harvest festival, the Thargelis, the Asiatic Greeks, performed a ceremony which entailed beating humans on their genitals with branches of the wild fig tree. This was designed to excite the generative powers of the man and woman who represented male and female fig trees and who, by their sexual union, would help the actual trees to bear fruit.

What is certain, however, is that in the days before cloth was woven early man would grab anything that came to hand to cover his nakedness. We can guess what materials he might use. He would use what primitive tribes use to this day; strips of bark, bunches of leaves, or feathers and skins from the birds and animals that he had killed and eaten.

The important question however is not *what* he used to cover himself but *why* he covered himself. Despite the Garden of Eden legend few modern psychologists or anthropologists believe that modesty had anything to do with it. Professor J. C. Fluegel argues that the three basic motives for our clothing ourselves are protection, modesty and decoration, and he ranks the motive of decoration as the most important and insistent. Among primitive peoples, he points out, there exist *unclothed* people but never *undecorated* people.

It is true that even anthropoid apes seem to enjoy decorating themselves, putting blades of grass or twigs or scraps of rag and rope on their shoulders; though it is surely significant that there is no account of their decorating their genitals. Children similarly find pleasure in decorating their bodies before they have developed consciousness of shame at exposure. They have an instinctive liking for finery like strings of beads or daisies round their necks. 'Of all motives for wearing clothes,' says Fluegel, 'those connected with sexual life have an altogether predominant position. Clothing for decoration originated largely through the desire to enhance the sexual attractiveness of the wearer and to draw attention to the genital organs of the body.' And he attaches significance to the fact that tribal body-painting and tattooing most often start near the genitals.

In fact the majority of psychologists and anthropologists agree that decoration was the prime motive, and few believe that protection had much, if anything, to do with it. They point out that primitive tribes do not wear clothes even in damp and chilly climates, and Darwin saw snow melting on the naked skins of savages in Tierra del Fuego.

Ernest Crawley is one of the few who warns against too much emphasis being given to the decoration theory. Crawley suspects that the painful tattooing around the genitals is similar to the boring and scarification of lips and ears and noses. The latter, he argues, are magic witch-doctor operations performed 'to secure the safety of these sense organs', and he suggests that what appear to be genital decorations are intended to serve a similar purpose.

I am sure Crawley is nearer to the truth than the others. The motive of protection is an instinctive animal necessity: decoration is merely a condiment, something thought up and thus intellectual. When humans became hunters and fishers they would inevitably feel a need to protect their bodies, particularly their sensitive genitals. The men especially. When a man began stalking game through the jungles, climbing trees to snare birds, wading into rivers and lakes to capture fish, he would have to cover his protrusive genitals, would have to fashion some kind of shield or apron to protect them against the pricks of briars and the slash of grasses. His mate, so long as she was restricted to family duties and suckling babies in the cave, might not have felt such urgent need for protection. In any case female genitals were less open to hazard than male ones; but it is likely she would copy her man. In her case it is just conceivable that her apron was imitative of her husband's and to that extent could be considered merely a decoration, but it seems likely that woman also, when she accompanied her man on treks across the savannahs, was moved by the motive of bodily protection. So we can imagine that even in the dawn of human life man was, as he is to this day, the dominant influence of female fashion, the couturier whose styles are imitated by imaginative and obedient seamstresses.

The covering of the genitals was a crucial moment in the development of human sexuality. Only after they had been covered and had in consequence become secret possessions could male and female genitals have assumed visual importance. Until that time the genital sensation of humans would have been merely tactile. Like those of the animals, for example. No animal shows the slightest visual interest in its mate's genitals: sexual attraction between animals is stimulated by touch and smell, not by voyeurism. It would be the same with humans so long as they were in their primal state of nakedness. But after genitals had been covered the sight of genitals uncovered would begin to have an erotic content. And when genitals became erotically attractive they would become important enough to merit decoration.

It was logical for man to decorate his genital shield. After he had covered his penis, that symbol of his maleness and the treasured organ which gave him pleasure, he would feel emasculated in appearance. He needed to distinguish himself as a man in the herd, to demonstrate that although his sex was concealed beneath bark or fur he was nevertheless a male. He would do so by decorating his protective apron with objects that struck him as appropriate symbols of masculinity: the teeth, horns, spines, tusks and tails of animals, or phallus-shaped shells. Later, to make doubly sure of his maleness being recognised, he extended male decorations to other parts of his body; painting or tattooing his chest with fierce arabesques, attaching plumes and skins and other trophies of the hunt to his brow and arms and ankles. Such decorations would in the course of centuries become accepted symbols for adorning the male body.

Similarly his women would adopt decorations symbolising their femininity and fertility, and it is conceivable that even then woman's decoration was designed not to compete with other women but to attract male eyes to her sexuality and arouse the desires of the man she needed as mate and protector.

Their children grew up through infancies of innocent nakedness, but as their sexual differences became apparent and as they themselves became conscious of being male or female, they in turn adopted aprons and decorations appropriate to their sex, or were initiated into them by elders in tribal ceremonies that had at first only domestic and sexual significance but were later elaborated into magical and religious ritual.

Eventually the symbolism of clothing would assume more importance than its original functional purpose. Genitals would then be dressed up not for protection but for display. We find Australian aborigines wearing genital medallions of stringy fur flattened into the shape of fans. Being less than two inches across they can neither cover nor protect, but, daubed with white, they draw attention to the wearer's masculinity.

In societies where decoration has become the chief motive for dress men are more amply clothed than women, but in societies where clothing has become synonymous with modesty women wear more than men. Among the most primitive people it is chiefly the male who assumes decoration. Crawley, noting that among the Indians of Guiana ornaments were worn by men rather than by women, points the contrast between primitive and civilised societies by remarking that 'for the last five hundred years of European ciivilisation decorative dress has been largely confined to women. During a previous period of some centuries . . . not only did the curve of luxury in dress reach its highest point, but there were attempts . . . to put down any attempt towards luxury on the part of women, prostitutes being excepted.' That exception is significant. It suggests social acceptance of the fact that, given the chance to adorn herself, woman does so primarily for sexual reasons.

The early humans of the forests and savannahs became settled communities, more civilised and adept. Weaving was invented, and in more advanced societies men and women discarded bark and skins and began to make their aprons of cloth. These developed naturally into the loincloth, the earliest of all fabricated garments; and the longest-lived, for it is still being worn over vast areas of the world thousands of years since its introduction.

By the time the loincloth was fashioned clothing had assumed not only sexual but also personal significance to the wearer. The particular bodily intimacy of the loincloth, that 'girdle of the loins', is emphasised in the Arabic where the word for a girdle, *'izar*, is also used as part of a phrase which identifies a particularly close friend.

As the personal significance of clothing increased, so did its sexual significance; clothes of men and women became more emphatically different in shape, more charged with sexual meaning, so that men and women, both primitive and civilised, were made ever increasingly conscious of the different sex nakedness beneath the clothes. The covering of their male and female bodies by sexually different costumes added to the erotic titillation experienced in uncovering those bodies.

This cultural development from nakedness to clothing can be traced in any individual human of today. The sense of pleasure and freedom we experience in the exercise and display of our naked bodies rises from our atavistic memories of that primal state of nudity when, before we had been intellectually shocked by the 'shameless novelty' and were free of the encumbrances of coverings, we experienced sensory impressions over every part of our completely exposed anatomies. Joy in nakedness certainly lies deeper in our subconscious than thoughts of either modesty or decoration. Because of the sense of decency now enforced upon us by society we suppress that joy, normally indulging in it only when we are alone or in the company of intimates, but we see the pleasure frankly enjoyed by children in the years before they are aware of shame. Children experience intense joy in nakedness and often find clothes restrictive to their play and pleasure. In fact Fluegel argues that clothes can distort the sexual development of a child. In sexually prohibitionist countries or in cold climates where protectively enveloping garments are necessary, he says, children can grow up without ever knowing the anatomical difference between the sexes, so that when their sexual impulses do evince themselves their desires might be directed indifferently upon beings of either sex or even on themselves. Just how susceptible children are to confusion and worry when 'it' is kept always secret was amusingly revealed by an eminent British personage when he confessed in a television interview that after being taken when a child to an art gallery he conducted furtive examinations of himself and for a long time was plagued with fears that his body was deficient because it had not grown that neatly curled leaf he had seen on statues of nude males.

Freud agreed that 'the progressive concealment of the body

which goes along with civilisation keeps sexual curiosity awake'. Curiosity is indeed one of the compulsive factors, some would say the most compulsive, in eroticism. This curiosity, the erotic desire to see what is underneath and to uncover it and the tendency to equate nakedness with sexuality, is exclusive to humans, and the narrator of Genesis, along with the narrators of all other books of the Bible, is writing in accord with his own fears and the strictures of his own society when he describes Adam as being so afraid of his nakedness. By the time Genesis was written it had become social custom and social law to keep the sexual organs covered. Therefore the sight of them uncovered, or even the mere thought of their being uncovered, became emotive. Not only in the Garden of Eden story but throughout the whole of the Bible we find repeated illustrations of the obsessive attitudes to nakedness in ancient civilisations. In fact Judaic law, the source of so much of our own law and so many of our moral attitudes, is neurotically disturbed by nakedness. The Bible reveals this neurosis in phraseology which makes nakedness and sexual gratification mean the same thing, so that either coitus or sodomy, each particularly condemned when it was of an incestuous nature, is referred to by such euphemisms as 'uncovering' or 'looking upon the nakedness' of members of one's family. Moslem law shows similar fears. The Sunnah prescribes that a man should not uncover himself even to himself; and in Arab countries I have met Moslem males who have insisted on wearing their drawers even in the privacy of shower baths.

However, as we have said, long before ancient civilisations framed these laws, humans conscious of nakedness and its erotic implications, were ashamed of it. There is evidence of that in existing communities, which are more primitive socially than those ancient civilisations. In such communities shames and fears of nakedness take bizarre form in tribal sexual taboos. At the core of these taboos are sexual phenomena which must strike any primitive as inexplicably mysterious; particularly the one Augustine tried to explain away, the erection of the penis, and also woman's menstruation.

The first hunter felt that his genitals needed protection against physical injury. His successor, with his genitals covered and now more erotically conscious of his maleness, felt that his sensitive excitable penis needed protection against visual harm. Crawley reports that among the Tannu and Malekula tribes 'the closest secrecy is adopted with regard to the penis, the sight even of that of another man being considered dangerous. They therefore wrap it around with many yards of calico, winding them and folding them until a preposterous bundle eighteen inches or two feet long is formed.' The observation provides a perfect parable to illustrate how sex fears can intensify prurient 'dressing up' and supposed modesty can result in the very opposite effect from what was intended. The frightened tribesman, instead of 'blotting out' his penis has magnified it into a gigantic codpiece, in the same way that more civilised peoples, when preoccupied with fears of sex, will by restrictive prudery actually foster sexual curiosity.

As clothing became more elaborate taboos became more exotic. The area of modesty shifted from the genitals to other parts of the body. Arab women are more intent on covering faces than genitals, and practically every anthropologist who has ever travelled among Arab peoples repeats stories of Arab women, when surprised naked, spreading their hands over their faces but leaving their genitals exposed. Until quite recently an Arab physician could usually examine a woman patient's arm only when it was extended through a hole in a wall or curtain; and it may well be so today in remote and primitive Arab communities. Chinese women were equally modest with their feet; at one time only a woman's husband was allowed to see her feet naked. The Negresses of Naga covered only their breasts from public gaze. They argued with some logic, that it was absurd to be modest about those parts of their bodies which everyone had seen from their birth, but it was very different with breasts, for breasts had come later than genitals and were more particularly signs of their mature femininity. On the other hand Quentin Bell reports that in some Himalayan communities a wife would show special respect for her husband's guests by receiving them with her breasts bare.

Freakish taboos about nakedness are confined neither to remote societies nor to primitive people. There have been plenty of taboos in our western society, and we still preserve many. In Henry VIII's time it was considered indecent not only for women but also for men to show their arms bare. The most persistent of western taboos has been that against the naked leg. From the beginning of western civilisation that limb which woman now shows so freely was with few exceptions covered. Even in eras when fashion encouraged women to the most provocative sexual exhibitionism, when breasts were pushed upward and outward to protrude dazzlingly from bodices, when waists were nipped and bustles and panniers hung around to enhance the luxury of female hips and buttocks, legs still remained covered. In Victorian days even the legs of pianos were clothed. In fact the very word 'leg' was considered too brutally explicit for polite lips. The rebuke that 'the Queen of Spain has no legs' is as historically characteristic as that of Queen Victoria not being amused, and when Ruskin's mother broke her leg she perforce had to report it as an accident to her 'limb'. This verbal taboo eventually extended from the leg itself to what covered the leg. Trousers became too vulgar to be referred to by name in society: they became 'unmentionables'.

When men and women who were visually aware of their differing sexuality began living in settled communities and framed socially necessary sexual taboos and laws it was inevitable that once a sexual code had been established moralists would appear on the human scene. Fluegel remarks that sexual desire is certainly one of the most disturbing elements in the primitive clan, but one wonders why on earth he so restricts his statement. Surely sexual desire is one of the most disturbing elements in any group of humans, in any clan and in any society, primitive or highly civilised. Instance the society into which the narrator of Genesis was born. It had reached a considerable degree of civilisation. Laws to control sexual life were already in operation. Therefore when that narrator began his story of how the world was created he faced the task of explaining why men and women were, unlike beasts of the field, ashamed of nakedness. His story of primeval Adam being tempted into sex by Eve and then trying to conceal his nakedness was a compelling legend because it was one with which all his readers could identify. It was in complete accord with their own secret desires to see 'what's underneath' and with their memories of shame and guilt after they had seen it.

The legend was most acceptable to the priests and rulers and moralists. It gave them God's sanction to enforce laws controlling sexual conduct; laws that would not only govern private things like marriage and punish grave sins of adultery, incest, sodomy, bestiality and other rebellious non-conformist acts, but could also be used to ensure public decency, even, for instance, to the extent of imposing regulations about dress and insisting that men and women would wear different clothes appropriate to their sex. By making nakedness and sin one the Garden of Eden legend buttressed both social law and religious belief, so that later we find powerful theologians like Augustine embroidering nakedness with scatalogical imagery and Clement of Alexandria declaiming 'On no account must a woman be permitted to show a man any portion of her body naked, for fear lest both should fall: the one by gazing eagerly, the other by delighting to attract those eager glances.' That sonorous warning might well be written in words of fire over the entrance of any strip club or the box office of many a modern revue. Far wiser than Clement really was that African chieftain, Pongo of Nigeria, who forbade wives to wear more than a string around their loins, 'because the wearing of clothes encouraged immorality'.

Although the fig-leaf complex survives, we are at the moment experiencing one of those periods of sex display which recur from century to century. On the stage complete nudity has become a vogue. This is generally diagnosed as a gesture of sexual liberty, and casually accepted as such by those who pay to see it. It is not. Those theatre audiences are not permissives indifferent to nudity. Those odd, in both senses of the word, members of the audience who disrobe themselves are actually more conformist in their nakedness than those who keep their clothes on. The rest of the audience, fully clothed, are peeping at something which they feel they ought not to see and thus re-enact the *frisson* they experienced under the bushes or other secret haunts in their separate, probably forgotten, infantile Edens. If society were truly 'permissive' of nakedness, and we met nudity at, say, every street corner, we would be less ready to pay guineas to see it on a stage, unless the nudity was 'clothed' in artistic expression.

Sporadic revolutionary impulses to pluck off the fig leaf have alarmed moralists in many eras of history. The society to whom the fresco of the Last Judgment was unveiled in the Sistine Chapel four hundred years ago was far more permissive than our society, yet Pope Paul III had to insist on Michelangelo painting drawers to conceal the private parts of those angels whose lovingly executed and explicit nudity had shocked ecclesiastics and others. Pietro Aretino, one of the leaders in the campaign which demanded emasculation of the angels or even the utter destruction of the fresco, reproached Michelangelo for indecency and exhorted the artist 'to imitate the modesty of the Florentines who had covered the shameful parts of their beautiful Colossus with golden leaves'. Although this Aretino who paraded so eloquently as a moralist was one of the most notorious blackmailers and libellers in all literary history as well as author of sonnets describing twenty-six different methods of coitus, he won his 'fig-leaf' battle and the drawers remain to this day.

It would be easy to fill pages with accounts of ludicrous efforts made by sex-scared societies to enforce what they called 'public decency', but we must content ourselves with a few of the more bizarre or naïve examples. Not many years ago the municipal council of Glasgow, Scotland, banned wax figures from the shops on the grounds that they were too erotically life-like in flesh-colour and shape. At the other side of the world, in Japan, the authorities actually made a law decreeing the exact height to which skirts could be lifted above ankles in rainy weather.

A decree issued by the Chief of Police of Long Beach near New York solemnly forbade 'couples walking on the beach or bathing to approach each other closer than six inches or 15 centimetres', and warned possible offenders that 'inspectors will be provided with footrules in order to make sure that bathers will preserve this distance'.

When sea-bathing became increasingly fashionable through the nineteenth century it found the moralists quite unprepared. As no one had as yet thought of such things as bathing drawers, young men resorted to distant beaches to bathe in the nude, and there were reports that the young ladies who promenaded at Yorkshire seaside resorts were noticed to be going ever farther afield along the cliffs and taking field-glasses and telescopes to watch 'wild-life'. When women began indulging in the sport of bathing, drawers and swimming costumes and bathing tents became necessary, and we are indebted to Havelock Ellis for tracing to Germany nearly fifty years ago a forbear of the bikinis now worn by women on any beach. Ellis reports: 'Valentin Lehr, of Freiburg in Bresgau, has invented a costume which is suitable for either public water-baths or air-baths, because it meets the demand of those whose minimum requirement is that the chief sexual centres of the body should covered in public, while it is otherwise fairly unobjectionable. It consists of two pieces, made of porous material, one covering the breasts with a band over the shoulders, and the other covering the abdomen below the navel and drawn between the legs. This minimal costume, while neither ideal or aesthetic, adequately covers the sexual region of the body, while leaving the arms, waist, hips, and legs entirely free.' Incidentally, a far more ancient ancestor of today's bikini is worn by the full-hipped maidens who disport themselves with discus, dumb-bells and parasol on the mosaic walls of a bathroom of a villa built in Sicily for a wealthy Roman in the third or early fourth century.

Havelock Ellis provides another little treasure. He quotes the report of a certain Dr. Shufeldt who 'once in the course of a photographic expedition in the woods came upon two boys, naked except for bathing-drawers, engaged in getting water lilies from a pond. He found them a good subject for his camera, but they could not be induced to remove their drawers, by no means out of modesty or mock-modesty, but simply because they feared they might possibly be caught and arrested.' We can form our own conclusions as to which of the three would be more likely to be arrested nowadays.

Fluegel gives us a whole collection of similar oddities. 'In the USA a "special assistant district attorney general" drew up some rules on the length of women's chemises, which required that these should fall below the knees; at Coney Island there were disputes as to whether women should be compelled to wear stockings while bathing; at Newport, an elegant watering-place, close fitting bathing dresses were forbidden, and a large notice warned bathers not to loiter on the platform in wet bathing costumes lest their too clearly outlined forms would inspire tabooed thoughts.

'For the same reason the Director of the Congregational Colony near Boulogne-sur-Mer in France took the children under his charge to a little-frequented beach where thirteen of them were drowned. When accused (December 1926) of manslaughter through neglect of reasonable precautions he said that his action had been dictated by a desire "to avoid arousing the children's curiosity". Judge B. Lindsey says a minister wanted a bill introduced to prevent the display of women's lingerie in shop windows.'

In 1928 the Hungarian authorities were so afraid of the erotic appeal of short skirts that they decreed that schoolgirls must wear trousers.

Finally we present the solemn promulgation of the 1926 Bishop of Angers, a twentieth-century Clement who was determined that provocative female flesh and curves should be concealed. 'For all ceremonies in church a high-necked dress should be worn. It should have long sleeves and should come down well below the knees. At marriage ceremonies the bride and bridesmaids should at most wear a slight décolletage "à la vierge". They should never have bare arms or merely cover them with a scarf. In town dresses should not cling closely to the body, they should have sleeves to the elbow, and the skirt should end distinctly below the knee. At most, a décolletage "en rond", not loose but neatly fastened, and not below the collar bone. Dresses must not be skin-tight, must have at least small sleeves, and must be two hand-breaths below the knee. At dances, gloves should be worn always. No dances which involve close bodily contact should be indulged in. At the seaside, the scanty bathing suit should be discarded in favour of the fuller bathing dresses formerly worn. Sun baths and games on the shore in bathing costumes are prohibited. Girls over ten years of age should wear long stockings and costumes which cover the knees.'

The prurient obsession of clerics with clothes and nakedness can result in grotesquely superstitious fears. After an earthquake in Italy in 1930 several Roman Catholic diviners said the disaster had been provoked by 'moral disorder and, in particular, shameful fashions' and said Naples had been saved from the catastrophe because the Neapolitans had 'resisted the present scandalous fashion'.

The 'clerics' of authoritarian governments show a similar desire to repress any sexual display in the clothing of their charges. In 1944, in an interview quoted by Simone de Beauvoir, Olga Michakova, secretary of the Central Committee of the Communist Youth Organisation, said, 'Soviet women should try to make themselves as attractive as nature and good taste permit . . . Girls are to be told to behave properly and walk like girls, and for this reason they will probably wear very narrow skirts which will compel a graceful carriage.'

But we have said enough to illustrate how the wearing of clothes has resulted in nakedness becoming synonymous with sin. In an earlier chapter we argued that in primitive societies where nudity of the sexual organs is the rule there is less evidence of those irritant and often dangerous neuroses which affect civilised people. At the very least there can be no possibility of finding transvestites among tribes where the costume of both man and woman consists, as it does in some savage tribes, of either a single length of cord, a pubic tassel of fur, a plait of hair or the dangling stem of a plant. Only in tribes sufficiently emerged from primitivism to attach importance to difference in male and female costume do we find the beginning of a preoccupation with what shape and conduct is appropriate to male and female, a preoccupation which lies at the root of so many of the sex and gender neuroses of civilised societies.

What most excited Victorian explorers and anthropologists, as was natural to a generation that had spent its infancy among pianos with clothed legs, was the nudity of the peoples they so thoroughly investigated and even more greedily photographed. Indeed we detect in the intimately detailed reports of such men as Richard Burton and his contemporaries a voyeurism and curiosity which often seems more prurient than scientific. In fact some of the explorers are ingenuous enough to express in naïve print their surprise that men and women who walked around in nakedness unabashed should show reluctance when these eager Victorians wanted, in scientific zeal, to examine more closely, even handle, their genitals. None of these writers seems to be aware that even heavily clothed and so-called civilised people might similarly show reluctance to having their genitals inspected and handled by inquisitive explorers, either in a crowded cinema or a marketplace.

Even the scientifically objective reports of Sir Harry H. Johnston, one of Britain's most talented explorers and empire-builders, occasionally reveal traces of subconscious Victorian prudery. Describing one African tribe he remarks, 'Both sexes have little notion or conception of decency, the men especially seeming to be unconscious of any impropriety in exposing themselves.' Knowing the man we know well enough that he intends no censure; it is only his vocabulary that is unfortunate. Man can only consciously 'expose' himself when he wears genital coverings which he can draw aside or unbutton. Or when, as in the case of male decorations like those aboriginal fur medallions, he considers his genitals covered if the decoration is dangling over them but considers them exposed, and consequently ready for a specific sexual purpose, when the medallion is removed.

Sir Harry chooses his words more fairly when, describing another African tribe, he comments that among them 'indecency does not exist, for they . . . walk about as nature made them, except when it is chilly or if they wish to look unusually smart, in which cases they throw cloth or skins around their shoulders'.

Beautifully significant there are the words 'indecency does

not exist'. For it can surely be argued that naked people are more civilised in an idealised sense of the word by their lack of shame of their nakedness, whereas we who claim to be civilised are teased and repressed and frightened by our 'dirty minds'. The contrast between the happy innocence possible to naked peoples and the obsessive sexual preoccupations of clothed ones is emphatically illustrated by Karl von den Steinen on the Baikairi Indians of Central Brazil who 'still live in the stone-age today without any metal weapons'. Paraphrasing Steinen's report Wilhelm Boelsche writes, 'They go about practically entirely naked. . . . A gentle trait pervades their social relations, which have been regulated from very early times, and there is a sunny joyousness about their whole nature. And art, a mirthful art sparkling with ornaments and colours and finding full self-expression in a highly imaginative manner, fills a large part of their existence. Ceilings and walls, straw mats and implements rise above the beautiful nakedness of their bodies in a veritable intoxication of art and applied art.'

The Garden of Eden legend of shame has eroded such innocence from vast areas of the world. Accompanying or following the explorers came the missionaries, zealots armed with the Word of God and pledged to rescue peoples from primal nakedness and savagery and to make them aware of the 'shameless novelty'. How abominably well these moralists succeeded! The reports of the anthropologists who followed them are packed with saddening stories of how within a generation, sometimes within even only a few years, naked innocents became prudishly aware of the sexual titillations of male and female clothing. Just as our own children in our civilised society are conditioned to awareness of the exciting differences hidden by trousers and skirts, these children of the other world were torn from their natural innocence into sophisticated awareness of how sexual differences could be hidden and yet provocatively emphasised by male and female clothing.

The loincloth began primarily as a functional garment, a protection and a cover and only secondarily, by its colour or embellishment, a decoration. But when early communities became more complex, when men instead of all being members of a herd and doing the same thing, chose individually fulltime occupations, they chose coverings appropriate for their work, so that the clothes they wore became the recognisable livery of their occupational roles. The introduction of concepts of caste and rank called for further distinctions in dress to indicate a man's status in society, and there have been periods in history when sumptuary laws were passed to enforce such distinctions.

The originally functional loincloth is the ancestor of every garment fashioned throughout all recorded history. When the headman and magicians of primitive communities and, later, the rulers and priests of cities and states needed distinctive dress to signify their rank, mantles gave dignity to rulers; robes emblazoned with mystic and religious insignia invested priests with sanctity. When robes draped a man's body from shoulders to feet the loincloth was no longer essential to decency, though it might still be worn for reasons of warmth, comfort or hygiene. But even when discarded as an intimate wrapping of the loins it survived in a symbolic fashion. It became an outer garment, first a rather utilitarian girdle, holding robes in position, and then merely decoratively as a sash, often gloriously resplendent like the one described by Josephus, 'so loosely-woven that you would think it was the skin of a serpent; embroided with flowers of scarlet and blue and fine linen'.

The bifurcated garments which have become the trousers of today developed from the loincloth. Crawley, who says there can be no doubt that for obvious anatomical reasons the naked male often finds it desirable to confine his genitals, conjectures that the use of a perineal cloth for men and of a mere apron or skirt for women is a sexual distinction of the earliest date and has been generally maintained. He sees 'the assigning of the skirt to women as the more sedentary and trousers to men as the more active sex'.

Certainly conditions of climate or occupation could dictate the length of the loincloth, and humans in the northern cold might be expected to extend it to cover their thighs or the whole of their legs, but in my opinion sufficient importance has not been given to the fact that it was when the horse was domesticated for riding that man would find it more necessary to wrap up his genitals and his legs. The Greeks considered trousers as 'barbarian dress', as well they might because trousers were worn by their invaders. But those men who swept down on the Mediterranean perhaps wore trousers not only because of their chilly native climate but also because they found them a practicable and comfortable garment to wear when astride a horse. Certainly 'barbarian trousers' were eventually adopted by civilised men of southern Europe. At first men of those races which in earlier times had worn tunics converted these tunics into bifurcated garments by sewing them up at the base and leaving two slits for the passage of the feet. 'Girding the loins' meant the tucking up of the folds to give freedom of movement. Eventually races as distant as Celts and Parthians and Persians were wearing knee-length lower garments. This conversion from tunic to trousers would not be necessary for women, for they rarely rode horses and were occupied with less active pursuits than men.

It has also been argued that man has always had to wrap himself up more than woman has because he lacks the natural warmth given to woman by her fatty deposits and feels the cold around his lower parts more than she did. On the other hand it is suggested that a woman's preference for trousers rather than a skirt may be an outward and visible sign of her psychological desire to assert her independence and her desire for equality with the male. There may be something in this theory in some cases, but many girls and women resort to jeans and slacks for practical reasons of convenience in an active working and travelling community as well as to be fashionably distinctive and especially decorative. Conversely any man who resorts to skirts is automatically considered to be a transvestite.

The concept of trousers as masculine and skirts as feminine is not world-wide, of course. In the Eastern wardrobe the sarong, a single sheet of cloth, is as 'unisex' as jeans are in the Western. The dhoti, the Indian loincloth, is the same garment whether bought for a man or woman, though it is worn in a different way. Wilfred Thesiger reports that when Arab-Saar women attempted to describe the men of north Arabia they remarked on the one thing that had most surprised and impressed them: 'They wear trousers: like women.' Women have in fact 'worn the trousers' in many parts of the world. Throughout India many adopted the Muslim fashion of drawers, wearing them under their saris; the Korean woman's national dress consisted of very full white cotton trousers and a robe tied under the arms.

In Western society, however, trousers in any form were considered so improper for a woman until late in the nineteenth century that even drawers were regarded as immodestly unfeminine; although on grounds of hygiene the gynaecologist Tilt did advocate drawers of fine calico, 'not to descend below the knee'.

Whatever women might think, trousers are rarely flattering to the female figure because a woman in trousers looks shorter than she does in a skirt. Rulers, priests and judges and the like wear what are essentially skirts. Robes of state and ceremony were designed for the purpose of increasing the impression of height and dignity.

Sexual distinctions are also seen in the kind of material chosen for the clothes of man and woman. It was natural for man the hunter to use tough materials, bark and skins for his coverings, and for woman to adopt softer coverings, even floral ornamentation. This distinction persists, quite apart from occupational necessity, in male and female clothes today.

When clothes began to denote status man became the arbiter of fashion. This was inevitable. Because the male had more free time than had the child-bearing infant-nursing female to devote to the conduct of affairs and the ruling of his clan he was the one most concerned in proclaiming his status. His was the decisive voice, therefore, in deciding how that status should be proclaimed and what trappings should be worn. By natural law also it was the male who had to be the craftsman or merchant or sailor or warrior, and so it was the male who had to have clothes appropriate to and indicative of his way of life.

Dress had an utterly different significance for woman. The fabric and embellishments of her costume would be sumptuous or frugal according to the status of her family or her husband, but the dress of any woman whether rich or poor, was the same in so far as the basic necessity in its design was to exhibit her as a woman, to decorate her feminine beauty, to heighten or preserve her sexual desirability. Thus historical sociological influences have intensified the sexual psychological influences in imposing fashions of status exhibitionism on the male and of sexual exhibitionism on the female.

Man, who could impress his fellows by the sumptuousness of his dress, could impress them also by the sumptuousness of the clothes he loaded on his consort. His most significant gifts to her or to any woman was fine raiment.

On her visit to King Solomon the Queen of Sheba must have carried an extensive personal wardrobe in her baggage train of 'seven hundred and ninety-seven camels, and mules and asses innumerable' apart from the 'very many precious gifts' and 'spices and very much gold and precious stones'. Yet it is significant that one account of that Royal Summit, the account given not in the Bible but in the Ethiopic *Kebra Nagast*, points out that it was Solomon who 'every day arrayed her in eleven garments which bewitched the eyes'. Obviously Solomon was wooing the Queen in the same manner as kings and bankers and tycoons have wooed distinguished ladies for centuries, even to this day of Gulbenkians and Onassis. But potentates and tycoons had another reason than bribery and conquest for the lavish way in which they adorned their wives and consorts and courtesans. To a man of the ancient world a woman was not only his mate but, far more important, his property. The clothes in which he dressed her signified more than the wealth and status or the poverty and mean position of the husband: it set her apart as a piece of personal property. The jewelled band or simple cord which a man put around a woman's brow or waist was as much a symbol of ownership as the fence or wall he built around his gardens or his grazing plot. Theodor Waitz has in fact gone so far as to argue, and other anthropologists have made similar claims, that 'male jealousy is the primary origin of clothing and therefore of modesty'.

That the Moslems were aware of this is somewhat indicated by the way they covered their women with enveloping robes, allowing them only a tiny slit around their eyes for contact with the outer world. The obvious reason for covering woman so completely was to avoid her arousing the sexual desire of another male. It was a natural precaution to take in a social system which stresses the view that each woman must be the personal and exclusive property of a man, first of her father and then of her husband. When the women of Turkey and later of other parts of the Moslem world were emancipated they did not by virtue of that emancipation become more 'like men' socially with equal rights and equal freedoms. By 1924 when the enveloping *charchaf* had been almost entirely replaced in Turkey by clothes of European style women actually became more feminine. They were now able to dress to show off their sexual charms and thus their sense of gender was intensified.

Western woman escaped from 'the harem' centuries earlier. Her successful battle against the humiliations of being merely man's 'property' is illustrated in the way she has for centuries had monopoly in beauty; the one most free to parade her sex and her attractions. In fact emancipation in dress which western woman gained centuries ago is far more valuable than the dubious emancipation in public affairs which she demands, often so unnecessarily, today.

Even so centuries of liberty to choose her own dress and indulge her every fancy has not rid woman of her feminine modesty fears. A woman, more than a man, is torn by two contradictory tendencies in her wearing of clothes: she is at one and the same time trying to display her sexual attractions and to hide her sexual shame.

We can detect this psychological conflict not so much in the kind of clothes a woman wears as in the way she wears them. Watch a woman's different attitudes in joining a company of friends or strangers. If she is confident and if she has no social or sexual timidities regarding the circumstances, she will without hesitation throw off her coat or let it fall open casually. If she is ill at ease, particularly if she does not want to invite the social, or for that matter the sexual, attentions of the others, she prefers to remain buttoned up; in every sense of the phrase.

Women, and men also, tend often unconsciously to draw their clothes more closely around them when in unfriendly company, and also do the same when meeting people with whom they do not wish to make contact, either because they feel these people are markedly superior or inferior to them or because there is no common interest. An actress wishing to portray a timid spinster will flutter nervous fingers around her demure scarf; an actor playing a nervous man will finger his tie. These assumed stage gestures, like our unconscious gestures of drawing our own clothes closely around us to signal that we wish to 'keep ourselves apart', are a direct reflection of our atavistic memories of that time when we humans first adopted clothes to cover us and drew them close around us for personal and intimate bodily protection. Although we have transferred our fidgeting to a neutral zone of our bodies we are nevertheless going through the motions of making sure we have 'adjusted' our dress.

We must not however imagine that it was for provocative sexual purpose, conscious or subconscious, that early man and woman put on their first genital coverings. Those tribal humans needed no outward declaration of their sex to attract the other. The first hunters and their women bundled naked together in their caves without, we should think, being too choosy as to who did what and to whom. The dressing-up did eventually become decorative and thus assumed provocative sexual differences intensifying the allure of woman for man is merely one of the many pleasant bonuses we humans have acquired during our progress. Even the narrator of Genesis admits that, for he makes it clear that Adam had already had his mate before he reached for fig leaves.

Nor has anyone ever succeeded in robbing us of that pleasure. Strict moralists who try to control sexual expression in dress find themselves in a perpetual Morton's fork of a dilemma. A conventional society feels that it must suppress blatant arousal of sexual desire, yet at the same time it has to insist, even to the extent of imposing laws to that end, that the sexual differences must be emphatic, and that men should dress as men and women as women. With the result that at every moment of every day sexual recognition in some form is inevitably announced each time a pair of trousers advances towards a skirt.

Clement of Alexandria, so conscious of the terrible lures of the flesh, knew well enough the dangers of sex difference in clothes. This theologian, so sex-aware that he could advise women on such a detail as not to drink from elegantly tall and narrow vessels 'that cause them indecently to throw back their heads, revealing to men their necks and breasts', made the valid point that as the object of clothing was merely to cover the body and protect it from cold there was no reason why woman's dress should differ from man's. That is the way he would have preferred it to be. If men and women were outwardly uniform there would be less lubricity around. Well, even in our day the frigid and loveless dictators of authoritarian states reveal similar preoccupations. Fortunately the human being remains at heart a rebel, a mutineer in Eden or in Hell against climate or environment, government or god. Even in communist overalls any Eve will still devise some artifice to signal that she has an apple for the eating.

2 SEX IN FASHION

'I must admit that no age ever produced anything so perverse as the clothing of the men of the present time who call themselves "pretty fellows". Their coiffures require nothing more than a row of hairpins to make them look completely feminine.'

Yes, it is London. But not London 1971. That observation was made in 1719. It should warn anyone away from attempting to write one of those histories of fashion in which the author attaches social significance to the width of a lapel or unearths common causes for the simultaneous rise and fall of bosoms and empires. That 1719 commentator reminds us that changes in fashion are merely superficial flourishes, that 'pretty fellows' who seem new and remarkable in 1971 seemed also so 250 years ago, as in fact they did in the Rome of Augustus. Of course the most bizarre manifestations of fashions are always what catch the eye, but a more statistical survey of our fellows soon show that the 'pretty fellows' and Mary Quants and Twiggys of this or any other day are and were only a few attractively gaudy figures prominent against a comparatively sober background of a vast populace which commonly wears far less exaggerated male and female costume.

One thing which fashion cannot change. Whatever lines its scissors cut and whatever frills and flounces it attaches to clothes, the irreversible social convention is that men shall dress differently from women. That, not the change in fashionable trimmings, is what concerns us in this book. In such an inquiry we must get under the frills of fashion, as it were, and uncover the essential sexual reasons for the difference in male and female clothing.

'What difference? There's little if any nowadays.' In 1971 such a comment comes as readily as it did to that 1719 writer. With the present vogue for 'unisex' clothes in boutiques where male and female can dress themselves in pants and shirts from the same peg, the comment might seem valid. There might, at a superficial glance seem little distinction between 'pretty fellow' and 'pretty girl'. But the similarity is as illusory in 1971 as it was in 1719, the sneer of perversity equally unfounded. Only a hangover of utilitarian nineteenth-century ideas could make anyone believe that personal decoration is in some ways unmanly or see anything perverse in long hair and frills and silver cloth. To do so shows ignorance of history. The gay blades of Renaissance Florence in parti-coloured hose and slashed beribboned sleeves and the fops of Bourbon France and Jacobean England in their brocade coats and frills and silken breeches were brilliantly decorative, and their 'manliness' even more incontestable than that of the original long-haired cowboys of the 'wild west'.

In any case colour and display in dress is basically a masculine characteristic; it satisfies man's desire to decorate himself and show himself off in competition with his fellows as well as proclaiming his status. Such a display is also, psychologists argue, a psychological necessity to the male. Without it he suffers 'satisfaction denial', and a man's subconscious dissatisfaction with the drab uniform imposed upon him by society can lead to sexual desires being inhibited or disordered.

In the more primitive societies of today, as in the early civilisations, man, not woman, is the decorated one, and his cockerel strutting in fine plumage is paralleled by the male's extra display in most animal species. The fact that flamboyant and colourful attire is essentially masculine has been shown for centuries by the gorgeous display of that most exclusively masculine of all clothing, military uniform. Only in recent history has the garb of the warrior become the drab colour of the earth on which men now die in anonymous masses, but the appeal that gaudy military habit makes to the masculine tendency for display was seen a few years ago when youths and young men adopted the fashion of wearing old military uniforms.

It is not a coincidence that the kind of sexual display in clothing which worries the moralists was at its flamboyant extreme in the Renaissance. An age of intellectual bursting-out and adventure makes its people more individually confident and self demonstrative: its men strut the more and its women seduce the more. Woman's reply to man's codpiece was to pad her belly: if man could pretend to be permanently tumescent then she could pretend to be permanently pregnant. Both women's and men's clothes were candidly decorative of their sex. Not only with codpieces but with cunningly designed garments man showed off his status as a man; his sleeves and trousers so tight that they had to be slashed at shoulder, elbow and knee so that he could move, and these slashes were gorgeously emphasised with coloured inserts and ribbons.

The mistake of thinking that colour and narcissistic display in clothing is effeminate is made only because dressing-up to show off has been woman's monopoly for so long. As we have said, the unisex fad, colourful and demonstrative though it is, is only a transitory swirl of fashion of no lasting significance. The feature of real significance in the fashion scene today is man's reassertion of his right as a male to decorate himself and show himself off in varied colours and fabrics. After more than a century of being a uniformed socialised drone he can once again be a sexual aristocrat, a 'pretty fellow' of individual colour and beauty.

The clothes worn today signify a welcome and double-edged rebellion: a political breaking-out and a sexual breaking-out. Both men and women are winning freedom from political uniformity and restrictive prudery. We see it most markedly in men's clothes, because there the change has been most intense. Up to the end of the eighteenth century man had been beautiful and had not been afraid to show it. Masculine decoration proclaimed, as it had done for centuries, his status or his wealth or both. Then came the revolutionary rise of the bourgeoisie. Any show of wealth or status was now suspect, even dangerous. Status or wealth had to be kept secret, or, at least, not shown off. Man, forced to abandon his instinctively masculine desire to strut around as a 'pretty fellow', was, throughout that drabbest of centuries, the nineteenth, encased in a working uniform as dreary as the age. The mills of the industrialists, grinding more finely and more exceedingly small than God's, reduced man to a fine powder of conformity. His clothes became more and more practical and utilitarian, more and more politically neuter. Only a 'sport', an eccentric, dared to be decorative and flamboyantly fashionable.

Every woman was to some extent drilled into uniformity, but because she had not yet achieved equality with man as a 'worker', except in the labouring classes, she escaped the full rigours of industrialisation and was still permitted to decorate. The male could therefore enjoy some vicarious dressing up by adorning his mate. The silks and jewels with which he draped her proclaimed, at a safe distance from his dull conformist self, his status and his wealth, though it was more politic to consider them as expressions of the devotion proper to a dutiful husband.

Parallel with the century's uniformity of dress was its doleful conformity of mind and, an inevitable accompaniment, sexual prudity. In a society so careful of its dividends and so frightened of the status quo being upset it was desirable that the most potentially revolutionary force of all, sexuality, should be buttoned up in 'unmentionables'. Woman, who because she was not a 'full member' of society had neither vote nor rights, could be allowed to indulge her sexual fancy in clothes, and even in our present sexually egalitarian age woman still indulges this fancy extravagantly. The hem of her skirt may sweep the pavements one month and almost disappear under her belt the next, but man's trousers still end up where they have ended for some 150 years, at his ankles. Even today, despite the increased attention paid to male fashion, a man could in most communities wear a suit as much as thirty years old without being noticeably out of fashion, whereas a woman in a dress equally old is startlingly noticeable, which is the prime reason why she now wears it.

Nevertheless the fact that our minds are free of many of the sexual fantasies and fears of the nineteenth century is shown by our discarding of that century's restrictive and prudish attitude to clothes and nudity. Moralists of the Clement stamp must see today's sexual parade as dangerous licence. Actually it shows a healthily candid attitude to male and female anatomy. Certainly today's Adam will not run in whimpering terror into the undergrowth if his fig leaf slips. He has already had many bites of the apple; the forbidden fruit is so available that neither Eve nor serpent can intensify the temptation of it by saucing it with sin.

There is a welcome loss of fear or shame. On occasions the new freedom encourages the exhibitionist to indulge in infantile displays. The display of pubic hair is enjoying a 'what the butler saw' attraction. But nakedness, losing its novelty by over-exposure, also loses its erotic impact, and it will soon be difficult for even so diligent an explorer as Kinsey to find such a one as he reported in America: a male who boasted he had 'laid' hundreds of girls and had never turned down an offer except on the occasion when a girl started to remove her clothing before coitus. That really shocked him. Such conduct, he said, showed that the girl was 'too indecent to have intercourse with'.

Up to a hundred years ago there was practically no sex difference in the clothes in which western society dressed its children. Boys as well as girls wore petticoats up to the age of six. Even into the 1870's any small boy in breeches would have been conspicuous among his skirted playmates. Until only a few years ago boys on the island of Marken in the Zuyder Zee were dressed in girl's petticoats and caps up to the age of seven, the only sex distinction being that the blouse worn by a boy had a light-coloured strip down the front. When the islanders were asked in 1924 the reason for this custom they had no idea, merely remarking, 'It's the fashion.' Bearing in mind the centuries when it was the fashion in Europe and that Marken was a somewhat isolated community, one is inclined to accept that fashion was the genuine reason, though the psychologists have thought up the more cunning theory that the little boys were dressed up as little girls because the adult males of Marken did not want there to be any masculine 'rivals', even merely symbolic ones such as little boys, alone with their womenfolk on the island when they were away on long fishing trips.

Orientals had a more defined aim for dressing boys as girls. They did so to avert the 'Evil Eye', tricking malevolence away from precious male heirs by camouflaging them as mere girls. The Indian Konkan carried this so far as to bore a boy's nose and put a female nose-ring on him.

I have tried in vain to discover the origin of the universal custom of 'blue for a boy and pink for a girl'. Certainly no preference for particular colours, individually or socially, ancient or modern gives a clue. Colour preferences vary widely and with no recognisable consistency from country to country and from race to race. Blue, of instance, was a sacred colour for the Mayas; priests were robed and sacred books bound in blue and for certain important ceremonies all the children were painted blue. On the other hand some peoples hate blue and have taboos against it, and in Roman Catholic countries blue or violet are symbolic of death.

One other difference in male and female clothing upon which scholars have spent great energy of research is the respective right and left overlap and buttoning of man's and woman's garments. Elaborately argued treatises have been written on this oddity. Brasch ascribes the difference between men's and women's clothes in this respect to the practical problems of daily life. He argues that buttons were introduced into common use in the Middle Ages, a time when men, commonly called upon to fight, had to keep the sword arm (usually the right one) free and warm. Cloaks would thus be worn with the left side overlapping the right, so that the left hand could control the cloak while the right hand was thrust inside to keep it warm. This custom of making men's clothes with left overlapping right continued when buttons were added. On the other hand women's main preoccupation was their children; they often carried their babies with them and had to breast-feed them in exposed places where it was desirable for the mother to shelter the baby and herself with her clothing. Since babies are almost always carried on the left arm, claims Brasch, the left breast was usually the most convenient for feeding, and the woman would protect the baby by pulling over it the right hand side of her clothing. Thus woman's clothing was customarily designed with the right overlapping the left.

In *The Naked Ape* Desmond Morris claimed that the vast majority of paintings of the Madonna and child show the baby on the woman's left arm. He ascribes this general tendency among mothers to the fact that the strong heartbeat is usually on the left-hand side, and the baby, having become accustomed to feeling the mother's heartbeat while in her womb, is apparently more contented if carried near to her heart during its early life. In experiments showing that babies fall asleep more quickly when recordings of various rhythmic sounds are played the effect of playing a recorded heartbeat is very strongly marked.

Brasch speculates also that if it is easier, as he suggests it is, to insert buttons with the right hand while controlling the buttonholes with the left hand, men would find the left overlap more convenient when dressing themselves, whereas maidservants would find the right overlap more convenient when they faced their ladies to dress them.

Some left-or-right theories are psychologically based. One in particular, advanced in *Revue Scientifique* ninety years ago, examined man's supposed tendency to perform movements centrifugally and woman's to perform them centripetally. We are asked to accept that the characteristically male attitude of aggression is centrifugal and the characteristically feminine attitude of defence is centripetal, and to compare as examples of this the poses of the Apollo Belvedere and the Venus de Medici. On such grounds it is claimed that if a woman put on a man's coat she would button it with the left hand with a centripetal movement.

Despite the impressive ingenuity of such arguments it does seem that on the question of buttons these earnest researchers are putting a very dubious cart in front of a very mythical horse. My belief is that buttons can have nothing at all to do with it. Long before buttons were invented, indeed long before men and women reached the stage of sewing any kind of fastening on their clothes, humans were already conscious of a need for a difference in male and female clothes. They had already made certain types of clothing and ways of wearing it appropriate for the different sexes. When buttons did come along they would be used to reinforce those distinctions on a sexually differing overlap that already existed. In which case it was neither breast feeding nor weapon-carrying nor any other occupational difference which created differing male and female overlap. Rather, I feel, it was the other way round: the overlap was deliberately employed to accord with and to emphasise already existing difference in male and female clothing.

If, however, I wanted to indulge in pseudo-scientific speculation on this point I could offer my own explanation about man's flies. The reason why they overlap left over right, whether buttoned or zipped, could be that they are therefore more easily opened one-handedly with man's dominant hand, the right. This leaves his left hand free to perform any ancillary operation that might be necessary while he is opening his flies: keeping the girl quiet, for instance. This as least was one problem Adam was spared.

2 WHEN BREASTS ARE MASCULINE

We reveal our sex every time we speak. Not only by masculine or feminine timbre of voice, but also by the words we use and the way we use them. Words add up to knowledge, and it is therefore with good reason sexual intercourse is described as having carnal *knowledge*.

Speech is the soul of human sexuality. By giving us the power to communicate and nourish our human intellect it also endowed us with the intellectual sexuality characteristic of human desire and love. Word-communication between man and woman is as essential to their sexual union as communication of penis and vagina; the imprint of words on our minds as necessary as the tactile sensations of coitus.

With a wink or a gesture or a smile we can of course convert any word in the language into a 'four-letter' word, but the sexual import of speech lies at a more subtle level of consciousness than a crude joke of sexual implication. This becomes apparent when we see how in all languages words assume individual sexual character. We find nouns that are immutably male or female. There are eunuch nouns too, neuter ones, and, if we think hard enough we could find deviant or at least transvestite ones.

As English-speaking peoples know, often to their exasperation, practically all other languages insist that words must be grammatically accorded a sexual distinction to which we must pay as polite and uniform attention as we do to the differences of man and woman. All the European languages of Greek or Latin derivation have masculine and feminine nouns. Ancient Latin and Greek had neuter nouns. Modern Greek retains neuter nouns, and German has neuter nouns.

The identification of human speech with human sexuality is obvious enough for us to understand that words could be given gender. Just how it happened is still the subject of professional dispute and research.

One lovely theory is my favourite among all other theories because it seems so illustrative and so sexily logical. Wheeler refers to it. It is the theory that noun-gender arose from the tendency natural to a human to personify himself with objects and to view them as persons. The most prominent characteristic of any person is a person's sex. Therefore objects that had been personalised would also inevitably become sexualised. More sophisticated linguistic theories elaborate this simple argument with detailed investigation into significant vowel endings found in primitive speech and in the languages of early civilisations. Frazer, among others, studied and eventually accepted a somewhat contrasting theory that objects assumed masculine or feminine gender not according to their own male or female 'personality' but according to the masculinity or femininity of the person who spoke their names. Others have argued that the higher and shriller voices of women eventually resulted in feminine endings to words.

But I favour that down-to-earth belief that objects were given male and female names because they represented in some way, by physical shape or feel or imagined purpose, the male penis and the female vagina. Confining ourselves to the European languages, the only languages I know anything about, we find that penis-vagina theory beautifully illustrated. Most things that are forceful, advancing, thrusting and hard are masculine; most things that are yielding, receptive and soft are feminine. There are, of course, inevitable exceptions, some of them exasperatingly inexplicable, but I retreat to the theoretically cowardly argument of saying that exceptions prove the rule.

Let us examine some penis-vagina nouns.

Latin had such classic examples as the masculine *ignis* for active fire and the feminine *aqua* for receptive water, and as I am writing this in Italy I grab an Italian dictionary to buttress my beliefs. As one would expect in this country the pen ejaculates sexy examples by the score. The masculine foot thrusts itself into the receptive feminine shoe. The male cork pushes itself into the feminine bottle. The male button more persuasively insinuates itself into the feminine button-hole. Though I cannot attempt to explain why an Italian sword should be feminine; unless there is some Freudian castration complex adhering to an instrument that kills men more often than it kills women.

To Italians Spring and Summer are feminine, Autumn and Winter are masculine. The world, a man-created thing, is masculine, but earth, the abode of Mother, is naturally feminine, as are the names of nearly all countries; with exceptions like Portugal and Belgium, which are masculine, a fact which can probably be accounted for only by complicated explanation relating to the phonetic demands of the Italian language. An interesting oddity is that although colours take the gender of the noun to which they are attached, the Italian word for pink, *rosa*, cannot be other than feminine.

In Spain sex seems to be determined more by size than by purpose. Things that are round but long are feminine, so that sometimes a larger object is feminine. In the Hamitic languages, similarly, big and important things are masculine, small and unimportant things are feminine. This has a divertingly unexpected result in Bedauyo. Woman's breasts, noticeably big and important, are masculine; man's nipples, small and unimportant, are feminine.

In some tribal languages word-gender is decided according to what is good or bad. In the minds of men what is good is masculine and what is bad is feminine. Darlington reports that when the smelters of iron ore in Bakitara in East Africa had to distinguish between good and bad stone, the better quality stone was given a masculine name, the poorer quality a feminine one. However, one must be careful here. The better quality was masculine in that it was *hard* to break and prepare for smelting, and the poorer quality was *softly* feminine.

More specifically a quality distinction is the use of the Amharic word *wand*, meaning male which, Levine reports, 'is employed in a way that indicates strong emotional approval. To say of someone *Essu Wand* now ("He is a male") is not to make a statement of biological fact; it is rather a eulogy of virtue, analogous to the American expression, "He's a real man." '

In our own society we have a very distinct sexually differentiated vocabulary for our garments: trousers and knickers, shirts and blouses. Petticoats and bloomers can never be other than feminine. Vests seem ambivalent.

Women, never men, are often given flower names. Flowers are so obviously feminine that a male can be slandered as being insufficiently masculine by calling him a pansy or a lily. Terms of abuse seem nearly always feminine. Just as 'effeminate' can be derogatorily applied to any weak or imperfect creative work, the vulgar names for parts of a woman's body can be used as epithets indicating an incompetent or futile person. Also a government that dithers or even a football team that loses is described as 'a lot of old women'. The term 'woman's work' is often used in a derogatory manner: 'women's gossip' describes trivial or vulgar chatter.

It is surely not preposterous to rope-in Chomsky as a possible recruit to support the penis-vagina theory of word gender. His theory that speech patterns are not developed from scratch when babies begin to utter words and we have some measure of grammar in our genetical inheritance can surely be linked to the fact that our sex is both physically and psychologically determined before and shortly after birth. We are born with an innate ability to be male and female and we can recognise masculinity and femininity before we can possibly be intellectually conscious of the masculinity and femininity of ourselves or others.

Applying this to the penis-vagina theory of speech we can imagine what probably happened when in their cultural infancy humans began to speak in a linguistically ordered manner. Incidentally that event did not happen all that long time ago; perhaps at the beginning of early civilised community life, only some 10,000 years ago.

Early human words would be words describing themselves and parts of their bodies, and having created words of such sexual implication primitive people would attach similar male and female labels to all the things they saw around them: sun and moon and stars, land and sea, trees and plants. Later they would extend their sexually constructed vocabulary to the objects they fabricated for daily life and which, because of their shape or feel or purpose, appeared distinctively male or female. Hence the penis-vagina concept of shoe and foot, cork and bottle, and the rest. This habit, once formed, would persist in the social subconscious even when the increasing sophistication of the human intellect disregarded primitive personifying, even down to our own day when the objects themselves have become more complex and less recognisable as penis or vagina symbols. So that in Italy it must still be a masculine train which plunges into the orifice of a feminine railway station. In the days of steam the expiring hiss which announced the train had come could be seen as the typical ending of any Mediterranean romance.

German is altogether more cautious and characteristically pedantic about sex. Man and woman are, naturally, respectively masculine and feminine, but the child and the girl are neuter: 'das Kind' and 'das Mädchen'. Obviously child and girl are not considered as having reached that stage of maturity which could merit their being sexed. German also extends this neuter convention in a class-conscious way. In polite language among better class folk the wife is 'die Frau', feminine, but an ordinary wife, the wife of the labourer down the street for instance, is 'das Weib', only neuter.

The Germans upset my theory and the whole European pattern by making trousers, 'die Hose', feminine, and the skirt 'der Rock', masculine. They go further. They also insist that the sun is feminine and the moon is masculine. Actually, however, in this they are in accord with most languages that have sex genders, though in modern Greek the moon is neuter. Those other languages are probably more logical in so far as that, after all, the sun can be considered, and physically is, the life-giver and, therefore, a mother. As for the moon we have always had a Man there.

It was, however, inevitable that because both Sun and Moon were always looked upon as deities whatever sex any language gave to one of them the opposite sex would have to be given to its so obviously contrasting partner.

The Greenlanders give a different slant to the sun-moon dichotomy by believing that the sun is feminine because it is a female spirit which kills men, and the female sun is constantly seeking revenge over the male moon because it rejoices at the death of women.

The attaching of sexual characteristics to objects is vividly demonstrated in the ancient Hindu ceremony performed for the purpose of ensuring the birth of a male child. Two different kinds of wood were rubbed together to kindle a male-inducing fire; the upper piece of wood was regarded as male and the lower as female.

Many words directly associated with sex sound vulgar to timidly polite ears. Some of them are the four-letter words with which many modern writers attempt, with decreasing effect, to shock us. Others are beguilingly affectionate nicknames for our physical possessions: John Thomas, Fanny, Pussy. Many men refer to their penis, with Freudian logic, as their tool. Equally Freudian is man's attitude to that obviously phallic instrument the gun; and the slangy American question 'Have you had your gun off?' needs no explanation.

The priest in Anthony Burgess' *The Wanting Seed* justifiably comments 'All dirty words are fundamentally religious. They are all concerned with fertility. God, we are told, is "love".'

The identification of speech with sexuality is so strongly felt in some societies that conversation is forbidden between persons who are socially precluded from having sexual relations. Even brothers and sisters fall under this ban. In fact sexual taboos abound in speech: consciously, by tribal law, among primitives; subconsciously, by social custom, among us. We still feel that certain words are appropriate for use only on masculine or feminine lips. Naturally this applies most markedly to words of a sexual significance and to the names of the sexual organs. In conversation about sex there are masculine and feminine argots.

Among primitives the sexual difference in speech often leads to the use of intricate euphemisms. For example, a Basuto woman, being forbidden by taboo from uttering her husband's name, cannot use that word at all even if it is also the name of a common object. If his name happens to be Lerotholi, meaning 'drop', she is unable to speak of a 'drop of water' but must exercise her ingenuity and convert the phrase into something like 'falling part of rain' or any phrase which, without use of the tabooed word will describe what she means. Similar conventions in speech are found among many primitive societies, along with taboos which forbid certain words to be uttered by women or men or in the hearing of one or the other.

When the Lord's Prayer was translated for the Kootenay Indians in British Columbia it had to be done in two languages, male and female. In Japan until recently female writing had to be different from masculine writing. Woman did not use ideograms. There still are marked differences between male and female modes of speech in Japanese, particularly noticeable in the refined elegances of speech used by aristocratic ladies.

These sexual intricacies of language show how insuperably difficult it would be, apart from the comparatively minor problem of creating a universal vocabulary, to formulate an international language. Yet there is one universal language, a language which needs neither vocal dexterity nor grammar, a language in which words can be expressed in a stare, a smile, a nod, a movement of the hand. The glances and gestures interchanged between man and woman as words inviting sexual communion are universally human. In this way sexuality, which has employed speech to communicate itself, can sometimes dispense with the elaboration of spoken words and become a silent language of unheard words which men and women all over the world translate into words of passion and desire.

12 The Emancipation Myth

I was driving south east towards the Sahara. About a half-a-mile from the track was a tent like an upturned boat, long and low and black and changing shape in the waves of heat rising from sand and scrub. I pulled up, and a Bedouin herdsman, tossing a stone at the heels of his goats to urge them towards denser scrub on a nearby slope, came forward to greet me.

He invited me to his home to refresh myself. As I stepped from sun to darkness I almost stumbled over two dark mounds of rags or clothing, just inside the entrance of the black tent. My host snapped his fingers. Tongue against teeth he made two sharp hissing noises, then added some monosyllables of command. The mounds rose and scuttled out. They were his wife and mother-in-law. From below the awning they picked up huge terracotta urns, then set off across the scrub, the urns balanced on their heads.

'They will bring you fresh water,' he explained.

While we waited I chatted with him about his life and his home. I asked about the flocks of goats cropping tough grass on the rocky slope.

Would he, I asked, move the tent, as Bedouins customarily do, when that sparse pasturage has been nibbled away? No, he told me. There was always enough grazing for his small flock.

'No,' he repeated, 'we stay here. It is a good place. And there is always fresh water. Only a mile away.'

The women came back. The massive urns on their heads were brimful of fresh spring water. My host began pouring water over my wrists and ankles 'to freshen me'. I motioned that I had used enough, but, insisting on hospitality, he continued pouring and emptied the whole of one urn. From the other we drank while the mother-in-law began preparing coffee. The wife hurried off with the emptied urn to refill it at the spring: only a mile away.

Now a story of another Arab encounter.

I was sitting on a daïs with Sheikh Suleiman, the Duke of Bedford of the Arab World who did the 'stately homes' trade of opening his tent in the Negev to tourists. The men facing us, sitting on a semi-circle of rugs rippling over sand, were his grandsons. The gaudy hilts of daggers gleamed at their waists. But the boy, only three years old, or perhaps four, who was given the honour of carrying my coffee to me on a brass tray, was one of his sons.

'How many sons have you?' I asked the Sheikh.

His face clouded. 'Allah forgive me,' he said. 'I do not know.'

My interpreter, the local schoolmaster, explained that when, years earlier, the Sheikh had accepted Israeli law he had sent all but one of his many wives away. Some were pregnant at the time. Perhaps they had borne sons.

'Do you know how many daughters?' I asked.

Grinning, the interpreter whispered my question to the Sheikh. The Sheikh choked over his coffee, then, still spluttering, bawled out the question to his grandsons. Their lips parted and their teeth flashed; they roared with laughter.

'Daughters!' The Sheikh laughed again. 'Who counts women?'

Such scenes fit our commonly accepted idea about the different status of women in east and west. We think of the desert particularly as 'a man's country': a country where man is still lord and master, and woman merely his slave, his bedmate, the mother of his sons and his domestic labourer.

There are, of course, parts of Europe where it is not all that different. For example, in Southern Italy, where I live, it is much the same. Not only in mountain villages and along rural roads but in the streets of apparently prosperous and progressive towns women are the carriers, baskets on their heads or burdens slung on their shoulders. From the terrace of my home in Amalfi I once watched my neighbour on a harvest morning superintending the labour of transporting his lemons to market. For hour after hour his wife and daughters heaved on to their shoulders skeps of lemons weighing well over a hundredweight and carried them down the granite stairways, 572 steps in all, to the waiting lorry. The husband's work was more exacting: he stood sweating in the sun with a pencil and paper making the essential record of the number of loads departing for the Naples market.

In the mountains of Greece I have seen women making profitable use of an hour's journey to their mountain home by spinning wool as they walked behind the mules on which their husbands rode. Even in Britain, in the Scottish Highlands, I have seen a crofter's wife yoked alongside a horse to pull the plough her husband directed with masculine skill through the stony soil.

Now a different story.

I was the guest in a penthouse of what I guess is the Riviera's most expensive hotel. My host is one of the richest and most powerful men of his profession. Every member of a vastly important firm hangs on his slightest command. Out of regard for him I will give no further clues.

His wife was in a petulant mood that morning. Diamonds and turquoises from a family necklace had been reset two days before into a brooch and ear-rings of a pattern specially designed to amuse and flatter a famous personage whose birthday party husband and wife had attended two days earlier. The jeweller had promised to collect the geegaws that morning and rebuild the gems back into the original necklace. She wanted to wear it at a dinner that weekend. The jeweller was unable to come along the coast that day.

My host, still suffering from a birthday-party hangover, did not feel like going out.

'Send them with Georges,' he suggested.

'No. It's too risky,' said the wife. 'You must take them.'

'That road!' he complained. 'Twelve miles!'

She shrugged.

With a grimace he pulled himself arthritically out of his chair, summoned the chauffeur, and set off. Only twelve miles. After all a shorter distance in a chauffeur-driven air-conditioned Mercedes than a desert mile with an urn on one's head.

At that point one might be tempted to drop the subject. There seems sufficient in those stories to crystallise all that could be thought or said about the relationship, social and political and economic and conjugal, of men and women, husbands and wives, over all the world and through all time. Every furious argument of feminist or anti-feminist is encapsulated there. Yet there is something which is not so apparent. The rhetoric blown up around the subject of the emancipation of women has obscured the real truth. It might be a valuable service to attempt to uncover that truth, to attempt to disperse here and now and forever the whole emancipation myth.

The sight of women bearing burdens across deserts or mountains while their menfolk jog along on camels or mules or sit smoking on café verandahs arouses the choler of the feminists, those ardent souls who plead so piteously or bawl so compellingly for equal rights for women.

At this point it is necessary to make an elementary observation. Feminists are not necessarily female. They come in both male and female shape. Though it is noticeable that the female of the species is often more doughtily and commandingly masculine than the male.

Feminists come also in two *classes*. One class comprises the political feminists, the propagandists in the field. These earnest men and women diligently strive to secure acceptance of the proposition that women should have equal rights, socially, politically, legally and economically, with men. No one but a reactionary or a fool would criticise their aims. Women should have equal pay for equal work, equal opportunity in professions and commerce and politics, equal rights in marriage and in law. No one can disagree with these laudable aims. That any dispute about woman's right to equality in such humdrum affairs has survived into this technological age is a historical absurdity; so grotesque an absurdity that one must think that only the grossest masculine tyranny or the crassest feminine ineptitude could be responsible for its continued existence. Until one examines feminist propaganda and sees how double-edged and misdirected it has been. Generations of feminists-in-the-field have failed to achieve acceptance of reasonable arguments because instead of confining them to demands for social justice they have been besotted with the illustration that women, being as *human* as man, should be considered the *same* as man. The noblest aspirations for sexual equality collapses if they are founded on a disregard for the essential differences, not only physical but also intellectual and emotional, between man and woman.

We have, most of us at least, grown out of the belief that woman is perhaps not human at all, and we consider only as an antique curiosity such a publication as *Women Are Not Human Beings* in Leipzig in 1595. Exactly a thousand years earlier, in 595, the doubts implicit in that title were learnedly debated at the Synod of Macon. Earlier still St. Thomas had declared that woman was only an 'occasional' and incomplete being, a kind of imperfect man. 'Man is above woman, as Christ is above man. It is unchangeable that woman is destined to live under man's influence, and has no authority from her lord.'

There indeed is anti-feminism. Though the ancients did not all hold such opinions. We must not forget the 'blue stockings' at Babylon's university 4,000 years ago, or the Lacedaemonian women who were too powerful to be suppressed by Lycurgus of Sparta, or the matrons of Rome and China. So we can smile at occasional pre-occupations with the 'woman problem'. We can even smile at Knox's mediaeval 'monstrous regiment'. Such expressions and arguments were merely the aberrations of bemused sex-superstitious minds.

The illusion that woman might not, after all, be human is not the one into which the political feminists have bogged themselves down. Their mistake lies in their confusion about the word 'equality'. They spend their breath trying to make *equality* mean *'the same'*. However eloquently they say it and whatever tone of voice they use, they are all making the same mistake. Some say it mellifluously, as does Simone de Beauvoir, who, intoxicated, not with liquor but with emotion, sobs out woman's woes upon your shoulder. Others, grinding cigar butts under their brogues, demand an equality with men which no one, at least physically, would dare deny them.

Leaving the political feminists we now come face to face with the second class of feminists, the philosophical ones. Most of these, both the men and the women, are eloquent writers. Of the women writers, a few, even those garbed in the most donnish robes, are brilliant expositors. High above the hurly-burly of practical arguments about equal pay and so forth they inhabit airy heights where scientific fact and scientific proof are cast aside as too crude to be acceptable. They believe, quite sincerely, in an infallible equality of woman. Indeed some of them are easily tempted into expressing the belief that woman is not only equal but superior. In a delightfully Shavian aphorism Brigid Brophy says, 'I obdurately insist on believing that some men are my equal.' We know, of course, that here Brophy is merely pulling our legs in her characteristically elegant way, but there are writers who actually say such things seriously with their tongues *out* of their cheeks. It is refreshing to turn to the candid words of the brilliant Mrs. Pearl Craigie. 'Women won't admit their absolute dependence on men. That is why I am dead against women's colleges, clubs, suffrage and the like. They make each other wretched, and they are, as influences on each other, utterly sterilising and devitalising.'

The philosophical feminists might argue bitterly against

such 'defeatism', but the point they always miss is the one point made by, among other perceptive writers on the subject, Lily Braun: 'Only the recognition that the entire nature of woman is different from that of man, that it signifies a new vivifying principle in human life, makes the women's movement, in spite of the misconception of its enemies and its friends, a social revolution.'

There it is: the difference in the 'entire nature'. The only way to eliminate that difference would be to eliminate the biological difference between sperm-carrier and egg-breeder; or to revert to a lower form of life in which the two functions can be performed in the one body. It is not, scientifically, beyond the bounds of possibility that humans could find an evolutionary path leading to the extinction of this father-mother disparity so that the whole burden of gestating and nursing human young would not be thrown upon only one half of the population.

Even today without scientific aids women are, as in the past, always able to opt out of maternity. Nuns have done so for centuries in the extreme form of completely renouncing sexuality to devote themselves body and soul to their vocation. Others, increasingly more of them in modern society, have avoided maternal commitments without forbidding themselves sexual enjoyments or sexual expression. Those who do, purposefully or inadvertently, become mothers after the still necessary nine months of gestating, avoid the chores of motherhood. Teats on bottles, baby foods, nurses and crèches can free them from the physical toils of rearing their young.

Here we find ourselves on the threshold of what true emancipation of woman would actually involve. Success in methods of artificial procreation could free men and women from the task, or the danger caused by accidents of propinquity, of creating children. Science, which can execute marvels, can also do humdrum jobs, and its invention of disposable diapers has taken from the landscape of domestic motherhood those lines of white squares fluttering in a drying breeze. Its further ingenuities of breeding-chambers and feeding-appliances could take from the landscape of femininity such out-moded symbols as menstruation, wide pelvises and pendant breasts.

Woman would then be completely emancipated. The political feminist Utopia would have dawned. If we manage, in the process, to retain our genitals they could become merely decorations or organs of pleasure no longer used in the present

Russian-roulette method of procreating ungenetically determined brats. Such emancipation would rid us of all the dangers and preoccupations and horrors of the sexual difference. And deprive us also of its joys.

1 MEN MUST WORK, AND WOMEN MUST WEEP

In a Tunisian village, having been impressed by the agility with which a young girl carried a load on her head, I attempted the same feat. The laughter that roared from the men on the café verandah was not because the load fell off, but because I had tried to do something exclusively feminine; to them my performance was as risible as that of a female impersonator getting laughs from a Palladium audience.

Let us look again at the scene of Arab women carrying burdens for their menfolk. It is time now to destroy the misconception to which our western minds leap at such a picture. The fact that in the more primitive communities woman's work is most often humbler and on occasions more arduous than man's does not always indicate that women are held in less regard by men.

It was St. Ambrose, a Christian, not an Arab, who declared 'Adam was led to sin by Eve. It is just and right that woman accept as lord and master him whom she led to sin.' That canonised gentleman speaks with the authority of the belief that has been the most persuasive force in forming our cultural and social attitudes, and the concept sticks, adheres to our subconscious even amid the chatter of feminist argument. Before the Koran, however, before that man-designed book emerged as a new cultural force, Bedouin women enjoyed a status quite superior to the one assigned to them now.

The wife with an urn on her head may actually be much more beloved by her husband than the woman with turquoises and diamonds around her flaccid neck. The Arab woman by virtue of her station and her, to masculine eyes, feminine need for protection, is more protected by her mate. And protection leads to tenderness. Between the Arab and his woman can be a deeper physical union than that experienced by the semi-independent man and wife of a more sophisticated community. There is a stronger duality, a more sensual appreciation of being of one body and one flesh. Leslie Finer, pointing out that similarly in Greece the males are more protective, draws attention to the fact that the rule is still generally observed that no son of a Greek family may marry until all his sisters have found husbands.

Among most primitive peoples, and even in more developed societies in which most of life has to be devoted to the growing or getting of food, man and woman work together as absolute partners and their roles are dually essential to the economy of their families. The concept of women of primitive tribes being downtrodden slaves of their menfolk is hardly borne out by the habit of Queen Shinga of the Congo who, Crawley says, on the eve of any new tribal adventure would sacrifice the handsomest man she could lay her hands on and dance with a 'sword hanging round her neck, an axe at her side and a bow and arrows in her hands'.

'Amhara women,' reports Levine, 'are regarded as a distinctly inferior class and are beaten as a matter of course for mistakes in their work or for apparent flirtations.' An Amharic proverb says 'Women and donkeys need the stick'. Even so they enjoy a number of important customary rights; retaining possession of all the land which they bring into marriage, and are considered to own one-half of all the property accumulated during the course of the marriage. Divorce may be obtained by the wife as readily as by the husband.

Havelock Ellis argued that although motherhood was woman's supreme function the idea that her activities should be confined to the home could now be regarded as almost extinct. He agreed with Friedrich Naumann and others who claimed that 'a woman is not adequately equipped to fulfil her functions as mother and trainer of children unless she has lived in the world and exercised a vocation'.

But what is it that makes a woman go into the world and exercise a vocation? To increase the family income? Yes, very often. Or because work is a self-realisation and she likes it? Also often. Or because it increases her sexual bargaining power at home and she can say to her semi-dependent husband, 'No, not tonight, darling! I've a conference at head office tomorrow?'

Women can now have both sex and career. This is the popular conception of the change in working habits in the western world. Implicit in the concept is the belief that woman's ambition has always been to have a career, but it could surely be argued that it is not because of a desire to compete with men that women now go out in greater numbers into the world to seek careers, but because the commercial values of modern life have devalued the home.

In Southern Italy where the tradition of home as an almost sacred entity is preserved we find woman's opportunities to educate herself and go out in the world restricted. Yet as wife and mother or even grandmother her position is one of power and privilege and it is her voice which dictates not only the family routine but the family economy. A Southern Italian woman in industry is a perpetual headache to the boss who tries to employ her. When it comes to the crunch her loyalty is always to her husband and his beliefs. To her, whatever might be the rules on the labour market, the laws of family life are more important, and at the ultimate she would rather carry skeps of lemons on her head for her husband without wages than press buttons among well-paid ranks of button-pressers in a factory. The justice of equal pay for equal work cannot be denied, but what is more relevant is that apart from unorthodox and exceptional women, like those who become Prime Ministers, women on the whole do not really want to do equal jobs.

Modern industrial techniques make it possible for women to do work as capably and as dexterously as men. Actually a woman has always had such capability. Anyone who has been anywhere near a farm knows that the farmer's wife can do anything her husband can do.

As we can see in other parts of the world there is often no marked difference between men and women in manual dexterity and strength. Mr. H. H. Hine of London University reported during 1928 excavations in Jordan that 'Our strongest woman, Handooma, one day carried a boulder so heavy that it took five men to lift it on her head'. And even in our western world women quite recently did manual jobs now considered as only suitable for male workers. To good effect, also it seems, for a nineteenth-century American, writing of pit-girls in Lancashire, said, 'You cannot find plumper figures, prettier forms, more shapely necks, or daintier feet despite the ugly clogs, in all of dreamful Andalusia.'

Nevertheless, from an employer's point of view a man is a more reliable economic investment for any job which requires as its first essential continuity of employment. Men or women are equally likely to be off work with flu or rheumatism, and any man might be more prone than a woman to come in with a sick head or not come in at all after a weekend's drinking. But apart from these exceptions, of one thing the employer of labour can be sure: a man is unlikely to be regularly off-colour once a month and will certainly never be pregnant.

There is another reason, a more subtle reason of which an employer might not be consciously aware, for the employer feeling that he gets more wage value out of a man. When he employs a man he is actually employing two people for one wage: he is employing a man and also the wife who sends the man to work lusty and well-fed, with all his creature comforts provided for and free to give all his time and energy to the job. So the employer has a worker who provides his own batman, valet, cook and housekeeper. The woman worker, on the other hand, will need to repair her stockings on the job.

An attitude even more mercenary is implicit in an objection to women workers made by the British Post Office in the '30's. They would have to supply separate lavatories, which was, for want of space, sometimes impracticable, and always expensive.

Division of labour between man and woman and the allocation of distinctive tasks to each varies throughout the world. For instance, all over the world it is usually the woman of the house who washes the family's clothes, but in Abyssinia this was considered a man's task in which women could not help him. An anecdote of Crawley's recalls my own experiences in Tunisia and Morocco. An English traveller horrified the women of a Moroccan village by sending a manservant to fetch water. They would not let him do what was a woman's task.

Distinctions between male and female vocations are found not only geographically but historically. Male clothes are today made by men, but the ancient Greeks and Romans had their clothes made by female slaves under the direction of the woman of the house.

There is always the danger of making slipshod generalisations from superficial observations on male and female aptitudes. Someone reported to Havelock Ellis that in Germany during the 1914–1918 War women employed as bus conductors were 'less amenable to discipline than men, less reliable and trustworthy, and more casual in their ways'. The dexterity of modern 'clippies' and the reliability of air-hostesses refute such prejudicial remarks. It is attractive to hear of a reverse process. One profession that has been for more than forty years the preserve of woman, that of personnel management, is now being invaded by men, who, according to women personnel officers, are not just seeking equality but are trying to get to the top.

Somewhat imaginatively Margaret Mead seems to think that in this technological age not only human beings but machines themselves are assuming sexual symbolism. At least she says that in America 'there is now a slight indication that motor cars are becoming female while aeroplanes become male'. As passengers we hope that neither car nor plane will become deviant.

Industrial psychologists argue that women are innately conservative in their work attitudes. In routine work they are 'quick, handy and patient', but they tend to be too concerned about their appearance and their dress; they also worry about the morals of their employer. Whereas any man is uneasy under a female supervisor, many women prefer receiving orders from a man and can display antipathy towards members of their own sex, either as competitors at similar work or in positions of command. Which makes employers chary of allowing women to rise in the hierarchial scale.

The woman at work also suffers a personal peculiarly feminine disadvantage. If she shows extreme competence she finds herself being classed as unfeminine: when she shows incompretence the comment is 'just like a woman!'

Despite the advances in technology and automation which have made the individual aptitudes and strengths of the sexes less and less important, schools and employers are still reluctant to encourage girls to acquire vocational skills. Girls' schools still receive remarkably fewer facilities for teaching science subjects. Although there are only three times more men than women at university there are forty male students to every one female student studying engineering, technology and applied science.

Yet as society becomes ever more sophisticated and increasingly dependent upon instruments the gap between the manual capabilities of man and woman narrows. Technological developments in industry make it possible for the physically weaker woman to control complex and powerful machinery as easily as any man can do, but now we have come to an age where this equality has wider implications.

Up to quite recently no one woman was ever physically strong enough to face up to a man in a fight; not with her fists, that is, though her stronger tongue muscles made her usually his superior in verbal battle. Today, however, with a rifle or for that matter an atom bomb in her hands a woman is equal to a man. Charlotte Corday d'Armont was no doubt a courageous assassin, but to have used a kitchen-knife to such good effect on Citoyen Marat she was probably, for all her feminine beauty, ferociously muscular. But the world will know that women have reached full physical occupational equality with men when it sees a President shot down by a woman even weaker in limb than an Oswald.

2 HOW WOMAN RULES

Recent memories of women chained to railings or flinging themselves in front of racehorses as a demonstrative short-cut to the ballot box make many believe that a battle for woman's rights is peculiar to this century. People a degree more aware of history seem to see the eighteenth century as the period when the 'oppressed class', women, began flinging off the chains of social servitude. These fictions are dispersed by a most cursory glance at the story of mankind.

One could think, from the shrill complaints against the subjection of women in past ages, that there had never been a Semiramis, a Queen of Sheba, a Boadicea, a Pilate's wife, a Caesar's wife and a Lady Macbeth, a flock of female de Guises and Medicis and a Rosa Luxemburg. They ignore those Empresses of Byzantium who wielded such immense political and financial power; daughters of Athenian professors and Frankish officers, some of them by birth princesses, but others tradesmen's daughters who had married into the purple and exercised sovereign authority. Even in Anglo-Saxon England women, apart from regal ones, occupied high position and held land in their own right.

Plato was advocating political equality for women all of 2,200 years ago, but long before his day the ancient world had already accepted it in various regions and in various guises. Four thousand years ago women of the Babylonian and Assyrian colony of Burus in Asia Minor were in positions of authority and although its University had a man as its Principal it was a woman's university with faculties of literature and art. After all, the primal 'boss' of the world was a woman; that old familiar personage we described on the first pages of this book, Mother Nature. Mankind had to recognise her dominance. Instinctively mankind accepted woman's biological importance, realising that the male, as Remy de Gourmont so neatly puts it, was merely 'the key which she requires to keep her wound up to go'.

In a society or time when man did not understand the part he had played in sowing the seed of a child woman's ability to give birth to children would seem as an attribute to the female's mysterious life-giving power. If she could give life, then surely she could take it away. Among the earliest known 'works of art' made by man more than 30,000 years ago, are miniatures of women in the last stages of pregnancy carved in stone. A mother-and-child group was painted as early as 10,000 B.C. The father does not appear as a subject in primitive art until the New Stone Age, about 5,000 B.C.

Because we fear most the power of those we adore or love superstitious reverence for Mother Earth and her coterie of goddesses infiltrated even into religions observed by fierce and necessarily aggressive societies. The Jews are one classic example of a masculine-dominated society, yet, despite the thunderous presence of Jehovah on every page, the Testament of Judaic history is permeated with warnings against the mysterious power of woman, from Eve, the eternal temptress, to Delilah, archetype of all women who suck man's strength away in his sleep. From such reverential awe of women it was a short and logical step to the belief that God on Earth could be born to us from so mysterious and wondrous a personage as a Virgin Mother. St. Paul found himself in the very centre of the transition from Goddess to God when at Ephesus he was faced by a demo of protestors yelling 'Great is Diana of the Ephesians'.

The ancient religions, those which through the medium of succeeding beliefs still permeate our social subconscious, worshipped the female principle. The Great Mother goddess unearthed at Susa, the Cretan earth-goddess figures with enormous buttocks and swelling breasts, Ishtar of Babylonia, Astarte of the Semites, Gaea, Rhea and Cybele of the Greeks, and Isis of Egypt show mankind's early reverence of Mother Nature. Even the 'god' of the Hindus, Siva, is half-female.

Of its very nature; civilisation is feminine. Civilisation means cities; cites mean homes; homes mean cocoons; cocoons wombs in which the female gestates and protects the race.

Bertrand Russell must have been nodding, or making a conditioned genuflection to the Left, when he argued that, 'The institution of private property brings with it the subjection of women', momentarily overlooking his own observation that in the Roman Empire, for instance, the influx of sudden wealth made women as free as they ever have been in human history. 'Women who had been virtuous slaves became free and dissolute; divorce became common, the rich ceased to have children.'

When China, a country where the sovereign personages had always been mother-in-law in the home and Queen Mother on the throne, moved towards modernisation, the dexterous dames established banks, and their menfolk were happy to relinquish the toils of financial and industrial responsibility. The banker women did not slacken their hold on the home; they intensified their power by marrying off their sons and assuming control of their clan in the supreme position first of mother-in-law and then grandmother.

Article 122 of the Soviet Constitution of 1936 declares: 'In Soviet Russia woman enjoys the same right as man in all aspects of economic, official, cultural, public and political life.' The time might yet come when some more enlightened society will have need to declare as authoritatively that in all aspects of life man must be allowed to enjoy the same rights as women.

When in primitive times conduct of affairs was a domestic family matter, politics were manufactured at home. When political success began to rely on armies and men marched forth as soldiers and it became inconvenient to have pregnant menstruating soldiery, women stayed at home. But when industrial development to positions of state and when modern techniques allowed the affairs of the nation to become conducted by universal suffrage women could play their part. There was no clank of the throwing off of chains; only the rustle of discarded silk as women stepped into the powerful cabinet of the bedroom.

It is argued that by asserting her social political and economic rights too vehemently and competing with man on equal terms, woman loses some of her erotic power over man. This can be true. A woman Cabinet Minister or a woman Judge is unlikely to lure a Samson into her bed, but the really feminine woman is by instinct too intuitively subtle to burden herself with the robes of government. By her central position in man's life and home woman can determine the social conditions and cultural patterns of nations and epochs. Additional to those few powerful female names which we have flashed across these pages there are women whose names we do not know, whose names we would probably be unable to unearth, who exercised in the past and exercise in the present decisive influence on the destinies of mankind: not in the seat of power, not from the benches of Senate or Parliament or Court House, but from bed. 'Petticoat government' conjures up a picture of women rulers occupying the seats of power. That is not the way in which woman holds sway over society. The reality of woman's rule could better be described as 'nightdress government'.

Very often woman's love for a man can be a projection of her ambitions. Through him she can gratify not only her sexual and maternal desires but also her political aspirations. She can identify herself with her husband's career. This intrigue can be entirely subconscious, not diminishing her love in the slightest; in fact often intensifying it.

No, the 'emancipation myth' which we must explode is not the fiction that women ever had need to fight against man for their rights. The myth is that the status of man and woman in civilised society reproduces the pattern of our ancient tribal ancestors. Because of common belief in the emancipation myth it is accepted that man has inherited the sexual status of his caveman grandfather. That forebear was hunter and warrior, and his female mate was the bearer of his children. Among such primitives there was need for such specialisation. Man had to hunt and fight, woman had to nurse and suckle. In those conditions man had to be dominant; consequently societies in cave and forest could not be other than what we now describe as 'masculine-dominated'.

It is, the emancipation myth tells us, just the same today. Man no longer stalks game in the forest, except for sport, nor adventures into alien territory to fight and kill, except in the political sport of war. But he still goes out into the world as hunter and fighter and adventurer. Nowadays he hunts wealth and fights industrial rivals and adventures in the jungles of commerce. Thus he continues the pattern of hunter-warrior man, while his mate at home tends the children and the fires of domestic comfort.

All wrong! The truth is that the man-woman status has been completely reversed. Today it is man who is the domestic slave and woman the free 'sport'. Man, whether he is the labourer in the factory and on the land or the tycoon behind a rosewood desk, is the domestic. Those activities of his in the world of work and business which are glamorised as being modern versions of his primeval role, all boil down to doing for women the jobs which primitive woman used to do for him. Man has become the one who draws the water and bakes the bread. He does neither, as primitive woman once did dutifully for him, with his own hands: but with his own hands and domestic skill he earns the money which brings the water through the tap and the bread from the bakery.

Anyone who would wish to make a field-study to prove this thesis can collect all the clinical material necessary in the U.S.A. America is not, as it is too often carelessly described, a matriarchy in the true sense. It still preserves the appearance of being a masculine-dominated structure, with male President and male political and industrial bosses. An American woman is still expected to assume her husband's name on marriage and give that name to their progeny, and there are still various marital and financial and social laws which appear to give man stronger status than woman. There, as in Britain, social attitudes and social vocabulary make it appear as though culturally woman is still only an accessory to man. On radio there are 'Women's Hours' and no 'Men's Hours'; in newspapers there are 'women's pages', and we still have publications described specifically as 'women's magazines' as though women were a class in society whose reading interests are confined only to exclusively feminine topics such as cooking, nursing, contraception and 'happy ever after' fiction.

But, although not a matriarchy, the U.S.A. has become a woman-dominated society, dominated by wives and widows. Socially it shows some of the characteristics that can be found among any herd of elephants where the leader is always an experienced female, or in a herd of deer, where, as Lorenz delightfully puts it, 'the old old females which are years past reproduction are the leaders and the most powerful social agents. Everybody obeys these old, very old ladies.' In America the 'old old ladies' are formidable matrons, blue-rinsed versions of the Earth Goddess. American man propitiates them with suitable awe.

Preoccupied in 1964 with questions of race we tended to overlook that the great American Civil Rights Act of that year not only provided a model for the British Race Relations Act but also covered sexual discrimination. In the first year of the

Act's operation more than 40 per cent of the cases under it were taken by women.

Not only American law but also American economy encourages a feminine equality which threatens to progress towards dependence on the female population. The way-of-life, its high-standard of living enjoyed by some and coveted by many, is based commercially upon woman's acquisitive desire to have, whether they are needed or not, or even if they are never used, the appurtenances of luxury life: furs and jewels or yachts and deep-freezers. Advertising is geared to attract the woman buyer. Any advertising directed at the male is subtly tailored to attract either those men who want to impress or 'buy' their women with the glamour of their possessions, or those men who are prone to that most feminine characteristic, acquisitiveness.

Historical examples of attempts to exclude women from having any say in public affairs can be produced by the thousand. One ludicrous one is sufficient. When a Royal Commission was appointed in Edwardian England to consider a reform of the divorce laws Edward VII, a monarch who was himself always enfolded by some ruling mistress, some rather debased version of a du Barry or a Pompadour, insisted that it would be decadent for any woman to sit on the Commission and hear the sordid arguments that would be necessary. Can it ever be believed that any one member of the Commission would fail, either at breakfast table or in bed, to report those arguments to his wife, or that he would not return to the deliberations filled with the opinions which she had expressed?

The truth is that the power of class and wealth has always been stronger and more significant than the power of one sex over the other. In all societies and in all eras men and women alike have stormed barriers, and if there are proportionately fewer women than there are men who were born slaves and became emperors or who tramped from log cabin to White House, it is not because women have lacked the outward thrusting ambitions considered as essentially masculine but because their ways of achieving their ambitions are less overt and more insidious.

So the ardent feminists are really fighting windmills. There is no battle between the sexes for control of human destiny and the government of political affairs. The trumpet-blaring march of women into the House of Commons has made no change, no change at all, in the development of British political life. There was and is no reason at all why women cut out for political life should not adopt politics as a vocation and flourish into Maggie Bonfields, or Bessie Braddocks or Golda Meirs. But let it be understood that they enter the chambers of governmental office by virtue of being good and successful politicians, not by virtue of their femininity or their breasts or their beguiling loveliness.

Women whose names we have never heard are probably doing far more to express the feminine point of view and realise certain feminine social ambitions than has been done by those three parliamentary Graces. A woman can exert as much or more influence on public affairs from behind the oven or from beside the cot in a politician's home than she ever can from behind the dispatch box. Votes won in bed endure longer than those dropped in ballot boxes.

PART FIVE

The Meaning of Love

Man is not a natural species, he is an historical idea
MERLEAU-PONTY

13 The Meaning of Love

There is an Arab saying that the beauty of man lies in the eloquence of his tongue. We can read into that word 'beauty' all the attributes that make us human. For in speech is all our human intellect, all our joy, and all our human capacity to love.

We humans, we men and women, are the only creatures on earth who derive more than mere physical pleasure from sexuality. In sex, in the exercise of or the sublimation of our sexual desires, in the appreciation of the difference between a man and a woman, we find intellectual and emotional ecstasies that are exclusively human. Agonies also we find, as well we know, but even when suffering those we must still treasure the knowledge that we are the only creatures on earth who know the meaning of love.

There, in essence, is the theme of this last chapter in which we shall attempt to see, or to surmise, or to argue, how human love evolved.

To begin that exploration into the origins of human love we must first try to see what we humans really are. Throughout this book the term *'human animal'* has been avoided, rigorously and purposefully. The term did serve some purpose in the past. It is now worn out, stale. It smells of that time when we discovered a few truths about our origins. From fossils, from skulls, from charred bones and middens, and from such romantic and evocative traces of human beginnings as the stump of a torch and a sooty handprint of a Neanderthal man found on the wall of his cave in Italy, we had learned something about our beginnings. Not much, but enough to make us realise that we were not, after all, sons and daughters specially fashioned in his own image by a terrible but doting father. We realised we were biological products of an earth which we inhabit along with billions of other creatures similarly biologically fabricated in billions of diverse patterns.

Lamarck, St. Hilaire, Linnaeus and Darwin, along with all their predecessors right back to those inspired Greeks Xenophanes of Ionia, Democritus, Leucippus and Anaximander, brought this knowledge to us. Accepting it, we went, as humans entranced with a new idea always do go, too far.

This new reason seemed to disperse superstitions which had made us uneasy for so long. We welcomed the grim but rational discovery that we humans were akin to all other creatures because, like them, we had emerged from a communal primeval slime. Following the fashion of this new enlightenment we discarded the old myths. Then we adopted a new one: the 'after all' myth. *After all* we were only a species of animal. *After all* we were cousins of the apes. We worshipped this law of evolution as we would have worshipped some new and unrelenting God. The genuflexions we made in its direction were religiously placatory: we were prepared to sacrifice our individual human dignity on the altar of science in the hope that this might protect us from the plagues and rages of our biological destiny. 'In the sackcloth and ashes of humility and in gratitude for your divine law, oh Biology, we prostrate ourselves and confess the sin of our humble animal beginnings.'

But, having performed our atonement for past errors, it is time now to atone for the 'evolutionary heresy'. It is time to renounce that Uriah Heep humility, that bobbing and curtsying to the other creatures on this earth. Man is not an animal. Out of our own untutored instinct and in defiance of learned and dexterous scholars and scientists we must now insist on that truth.

Man, naked or hairy or both, is *not* an ape. He is man, and he is unique. So unique that he is the only creature on earth who has any concept of there being such things as higher and lower species. He, the sovereign creature, has ordained the order of precedence. He is 'the greatest'.

When we survey the spectrum of what we call the animal kingdom we can see the immense difference, a vast sweep of difference, between the highest species of animal and those lowest species which zoologists dredge from puddles. But all that difference, the whole stretch of it from highest animal to lowest animal, is minute compared with the gap, cosmic in its width, between human beings and the noblest or most intelligent animal any zoologist might parade for our admiration. In intelligence, in dexterity, and also in beauty, we are light years above and apart from all other inhabitants of this earth.

We admit, of course, that we share many physical characteristics with animals. We live on an earth where air and water and food and perceptive movements are essential to life.

Therefore we also must have noses, eyes, ears, lungs, limbs, blood and veins and nerves, genitals and guts. But above the level of those shared characteristics our resemblance to animals, even to those caricatures of us, the apes, stops.

So let us here and now expel the apes from our hearth, kick these impostor relatives out of our home. Some of them do seem to walk upright on two feet and swing two hands, though what they possess can better be described as four hands.

And they are hairy, whereas we, zoologists try to tell us, are naked. We are not naked at all. A human has more hair than a chimpanzee, but, as can be expected in so exquisitely designed a creature as a human, our hairs are shorter, fairer and more delicate than the coarse and brutish hair of chimpanzee or of any other creature on earth. Our so subtle hairiness is a sophisticated biological endowment with which we have perfected our human sensitivity of touch; two million delicate antennae convey impressions to our nervous system. Admittedly those fine hairs cannot keep us warm. But what matter? There is no need for humans to grow their own fur for such a mundane purpose. Our human brains can find other ways of keeping warm. We can strip fur or wool from other creatures or crop plants and weave cloth to protect our smooth and lovely skin. We can build fires and walls to keep the wind at bay. We can, eventually, design central heating. Furthermore, having learned how to make clothes and put them on, we learned the extra joys we could experience in taking clothes off. No un-naked ape or other animal ever has the pleasure of disrobing its mate or being disrobed.

Nor has any animal that exclusively human attribute of finding joy at the sight of the body of another, of experiencing erotic ecstasy on seeing difference between male and female. Here we come close to the human mystery, the human's own individual and beautiful secret. A human does not need the rutting touch or brutish stink of male or female body for the arousal of sexual desire. A marvel that distinguishes human from animal is that the sight of a body, or the sight of a mere part of a body, or even a concealed and imagined part of it, can provoke sexual longing. Or, flying higher, can provoke a poem or a drama or a symphony, and, less idyllically, a rape, a crime or a war.

1 'MAKING LOVE' OR BEING IN LOVE

Only men and women have been able to enrich and elevate sexual desire and the sexual act itself into a sacrament. Endowing sex with imagery and sentiment and ritual the human has made it one of the arts of life: the passionate art. So much an art that sometimes, completely regardless of beauty of shape or other sexual attraction, in the absence of the loved one or in the presence only of a non-existent or imagined loved one, a human being can experience intellectual passions more ecstatic, or more agonising, than any physical passion.

In sexuality of such creative calibre the human has attained what could be considered the ultimate achievement of art: the ability to imagine art in the abstract without needing the presence of the substance of art. As a prisoner in the black blindness of a totalitarian cell can still imagine and believe in ideals of freedom and justice existing beyond his present darkness, or as a blinded man continues to see paintings and statues and human glories in the lenses of his memory, or a deafened one hears music and verse, so can a human deprived of sexual union remember past ecstasies and dream of ecstasies to come.

There is a dark side to the argument, of course. If humans get more joy from sex than any other living creature, they also get more agony from it; more torture of mind and sometimes more torture of body. They can degrade and distort it. We do not mean here physical degradation or distortion, but the mental degradation and distortion which perverts sex into a weapon of fear or submission or hatred; in other words makes it stink. No animal does that either.

Therefore, it is in human vision, in the human talent for imagery and intellectual appreciation, that we must seek the meaning of human love.

Here we must use our words carefully, because, to our shame, we often debase that most precious human possession which we call language; and the one word in our vocabulary which we have most debased is the word 'love'. We use it appallingly carelessly. We use it to describe years of devotion and years of physical ecstasies or romantic agonies. We use it also to describe a hurried caress, an erection, an orgasm, a buttoning-up and a goodbye.

'Making love' can describe nothing more than grubby sexual intercourse in a back alley, in a field or on a beach, behind a door or a couch at a party, even in a brothel or a lavatory. In short, we use the word 'love' as a synonym for coitus. At such a level animals also 'make love' and, apart from their sexual seasons restricting the operation to certain weeks in the year, are our equals in performing it.

Therefore, it must be emphasised that human love, the love it is hoped to talk about in this chapter, is not the love implied in the phrase 'making love'. Indeed, it is not something we can *make*: it is something we must *be*.

'*Being*' in love is something no other creature on earth can come anywhere near. All those mating ceremonies and dances dotingly described by zoologists as animal ceremonies of love are the result not of love but of instinctual sex urges. Only human observers, because they are human and are therefore capable not only of being in love but also of being in love with love, could make the imaginative mistake of seeing semblance of love in animal gyrations and nuzzlings and bitings and howlings. Neither is the so-called 'love' of animal parents for their young anything more than protective instinct. As can be proved, the love of animal parents for their young has neither the intelligence nor emotional qualities of the love of a man and woman for their child. Only sentimental anthropomorphists could believe that animals can love their mates or their progeny or that the jackdaw popping minced worm into Konrad Lorenz's ear was doing anything but instinctively filling with food what it saw only as a void agape with hunger.

Of necessity Nature had to fashion the physical acts of copulation and impregnation into compulsive instincts; had to make the performance attractive to plants and insects, birds and fishes and animals, and thus ensure the procreation of young and the perpetuation of species. Knowing this we have mistakenly extended the 'after all we are only animals' argument to an 'after all it is only sex' description of the relationship between man and woman. Enmeshed by the brilliance of Freud, or our misunderstanding of him, we have accepted the error of believing that human sex is only one of the instincts, as it is with animals, and that it can therefore be equated with sensual desires for drink and food and warmth. We must refute that repulsive implication that in our love we humans are merely the jerking puppets of physical instincts. To support that refutation we need mention only one fact which even the 'only animal' physiologists have to admit. It is this. When we examine the range of species of living creatures from lowest to highest we find that only in the highest species is the cortex of the brain, the reasoning part of the brain, involved in the performance of the sexual act.

Down among the lowest of creatures the sexual difference is non-existent. Even where, a little higher in the scale, sexual reproduction does occur, it is a sluggish unexciting process of procreating young in monotonous cycles of unchanging generations. A few steps higher we find the insects and reptiles and fish performing their procreative functions almost as automatically although some of them do use methods which seem inventively bizarre. The female mantis, for example, gobbles up her mate as soon as he has done his masculine duty; a performance which has stirred the imagination of many writers to reflect that often a woman analogously mentally 'gobbles' up her man with similar gusto. One species of male spider wears a kind of syringe on his head with which he sucks up sperm from his reproductive system and then squirts it into the female. The male octopus uses one of his arms as a penis. He loads it with sperm and plants it inside the female. Another species detaches a sperm-charged arm and lets it swim off to copulate with any female it might meet. Neither mantis nor spider nor octopus, we dare say, is given to daydreaming or jealousies about the indifferently chosen partner. Their sexual habits are physically dramatic but we cannot imagine they are mentally traumatic. No emotions of imaginative desire or sense of joy or nostalgic memories can be caused by, respectively, the gobbling up of a husband, or by the almost surgical injection of sperm, or by the dispatching of a limb. Neither, of course, will ever mantis, female spider nor female octopus ever be sufficiently worried about his or her ability to perform the sexual act as to feel need for any psychological guidance.

Nathan describes how 'Wasps recognise female wasps entirely by their sense of smell . . . So important is the sense of smell that after the female's scent glands have been dissected out, many male insects attempt to copulate with the glands and not with the female herself'. Can we imagine a man ignoring the whole woman and attempting to make love only to her ovaries?

Higher in the category of species, birds perform colourful

courting rituals, cats howl, stags bay, but the result of such wooing is usually nothing but a deft and speedy coitus, confined, except for some scratches and bites, to genital gratification. See the way in which a hen, after the cock's momentary mounting, primly ruffles disordered feathers into place and continues pecking corn. That illustrates as well as anything all that 'making love' signifies to the animal world.

Perhaps the nearest simulacrum to the community of man is the community of the ant. Ants can build tenements and cities, they can employ slaves and organise armies, they can tend cattle and cultivate mushrooms. Some of them have even mastered authoritarian techniques of birth control. But the level of civilisation achieved by the industrious community-minded ant has never and can never progress a step upward to the level achieved by often lazy and frequently rebellious man. Lacking imagination and lacking emotion, in other words lacking the ingredients necessary to human aspirations and human love, an ant will never build a temple, nor ever write a verse or compose a symphony or paint a picture.

Nathan, a scientist who would be among the first justly to rebuke anyone at my level of scientific knowledge for making crude assumptions about animal thoughts, does point out in *The Nervous System*, 'We think of the brain as being able to plan the future, making use of its experience of the past. But that the brain should possess this kind of intuitive or instinctive knowledge comes to us as a surprise. We always overestimate consciousness. For really it is unnecessary for animals to know the purpose of their activities. All that is needed is that they should carry out the right behaviour.'

Animals copulate: so do humans. Animals cannot make love: humans can. Animals, the female driven mad by her intense sexual urge during her recurrent restricted period of sexual receptivity and the male sniffing hungrily at the inviting odours she emits, desire each other during periods of heat without any intellectual appreciation of themselves being male or female or their mates being male or female. Men and women can desire each other for all the year and through all their lives in accordance with their imagined ideal of male or female lover. Even in its primary and probably simplest manifestations human love shows an essential difference from animal rut in that the human *consciously* selects his or her mate, whereas the animal in rut falls on or surrenders to the most available sexual partner.

No animal can attain the higher level of intellectualising sex and extract from sensual gratification in coitus that extra that the human extracts from it, the mental essence of passion, let alone luxuriate in the thought of love before or after or even without the hope of copulation. Humans can enjoy the instinctual animal drive sex immensely; but love is an exclusively human adornment of that instinct.

We can embalm love in our memories. Only humans can enjoy or suffer this nostalgia. A dog does not remember, either with affection or regret or anger, his last bitch. Nor does he ever sit thinking with mounting desire about the one he might meet in the park next Sunday. Unlike the animal which performs the act at the crack of the biological whip and, having done its racial duty, trots off without memory or souvenir towards the accident of some other chance mating, a human lover, man or woman, can recall not only last night's journey, each moment of sex play that preceded it and the orgiastic ecstasy that ended it, but can recall also innumerable other acts of love in the past; can recall perhaps even in old age the very first love, remembering all the ambience of its occurrence: the furnishings of the room, turned-back sheets on a bed or dapplings of shadows on the grass, the pressure of fingers caressing breast and buttocks, the scent of unloosened hair or the sheen of silk. Around such a memory a man or woman can weave romance, and adorn the picture of an act performed years ago in poetry or in shame.

Eminent and qualified scholars warn me away from arguing that the sex drive of animals is merely sex appetite lacking emotional coloration. Their finely tuned arguments can lead us to a profound study of the instinct-emotions of animal mentality and, at the last resort, we might have to confess our inability as yet to be sure what an animal is thinking. I retreat from such engulfing arguments to say that the sum total of everything which humans, scientists or others, might produce as evidence of animal thoughts exists only because of human theoretical observation of the digits and can ultimately be added up only in human terms. In the same degree that human thoughts and emotions are impenetrably beyond the understanding of whatever mind an animal has, the thoughts and emotions in an animal are beyond any human valuation of acceptable precision. Admittedly we might by measuring animal behaviour reflexes translate them into evidence of what might be described as 'animal emotion'. But if there is such emotion, then, because its abode is in an animal mind, it is far too primitive in expression to merit any consideration in the same context as human emotion with its exclusively human accretions of imagination and aspiration and selective love.

Everything we say in this chapter depends on accepting that the emotion of *love* is exclusive to humans.

2 SEX IN THE BRAIN

How can we accept this? How can we claim that our human minds are more perceptive of and more receptive to emotions than the minds of other living creatures also built of flesh and bone?

We can best begin to answer those questions by recalling how physical investigation of the brains of both animals and humans has established that sexual desire has a biological construction and that the dynamo of sexual desire is found, in both animals and humans, in the very place where he should expect to find it: in the brain, in that 'sex area' known as the hypothalamus.

By counting the number of times a mouse inserts its penis before it ejaculates and the amount of time it takes to repeat the process behaviourist psychologists have substantiated the claim that even in an animal a pattern of sexual behaviour, once well established, becomes a little less dependent on the biology of the creature. Not entirely sexual instinct then, but a little bit of sex thought goes into 'making love' between mice. But 'thought' to what extent? Only to mouse extent. Such biological proof of the fact that both human brains and animal brains have an area which can 'think' about sex and can, to mouse-extent or man-extent, control sexual behaviour does not conflict with the argument that the capacity to idealise and intellectualise sexuality is exclusive to human beings. Indeed, the very fact that the source of current for our sexual drive is found in the brain increases the conviction that what we define as love must be exclusive to humans. For, as the human brain has been perfected into an instrument of intellectual capabilities astronomically excelling any possessed by any other inhabitant of earth, it would be surprising if the sexuality built into the brain of a human did not similarly excel in intricacy and gradations of emotion the sexuality built into the brains of other creatures.

We have the whole world and the record of man's life in the world to prove that the human brain does possess an extra potentiality which is non-existent in other creatures: the potentiality of creative imagination. Every product of man's hands is a diploma of his intellectual superiority. But every product is something more: it is also a monument to the glory of human love. This relationship between all human artefacts and human love is of course plainly seen in such obvious expressions of human love as art and music and literature, cathedrals and mosques and palaces. But every other man-created thing, from the merest utensil of domestic need to the most complex creation of our technological age, has its origin in human love in the sense that human love was the original emotion which enforced the concept of family and home. Every object we possess is the result of that.

In human evolution, therefore, the initial motivation was for 'improvement': not, as it was and remains in animal evolution, the blind driving force of the genitals but the inspired driving force of love. Admittedly the essential physical ingredient to spark off that force was the difference between male and female bodies, but the ingredient more essential to evolution has been intellectual appreciation and the intensifying of that more pervasive difference, the difference in emotion and intellect.

We now know that the organisation of the sex drive is under the physical control of the hypothalamus; but to consider the more intelligent way humans use this sex trigger in the brain we must step beyond physiological investigation and indulge in evolutionary speculation.

The growth of human intelligence, says Julian Huxley, involved not only a biological but a cultural change, and he rightly insists that the evolution of man is as much an evolution of human intelligence as an evolution of the human body. 'Evidently,' he says, 'in the line leading to man, the organisation of awareness reached a level at which experience could be not only stored in the individual but transmitted accumulatively to later generations.' Man, he continues, owes his triumphant emergence on the scene as a thinking and creative being by virtue of his human 'capacity for transmitting experience and the fruits of experience from one generation to the next'.

Here the philosopher is supported by the scientist, for Nathan says, 'In the case of man, apart from physiological facts behaviour is affected by all he has learned and experienced, including the immense influence of other people in the present and, more important, in the past. In man, the organisation of behaviour in accordance with cultural factors has become overwhelmingly important. This means in anatomical and physiological terms that the fore-brain is very important and that the influence of hormones is correspondingly less important.'

We can see in those words a hint that the essence of human love must lie more in the mind than in the body. It is always a delight to find scientist and philosopher joining company: it is an additional delight to draw into that company the visionary Mellersh who, in a reference to the evolution of sex and of the brain and their combined influence upon mammalian behaviour, beautifully describes it as 'a saga of increasing sensitivity, culminating triumphantly in man'.

It would be sad indeed to ignore that expression of faith in human ascendancy. It would be more than sad, it would be cynical, to imagine that our human brain which automatically controls the manifold processes connected with such processes as breathing and the beating of the heart and the oxygenising of blood and also automatically controls our tactile sexual responses should also control our sexual desires with similar automatic indifference. A woman locked in the sexual embrace of a man would find it depressing to believe that the motions of his hand and body as well as the words he whispers are merely biologically engineered emanations from a clot of tissue inside his skull. Marvellous and ingeniously staged though it is, the scientific drama of two hypothalamuses enjoying a night in bed seems but a miserably mechanistic substitute for *Romeo and Juliet*.

3 THE FIRST LOVERS

Our earliest ancestors, those first lovers, human father and mother of half-a-million or more years ago, have left us few clues about themselves. Now and again we dig up some scraps of their remains. But up to now the accumulated treasure of our discoveries amounts to little more than a hoard of skulls, an occasional femur or thigh bone, a handful of teeth and other bits of bones. Lying alongside them we find the bones of their contemporary animals as well as fossilised prints of their contemporary vegetation. These help us to construct a scene of their way of life.

Guided by such sparse clues palaeontologists and other scientists and sages can as yet lead us only so far as the banks of the river of human evolution and point across it to stepping stones so wide apart that they offer a daunting path leading uncertainly to our beginnings. The stepping stones are the proved biological and palaeontological, anthropological facts. Between them are the savage currents over which we must build the frail bridges of our individual theories.

The scientist can buttress those bridges for us. For the scientist is an artisan of theories and the supporters of speculation, and ultimately he proves what the visionary has earlier imagined. The dream comes first: the scientist with his rules and microscope comes later.

We must be cautious with the scientist, however. As cautious with him as with a robed priest or a monkey-tailed voodoo man. For the wisdom of geneticists and biologists can become as clotted with superstitious reverence as are the dogmas of any priestly faith. We must treat the scientist's psycho-mathematical theory that humans are merely a ten-billion-to-one accident of mutation self-defensively; in the same way that we treat the equally picturesque legends of mythology and religion. For such a theory can be even more destructive of human dignity than a doctrine declaring that we are merely puppets of some divine creation. We must hold courageously to our lonely confidence in ourselves, to our conviction that no other creature but man created man. No outside power breathed life into him. Man created himself. No other personage could have had the intelligence or the sheer impudence to do it.

Now that man, in this approximate 5,000th century of his existence on earth, has found the courage to conquer his dependent fear of an imagined Father, it is time for him to realise that in the course of his existence he has defeated a force which he had greater reason to fear than any god; the oppressive tyranny of evolutionary law. Man has made that conquest. On every hand is evidence of the triumph he has not yet dared to proclaim. Man's successful revolt against the dictates of evolution is what has raised him uniquely above all living creatures on earth. Any teaching, religious or scientific, which seeks to deny or ignore the individual effort of the human being to create itself human, or tries to find some religious or chemical or biological explanation, leaves in the mouth the same bitterness of forbidden fruit as was tasted in the Garden of Eden.

Other creatures submitted to and obeyed the laws of Nature: the human refused. All other creatures blindly followed the evolutionary path. Some achieved heights of animal intelligence and wild beauty of form or colour or plumage. Some, because Nature wished it so, became grotesque, nightmarish and obscene. Others reached their evolutionary cul-de-sac, became outmoded, and perished, leaving no mark on earth but the curve and crack of fossil bones.

Only humans had the brain and guts to turn aside, to adventure along new paths, to explore new territory. In courage and in arrogance the human fashioned himself in the image of his imagined Father. He fought and slaughtered other creatures, or tamed and used them. He scratched and ploughed the earth, scattered seed and reaped crops, dug homes in earth and rock, and then raised temples and tenements of the stone and glass and steel which he quarried and forged from the body of that very earth which would have him enslaved but which he enslaved.

But how? What gave the human the strength to achieve this revolutionary, evolutionary break-through? What else but that visual recognition of the difference between man and woman which fired the charge of human love? It happened in this way.

When our pre-human biological ancestors scampered on four feet their sex life would be the same as that of other four-footed creatures. The male, excited by the odour which the female emitted, tracked her down for his sexual purpose. He did not worry about the colour of her eyes. He followed his nose; he used his sense of smell and showed no selective preference for any female's vital statistics.

They lived like their animal contemporaries in a continual present. Animals always do so. They have no sense of past or future. We can ignore in this context those instincts and conditioned reflexes which might be said to represent an animal's 'memory' because those reflexes are merely sensory to received impressions and mean no more than 'This happened to me before, and my response to it is . . .' They are not saying, 'This happened to me on the last Thursday in August'. Neither had our pre-human ancestors any concept of the last Thursday in August. They foraged for food and water when they felt the need to eat or drink; they slept when they were exhausted. They also copulated whenever the sexual urge arose, and the male would never remember, even if he could so much as consciously notice, the colour of the female's hair, let alone the shape of her ankles.

What altered all this? The answer is a change in position, a change in stature, a magnificent rising up.

In the Miocene Age, somewhere between 28 and 12 million years ago, there was an ecological crisis. Forests receded and gave way to open grassy savannah. The four-footed pre-humans, having no trees to swing from, were forced to migrate into immense open plains. A dangerous performance this trekking across open spaces. They had to keep their wits about them. They had to look ahead and around not only to spot predators but to see where the hell they were going. To do that they had to do what a platoon on the march through enemy territory has to do: keep their heads up and their bloody eyes open. Doing so they found they had to lift their fore-feet from the ground and use only their hind feet for locomotion. The fore-feet, being unoccupied, found, as idle hands are reputed to find, other work to do. Hands could scrabble amid earth and grasses for food. They could eventually become dexterous enough to grab hold of a stick or a piece of rock to clonk over the head anyone who tried to attack them or anyone they did not like. Before long they would choose pointed stones to make the clonking more effective. Later they would strike one stone upon another to crack it into an even more effective splinter. They had made the first weapon. We are a few million years uncertain just when man's first weapon was made: we are sure only about the date of his last.

Meanwhile not only their hands were developing, but also their eyes. All that looking around proved to be effective optic therapy. They developed an acuity of vision which made them less dependent upon their noses. When they relied less and less on their sense of smell the odours of the female became less insistent.

But look! She might not be emitting inviting odours, but there she is in a posture that can mean only one thing. What was more, as well as having more perceptive eyes to see each other, they had hands to grasp each other. There was no need for man to sneak up behind her or 'cover her' in animal fashion. And she for her part was now free of the danger of his doing so. Now she too was upright. She too had hands. And she too could turn and look at him face to face. At last man saw the colour of her eyes; at last she saw the hairs on his chest.

This is the real confrontation, the one that means most in the whole story of the human race: the moment when man and woman first came face to face and saw each other and reached out their desirous hands. Of all traumas this is the fundamental human trauma, the pre-natal trauma of the human being. It was only the beginning, the mere flicker of a dawn millions of years distant on the human horizon, but it was the recognition of the visual difference of man and woman which, after millions of years, could burgeon into that human love rightly described by Stendhal as 'the miracle of civilisation'.

When man and woman began walking upright the whole position was changed. Here 'position' can be used in every imagined sense of the word. We might as well, in this chapter on sex and love, deal first with the sexual positions. Early man, who when he was pre-human had formerly merely sniffed an invitation in the air, could now see that invitation facing him. Early woman could also see the rising promise of male desire. Walking upright also developed muscles into different shape, particularly strengthening and increasing the buttocks. This enlargement, making the pre-human sexual attacks from behind somewhat more awkward, encouraged the frontal sexual approach which is still almost unique to human beings. Prehensile or even more sensitively dexterous hands, first for grasping and holding, and later for embracing and erotic caresses, made the frontal position increasingly ecstatic.

There are psychological complexities buried deep in frontal sex. These burgeoned only as humans became psychologically intellectual beings. The frontal position puts the male, even when adult, in a position similar to that of the suckling infant, and this can 'enhance the diffusion and complexity of social feelings'. That comment by Hockett and Ascher is surely borne out by the joy adult man and woman can experience by simulating suckling in making love. This natural joy can also enhance a mother's love for her baby as she translates the infant's suckling into remembered joys which she experienced in the kisses and nuzzlings of the infant's father.

We have had to pay for the joys and dignity of walking upright. Medical science gives us a sombre list of all the physical ills it has brought to us: our tendency to hernia, stone, diseases of the appendix, contraction of the lungs, as well as disorders of the liver which are caused by the gravitational difficulty of pumping blood up through the ascending venae-cava from what was once our horizontal back end but is now the vertically lower part of our body.

Woman paid a slightly higher price because of peculiarly female needs. The erect posture affected her sexual organs very seriously. To begin with she had to bring them more to the front and, it seems, is still in the evolutionary process of perfecting the transition. Her erect posture interfered with maternal functions which she had performed more comfortably in pre-human days. Woman suffers from displacements of the uterus that are almost unknown in quadrupeds, and it is delightfully illustrative of her pre-human origin that in cases of displacement of the uterus one of the most effective methods for restoring the organ to its proper place is for the woman to assume a knee-elbow position, the bodily position of a four-footed animal.

All those trivial physical disadvantages men and women have taken 'in their stride'. Those words also can be read in every sense of the term. Varicose veins and the like are a small price to pay for the dignity of striding the earth upright as lord of all creation. With the powers latent in our human brains we will learn how to deal with those just as we have learned how to protect and keep warm our delicate non-naked skins.

The rewards we gained have astronomically outstripped the mediocre penalties we have suffered. The conversion of forefeet into human hands gave us human manual dexterity, first for the primitive fashioning of implements of attack and defence, utensils, clothes, bricks and quarried stone, and, hundreds of thousands of years later, for holding styles and pens, the paint-brushes of the artist, the chisel and mallet of the sculptor.

Of greater import than the creation of hands, however, was the bursting out of that human inspiration of mind which was to guide those hands to their delicate and formative creative acts, good and evil, noble and ignoble. That inspiration was born in the awakening of being upright, in the immense widening of human horizons which forced upon us the glory of human vision and, most important of all, human speech.

Those two human attributes are complementary.

Developed acuity of sight created new modes of life, a new visual perception of the world. It gave humans something else; something which is the fulcrum of our evolutionary revolution: the capacity for men and women to recognise their sexual difference. This is what changed packs of scampering pre-humans into human communities. It can be considered as the birth of what today we call marriage. No longer following the scent blown on the breeze by any anonymous female but now *seeing* his mate man could recognize her. In that stare of recognition was conscious selection of the love-object; that conscious selection which, as we have mentioned, is unique to humankind. Seeing and selecting and recognising each other man and woman became partners and nourished conjugal desire as distinct from the accidental desires of rut.

But the act of facing each other forced upon humans a new demand. Eye to eye was no longer enough. Now they had to communicate. Grunts and chatterings and squeaks of fear and pleasure were not enough to translate all that they now saw and felt. They had to find noises, sculptured noises, to translate vision one to another. Came words. The forming of words required the bringing into operation a part of the human brain's potential which had never been used before. The forming of words also gave new structures to human thought. Things talked about had to be thought about. Calculation became necessary. Evaluation too. Then imagination. And finally emotion with its glories of human understanding and human love.

Today's palaeontologists can produce physical clues to the development of human speech: fossil evidence that in the vocal tract of the human has taken place a series of changes apparently necessary for the generating of speech. That speech is an exclusively human achievement is supported by computerised analyses of the vocal tracts of monkeys which prove that these creatures are anatomically incapable of producing the full range of sound available to the human.

The human sexual drive, exploded by the visual and spoken revelation of desire between man and woman, is what gave humans the power and the courage to rebel against and avoid any cul-de-sac development evolution had designed for them. Mankind could now frame its own laws of evolution, could choose its own pattern of 'natural selection'. 'We must assume,' said Ewald Hering, in a lecture quoted by Bloch, 'that for untold generations always those animals and men have had the most numerous descendants in whom the sexual act was the most powerful; this powerful impulse being inherited was transmitted to the next generation and tended by natural selection continually to increase.' Bertrand Russell, declaring that evolution is unpredictable and that determinism cannot refute the advocates of free will, superbly crystallises his declaration in one comment he makes on the Greeks. 'It was the combination of passion and intellect that made them great.'

It is a sentence that can apply to us all, to all humans. It is the combination of passion, the combined physical passion and intellectual passion which is an exclusively human possession, that has made humans great.

Dare we go further? Dare we step beyond this observation into an area of speculation of terrifying immensity? Well, if we do accept the theory that the capacity to evaluate sexual desire to the dignity of love is a capacity exclusive to the human, then we might inch forward into the belief that this one human aptitude explains that great mystery in the history of human life when, for no reason that the greatest scientist has yet discovered, the brain of pre-human man expanded suddenly into a wondrous instrument which was to make man master of his world and everything within it, even to the point of creating gods in his own magnificent likeness.

If we dare take that step, then we dare say that it was the visual consciousness of the difference between man and woman and its development to emotional love that transformed man from pre-human to human. By becoming aware of love, by realising that the sexual difference could mean something greater and nobler than instinctive animal copulation, human beings needed that new and bigger enlarging brain to enjoy more intensely the creativity implicit in love and to inquire more deeply into the romantic exhilaration of it.

After that step all seems more clear. Although the physical difference between man and woman was crudely initiated by Nature as a biological necessity to ensure the perpetuation of a species, it was the human who cultivated that difference into the art of intellectual sexuality. Through millenniums of changing and ever-developing culture man deliberately fostered the difference, raising human sexuality to the status of human love.

The lover sees something an animal cannot see. He sees difference between man and woman as the difference between a key and a lock who must come together not only in the physical act of sex but also in a union of spirit to keep secure the door that guards the treasure of love and to open it for the children who will inhabit and enrich all our futures. There we have rescued that soiled and shabby phrase 'making love' from the vulgar and brutal misuse it suffers today, and we can instead recognise it as the well-spring of all the human creativity and glory which lies embalmed in the eight words which compose the title of this book.

Selected Bibliography

ASHLEY, David James Burrows: *Human Intersex* (E. & S. Livingstone, Edinburgh & London, 1962).

BAKER, J. R.: *Sex in Man and Animals* (G. Routledge & Sons, London, 1926).

BARCLAY, A., et al.: *Father Absence, Cross-Sex Identity and Field-Dependent Behaviour in Male Adolescents* (Child Development, Lafayette, Indiana, March 1967).

BEAUVOIR, Simone de: *The Second Sex*. Trans. Peter Green (Alfred A. Knopf Inc, New York, 1962).

BEACH, Frank A., ed.: *Sex and Behaviour* (John Wiley & Sons, New York, 1965).

——: *Characteristics of Masculine 'Sex Drive'* (Nebraska Symposium on Motivation, 1956).

BEDALE, E. M., with SOWTON, S. C. M., and MYERS, C. S.: *Two Contributions to the Experimental Study of the Menstrual Cycle* (Industrial Fatigue Research Board Report No. 45, London, 1927).

BEIGEL, Hugo C.: *Body Height in Mate Selection* (Journal of Social Psychology, Provincetown, 1954).

BELL, Quentin: *On Human Finery* (Hogarth Press, London, 1947).

BELL, Richard and DARLING, Joan F.: *Prone Head Reaction in the Human Neonate* (Child Development, Lafayette, Indiana, December 1965).

BELL, William Blaire: *The Sex Complex: A Study of the Relationships of the Internal Secretions to the Female Characteristics and Functions in Health and Disease* (Ballière & Co., London, 1934).

BLOCH, Iwan: *Studies of Sex Life in England*. Trans. Richard Deniston (Falstaff Press, New York, 1934).

——: *Sexual Life in England*. Trans. W. H. Forstern (Francis Aldor; London, 1938).

——: *The Sexual Life of our Time*. Trans. M. Eden Paul (Rebman, London, 1908).

BODMER, Frederick, ed. Lancelot Hogben: *Loom of Language* (G. Allen & Unwin, London, 1943).

BOEHM, Felix: *The Femininity Complex in Man* (International Journal of Psycho-analysis, London, January 1930).

BOELSCHE, Wilhelm: *Love-Life in Nature*. Trans. Cyril Brown, ed. Norman Haire (Jonathan Cape, London, 1931).

BOOK, Hannah M.: *A Psycho-Physiological Analysis of Sex Differences* (Journal of Social Psychology, November 1932).

BOUSFIELD, Edward George Paul: *Sex and Civilisation* (Kegan Paul & Co., London, 1925).

BOWLBY, Edward John Mostyn: *Child Care and the Growth of Love*, ed. Margery Fry (Penguin Books, London, 1953).

BRASCH, Rudolph: *How did it Begin?* (Longmans, Croydon, Victoria, 1965).

BRETON, Peter: *Vocabulary of Names of Parts of the Body* (Government Lithographic Press, Calcutta, 1825).

BRIFFAULT, R.: *The Mothers* (G. Allen & Unwin, London, 1927).

BROPHY, Brigid: *Mozart the Dramatist* (Faber & Faber, London, 1964).

——: *Black Ship to Hell* (Secker & Warburg, London, 1962).

——: *Don't Never Forget* (Jonathan Cape, London, 1966).

BROWN, J. A. C.: *Freud and the Post-Freudians* (Penguin Books, London, 1967).

BURKE, R. J.: *Differences in Perception of Desired Job Characteristics of The Opposite Sex* (Journal of Genetic Psychology, Provincetown, September 1966).

CAMERON, P.: *Notes on Times Spent Thinking About Sex* (Psychological Reports, Missoula, June 1967).

CAPLAN, Gerald: *An Approach to Community Mental Health* (Tavistock Publications, London, 1961).

CARTER, C. O.: *Human Heredity* (Penguin Books, London, 1962).

CHODOFF, P.: *Critique of Freud's Theory of Infantile Sexuality* (American Journal of Psychiatry, Hanover, November 1966).

CLARK, E. T., et al.: *Ability of Females to Draw Sexually Undifferentiated Human Figures* (Perceptual and Motor Skills, Missoula, August 1965).

COMFORT, Alex: *Sex in Society* (Duckworth, London, 1963).

COSTA, Mario A.: *Reverse Sex*. Trans. Jules J. Block (Challenge Publications, London, 1961).

CRAWLEY, Ernest: *Dress, Drinks, and Drums* (Methuen & Co., London, 1931).

——: *The Mystic Rose* (Methuen & Co., London, 1927).

CULLIS, M. A.: *Farthingale: A Suggested Derivation* (International Journal of Psycho-analysis, London, Vol. XI, 1930).

CURLE, Richard Henry Parnell: *Women* (Watts & Co., London, 1947).

DAHLSTROM, Edmund (ed.): *The Changing Roles of Men and Women* (Duckworth, London, 1967).

DAMON, A., et al.: *Parental Smoking and Sex of Children* (American Journal of Epidemiology, Baltimore, May 1966).

DARLINGTON, C. D.: *The Evolution of Man and Society* (George Allen & Unwin, London, 1969).

DARLINGTON, H. S.: *The Secret of the Birth of Iron* (International Journal of Psycho-analysis, London, 1928).

DAY, Michael H.: *Fossil Man* (Paul Hamlyn, London, 1969).

DEARBORN, C. von Ness: *The Psychology of Clothing* (Psychological Monographs, Washington, Vol. XXVI No. 1, 1918).

DEUTSCH, Helene: *Psychology of Women* (Grune & Stratton, New York, 1945, Research Books, London, 1946).
DINGWALL, E. J.: *Male Infibulation* (John Bale, Sons & Danielsson, London, 1925).
DIXON, W. E.: *The Tobacco Habit* (British Medical Journal, London, October 1927).
DREVER, James: *Instinct in Man* (Cambridge University Press, 1921).
DUNLAP, Knight: *The Development and Function of Clothing* (Journal of General Psychology, Provincetown, Vol. I, 1928).
EDEN, Paul: *The Sexual Life of the Child* (British Society for the Study of Sex Psychology, London, 1921).
EISELEY, Loren: *The Immense Journey* (Gollancz, London, 1958).
EJLERSEN, Mette: *I Accuse*. Trans. Marianne Kold Modsen (Tandem, London, 1969).
ELLIS, Henry Havelock: *Studies in the Psychology of Sex* (F. A. Davis & Co., Philadelphia, 1920).
———: *Man and Woman* (William Heinemann, London, 1934).
ENDLEMAN, Robert: *Reflections in the Human Revolution* (Psychoanalytic Review, New York, Summer 1966).
EVANS, Mary: *Costume Throughout the Ages* (J. B. Lippincott Co., Philadelphia & New York, 1950).
EYSENCK, H. J.: *Uses and Abuses of Psychology* (Penguin Books, London, 1953).
———: *Fact and Fiction in Psychology* (Penguin Books, London, 1965).
FINCK, H. T.: *Romantic Love and Personal Beauty* (Macmillan & Co., London, 1887).
FISHER, Ronald Aylmer: *The Genetical Theory of Natural Selection* (Clarendon Press, Oxford, 1930).
FLACCUS, Louis W.: *Remarks on the Psychology of Clothes* (Pedagogical Seminary, Worcester, Mass., Vol. XIII, 1906).
FLUGEL, John Carl: *The Psychology of Clothes* (L. & V. Woolf, Institute of Psycho-analysis, London, 1930).
FLUKER, J. L.: *Recent Trends in Homosexuality in the West End* (British Journal of Venereal Diseases, London, March 1966).
FORD, Clellan Stearns, with BEACH, Frank Ambrose: *Patterns of Sexual Behaviour* (Eyre & Spottiswoode, London, 1965).
FORREST, T.: *The Paternal Roots of Male Character Development* (Psycho-analytic Review, New York, Spring 1967).
FORSTER, J. R.: *Observations Made During a Voyage Round the World* (London, 1778).
FRANCK, K., and ROSEN, E.: *A Projective Test of Masculinity-Femininity* (Journal of Consulting Psychology, New York, 1949).
FRAZER, J. G.: *A Suggestion as to the Origin of Gender in Language* (Fortnightly Review, lxvii, 1900).

FRAZER, J. G.: *The Golden Bough* (Abridged Edition, Macmillan, London, 1923).
FRIEDAN, Betty: *The Feminine Mystique* (Gollancz, London, 1963).
FREUD, Sigmund: *The Standard Edition of the Complete Psychological Works*, ed. James Strachey (The Hogarth Press and Institute of Psychoanalysis, 1966).
GERSHMAN, H.: *The Changing Image of Sex* (American Journal of Psycho-analysis, New York, 1967).
GESELL, Arnold, with ILG, Frances L., and AMES, Louise Bates: *Youth: The Years from 10 to 16* (Harper & Bros., New York, 1956).
GESELL, Arnold, with HALVERSON, Henry M., THOMPSON, Helen, ILG, Frances L., CASTNER, Burton M., AMES, Louise Bates, and AMATRUDA, Catherine S.: *The First Five Years of Life* (Harper & Bros., New York, 1946).
GIAFFERI, Paul Louis de: *The History of the Feminine Costume of The World from 531 BC to Our Century* (Foreign Publications, New York, 1927).
GINOTT, Hain G.: *Between Parent and Child* (Staples Press, London, 1968).
GODFREY, Elizabeth: *English Children in the Olden Times* (Methuen, London, 1923).
GOLDSCHMIDT, Richard Benedict: *The Mechanism and Physiology of Sex Determination* (Methuen, London, 1923).
GREEN, R., with MONEY, J.: *Stage-Acting, Role-Taking, and Effeminate Impersonation During Boyhood* (Archives of General Psychiatry, Chicago, November 1966).
GULIK, Robert Hans van: *Sexual Life in Ancient China* (E. J. Brill, Leiden, 1961).
GUYON, Rene: *Sexual Freedom* (Alfred A. Knopf, New York, 1950).
HAIRE, Norman: *Hymen, or the Future of Marriage* (Routledge & Kegan Paul Ltd., London, 1927).
———: *The Importance of Sexual Disorder and Disharmonies in the Production of Ill-Health* (Third Sexual Reform Congress, 1929. Congress Report).
HAYS, Peter: *New Horizons in Psychiatry* (Penguin Books, London, 1964).
HEBB, D. O.: *Textbook of Psychology* (W. B. Saunders Co., Philadelphia & London, 1958).
HENRY, George William: *All the Sexes* (Holt, Rinehart & Winston, Inc., New York, 1965).
HOCKETT, Charles, with ASCHER, Robert: *The Human Revolution* (Current Anthropology, June 1964).
HOROWITZ, E. M.: *The Male Climacteric* (East African Medical Journal, November 1960).
HOUSDEN, J.: *An Examination of the Biologic Etiology of the*

Transvestism (International Journal of Social Psychiatry, London, Autumn 1965).
HOUSTON, M. G., with HORNBLOWER, Florence S.: *Ancient Egyptian, Assyrian and Persian Costume* (A. & C. Black, London, 1920).
HUNTER, I. M. L.: *Memory* (Penguin Books, London, 1964).
HUXLEY, J. S.: *Evolution: The Modern Synthesis* (George Allen & Unwin, London, 1963).
HUXLEY, J. S.: *Essays of a Humanist* (Chatto & Windus, London, 1964).
HUXLEY, Thomas Henry: *Evidence as to Man's Place in Nature* (Williams & Norgate, London, 1863).
JOHNSON, G. B.: *Penis-Envy? or Pencil-Needing* (Psychological Reports, Missoula, April 1967).
JONES, Ernest: *Papers on Psycho-Analysis* (Baillière, Tindall and Cox, London, 1948).
KELSEY, F. D.: *Androgomymy in Schizophrenics and Their Relatives* (British Journal of Psychiatry, London, December 1965).
KEY, E. K. S.: *The Woman Movement*. Trans. Mamah Bouton Borthwick (G. P. Putnam's Sons, New York & London, 1946).
KLEIN, Viola: *The Feminine Character* (Kegan Paul & Co., London, 1946).
KOHLBERG, L., et al.: *The Impact of Cognitive Maturity on the Development of Sex-Role Attitudes in the Years 4–8* (Genetic Psychology Monographs, Provincetown, February 1967).
KREITLER, Hans and Shulamith: *Children's Concepts of Sexuality and Birth* (Child Development, Lafayette, Indiana, June 1966).
KRICH, Aron: *Before Kinsey*: Continuity in American Sex Research (Psychoanalytic Review, New York, Summer 1966).
LANDY, E. E.: *Sex Differences in Some Aspects of Smoking Behaviour* (Psychological Reports, Missoula, April 1967).
LAVER, James: *Taste and Fashion from the French Revolution to the Present Day* (G. G. Harrap & Co., London, 1945).
LEVINE, Donald N.: *Masculinity in Ethiopian Culture* (International Journal of Social Psychiatry, London, Winter 1966).
LUCKEY, E. B.: *Helping Children Grow Up Sexually. How? When? By Whom?* (Children, Washington, July–August 1967).
LUNDBERG, Ferdinand, and FARNHAM, Marynia, Foot, L.: *Modern Woman: The Lost Sex* (Harper & Bros., New York & London, 1947).
MACAULAY, Eve: *Some Notes on the Attitude of Children to Dress* (British Journal of Medical Psychology, London, Vol. IX, 1929).
MARANON, G.: *The Evolution of Sex*. Trans. Warre B. Wells (G. Allen & Unwin, London, 1938).
MARKEL, N., with ROBLIN, Gloria, L.: *The Effect of Content and Sex-of-Judge on Judgements of Personality from Voice* (International Journal of Social Psychiatry, London, Autumn 1965).
MCCARTHY, Mary: *On the Contrary* (Heinemann, London, 1962).

McCONAGHY, N.: *Penile Volume Change to Moving Pictures of Male Female Nudes in Heterosexual and Homosexual Males* (Behaviour Research and Therapy, Oxford, February 1967).

MAYER-GROSS, W., with SLATER, Eliot, and ROTH, Martin: *Clinical Psychiatry* (Cassell, London, 1960–3).

MAYR, Ernst: *Animal Species and Evolution* (Belknap Press of Harvard University Press, Cambridge, Mass., 1963).

MEAD, Margaret: *Male and Female* (Gollancz, London, 1949).

——: *First Discussion: The Childhood Genesis of Sex Differences in Behaviour in Discussions on Child Development* (J. M. Tanner and Barbel Inhelder; Eds.) (Tavistock Publications, London, 1958).

——: *Sex and Temperament in Three Primitive Societies* (G. Routledge & Sons, London, 1935).

MELLERSH, N. E. L.: *The Story of Life* (Arrow Books, London, 1961).

MEYERS, T. J.: *The Cliteroid Woman* (Psychiatric Quarterly, Utica, April 1966).

MICHAEL, Richard P.: *Controlling Sexual Behaviour* (Research Reviews, 1962–3).

MICHELET, Jules: *Love.* Trans. J. W. Palmer (Rudd & Carlton, New York, 1960).

MITCHELL, G. A. G., with PATTERSON, E. L.: *Basic Anatomy* (E. & S. Livingston, Edinburgh & London, 1967).

MITTWOCH, Ursula: *Do Genes Determine Sex?* (Nature, London, February 1969).

MOLL, Albert: *The Sexual Life of the Child.* Trans. Dr. Eden Paul (George Allen & Unwin, London, 1912).

MONEY, J.: *Components of Eroticism in Man. II: The Orgasm and Genital Somesthia* (Journal of Nervous and Mental Disease, Baltimore, July 1967).

——: *Progress of Knowledge and Revision of the Theory of Infantile Sexuality* (International Journal of Psychiatry, July 1967).

MONEY, J., with NEILL, J.: *Precocious Puberty, IQ and School Acceleration* (Clinical Pediatrics, Philadelphia, May 1967).

MONEY, J., with EPSTEIN, R.: *Verbal Aptitude in Neonism and Prepubertal Effeminacy: A Feminine Trait* (Transactions New York Academy of Sciences, February 1967).

MONRO, Isabel Stevenson, with COOK, Dorothy Elizabeth: *Costume Index* (H. W. Wilson Co., New York, 1937).

MONTAGU, M. F. Ashley: *The Natural Superiority of Women* (George Allen & Unwin, London, 1954).

MONTAGU, M. F. Ashley (Ed.): *Genetic Mechanisms in Human Disease: Chromosomal Aberrations* (Charles C. Thomas, Springfield, III, 1961).

MORRIS, Desmond: *The Naked Ape* (Jonathan Cape, London, 1967).

MYRDAL, A., with KLEIN, Viola: *Women's Two Roles* (Routledge & Kegan Paul, London, 1968).

NATHAN, Peter: *The Nervous System* (Penguin Books, London, 1969).

NEEDLES, W.: *The Defilement Complex: A Contribution of Psychic Consequences of the Anatomical Distinction Between the Sexes* (Journal of the American Psychoanalytic Association, New York, October 1966).

NIETZSCHE, Friedrich Wilhelm: *The Complete Works*. Ed. Oscar Levy (J. N. Foulis, Edinburgh & London, 1909–13).

OAKLEY, Kenneth: *Man the Tool-Maker* (Department of Geology and Palaentology, British Museum, 1963).

PERLS, F. S., with HEFFERLINE, Ralph F., and GOODMAN, Paul: *Gestalt Therapy* (Julian Press, New York, 1951).

PLACZEK, S.: *The Sexual Life of Man*. Trans. W. C. Rivers (J. Bale & Co., London, 1923).

PLANCHE, J. R.: *A Cyclopedia of Costume* (London, 1876–79).

PLOSS, Herman Heinrich, with BARTELS, Max and Paul, *et al.*: *Woman* (William Heinemann, London, 1935).

POLANYI, Michael: *Knowing and Being*. Ed. Marjorie Grene (Routledge & Kegan Paul, London, 1969).

RANK, Otto: *The Trauma of Birth* (Kegan Paul & Co., London, 1929).

REICH, Wilhelm: *The Function of the Orgasm: Vol. I of The Discovery of the Orgone*. Trans. Theodore P. Wolfe (Orgone Institute Press, New York, 1942).

REIK, Theodor: *The Creation of Woman* (George Braziller, New York, 1960).

RICHTER, Derek (Ed.), TANNER, J. M., LORD TAYLOR; ZANGWILL, O. L.: *Aspects of Psychiatric Research* (Oxford University Press, London, 1962).

ROEBUCK, J., *et al.*: *The Cocktail Lounge: A Study of Heterosexual Relations in a Public Organisation* (American Journal of Sociology, Chicago, January 1967).

ROMANES, G. J.: *Mental Differences Between Men and Women* (Nineteenth Century, May 1887).

ROMER, A. S.: *Man and the Vertebrates* (University of Chicago Press, Chicago, 1941).

ROTHBART, M. K., *et al.*: *Parents Differential Reactions to Sons and Daughters* (Journal of Personality and Social Psychology, Washington, October 1966).

RUSSELL, Bertrand: *History of Western Philosophy* (George Allen & Unwin, London, 1948).

SCHEINFELD, Amram: *Women and Men* (Harcourt Brace & Co., New York, 1944).

SCHNEIDERMAN, Leo: *A Theory of Repression in the Light of Archaic Religion* (Psychoanalytic Review, New York, Summer 1966).

SCHWARZ, Oswald: *The Pyschology of Sex* (Penguin Books, London, 1965).

SEELEY, J. R., with SIM, R. A., LOOSLEY, E. W., BELL, Norman W., and FLEMING, D. F.: *Crestwood Heights* (Constable & Co., London, 1956).
SEITZMAN, Daniel: *Salinger's Franny, Etc. Etc.* (American Imago, New York, Spring 1965).
SHAW, Otto L.: *Maladjusted Boys* (George Allen & Unwin, London, 1965).
SHAW, R. Claye: *The Sexes in Lunacy* (St. Bartholomew's Hospital Reports, 1888).
SHEARER, M.: *Homosexuality and the Pediatrician* (Clinical Pediatrics, Philadelphia, 1966).
SLOVIC, Paul: *Risk-Taking in Children: Age & Sex Differences* (Child Development, Lafayette, Indiana, March 1966).
SPENCER, Sir W. B., with CILLEN, F. J.: *The Native Tribes of Central Australia* (Macmillan & Co., London, 1938).
STEKEL, Wilhelm: *Impotence in the Male*. Trans. Oswald H. Bolts (Vision Press, London, 1953).
STOLLER, Robert J.: *Sex and Gender* (Hogarth Press, London, 1968).
STRASSBURGER, F.: *Steeple Effect* (Journal of Nervous and Mental Disease, Baltimore, March 1966).
SULLY, James: *Studies in Childhood* (Longmans & Co., London, 1903).
TANNER, J. M.: *Education and Physical Growth* (University of London Press, London, 1961).
TAYLOR, G. Rattray: *The Science of Life* (Panther Books, London, 1967).
TAYLOR, Henry Osborn: *Greek Biology and Medicine* (Norwood, Mass., 1923).
TILNEY, F., with RILEY, Henry Alsop: *The Brain From Ape to Man* (H. K. Lewis & Co., London, 1928).
TILT, Edward John: *Elements of Health and Principles of Female Hygiene* (Henry G. Bohn, London, 1852).
URBAN, Rudolf von: *Sex Perfection* (Rider, London, 1958).
VENER, A. M., et al.: *The Preschool Child's Awareness and Anticipation of Adult Sex Roles* (Sociometry, Albany, June 1966).
WALKER, Kenneth: Human Physiology (Penguin Books, London, 1963).
———: *The Physiology of Sex and its Social Implications* (Penguin Books, London, 1964).
WALTER, W. Grey: *The Living Brain* (Gerald Duckworth & Co., London, 1953).
———: *The Development and Significance of Cybernetics* (Civilta delle Macchine, Rome, November–December 1962).
WEBB, Wilfred Mark: *The Heritage of Dress* (E. Grant Richards, London, 1907).
WEIL, M. W.: *An Analysis of the Factors Influencing Married*

Women's Actual or Planned Work Participation (American Sociological Review, New York, 1961).
WEININGER, Otto: *Sex and Character* (William Heinemann, London, 1906).
WELLS, H. G., with HUXLEY, J. S., and WELLS, G. P.: *The Science of Life* (Cassell & Co., London, 1934–37).
WESTERMARCK, Edward Alexander: *The Origin of Sexual Modesty* (British Society for the Study of Sex Psychology, London, 1921).
——: *On the Position of Women in Early Civilisation* (Sociological Society, Sociological Papers, Vol. I, 1905).
WRIGHT, Benjamin, with TUSKA, Shirley: *The Nature and Origin of Feeling Feminine* (British Journal of Social and Clinical Psychology, Cambridge, June 1966).
WRIGHT, Helena: *More About the Sex Factor in Marriage* (Williams & Norgate, London, 1954).
YAP, P. M.: *Koro: A Culture-Bound Depersonalisation Syndrome* (British Journal of Psychiatry, London, 1965).
ZIPPIN, D.: *Sex Differences and the Sense of Humour* (Psychoanalytic Review: New York, Summer 1966).
ZWEIG, F.: *Women's Life and Labour* (Victor Gollancz, London, 1952).

General Reference

DORLAND's *Medical Dictionary* (Saunders, 1968).
Encyclopedia Biblica (Adam & Charles Black, London, 1899).
GRAY's *Anatomy* (Longmans, Green, 1967).
MORRIS's *Human Anatomy* (McGraw-Hill Book Co., New York, 1966).
Penguin Dictionary of Biology (Penguin, 1963).

Index

An asterisk denotes a mention in the Bibliography

abdomen, 58, 165, 174
accident risks, 77-8, 80
adolescence *see* puberty
alcohol, 28-9, 188, 235, 300
Angus, H. Crawford, 163-4
anus, 70, 177
Are Women Human? by M. Funke, 225
Aretaeus, 73
arms, 63-4, 66, 83, 94, 114, 238, 310
artificial insemination, 30-2
*Ascher, R. *see* Hockett, C., and Ascher
Ashley, April, 52-3

baldness, 70, 244
*Beach, Frank A., 157
beard, 70, 142
Beardsley, Aubrey, 175
*Beauvoir, Simone de, 32, 125, 176, 211, 259, 324, 350
Beethoven, 199, 208, 214, 216, 222, 227, 239
*Beigel, Hugo C., 60
*Bell, William Blaire, 94-6, 254-5, 261
Benjamin, H., 53
birth, 113, 141, 175
 hazards and abnormalities, 79-81, 84
 trauma, 104-7, 114
birth pill *see* contraception
bisexuality, 116, 150-3
bladder, 40, 62, 72-3
*Bloch, Iwan, 68, 383
blushing, 68
*Boehm, Felix, 51
*Boelsche, Wilhelm, 326
bones, 57, 61, 94-5, 252-3, 377-8
brain, 24, 105, 188, 224, 278, 372-3
 evolutionary development, 241-53
 in evolution of love, 375-8, 383, 384
 intellectual potential, 230-41
 'sex area', 179-81
 sexual desire, 375-7
 source of thought, 225-30
breasts, 24, 47, 126, 165, 263-4, 309-10, 339, 341
 as secondary sexual characteristic, 19, 22, 49
 at puberty, 144
 clothing, 104, 141, 309-10, 319-20, 332, 337-8, 339
 erogenous zone, 177-8
 milk and feeding, 95, 111-13, 337-8, 339
 sexual symbolism, 292, 358
 shape, 57, 67
 weaning, 108, 111-12, 114-16

British Journal of Psychiatry, 153
British Medical Journal, 93, 261
*Brophy, Brigid, 215-16, 350
*Brown, J. A. C., 117
Burden Neurological Institute, 228-9, 240
Burgess, Anthony, 344
Burt, Sir Cyril, 205
Busch, Wilhelm, Heinrich, 58
buttocks, 56, 66, 71, 310, 320, 358, 374, 381

*Carter, C. O., 81, 249-50, 252, 260
castration, 179, 341
 effect on voice, 71
 fears, 120-1, 123-6, 129, 131, 187, 293-4
Catherine the Great, 178, 218
cells, 25-7
Chaminade, Cecile, 196
'change of life' *see* menopause
chastity *see* virginity
child mortality, 35. *See also* life expectancy
childbirth *see* birth
Chisnall, A., 147
chromosomes, 19, 25-31, 38, 51, 55, 80, 97, 205, 216, 241
Clement of Alexandria, 322, 336
clitoris, 37-40, 41, 47, 68, 122, 145-6, 147, 174, 178, 269
clothes, 103-4, 141, 287, 355
 as psychological necessity, 305-7
 fashion, 332-9
 fetishism, 153
 linguistic description, 339-45
 nudity and modesty, 307-32, 369
 sexual symbolism, 21
 See also trousers, skirts
club-foot, 81
coccyx, 63
codpiece, 308, 310, 312, 319, 334
coitus, 91-2, 109, 116, 148-9, 156-7, 268, 285-6, 303-4
 after menopause, 185-6
 deviation, 150, 154-5
 evolution of love, 370-5, 379-84
 hymen, 167-71
 impotence, 187, 188-9
 in animals, 300
 nudity, 317-18, 321, 336
 orgasm, 172-8, 180, 181
 sexual education, 161-6
 taboos, 290-1

395

colour blindness, 81
contraception, 46, 156, 190, 219, 373
convolute roscocoffinis, 99
Cook, Robert, 9
copulation *see* coitus
cortex, 233-4, 239, 248, 372
*Crawley, E., 171, 287, 294, 296, 314-16, 318, 327, 355
Curie, Marie, 196, 218
curvature of spine, 83

Dacey, J., 206
*Dahlstrom, Edmund, 139
Dalton, K., 258-9
*Darlington, H. S., 341
Darwin, Charles Robert, 59, 200, 240, 255, 314, 367
*Day, Michael H., 231-3
delinquency, 138, 145-6
*Deutsch, Helene, 48, 68, 98, 106 127, 168
deviations and changes of sex, 41-2, 48-55, 69, 103-4, 142, 146, 148-55
Dewhirst, C. J., 52
dimples, 72
Doyle, Christine, 54
*Dunlap, Knight, 173

education *see* sexual education. *See also* intelligence and intellect
eggs, 39, 126, 133, 165, 286, 351
 fertilisation, 23, 25-6, 27-32, 37
 menopause, 184
 menstruation, 90-4, 95-6, 99
 produced in ovaries, 40-1
 shape of body, 56-7, 65-6
 woman as egg-breeder, 22, 184, 224, 238, 261
*Eiseley, Loren, 10
ejaculatio praecox, 173, 189
Eliot, George, 208, 216
*Ellis, Henry Havelock, 94-6, 125, 203, 254-6, 261, 277, 322-3, 353, 355
Ellis, Sir William, 128
Ellman, Mary, 210-11
embryo and foetus, 62, 95, 143
 abnormality, 79-81
 at birth, 106-7
 development, 37-9, 41, 45, 69
 dreams, 33-4
 parthogenesis, 31
 primitive ideas, 165-6
empid fly, 301
endomorphy, 61-2
evolution
 brain, 241-53
 love, 367-70, 377-85
 pelvis, 252
 sex differences, 284-7
 sexual laws, 287-97
extra-sensory perception, 272-3

*Eysenck, H. J., 200, 274

fat, 19, 61-2, 65-6, 79, 179, 328
fears, 106, 115-16, 185, 276, 318
 of castration, 120, 123-5, 131-2, 187-9
 of primal man, 289, 293, 294-6
feet, 64-5, 178, 181, 310, 319, 341
fertilisation of egg, 23, 35, 40-1, 76, 80, 91, 95, 261
fetishism, sexual, 153, 306
*Flinck, H. T., 58
Finer, Leslie, 352-3
*Fluegel, J. C., 170, 313-14, 317, 320, 323
foetus *see* embryo and foetus
Foote, Nelson, 175
Fossil Man by Michael H. Day, 231
France, Anatole, 230
Franklin, Rosalind, 196-7
*Frazer, J. G., 340
Fremont-Smith, F., 54
*Freud, Sigmund, 33, 104, 140, 144-6, 151, 157-8, 169, 174, 191, 275, 317-18, 371
 on fantasies, 147
 humour, 265-6
 infantile sex, 108-9, 110-11, 116-21
 marriage, 303
 neurotic symptoms, 259
 penis-envy and castration fears, 123, 125, 128-9, 187
Freud and the Post-Freudians by J. A. C. Brown, 117
*Friedan, Betty, 217
frigidity, 188, 189, 190. *See also* impotence
Funke, Max, 225

Gall, Francis, 179
genes, 25-6, 205, 216, 285
genital folds, 38-9, 49
genital tubercle, 38
genitals, 48-53, 58, 177, 187, 269, 294, 351
 clothing, 103-4, 135, 141, 307-31 *passim*
 erogenous zones, 177-8, 181
 Freudian theories, 120-1, 123, 129, 132
 malformation, 79-80
 puberty, 69, 143-5
*Gesell, Arnold, 115, 201-2, 268
Gesensius, F. H. W., 312-13
gestation, 93, 237-8
'Gibraltar woman', 242-4, 246, 249-50
glands, 19
 adrenal, 46
 endocrine, 42-7
 pituitary, 47, 79
 sex, 40-2, 44, 151, 177, 179, 184
 thyroid, 44, 79, 261

glans, 39, 49, 68
Glanville, Brian, 84
Goethe, 205–6
goitre, 78
Goncourt, Edmond de, 192, 238
gonadotrophins, 97
growth rates, 96–7
*Guyon, Rene, 156, 182–3

hair, 19, 21, 49, 60, 86, 369
  differences in growth, 63, 68–70, 244
  fashion, 333–4, 336
  pubic, 118, 141
*Haire, Norman, 156, 165, 170, 182
hands, 64, 66, 82, 181, 245–6, 369, 380, 382
harelip, 81
*Hebb, D. O., 201
*Henry, George William, 142, 162
Hepworth, Barbara, 241
hermaphroditism, 38, 45, 49–50, 142, 305
Herodotus, 22
heterosexuality, 19, 53, 116, 135, 152–3
Hippocrates, 39
hips, 22, 56–9, 309–10
*Hockett, Charles with Ascher, Robert, 381
homosexuality, 19, 53–5, 103, 148, 150–5, 215, 318, 320
hormones, 19, 56, 204–5, 262, 377
  sex hormones, 42–8, 73, 80, 97, 256–7, 270
*Horowitz, E. M., 9, 185
Horsman, R. H., 9
*Housden, J., 54–5
*Human Anatomy by Sir Henry Morris, 230
*Human Heredity by C. O. Carter, 81, 249, 260
humour, 265–9
*Hunter, I. M. L., 17
Huxley, J. S., 376
hymen, 165, 167–71
hypothalamus, 179–80, 183, 188, 190, 375–7

*Immense Journey, The, by Loren Eiseley, 10
impotence, 179, 186, 187–91
incest, 111, 155–6, 289–90, 298, 320
Industrial Fatigue Research Board, 98–9, 259
'inferiority complex', 124
instinct, 22
Institute of Actuaries, 77
intelligence and intellect, 19, 113
  artistic achievement, 208–16
  brain as source of, 225–9
  choice of mate, 298–300, 373
  distinction between these terms, 195–8

  effect of menstruation on, 257–62
  evolutionary development, 244–53
  I.Q. of men and women, 199–208
  in evolution of love, 369, 376, 377–84
  intuition, 270–8
  masculine and feminine attitudes, 263–5
  potential of brain, 230–41
  social factors, 216–22
  women's inferior intellect, 223–4
intercourse see coitus
intersexuality, 51, 53
intuition, 19, 263–78

Jamieson, George now April Ashley, 52–3
James IV, King of Scotland, 159
jealousy, 127
Jeffrey, Lord Francis, 225–6, 229
Johannsen, W. L., 26
Johnston, Sir Harry H., 82, 325
Johnstone, R. W., 74
Judaism, 155, 291, 294, 297, 328, 358

Kinsey Report, 10, 172–3, 190, 336
kissing, 178
Klein, Melanie, 121
Klobukowska, Eva, 55
Koro disease, 186–7, 191
Krafft-Ebing, Richard Freiherr von, 146, 151
*Kreitler, Hans and Shulamith, 128–30, 166
*Krich, Aron, 162

labia, 38–9, 49, 68, 129
The Lancet, 258, 259
language see speech and language
Langton, Mrs. Jean, 9
legal attitudes, 52–3
legs, 60, 65–6, 157, 238, 260
  shorter in women, 58, 63, 65, 224
  clothing, 310, 319–20, 327–8
  thigh muscles, 83, 215
Lennon, John, 175
lesbians, 103
*Levine, Donald N., 341, 353
Lewin, Bertrand, 111
life expectancy, 35, 75–8, 90–1
Linken, Arnold, 146
The Living Brain by W. Grey Walter, 228
Loeb, Jacques, 31
Lorenz, Konrad, 53–4, 361, 371
love, 19, 22, 142, 158, 181, 209, 277, 308
  animal and human aspects, 370–5
  at puberty, 145, 147–8
  denial of, at weaning, 109–15
  evolution of, 246, 367–9, 375–85
  in Bible, 155

love—contd.
  making love, 159–67, 176–8
  marriage, 303–4
  Platonic, 181
  romantic, 152, 183
  ruling power of women, 359–60
Lucretius, 155
*Lundberg, Ferdinand and Farnham, Marynia Foot L., 172

Mackay, Donald, 9
McLung, C. E., 26
*Maladjusted Boys by Otto L. Shaw, 112
*Male and Female by Margaret Mead, 287, 391
*Man and the Vertebrates by A. S. Romer, 242
marriage, 92, 301–4, 308, 320, 353, 361, 383
Martin, Ruth, 174
masturbation, 121, 132, 137, 154, 178
*Mead, Margaret, 10, 54, 135, 139, 165, 203, 219, 287, 356, 391
*Mellersch, N. E. L., 377
menopause, 79, 181, 183–6, 190–1
menstruation, 73, 79, 170, 175, 181, 268, 351, 359
  at puberty, 144
  effect on intellectual development, 254–62
  mystery of, 90–100
  taboos, 290, 318–19
Merleau-Ponty, 366
mesomorphy, 61–2
metabolism, 78–9, 179, 253
Michaelangelo, 321
Michaelis Rhomboid, 71–2
milk, 67, 95, 184, 237–8, 286
  weaning, 109, 111–12, 114–15
modesty, 307–32
More, Sir Thomas, 299
*Morris, Desmond, 338
Morris, Sir Henry, 57, 230
mortality rate see life expectancy
moustache, 142
mouth, 178, 181
movement, 21, 56, 65–7
'Murrian man', 242, 246, 249–51
muscles, 57, 61, 182
  clothing, 103–4, 310
  larger in men, 198, 237, 278
  speech, 115, 356
  strength, 82–5, 381

*Naked Ape, The, by Desmond Morris, 338
*Nathan, Peter, 9, 180, 183, 188, 372–3, 377
Nature, 22–3, 65, 73–4, 75–6, 110, 131, 167, 371, 379, 384
  as feminine principle, 23–7, 357–8

menopause, 185
menstruation, 90–1, 96–8
'premium' pleasure, 174–5
pro-feminine prejudices, 27–8, 33, 35, 41–2, 47–8
navel, 58
*The Nervous System by Peter Nathan, 373
Nietzsche, 60, 172, 190, 214, 295
nipples, 39, 67, 81, 108, 110–13, 132, 177, 341
North, Jane, 9
North, Jon, 9
nudity, 307–32, 336

Obscene Publications Acts 1959 and 1964, 158
'oedipus complex', 120–1
oestrin, 44–6
oestrogen, 45–6, 180, 258
orgasm, 154, 160–2, 172–83, 370–1
ovaries, 28, 44, 47, 49, 51, 180
  deficiency, 56–7
  development, 40–2
  hormone treatment, 50
  menopause, 184–5
  ovulation, 91, 93
  removal, 46

palolo worm, 99–100
parents, 32–5, 61
  distinguished by baby, 20–3, 114–16
  influence, 134–7, 138–42, 146, 164
parthenogenesis, 31–2
pelvis, 65, 74, 79, 252, 351
penis, 20, 23, 74, 104, 114–16, 132, 165, 263–4, 339–44, 373, 375
  abnormalities, 49, 51
  as secondary sexual characteristic, 17–19, 22, 41
  clothing, 308, 315, 316, 318–19
  development, 37–40, 47, 150
  impotence, 187–91
  involuntary erection, 160
  orgasm, 176–8
  perforation of hymen, 167, 171
  puberty, 145–6
  superstition and taboo, 165–6, 292–4
penis-envy, 120, 121–32
phallic symbols, 131, 292
phallus see penis
*The Physiology of Sex by Kenneth Walker, 30
Plato, 181, 208, 357
Pliny, 93
*Ploss, Hermann Heinrich, 145, 171, 181
Plutarch, 61
*Polanyi, Michael, 225, 273
Poppaea, 169

pregnancy, 78-9, 95, 148, 170, 175, 188, 309, 334, 355
  abnormality, 79-81, 106
  in primitive societies, 135, 141, 165, 290-1, 358, 359
prepuce, 39, 68
Prince, Dr. Charles (also known as Dr. Virginia), 54
progesterone, 46-7, 258
prolactin, 47
prostitution, 19, 71, 147, 163, 165, 296, 308, 316
Psychology of Women by Helene Deutsch, 106
puberty, 79, 162, 177, 181, 268, 275, 308
  general development at, 142-9
  in primitive societies, 144, 161, 171
  mental changes, 203-5, 257-8, 260-1
  physical changes, 69-72, 73-4, 90, 96-8, 144-5
pudendal cleft, 38
pyloric stenosis, 81

Quilligan, E., 33

retirement, 77
Roeder, F., 180
Roman Catholicism, 156, 291, 297, 324, 337
*Romanes, G. J., 203
*Romer, Alfred Sherwood, 242-3, 245, 248, 251, 284, 285
*Russell, Bertrand, 358-9, 384

St. Augustine, 308, 318, 321
St. Paul, 358
St. Teresa, 183
St. Thomas's Hospital, London, 81
Salinger, J. D., 211
'Samaunda' disease, 148
Sarto, Andrea del, 64
schizophrenia, 80
*Schneiderman, Leo, 291
scrotum, 38-9, 40, 49, 129
The Second Sex by Simone de Beauvoir, 125, 259
*Seeley, J. R., 185
semen *see* sperm
Sex and Gender by Robert J. Stoller, 129
Sex Complex, The, by William Blaire Bell, 94
sexual
  ambivalence *see* deviation
  characteristics distinguished as primary and secondary, 19, 22, 61, 103-4
  changes *see* deviation
  curiosity, 18, 144, 147, 318
  education, 20-1, 134, 140-1, 162-4
  pleasure, 40, 172-8, 180-1, 186, 190

shape of body, 56-8
Shakespeare, 199, 203, 208-9, 212, 227, 240
*Shaw, Otto L., 112
sight, 245-6, 382-3, 384-5
skin, 67-9, 110
skirts, 127, 131, 141, 343
  fashion, 333-9
  sexual distinction in clothes, 305-32
skull, 62-3, 95, 214, 224, 226, 229-30, 232
  evolutionary development, 241-53
*Slovic, Paul, 138
smell, sense of, 73, 114, 245-6
smoking, 30, 188
Smyth, Dame Ethel, 195-6
social conditioning, 18, 19, 107, 203, 361
sodomy *see* homosexuality
Soviet Russia, 156-7, 217
speech and language, 20, 115, 201-3, 339-45, 367, 370, 382-3
sperm, 24, 25, 35, 40, 80, 156, 176-7, 181, 238, 372
  change of life, 183-4
  ejaculatio praecox, 173
  fertilisation of egg, 23, 27-8, 32, 37, 41, 76, 93
  hymen, 167-8, 170
  Y-bearing spermatozoa, 81-2
Starling, Ernest, 43-4
status of women
  emancipation, 346-52
  employment, 351-7
  ruling power, 357-63
*Stekel, Wilhelm, 163, 173, 189-90
*Stoller, Robert J., 129, 132
strength, 82-5, 96, 113
  of character, 85-90
structure of body, 62-5
suicide, 78, 190
Sullerot, Evelyne, 204
Superstitions *see* taboos
'Swanscombe man', 246, 248-51
Symposium, The, by Plato, 181

taboos and superstitions, 287-97, 298, 300, 318-20, 337, 344
*Tanner, J. M., 61
tattooing, 314
Tavistock Clinic, symposium, 139, 147, 202
Taylor, M. A., 80
telepathy, 272-3
testicles, 22, 24, 44, 47, 49, 51, 56, 185, 286
  development, 38, 40-2
testosterone, 44-5, 80
Textbook of Psychology, A, by D. O. Hebb, 201
Tiger, Lionel, 197

trans-sexuality, 51, 116
transvestism, 53–5, 328
trousers, 18, 127, 129, 131, 141, 343
    fashion, 333–9
    sexual distinctions in clothes, 305–32

urination, 21, 22, 40, 49, 72–3, 122–3, 129, 187
uterus, 28, 33–5, 39, 51, 79, 84, 126, 178, 184, 358
    birth, 104–7, 113–14
    development of embryo, 45, 95
    displacement, 382
    in relation to ovaries, 40–1
    menstruation, 96
Utopia by Sir Thomas More, 299

vagina, 18–19, 53, 116, 132, 140, 186, 220, 292, 339, 340, 342–3
    coitus, 162, 163–4
    hymen, 167–71
    orgasm, 174, 176, 178
    puberty, 144–6, 147
    sexual abnormality, 129, 150–1
virginity, 31–2, 67, 79, 167–70, 308

virility, 69, 85, 187
voice, 21, 42, 70–1, 115, 118, 134, 144, 179. *See also* speech and language

Waitz, Theodor, 330
*Walker, Kenneth, 30, 38, 73, 81, 166, 173–4, 198, 260, 273, 303
*Walter, W. Grey, 9, 228, 235–6
Wanting Seed, The, by A. Burgess, 344
weaning, 108, 114–16, 134
Welch, Raquel, 178
widowhood, 75–7
Woman's Own, 174
womb *see* uterus
Women are Not Human Beings, 349
Woolf, Virginia, 195, 211
World League for Sexual Reform, 158

X- and Y-chromosomes, 26

Yale New Haven Hospital, Connecticut, 33

Zazzo, Rene, 147, 202

All Sphere Books are available at your bookshop or newsagent, or can be ordered from the following address:

Sphere Books, Cash Sales Department,
P.O. Box 11, Falmouth, Cornwall.

Please send cheque or postal order (no currency), and allow 7p per copy to cover the cost of postage and packing in U.K. or overseas.